THE
IDEA OF HISTORY

THE
IDEA OF HISTORY

R. G. COLLINGWOOD

A GALAXY BOOK

NEW YORK • OXFORD UNIVERSITY PRESS

1956

First English edition, 1946

First published as a Galaxy Book, 1956

Eighth printing, 1965

EDITOR'S PREFACE

§ 1. *Disiecta membra*

DURING the first six months of 1936 Collingwood wrote thirty-two lectures on *The Philosophy of History*. The manuscript falls into two parts, each of which he intended to work up into a book. The first is an historical account of how the modern idea of history has developed from Herodotus to the twentieth century; the second consists of 'metaphysical epilegomena' or philosophical reflections on the nature, subject-matter, and method of history.

Of the two projected books the second began to take shape in the spring of 1939 when, during a short stay in Java, Collingwood started to write *The Principles of History*. In this work he proposed to discuss the 'main characteristics of history as a special science' and then to consider its relations with other sciences, particularly natural science and philosophy, as well as its bearing on practical life.

In 1940 he revised part of the 1936 manuscript, especially the section on Greece and Rome, and rechristened it *The Idea of History*. But though he meant eventually to make it a companion volume to *The Idea of Nature*, he was unfortunately unable to work on it any further.

It was Collingwood's wish that his posthumous papers should be judged by high standards when their publication was under consideration, and the decision to construct a book out of these manuscripts on history has not been taken without some hesitation. It was thought, however, that they contained material which might be useful to historians as well as to philosophers and which was too good not to be published.

Since the greater part of the available material was little more than a first draft, much more editing has been necessary here than in *The Idea of Nature*. But I think it right to say that although the layout of the book and some of its form are due to the editor, the content is everywhere Collingwood's. The design of the book makes some repetitions almost inevitable (particularly in the separate essays which I have chosen and grouped together to form Part V and which it seemed best to print almost exactly as they were written), and the various dates at which different parts were composed, as well as the development of the author's thought even during the writing of the 1936 manuscript, may serve to account for such occasional inconsistencies as still remain.

With the exceptions noted below, the basis of the book is the 1936 lectures, and I have followed the plan of those lectures by making one book instead of two. My reason for this is that while there are available sufficient unpublished manuscripts and published essays to make a separate book of papers on the nature of history, I am not satisfied that the quality of all the unpublished material is sufficiently high to warrant publication.

The manuscript of *The Principles of History* is a fragment, containing only one-third of what was planned, but Collingwood wrote on it a note authorizing its publication with a preface 'explaining that it is a fragment of what I had, for twenty-five years at least, looked forward to writing as my chief work' In spite of this authority, I have not felt justified in printing more than the three excerpts which appear below as Part III, § 8 and Part V, §§ 3 and 6. And even these I have included with some misgivings. They are written in Collingwood's later manner, and their style and temper is sometimes rather out of key with the rest of the book; but their inclusion serves to round off his view of history and to expound in more detail some points only briefly indicated elsewhere.

In Part V, §§ 1 and 2, I have included two essays on history which have been published already: the Inaugural Lecture which Collingwood delivered as Waynflete Professor of Metaphysical Philosophy on 28 October 1935 (published as a pamphlet by the Clarendon Press) and the lecture which he gave to the British Academy on 20 May 1936 (published in the *Proceedings* of the Academy, vol. xxii, and now reprinted with the Academy's consent). It has not seemed worth while to reprint other essays on history which he published from time to time, either because they represent positions which he later abandoned, or else because their substance has been absorbed into the contents of the present volume. Particulars of these essays may be found in the list of his philosophical writings appended to an obituary notice in the *Proceedings of the British Academy*, vol. xxix. To that list the following items should be added:

Thanks are due to the editors, and to Messrs. Longmans, Green, & Co., the publishers, of the *English Historical Review* for permission to make use, in this book Part IV, § 1 (iv), of a book-review contributed by Collingwood to that periodical.

§ 2. *Magis amica veritas*

If Collingwood's wishes about his posthumous papers continue to be observed, this will be the last of his philosophical books, and it may be appropriate to make some general remarks in this section about his philosophical work, and, in § 3, about his personality and his position in the world of philosophy.

He always claimed that philosophy should be systematic, but his philosophical writings make up not so much one system as a series of systems. They may perhaps be divided into three groups, although some development of thought may be traceable within the works of each group. The first consists of what he came to regard as juvenilia, *Religion and Philosophy* (1916) and *Speculum Mentis* (1924). The second begins with the *Essay on Philosophical Method* (1933) and continues with *The Idea of Nature* (which dates, except for its Conclusion, from 1934) and much (1936) of *The Idea of History*. The last comprises the *Autobiography* (1939), the *Essay on Metaphysics* (1940), and *The New Leviathan* (1942). *The Principles of Art* (1938) is akin in part to the second group, in part to the third.

A full appraisal of work so many-sided as that which these volumes contain would take more space than can here be allowed, and therefore it may be well if the discussion is mainly confined to only one of its facets, namely to Collingwood's conceptions of the relation between philosophy and history. He said himself in his *Autobiography* that his aim in philosophy had been to bring about a *rapprochement* between these two disciplines, and since so much of what I have to say in this section is critical in tone, it must be affirmed at the outset that this aim is successfully achieved in the books written at the zenith of his powers, i.e. in what I have just described as the second group of his philosophical writings. The *Essay on Philosophical Method* argues that the subject-matter of philosophy resembles history rather than nature and that its method must be constructed accordingly. *The Idea of History* forces on the attention of philosophers the epistemological problems to which the existence of history gives rise, and, like *The Idea of Nature*, it shows how philosophical questions can be illuminated and solved by an historical approach. It is not too much to say that after these books English philosophers will be able to continue ignoring history only by burying their heads in the sand.

Collingwood's views on philosophy and history, as well as on other matters, have often been compared with Croce's, and certainly there is an interesting parallel between the philosophical development of the two men. Croce's first interest in philosophy was kindled by the Herbartian and anti-Hegelian Labriola; Collingwood was indoctrinated as an undergraduate with Cook Wilson's realism. It was their artistic and historical interests that made both of them dissatisfied with the philosophy they had been taught; they both proceeded to study Hegel for themselves and to do original work in history; and they both worked their way to a form of idealism and eventually to an identification of philosophy with history. But although Collingwood learnt much from Croce about aesthetics and something about history, it would be a mistake to regard him as essentially a follower of his. For instance, many of the ideas in *The Idea of History* are similar to Croce's, but they were in large measure arrived at independently as a result of his own historical work and they are elaborated in more detail and argued more carefully. Moreover, he used to say that his favourite philosopher was Plato and that Vico had influenced him more than anyone else; and if in his final years he came to adopt an historicism not unlike Croce's, he had earlier keenly criticized him and had started to work out a philosophy of his own which differed considerably from parts at least of the Philosophy of Spirit. The philosophy in question is the one implied, rather than specifically expounded, in the *Essay on Philosophical Method*.

In that *Essay* distinctions are drawn between historical study and philosophical criticism, between historical thought as concerned with the individual and philosophical thought as concerned with the universal, and between the attitudes appropriate to the study of philosophy and the study of history. If these distinctions may be relied upon, the book itself is philosophy and not history. Nevertheless, it is plain that the philosophy in it has learnt from history, as well as from natural science, because its core is the doctrine that philosophical concepts are specified on a scale of forms related to one another as lower to higher in a process of development. Just as we have to call on the scientific conception of evolution in order to understand the physical world, and just as we cannot understand the British Constitution without investigating the historical process through which it has been created, so, Collingwood argued, we must not treat pleasure, utility, and moral goodness as mere specifications of goodness, existing side by side (like the biological species of pre-evolutionary biology) since a simultaneous creation; we must discover their genetic interconnexion and exhibit them as stages in the process through which the conception of goodness has developed. In dealing with concepts, however, we are dealing with thoughts dialectically related to one another and therefore with material more akin to that of history than to that of natural science.

From this point of view, philosophy is like science in dealing with a universal (e.g. with truth or goodness); but it is like history in that the specifications of this universal are linked together somewhat like the stages in an historical process, each incorporating in itself the characteristics of its predecessors and being pregnant with those of its successors. It might be thought that if categories thus have a sort of history of their own, philosophy, as a study of them, is itself history. But this is not Collingwood's view, because he argues that history is the study not of all processes but only of human affairs, and that it proceeds, by the interpretation of evidence, on the lines described in Part V, § 3 of *The Idea of History*. This implies that philosophy, as well as the sciences, including biology, falls outside history and cannot be incorporated into it until it ceases to ask 'What is goodness?', as in the *Essay on Philosophical Method* it is still permitted to do, and stops short at such questions as 'What was Plato's conception of goodness?'

Thus the philosophy which would have resulted from a use of the method that Collingwood advocated in his *Essay* would have the conception of development as its *leit-motiv*, and it would be to that extent a philosophy under historical influences, but it would still be distinct from history even if it were confined to a study of the categories which some thinkers have regarded as history's groundwork. But, at this point in Collingwood's thought, it was not so confined, because he then held that in addition to writing a history of the idea of nature, for example, the philosopher should construct a cosmology, the result of his reflections on that history: in addition to being an historian of philosophy, he should work out a philosophy of his own.

This *Essay* explicitly excludes 'ultimate problems' from consideration, and the reader is left to construct for himself the metaphysics, logic, and ethics which it entails. Collingwood did begin to apply his method to cosmology, and he outlined his results in a paper read to an Oxford society in 1935 and also in the original conclusion to his lectures on the philosophy of nature. That conclusion he later suppressed; and he did not return to the task of writing out in full the philosophy which the *Essay* had been meant to introduce. The reason for this is that he changed his mind. Like Croce, he came to think that 'philosophy as a separate discipline is liquidated by being converted into history'. (This quotation, like others in this section for which no source is quoted, is from a series of notes written early in 1939 for *The Principles of History*.)

How did this change of view come about, and how does the view he finally held compare with those he had held earlier?

The inference from chapters vii and x of his *Autobiography* is that he had elaborated his doctrine of 'absolute presuppositions' and the purely historical character of metaphysics (expounded in the *Essay on Metaphysics*, published in 1940 but prepared in 1938) before he wrote the *Essay on Philosophical Method* in 1932. This is hardly credible. Not only did the earlier *Essay* clearly distinguish philosophy from history, as we have seen, but the 1936 lectures on the philosophy of history still draw the same distinction; and I have documentary evidence that in 1936 he still believed in the possibility of metaphysics as a separate study, distinct altogether from history, a study of 'the One, the True, and the Good'. Hence I am compelled to believe that his philosophical standpoint radically changed between 1936 and 1938, even though no such change is recorded in his *Autobiography*, and even though others maintain that, while his views developed, the development was gradual and always along the same track.

These differences of view can be reconciled to some extent, because the change to which I have referred was not an unheralded revolution; it was caused when the sceptical and dogmatic trends, present in Collingwood's earlier thought, triumphed over the temporary defeat they had sustained bewteen 1932 and 1936, so that the philosophy which 'emerged' after 1936 was not an entirely new growth but had its roots in its author's past.

At the end of the *Essay on Philosophical Method* Collingwood said that he could never plead guilty to a charge of scepticism, but when this charge was pressed on the ground of certain passages in *Speculum Mentis*, the peculiar vehemence with which he denied it did little to produce an assurance of his innocence. In the same *Essay* he pointed out that scepticism was a covert dogmatism and that this was particularly true of the Oxford philosophy which he had himself been taught. Yet from the sceptical strain in that philosophy (and *eo ipso* from a corresponding dogmatism) he was finally unable to free himself, and it is interesting to observe the influence of this strain on his thought as he developed his theory of history. Philosophical scepticism in one form or another was the price he paid for the endeavour to compress philosophy into history.

In the *Autobiography* he considered the view, commonly held by his Oxford teachers, that in studying the history of philosophy it is necessary to ask, first, 'What did Plato think?' and secondly, 'Was he right?' The first question was said to be historical and the second philosophical. But, he argues, there is really only one question, and that an historical one; it is impossible to understand what Plato thought without discovering what problem he tried to solve; and if the problem can be identified, that is proof that he solved it, because we only know what the problem was by arguing back from the solution. It follows that it is impossible to discover what Plato thought without simultaneously discovering whether his thought was

true. This argument is not made easier of acceptance by the
analogies used to illustrate it: since Nelson won the battle of
Trafalgar, we are told, he solved his tactical problems, and we
can discover what these were, and what his plan was, by arguing
back from the tactics he used in the battle: Villeneuve, however, lost the battle; he failed to solve his problems, and we
thus cannot discover what his plan was. If this analogy be
pressed, the inference would seem to be that we can understand
a philosopher's problem only when he has won his battle, or
solved his problem correctly, so that all philosophical writings
are either true or unintelligible. This startling result is hard to
reconcile with Collingwood's own criticism of Plato in the same
chapter of his book, where he remarks that Plato was wrong to
suppose that in the *Republic* he had described the form of
political life as such, instead of the form of Greek political life
only.

Elsewhere there appears a different but no less difficult view
of the connexion between 'historical' and 'philosophical'
questions. In a manuscript written in 1936 Collingwood says:
'St. Augustine looked at Roman history from the point of view
of an early Christian; Tillemont, from that of a seventeenth-
century Frenchman; Gibbon, from that of an eighteenth-century
Englishman; Mommsen, from that of a nineteenth-century
German. There is no point in asking which was the right point
of view. Each was the only one possible for the man who
adopted it.' Contrast this passage with what he says in *The
Idea of History* (Part III, § 5) about the varying attitudes of
past historians to the Middle Ages, attitudes there described as
'historical errors'. If there is no point in asking whether a past
thinker is right or not, the 'philosophical' question is no longer
'incapsulated' into history; it is set aside altogether as one that
cannot arise. And in 1939 Collingwood put this explicitly when
he wrote that 'history is the only kind of knowledge' and proceeded to explain what he meant by adding that 'logic is an
attempt to expound the principles of what in the logician's own
day passed for valid thought; ethical theories differ but none
of them is therefore erroneous, because any ethical theory is an
attempt to state the kind of life regarded as worth aiming at,
and the question always arises, by whom? Natural science
indeed is distinct from history and, unlike philosophy, cannot

be absorbed into it, but this is because it starts from certain presuppositions and thinks out their consequences, and since these presuppositions are neither true nor false, thinking these together with their consequences is neither knowledge nor error.' And presumably an essay on philosophical method is not an exposition of the method which philosophers ought to adopt because it is the right one, but simply a description of the method which the essayist or one or other of his predecessors happens to use.

It surely must be a radical scepticism about both philosophy and natural science which leads a thinker to hold that knowledge is to be gained only by historians and only from interpreting historical evidence. From *The Idea of History* onwards, Collingwood's writings contain an impressive argument for the recognition of history as productive of results no less entitled to be called knowledge than those of natural science. But he was not content merely to argue, as he did so vigorously and convincingly, against positivistic attempts to absorb philosophy into natural science as the sole form of knowledge; he went farther and took up a position equally intransigent, and at bottom for the same sceptical reasons, claiming for history precisely what his opponents claimed for science. A mere *rapprochement* between philosophy and history had ceased to content him.

An example drawn from his later writings may show how the leaven of philosophical scepticism worked in his thought. In *The Idea of History* there is a sharp rejection of Dilthey's idea that the philosophy a man adopts depends on his psychological make-up. Was the sharpness due to a still unconscious suspicion that a similar and no less sceptical view was implicit in the historical relativism to which he became more and more attracted? As we have seen, he came to think that there is no sense in asking whether St. Augustine's view of Roman history is right or wrong, because he could not have thought otherwise than he did under the conditions of his own epoch. But if we ask exactly why he could not have thought otherwise, part at least of the answer must be 'because of his psychological make-up', and indeed this answer receives some confirmation from the *Essay on Metaphysics*.

In that book it is argued that a body of knowledge ultimately

depends on the acceptance of a group of 'absolute presuppositions'; for instance, 'God exists' is said to be among the absolute
presuppositions of 'science and civilization'. But Collingwood's own historicist principles compel us to ask 'Whose
science?', 'Whose civilization?' And we cannot answer 'Modern
science' or 'Western civilization' without supposing that these
are unities far more integrated than a critical review of the
history of thought would allow them to be. Could it be seriously
maintained that 'Western civilization' is a sort of climate,
common to all those who participate in it or live under it, or
that all workers in the field of modern science must necessarily
share precisely the same group of absolute presuppositions?
Scientists are men, whose interests outside science may have
an impact on their scientific work and whose differences in
nationality, education, and tradition would seem to imply or at
least to permit of variations in the presuppositions of their
work. The logic of Collingwood's argument would ultimately
force him to descend from generalities, like 'science' and
'civilization', to the individual, and to hold that the work of
any individual thinker is made what it is in the last resort by
the particular set of absolute presuppositions which he himself
has adopted. Now it is a vital question how a man comes to
hold the presuppositions he does and how they come in course
of time to be rejected in favour of others. To this question
Collingwood turns only in a footnote, as if by an afterthought,
and his answer is that they are unconsciously adopted and are
changed by a process of 'unconscious thought'. In its context
this obscure phrase seems to imply that since these presuppositions, together with their acceptance and alteration, fall
into the sphere of the 'unconscious', they belong to the field
which Collingwood thought was legitimately occupied by
psychology. Agreement with Dilthey's doctrine turns out to
be surprisingly near.

It was perhaps Collingwood's very absorption in the many
different branches of study he had made his own which blurred
for him the distinctions between them. In his first book, for
instance, religion, theology, and philosophy are all said to be
identical. In *The Principles of Art* (despite the argument in the
last chapter of the *Essay on Philosophical Method*) there is no
sure way of distinguishing between philosophy and poetry as

species of literary composition. If natural science escapes being identified with history at the end, this may be because Collingwood never really worked at it himself, although he was well versed in its history. He brought a powerful mind to bear on whatever happened to be engrossing his energies, theology, art, or history; he was conscious that it was the same questioning mind at work, whatever its object, and he seems to have been inclined to draw the conclusion that philosophy was simply identical with whatever he happened to be studying most intensively at the time. In 1935–6—the period which divides the *Essay on Philosophical Method* from the historicism of later years—it was history which was absorbing most of his attention; the 'liquidation' of philosophy, which began at that time, was due to this fact as well as to a combination of the sceptical strain in his thought, which I have been illustrating, with the dogmatic strain which was its inevitable accompaniment.

The dogmatic element in Collingwood's work has been more commonly recognized than the sceptical; if we except the *Essay on Philosophical Method*, *The Idea of Nature*, and much of *The Idea of History*, there is an air of confidence, and sometimes of bombast, about parts of his mature philosophical writings, and critics noticed the same air of over-assurance about his later lectures. This obtrusive dogmatism was not merely the obverse of his scepticism; nor did it merely colour the form of his later work; it affected its content and it was linked with a change in his attitude to religion, always one of his strongest interests. In *Speculum Mentis* he explicitly withdrew from his earlier identification of religion with theology and philosophy and adopted instead a view of religion reminiscent, for instance, of Hegel and Croce: religion mistakes imagining for thinking and asserts the reality of what is only symbol. Christianity solves the religious problem of reconciling God with man and thus prepares the way for its supersession by philosophy; it continues in existence only because it is the sole means of escaping the superstition which is a constant pitfall for the human mind. Here, it will be noticed, the sceptical strain in Collingwood's thought appears in his attitude to Christian doctrine, while it is the claims of philosophy which tend to be dogmatic.

He did not long remain content with *Speculum Mentis* and,

so far as religion is concerned, he put forward a new view in a pamphlet on *Faith and Reason* (1928). This essay is one germ of the *Essay on Metaphysics* and it forms a valuable commentary on that book. Reason and faith, he holds, are indispensable to one another. Each is an independent source of knowledge, reason providing us with knowledge of the world in its details, faith with knowledge of the world as a whole. Scientific thought rests on a foundation consisting of certain pieces of knowledge about the world which we did not acquire and cannot criticize by scientific methods: instances are the existence of God, the reality of free-will and immortality, and the fact that there are laws of nature. For these pieces of knowledge we have no reasons; they are the fruit of faith, not mere faith, but a rational faith universal in everyone and necessary to all thought, even to the thought whereby a critic may pretend to criticize it. Here there is no attempt to ascribe a monopoly of truth to any discipline; nor is there any scepticism about finding a truth which shall be universal and valid for all thought. The shoals of scepticism and the billows of dogmatism have been safely passed and the ship is at anchor in the calm sea of that philosophical serenity which produced the *Essay on Philosophical Method* and the philosophical theology which in 1933 closed his lectures on ethics.

With the *Essay on Metaphysics*, however, important differences emerge. The absolute presuppositions (i.e. the content of religious faith) are no longer said to be knowledge; as presuppositions they are neither true nor false. And they are no longer universal characteristics of all thought; they are always historically conditioned. With the philosophical scepticism thus reintroduced there is bound up a new dogmatism; our attitude to our own absolute presuppositions (i.e. to our own religion) is to be one of 'unquestioning acceptance'. Collingwood tells us in the same book that realism is based on 'the grandest foundation a philosophy can have', namely human stupidity. A reader may sometimes be forgiven for wondering whether Collingwood was trying instead to erect his philosophy on the foundation of human credulity.

Whither his later speculations on religion led him it is hard to say, though some hints may be found in *The New Leviathan* where there is a significant passage on Christianity as an anger

religion. It may suffice to remark that while his final historicism
has affinities with Dilthey and Croce, his doctrine of absolute
presuppositions, with its religious and theological background,
has affinities with Kierkegaard and even Karl Barth. Collingwood believed in the *coincidentia oppositorum*, as many passages
in his writings testify. I am suggesting that his own later
philosophy provides a striking illustration of this phenomenon.

The preceding paragraphs have drawn attention to the
sceptical and dogmatic elements which exist side by side in
Collingwood's later work as unreconciled opposites. Any form
of historicism is confronted by the difficulty of avoiding complete scepticism. (If Hegel's philosophy is due to his own
psychological make-up or is a function of conditions, economic
or other, prevailing in his own time, the same is true of the
historian's own methodology and of any possible standard
of criticism. In these circumstances questions of truth and
falsity cannot arise.) Driven by what seems to have been a
somewhat dogmatic solution of religious difficulties, Collingwood avoided this Scylla only by falling into the Charybdis of
'unquestioning acceptance', and it is doubtful whether in his
writings he was able to make his historicism plausible by
providing sailing directions plain enough to enable the mariner
to escape both these hazards.

Why did he never finish *The Principles of History*? Dimi-
nished physical strength, and preoccupation with *The New
Leviathan*, are two obvious answers. But the true answer is
that his project had become either impossible or unnecessary.
The Principles of History was either a philosophical work, an
attempt to describe what history is and to explain how historical
knowledge is possible, or else it was no more than autobiography, an account of how the author as a matter of fact proceeded in his own historical work. For Collingwood by 1939 it
could not be the former, because philosophy had been absorbed
by history; and it was useless for him to write the latter because
his *Autobiography* was already in print. By this time it was not
even open to him to distinguish his practice as an historian
from his philosophical theory about his practice, because in the
Autobiography theory and practice had been identified.

By setting limits to criticism he had even closed the door
on the possibility that his philosophy might be the historian's

reflective self-criticism. This conception of philosophy is adumbrated in § 1 of the Introduction to *The Idea of History* where, as elsewhere, he distinguished between a thought and our awareness of the thought, or between thought of the first degree (e.g. history) and thought of the second degree (philosophy). Further, he used to hold that to be conscious that one thinks x is at once to be in a position to criticize x, because self-knowledge is the possibility of self-criticism. Now it may well be that our thinking proceeds on presuppositions of which we are not at first aware, but if it is possible to become aware of them, and Collingwood thought it was, how can we resist criticizing them? An objector may ask, 'By what criterion?' but, in his earlier years, Collingwood would have replied that reason needed none save itself. Reasoning, he then held, is self-critical at least to the extent of being able to criticize and revise its categories and to detect its own errors; to be aware that one has a bias is already to have transcended that bias. Our unknown presuppositions are doubtless accepted unquestioningly, but to hold that when known they must be accepted in the same spirit is to hold that our awareness of our beliefs is of a kind different from that knowledge of them which would expose them to criticism. If Collingwood came to accept this doctrine and to abandon a philosophy of history, the reason seems to have been that he was driven by a ghost arising out of his past, because the doctrine at once calls to mind the realist denial of self-knowledge and, for instance, Alexander's argument that the self is 'enjoyed' but not known. That argument Collingwood rejected in *The Idea of History* (Part IV, § 1 (ii)), and this is consistent with the passage to which I have referred in the Introduction to that work; but in the *Essay on Metaphysics* an antitype of that argument is implicit and this is not that book's only relapse into the realism of its author's youth. It also contains a denial of any overlap of faith and reason, of presupposing and propounding. What is this save a reversion from the doctrine of the *Essay on Philosophical Method* to the Cook Wilsonian doctrine of a difference in kind alone, and not in degree as well, between belief and knowledge?

To find in Collingwood's later works certain doctrines which he had earlier repudiated does not prove those doctrines false. But it is sometimes hard enough to make the later works consistent even with themselves. The *Essay on Metaphysics* professes not to expound the author's own metaphysical ideas, but to explain what metaphysics is 'and always has been'. If so, then, on his own principles, it can hardly be a work of history; and indeed the argument of a crucial chapter 'On Presupposing' is set forth *more mathematico*; even if this were only a matter of form, the argument can still not be made into an historical one so long as we accept what is said about historical evidence and inference in the passage from *The Principles of History* printed below as Part V, § 3. Philosophy would thus seem to have resisted absorption into history at the very time when its absorption was being proclaimed. To this criticism Collingwood might have replied that it depended on a false view of history; it is sponsors of this kind of criticism, he wrote, who 'feel it necessary to amend history by adding to it what they have left out (and correcting the errors they have put in) by calling a conception of philosophy into existence to redress the balance of their conception of history'. To which one might retort that Collingwood apparently required a dogmatic type of theology to counterbalance *his* conception of history, but perhaps the proper reply is that he has still left us not clearly enlightened on the true conception of history. If he solved the problem of combining what is generally known as philosophy with what is generally known as history to form a new discipline to be called History and (as he suggested in his *Autobiography*) to be the means of solving all the problems of human affairs, he never clearly expounded his solution in his writings.

To read Collingwood's later philosophical works is to be sadly reminded of what he wrote himself about Bury (see Part IV, § 1 (iv) below). By 1932 he had succeeded by 'great toil' in freeing himself from the scepticisms of his youth and had forged in the *Essay on Philosophical Method* a weapon which might have enabled him to cut his way through the forest of philosophical problems and erect for himself a habitation which might long have stood secure against the winds of criticism. By 1938, when the *Autobiography* was written, he had relapsed into scepticisms whose falsity he had discerned six years earlier, and, consequentially, had fallen into a dogmatism which in the *Essay on Philosophical Method* he had outsoared; and the result is that enthusiasm for history tended to make him 'turn traitor' to his philosophical vocation. The multitude of his absorbing interests, together with the presage of an early death, induced him to work fast. Did he perhaps write too quickly to be aware of all the implications in his own arguments? Was the price of attempting too much the loss of the wisdom that might have come by waiting?

§ 3. *Amicitiae sacrum*

In *The Idea of Nature* Collingwood laid down his own test for detecting the greatness of a philosopher. The grand manner in philosophy 'is the mark of a mind which has its philosophical material properly controlled and digested. It is thus based on width and steadiness of outlook upon its subject-matter; . . . it is marked by calmness of temper and candour of statement, no difficulties being concealed and nothing set down in malice or passion. All great philosophers have this calmness of mind, all passion spent by the time their vision is clear, and they write as if they saw things from a mountain-top. That is the tone which distinguishes a great philosopher; a writer who lacks it may or may not be worth reading, but he certainly falls short of greatness.' Judged by this test there is only one book of Collingwood's which could be called great, namely the *Essay on Philosophical Method*, though it must be added that the same philosophical temper is to be found in most of *The Idea of Nature* and *The Idea of History*. The rest of his philosophical books were certainly not free from passion and they cannot be thought calm.

In reviewing the *Essay on Philosophical Method* I was bold enough to call it 'a philosophical classic'. Some of my contemporaries were derisory, others were kind enough to excuse my judgement as due to the partiality of a friend. Certainly I found myself in a minority amongst reviewers. The review in *Philosophy* was unfavourable; that in *Mind*, though not unappreciative, was almost wholly based, as its author subsequently admitted in conversation, on a failure to read Collingwood's Introduction with sufficient care. Nevertheless, nothing that other critics said led me to change my opinion, and I was fortified in it by seeing a letter about the book from Alexander to Collingwood and, some years later, by a talk with

Joachim, who described the *Essay* as a philosphical work 'of the first order'.

However good the book may be, it remains little more than an introduction to a philosophy not yet written. It is full of promise, but it is insufficient by itself to earn for its author many pages in the history of philosophy. This may be one reason why the most recent English book on modern philosophy (*Recent Philosophy*, Home University Library, 1936) contains no mention of his name. His affinity with Croce in aesthetics, as well as personal friendship, may explain the dozen pages devoted to *Speculum Mentis* by G. da Ruggiero in *Filosofi del Novecento* (Bari, 1934).

How was it that the promise of the *Essay on Philosophical Method* was fulfilled, if at all, only in *The Idea of Nature* and *The Idea of History* and not in the later works? In the preceding section I have made some suggestions about the way his thought developed and the reasons why the development took the line it did. But what I said was incomplete because I did no more than hint at one decisive factor which cast a dark shadow over all his later work: his ill health.

The *Essay on Philosophical Method*, worked out in connexion with lectures on ethics written and rewritten from 1922 onwards, was prepared for publication during the spring of 1932. At about the same time Collingwood's health began to give trouble and he was given a term's leave of absence from his college work. It was not then realized that this was the beginning of the ill health against which the rest of his life was to be an heroic struggle. What started to happen at some point during the following years was that tiny blood-vessels began to burst in the brain, with the result that the small parts of the brain affected were put out of action. It was only an intensification of this process when in 1938 he had the first of a series of strokes which eventually reduced him to helplessness, so that his death from pneumonia in 1943, when he was fifty-two, was in some ways no unfortunate end.

In these circumstances the wonder is not that his later books should lack serenity or be marred by febrility and overweening confidence, or contain matter which dismayed his friends; the wonder is that they were written at all, and still more that they should contain passages of outstanding worth. *The Principles of Art* has a section devoted to a carefully elaborated theory of imagination, which deserves more study than it seems yet to have received from professional philosophers (whose attention may have been diverted from the book by the fact that *Mind* never reviewed it). The *Autobiography* outlines an interesting logic of question and answer which has begun to be noticed by contemporary logicians. The *specimina philosophandi* in the *Essay on Metaphysics* are brilliant essays in the history of thought. *The New Leviathan* gives some hint of the fruitfulness of applying to ethics the method expounded in 1933, and the value of its sustained defence of our civilized way of life has been recognized even by reviewers not very favourably disposed to Collingwood's other books.

Nevertheless, whatever the value of these and other passages in his later works, the fact remains that the range and depth of Collingwood's philosophical mind was greater than his publications reveal. If I am asked how good a philosopher he was, I must distinguish his promise from his performance. Those who knew him best (and these are not many, because his devotion to study, and latterly his ill health, made him something of a recluse) are those least likely to object if I say that, in his prime, the power of his mind promised to place him on a level, not with his contemporaries, but with his seniors, Alexander and Whitehead. In addition to a keenly critical gift and a power of entering sympathetically into philosophies very different from his own, he had a constructive mind of a sort that promised to be comparable, in recent English philosophy, with that of the philosophers just named. But the promise never became performance; and it is perhaps not surprising that those who know him only or mainly through his philosophical writings should regard him as an able, an ingenious, and sometimes a perverse writer, but hardly anything more.

Reviewers sometimes accused him of 'trailing his coat' and even of 'wilful perversity', though they have been apt to evade rather than answer the arguments by which some of his paradoxes were supported. Two instances may be given from the *Essay on Metaphysics* and the *Autobiography*: first, his argument that psychology, legitimate and invaluable as a science of feeling, becomes the 'propaganda of irrationalism' when it masquerades as a science of thought; secondly, his belief that modern analytic and positivistic philosophies, despite their avowed aims, are essentially irrationalistic in tendency and dangerous to civilization. The former was challenged in *Mind* (1942), but it is doubtful if the challenger had really grasped Collingwood's argument, perhaps because of the rather intemperate way in which it was put forward. The second has aroused amusement, but it has hardly been answered at all, although a hostile critic might have asked Collingwood whether his own historicism was at bottom any less irrationalist or any less prejudicial to civilization than the philosophies he so unsparingly attacked. In any case, whether Collingwood was right or wrong on these matters, he was in earnest about them. He was not writing for effect or to shock his readers out of complacency; he meant what he said and he did give his reasons; but he might have produced more conviction if he had been able to express himself less passionately.

The rather hectoring style of the later books gives the impression that their author had a proud consciousness of considerable superiority. The real Collingwood was not like that. Before ill health changed him, he was essentially modest; he was conscious of possessing abilities above the ordinary, but equally conscious of their limitations; he was patient of criticism and even went out of his way to seek it. If here I have been critical of his work, that is but what he would have expected and desired. The mass of unpublished manuscripts he left behind him is evidence of the immense toil which he gave himself in order to clarify his ideas and develop them in detail; and it must be remembered that his philosophical work is only a portion of his total scholarly output; for an estimate of Collingwood, the historian of Roman Britain, I need only refer to Mr. I. A. Richmond's graphic essay, together with a bibliography of Collingwood's historical publications, in the *Proceedings of the British Academy*, vol. xxix.

Collingwood was endlessly painstaking with his college pupils, although few of them took much interest in philosophy; but a great deal of his best work was put into his university lectures which attracted very large audiences and widened his influence as a philosophical teacher. Speaking in a thin but clear voice, he always gave the impression that he had something important to say; this made it interesting, and the orderly argument, couched in clear-cut and well-chosen phraseology, made it intelligible to anyone who would listen. To many an undergraduate his lectures on ethics, especially in earlier years, came as a revelation. His abilities brought him respect, though his aloofness was apt to inhibit affection; but in the company of those privileged to enjoy his friendship he was never aloof, and it is hard for me at least to say which was the greatest, the affection inspired by Collingwood the man, the stimulus derived from the tutor, or the admiration evoked by the gifts of the philosopher and historian from whom I have learnt 'more than I can hope to acknowledge'.

T. M. KNOX

ST. ANDREWS
30 *October* 1945

CONTENTS

THE
IDEA OF HISTORY

INTRODUCTION

§ 1. *The philosophy of history*

THIS book is an essay in the philosophy of history. The name 'philosophy of history' was invented in the eighteenth century by Voltaire, who meant by it no more than critical or scientific history, a type of historical thinking in which the historian made up his mind for himself instead of repeating whatever stories he found in old books. The same name was used by Hegel and other writers at the end of the eighteenth century; but they gave it a different sense and regarded it as meaning simply universal or world history. A third use of the phrase is found in several nineteenth-century positivists for whom the philosophy of history was the discovery of general laws governing the course of the events which it was history's business to recount.

The tasks imposed on the 'philosophy' of history by Voltaire and Hegel could be discharged only by history itself, while the positivists were attempting to make out of history, not a philosophy, but an empirical science, like meteorology. In each of these instances, it was a conception of philosophy which governed the conception of the philosophy of history: for Voltaire, philosophy meant independent and critical thinking; for Hegel, it meant thinking about the world as a whole; for nineteenth-century positivism, it meant the discovery of uniform laws.

My use of the term 'philosophy of history' differs from all of these, and in order to explain what I understand by it I will first say something of my conception of philosophy.

Philosophy is reflective. The philosophizing mind never simply thinks about an object, it always, while thinking about any object, thinks also about its own thought about that object. Philosophy may thus be called thought of the second degree, thought about thought. For example, to discover the distance of the earth from the sun is a task for thought of the first degree, in this case for astronomy; to discover what it is exactly that we are doing when we discover the distance of the earth from the sun is a task for thought of the second degree, in this instance for logic or the theory of science.

This is not to say that philosophy is the science of mind, or psychology. Psychology is thought of the first degree; it treats mind in just the same way in which biology treats life. It does not deal with the relation between thought and its object, it deals directly with thought as something quite separate from its object, something that simply happens in the world, as a special kind of phenomenon, one that can be discussed by itself. Philosophy is never concerned with thought by itself; it is always concerned with its relation to its object, and is therefore concerned with the object just as much as with the thought.

This distinction between philosophy and psychology may be illustrated in the different attitudes adopted by these disciplines to historical thinking, which is a special kind of thinking concerned with a special kind of object, which we will provisionally define as the past. The psychologist may interest himself in historical thinking; he may analyse the peculiar kinds of mental event that go on in historians; he might for example argue that historians are people who build up a fantasy-world, like artists, because they are too neurotic to live effectively in the actual world, but, unlike artists, project this fantasy-world into the past because they connect the origin of their neuroses with past events in their own childhood and always go back and back to the past in a vain attempt to disentangle these neuroses. This analysis might go into further detail, and show how the historian's interest in a commanding figure such as Julius Caesar expresses his childish attitude to his father, and so on. I do not suggest that such analysis is a waste of time. I only describe a typical case of it in order to point out that it concentrates its attention exclusively on the subjective term in the original subject-object relation. It attends to the historian's thought, not to its object the past. The whole psychological analysis of historical thought would be exactly the same if there were no such thing as the past at all, if Julius Caesar were an imaginary character, and if history were not knowledge but pure fancy.

For the philosopher, the fact demanding attention is neither the past by itself, as it is for the historian, nor the historian's thought about it by itself, as it is for the psychologist, but the two things in their mutual relation. Thought in its relation to its object is not mere thought but knowledge; thus, what is for psychology the theory of mere thought, of mental events in abstraction from any object, is for philosophy the theory of knowledge. Where the psychologist asks himself: How do historians think? the philosopher asks himself: How do historians know? How do they come to apprehend the past? Conversely, it is the historian's business, not the philosopher's, to apprehend the past as a thing in itself, to say for example that so many years ago such-and-such events actually happened. The philosopher is concerned with these events not as things in themselves but as things known to the historian, and to ask, not what kind of events they were and when and where they took place, but what it is about them that makes it possible for historians to know them.

Thus the philosopher has to think about the historian's mind, but in doing so he is not duplicating the work of the psychologist, for to him the historian's thought is not a complex of mental phenomena but a system of knowledge. He also thinks about the past, but not in such a way as to duplicate the work of the historian: for the past, to him, is not a series of events but a system of things known. One might put this by saying that the philosopher, in so far as he thinks about the subjective side of history, is an epistemologist, and so far as he thinks about the objective side a metaphysician; but that way of putting it would be dangerous as conveying a suggestion that the epistemological and metaphysical parts of his work can be treated separately, and this would be a mistake. Philosophy cannot separate the study of knowing from the study of what is known. This impossibility follows directly from the idea of philosophy as thought of the second degree.

If this is the general character of philosophical thinking, what do I mean when I qualify the term 'philosophy' by adding, 'of history'? In what sense is there a special philosophy of history different from philosophy in general and from the philosophy of anything else?

It is generally, though somewhat precariously, agreed that there are distinctions within the body of philosophy. Most people distinguish logic or the theory of knowledge from ethics or the theory of action; although most of those who make the distinction would also agree that knowing is in some sense a kind of action, and that action as it is studied by ethics is (or at least involves) certain kinds of knowing. The thought which the logician studies is a thought which aims at the discovery of truth, and is thus an example of activity directed towards an end, and these are ethical conceptions. The action which the moral philosopher studies is an action based on knowledge or belief as to what is right or wrong, and knowledge or belief is an epistemological conception. Thus logic and ethics are connected and indeed inseparable, although they are distinct. If there is a philosophy of history, it will be no less intimately connected with the other special philosophical sciences than these two are connected with each other.

We have then to ask why the philosophy of history should be a subject of special study, instead of being merged in a general theory of knowledge. Throughout the course of European civilization people have in some degree thought historically; but we seldom reflect on the activities which we perform quite easily. It is only the difficulties which we encounter that force upon us a consciousness of our own efforts to overcome them. Thus the subject-matter of philosophy, as the organized and scientific development of self-consciousness, depends from time to time on the special problems in which, at any given time, men find special difficulties. To look at the topics specially prominent in the philosophy of any given people at any given period of their history is to find an indication of the special problems which they feel to be calling forth the whole energies of their minds. The peripheral or subsidiary topics will reveal the things about which they feel no special difficulty.

Now, our philosophical tradition goes back in a continuous line to sixth-century Greece, and at that time the special problem of thought was the task of laying the foundations of mathematics. Greek philosophy therefore placed mathematics in the centre of its picture, and when it discussed the theory of knowledge it understood by it first and foremost the theory of mathematical knowledge.

Since then there have been, down to a century ago, two great constructive ages of European history. In the Middle Ages the central problems of thought were concerned with theology, and the problems of philosophy therefore arose out of reflection on theology and were concerned with the relations of God and man. From the sixteenth to the nineteenth centuries the main effort of thought was concerned with laying the foundations of natural science, and philosophy took as its main theme the relation of the human mind as subject to the natural world of things around it in space as object. All this time, of course, people were also thinking historically, but their historical thought was always of a comparatively simple or even rudimentary kind; it raised no problems which it did not find easy to solve, and was never forced to reflect upon itself. But in the eighteenth century people began thinking critically about history, as they had already learnt to think critically about the external world, because history began to be regarded as a special form of thought, not quite like mathematics or theology or science.

The result of this reflection was that a theory of knowledge proceeding on the assumption that mathematics or theology or science, or all three together, could exhaust the problems of knowledge in general, was no longer satisfactory. Historical thought has an object with peculiarities of its own. The past, consisting of particular events in space and time which are no longer happening, cannot be apprehended by mathematical thinking, because mathematical thinking apprehends objects that have no special location in space and time, and it is just that lack of peculiar spatio-temporal location that makes them knowable. Nor can the past be apprehended by theological thinking, because the object of that kind of thinking is a single infinite object, and historical events are finite and plural. Nor by scientific thinking, because the truths which science discovers are known to be true by being found through observation and experiment exemplified in what we actually perceive, whereas the past has vanished and our ideas about it can never be verified as we verify our scientific hypotheses. Theories of knowledge designed to account for mathematical and theological and scientific knowledge thus do not touch on the special problems of historical knowledge; and if they offer themselves as complete accounts of knowledge they actually imply that historical knowledge is impossible.

This did not matter so long as historical knowledge had not yet obtruded itself on the consciousness of philosophers by encountering special difficulties and devising a special technique to meet them. But when that happened, as it did, roughly speaking, in the nineteenth century, the situation was that current theories of knowledge were directed towards the special problems of science, and inherited a tradition based on the study of mathematics and theology, whereas this new historical technique, growing up on all sides, was unaccounted for. A special inquiry was therefore needed whose task should be the study of this new problem or group of problems, the philosophical problems created by the existence of organized and systematized historical research. This new inquiry might justly claim the title philosophy of history, and it is to this inquiry that this book is a contribution.

Two stages are to be expected as the inquiry proceeds. First, the philosophy of history will have to be worked out, not, indeed, in a watertight compartment, for there are none in philosophy, but in a relatively isolated condition, regarded as a special study of a special problem. The problem requires special treatment just because the traditional philosophies do not deal with it, and it requires to be isolated because it is a general rule that what a philosophy does not assert it denies, so that the traditional philosophies carry with them the implication that historical knowledge is impossible. The philosophy of history has therefore to leave them alone until it can build up an independent demonstration of how history is possible.

The second stage will be to work out the connexions between this new branch of philosophy and the old traditional doctrines. Any addition to the body of philosophical ideas alters to some extent everything that was there already, and the establishment of a new philosophical science necessitates a revision of all the old ones. For example, the establishment of modern natural science, and of the philosophical theory produced by reflection upon it, reacted upon the established logic by producing widespread discontent with the syllogistic logic and substituting for it the new methodologies of Descartes and Bacon; the same thing reacted upon the theological metaphysics which the seventeenth century had inherited from the Middle Ages and produced the new conceptions of God which we find for example in Descartes and Spinoza. Spinoza's God is the God of medieval theology as revised in the light of seventeenth-century science. Thus, by the time of Spinoza, the philosophy of science was no longer a particular branch of philosophical investigation separate from the rest: it had permeated all the rest and produced a complete philosophy all conceived in a scientific spirit. In the present case this will mean a general overhauling of all philosophical questions in the light of the results reached by the philosophy of history in the narrower sense, and this will produce a new philosophy which will be a philosophy of history in the wide sense, i.e., a complete philosophy conceived from an historical point of view.

Of these two stages, we must be content if this book represents the first. What I am attempting here is a philosophical inquiry into the nature of history regarded as a special type or form of knowledge with a special type of object, leaving aside, for the present, the further question how that inquiry will affect other departments of philosophical study.

§ 2. *History's nature, object, method, and value*

What history is, what it is about, how it proceeds, and what it is for, are questions which to some extent different people would answer in different ways. But in spite of differences there is a large measure of agreement between the answers. And this agreement becomes closer if the answers are subjected to scrutiny with a view to discarding those which proceed from unqualified witnesses. History, like theology or natural science, is a special form of thought. If that is so, questions about the nature, object, method, and value of this form of thought must be answered by persons having two qualifications.

First, they must have experience of that form of thought. They must be historians. In a sense we are all historians nowadays. All educated persons have gone through a process of education which has included a certain amount of historical thinking. But this does not qualify them to give an opinion about the nature, object, method, and value of historical thinking. For in the first place, the experience of historical thinking which they have thus acquired is probably very superficial; and the opinions based on it are therefore no better grounded than a man's opinion of the French people based on a single week-end visit to Paris. In the second place, experience of anything whatever gained through the ordinary educational channels, as well as being superficial, is invariably out of date. Experience of historical thinking, so gained, is modelled on text-books, and text-books always describe not what is now being thought by real live historians, but what was thought by real live historians at some time in the past when the raw material was being

created out of which the text-book has been put together. And
it is not only the results of historical thought which are out
of date by the time they get into the text-book. It is also
the principles of historical thought: that is, the ideas as to the
nature, object, method, and value of historical thinking. In the
third place, and connected with this, there is a peculiar illusion
incidental to all knowledge acquired in the way of education:
the illusion of finality. When a student is *in statu pupillari* with
respect to any subject whatever, he has to believe that things
are settled because the text-books and his teachers regard them
as settled. When he emerges from that state and goes on studying the subject for himself he finds that nothing is settled. The
dogmatism which is an invariable mark of immaturity drops
away from him. He looks at so-called facts with a new eye.
He says to himself: 'My teacher and text-books told me that
such and such was true; but is it true? What reasons had they
for thinking it true, and were these reasons adequate?' On the
other hand, if he emerges from the status of pupil without continuing to pursue the subject he never rids himself of this dogmatic attitude. And this makes him a person peculiarly unfitted
to answer the questions I have mentioned. No one, for example,
is likely to answer them worse than an Oxford philosopher who,
having read Greats in his youth, was once a student of history
and thinks that this youthful experience of historical thinking
entitles him to say what history is, what it is about, how it
proceeds, and what it is for.

The second qualification for answering these questions is that
a man should not only have experience of historical thinking but
should also have reflected upon that experience. He must be
not only an historian but a philosopher; and in particular his
philosophical thought must have included special attention to
the problems of historical thought. Now it is possible to be a
quite good historian (though not an historian of the highest
order) without thus reflecting upon one's own historical thinking. It is even easier to be a quite good teacher of history
(though not the very best kind of teacher) without such reflection. At the same time, it is important to remember that
experience comes first, and reflection on that experience second.
Even the least reflective historian has the first qualification. He
possesses the experience on which to reflect; and when he is

asked to reflect on it his reflections have a good chance of being to the point. An historian who has never worked much at philosophy will probably answer our four questions in a more intelligent and valuable way than a philosopher who has never worked much at history.

I shall therefore propound answers to my four questions such as I think any present-day historian would accept. Here they will be rough and ready answers, but they will serve for a provisional definition of our subject-matter and they will be defended and elaborated as the argument proceeds.

(a) *The definition of history*. Every historian would agree, I think, that history is a kind of research or inquiry. What kind of inquiry it is I do not yet ask. The point is that generically it belongs to what we call the sciences: that is, the forms of thought whereby we ask questions and try to answer them. Science in general, it is important to realize, does not consist in collecting what we already know and arranging it in this or that kind of pattern. It consists in fastening upon something we do not know, and trying to discover it. Playing patience with things we already know may be a useful means towards this end, but it is not the end itself. It is at best only the means. It is scientifically valuable only in so far as the new arrangement gives us the answer to a question we have already decided to ask. That is why all science begins from the knowledge of our own ignorance: not our ignorance of everything, but our ignorance of some definite thing—the origin of parliament, the cause of cancer, the chemical composition of the sun, the way to make a pump work without muscular exertion on the part of a man or a horse or some other docile animal. Science is finding things out: and in that sense history is a science.

(b) *The object of history*. One science differs from another in that it finds out things of a different kind. What kind of things does history find out? I answer, *res gestae*: actions of human beings that have been done in the past. Although this answer raises all kinds of further questions many of which are controversial, still, however they may be answered, the answers do not discredit the proposition that history is the science of *res gestae*, the attempt to answer questions about human actions done in the past.

(c) *How does history proceed?* History proceeds by the interpretation of evidence: where evidence is a collective name for things which singly are called documents, and a document is a thing existing here and now, of such a kind that the historian, by thinking about it, can get answers to the questions he asks about past events. Here again there are plenty of difficult questions to ask as to what the characteristics of evidence are and how it is interpreted. But there is no need for us to raise them at this stage. However they are answered, historians will agree that historical procedure, or method, consists essentially of interpreting evidence.

(d) Lastly, *what is history for?* This is perhaps a harder question than the others; a man who answers it will have to reflect rather more widely than a man who answers the three we have answered already. He must reflect not only on historical thinking but on other things as well, because to say that something is 'for' something implies a distinction between A and B, where A is good for something and B is that for which something is good. But I will suggest an answer, and express the opinion that no historian would reject it, although the further questions to which it gives rise are numerous and difficult.

My answer is that history is 'for' human self-knowledge. It is generally thought to be of importance to man that he should know himself: where knowing himself means knowing not his merely personal peculiarities, the things that distinguish him from other men, but his nature as man. Knowing yourself means knowing, first, what it is to be a man; secondly, knowing what it is to be the kind of man you are; and thirdly, knowing what it is to be the man *you* are and nobody else is. Knowing yourself means knowing what you can do; and since nobody knows what he can do until he tries, the only clue to what man can do is what man has done. The value of history, then, is that it teaches us what man has done and thus what man is.

§ 3. *The problem of Parts I–IV*

The idea of history which I have just briefly summarized belongs to modern times, and before I proceed in Part V to expound and elaborate this idea in more detail I propose to cast light upon it by investigating its history. Historians nowadays think that history should be (a) a science, or an answering of questions; (b) concerned with human actions in the past;

(c) pursued by interpretation of evidence; and (d) for the sake of human self-knowledge. But this is not the way in which people have always thought of history. For example, a recent author[1] writes of the Sumerians in the third millennium before Christ:

'Historiography is represented by official inscriptions commemorating the building of palaces and of temples. The theocratic style of the scribes attributes everything to the action of the divinity, as can be seen from the following passage, one of many examples.

'"A dispute arises between the kings of Lagash and of Umma about the boundaries of their respective territories. The dispute is submitted to the arbitration of Mesilim, king of Kish, and is settled by the gods, of whom the kings of Kish, Lagash, and Umma are merely the agents or ministers:

'"Upon the truthful word of the god Enlil, king of the territories, the god Ningirsu and the god Shara deliberated. Mesilim, king of Kish, at the behest of his god, Gu-Silim, . . . erected in [this] place a stela. Ush, *isag* of Umma, acted in accordance with his ambitious designs. He removed Mesilim's stela and came to the plain of Lagash. At the righteous word of the god Ningirsu, warrior of the god Enlil, a combat with Umma took place. At the word of the god Enlil, the great divine net laid low the enemies, and funerary *tells* were placed in their stead in the plain."'

Monsieur Jean, it will be noticed, says not that Sumerian historiography *was* this kind of thing, but that in Sumerian literature historiography *is represented by* this kind of thing. I take him to mean that this kind of thing is not really history, but is something in certain ways resembling history. My comment on this would be as follows. An inscription like this expresses a form of thought which no modern historian would call history, because, in the first place, it lacks the character of science: it is not an attempt to answer a question of whose answer the writer begins by being ignorant; it is merely a record of something the writer knows for a fact; and in the second place the fact recorded is not certain actions on the part of human beings, it is certain actions on the part of gods. No doubt these divine actions resulted in actions done by human beings; but they are conceived in the first instance not as

[1] Monsieur Charles F. Jean, in Edward Eyre, *European Civilization* (London, 1935), vol. i, p. 259.

human actions but as divine actions; and to that extent the thought expressed is not historical in respect of its object, and consequently is not historical in respect of its method, for there is no interpretation of evidence, nor in respect of its value, for there is no suggestion that its aim is to further human self-knowledge. The knowledge furthered by such a record is not, or at any rate is not primarily, man's knowledge of man, but man's knowledge of the gods.

From the writer's point of view, therefore, this is not what we call an historical text. The writer was not writing history, he was writing religion. From our point of view it can be used as historical evidence, since a modern historian with his eye fixed on human *res gestae* can interpret it as evidence concerning actions done by Mesilim and Ush and their subjects. But it only acquires its character as historical evidence posthumously, as it were, in virtue of our own historical attitude towards it; in the same way in which prehistoric flints or Roman pottery acquire the posthumous character of historical evidence, not because the men who made them thought of them as historical evidence, but because *we* think of them as historical evidence.

The ancient Sumerians left behind them nothing at all that we should call history. If they had any such thing as an historical consciousness, they have left no record of it. We may say that they must have had such a thing; to us, the historical consciousness is so real and so all-pervasive a feature of life that we cannot see how anyone can have lacked it; but whether we are right so to argue is very doubtful. If we stick to facts as revealed to us by the documents, I think we must say that the historical consciousness of the ancient Sumerians is what scientists call an occult entity, something which the rules of scientific method forbid us to assert on the principle of Occam's Razor that *entia non sunt multiplicanda praeter necessitatem.*

Four thousand years ago, then, our forerunners in civilization did not possess what we call the idea of history. This, so far as we can see, was not because they had the thing itself but had not reflected upon it. It was because they did not possess the thing itself. History did not exist. There existed, instead, something which in certain ways resembled what we call history, but this differed from what we call history in respect of every one of the four characteristics which we have identified in history as it exists to-day.

History as it exists to-day, therefore, has come into existence in the last four thousand years in western Asia and Europe. How did this happen? By what stages has the thing called history come into existence? That is the question to which a somewhat bald and summary answer is offered in Parts I–IV.

PART I

GRECO-ROMAN HISTORIOGRAPHY

§ 1. *Theocratic history and myth*

By what steps and stages did the modern European idea of history come into existence? Since I do not think that any of these stages occurred outside the Mediterranean region, that is, Europe, the Near East from the Mediterranean to Mesopotamia, and the northern African coastlands, I am precluded from saying anything about historical thought in China or in any other part of the world except the region I have mentioned.

I have quoted one example of early Mesopotamian history from a document of about 2500 B.C. I say history, but I ought rather to say quasi-history, because, as I have pointed out, the thought expressed in this document resembles what we call history in making statements about the past, but differs from it, first, in that these statements are not answers to questions, not the fruits of research, but mere assertions of what the writer already knows; and secondly, that the deeds recorded are not human actions but, in the first instance at any rate, divine actions. The gods are conceived on the analogy of human sovereigns, directing the actions of kings and chiefs as these direct the actions of their human subordinates; the hierarchical system of government is carried upwards by a kind of extrapolation. Instead of the series: subject, lower official, higher official, king, we have the series: subject, lower official, higher official, king, god. Whether the king and the god are sharply distinguished so that the god is conceived as the real head of the community and the king as his servant, or whether the king and the god are somehow identified, the king being conceived as an incarnation of the god or at any rate as in some way or other divine, not merely human, is a question into which we need not enter, because, however we answer it, the result will be that government is conceived theocratically.

History of this kind I propose to call *theocratic history*; in which phrase 'history' means not history proper, that is scientific history, but a statement of known facts for the information of persons to whom they are not known, but who, as worshippers of the god in question, ought to know the deeds whereby he has made himself manifest.

There is another kind of quasi-history, of which we also find examples in Mesopotamian literature, namely the *myth*. Theocratic history, although it is not primarily the history of human actions, is nevertheless concerned with them in the sense that the divine characters in the story are the superhuman rulers of human societies, whose actions, therefore, are actions done partly to those societies and partly through them. In theocratic history humanity is not an agent, but partly an instrument and partly a patient, of the actions recorded. Moreover, these actions are thought of as having definite places in a time-series, as occurring at dates in the past. Myth, on the contrary, is not concerned with human actions at all. The human element has been completely purged away and the characters of the story are simply gods. And the divine actions that are recorded are not dated events in the past: they are conceived as having occurred in the past, indeed, but in a dateless past which is so remote that nobody knows when it was. It is outside all our time-reckonings and called 'the beginning of things'. Hence, when a myth is couched in what seems a temporal shape, because it relates events one of which follows another in a definite order, the shape is not strictly speaking temporal, it is quasi-temporal: the narrator is using the language of time-succession as a metaphor in which to express relations which he does not conceive as really temporal. The subject-matter which is thus mythically expressed in the language of temporal succession is, in myth proper, the relations between various gods or various elements of the divine nature. Hence myth proper has always the character of *theogony*.

For an example, let us consider the main outline of the Babylonian *Poem on the Creation*. We have it in a text of the seventh century B.C., but this professes to be, and doubtless is, a copy of very much older texts, probably going back to the same period as the document I have already quoted:

'The poem begins at the origin of all things. Nothing exists as yet, not even the gods. Out of this nothingness appear the cosmic principles *Apsu*, fresh water, and *Tiamat*, salt water.' The first step in the theogony is the birth of *Mummu*, the first-born son of Apsu and Tiamat. 'The gods increase and multiply.

Then they become rebellious against [this original] divine triad. Apsu decides to destroy them. . . . But the wise *Ea* triumphs by the use of magic. He casts a powerful spell upon the waters, Apsu's element, puts his ancestor to sleep', and makes Mummu captive. Tiamat now 'plans to avenge the conquered. She marries Qingu, makes him head of her army, and confides to his care the tablets of fate.' Ea, divining her plans, reveals them to the ancient god Anshar. At first Tiamat triumphs over this coalition, but now arises Marduk, who challenges Tiamat to single combat, kills her, cuts her body in two 'like a fish', and makes out of one half the heavens, in which he places the stars, and out of the other the earth. Out of Marduk's blood, man is made.[1]

These two forms of quasi-history, theocratic history and myth, dominated the whole of the Near East until the rise of Greece. For example, the Moabite Stone (ninth century B.C.) is a perfect document of theocratic history, showing that little change has taken place in that form of thought for between one and two millennia:

'I am Mesha, the son of Kemosh, king of Moab. My father was king over Moab thirty years and I became king after my father. And I made this high-place for Kemosh, for he saved me from my downfall and made me triumph over my enemies.

'Omri, king of Israel, was the oppressor of Moab for many long days because Kemosh was angered against his country. His son succeeded him, and he also said "I will oppress Moab". It was in my day that he said it. And I triumphed over him and his house. And Israel perished for ever.

'And Omri took possession of the land of Mehedeba and lived there during his life and half his sons' lives, forty years; but Kemosh restored it to us in my lifetime.'

Or again, here is a quotation from the account, put into the mouth of Esar-Haddon, king of Nineveh early in the seventh century B.C., of his campaign against the enemies who had killed his father Sennacherib:

'The fear of the great gods, my lords, overthrew them. When they beheld the rush of my terrible battle, they were beside themselves. The goddess Ishtar, goddess of battle and of fighting, she

---

[1] Jean, in Eyre, op. cit., pp. 271 ff.

who loves my priesthood, remained at my side and broke their line. She broke their battle-line, and in their assembly they said "It is our king!"[1]

The Hebrew scriptures contain a great deal of both theocratic history and myth. From the point of view from which I am now considering these ancient literatures, the quasi-historical elements in the Old Testament do not greatly differ from the corresponding elements in Mesopotamian and Egyptian literature. The main difference is that whereas the theocratic element in these other literatures is on the whole particularistic, in the Hebrew scriptures it tends to be universalistic. I mean, the gods whose deeds are recorded in these other literatures are on the whole regarded as the divine heads of particular societies. The God of the Hebrews is certainly regarded as in a special sense the divine head of the Hebrew community; but under the influence of the 'prophetic' movement, that is, from about the middle of the eighth century onwards, they came to conceive Him more and more as the divine head of all mankind; and therefore expected Him no longer to protect their interests as against those of other particular societies, but to deal with them according to their deserts; and to deal with other particular societies in the same way. And this tendency away from particularism in the direction of universalism affects not only the theocratic history of the Hebrews but also their mythology. Unlike the Babylonian creation-legend, the Hebrew creation-legend contains an attempt, not indeed a very well-thought-out attempt (for every child, I suppose, has asked its elders the unanswerable question, 'Who was Cain's wife?'), but still an attempt, to account not only for the origin of man in general but for the origin of the various peoples into which mankind, as known to the authors of the legend, was divided. Indeed one might almost say that the peculiarity of the Hebrew legend as compared with the Babylonian is that it replaces theogony by ethnogony.

§ 2. *The creation of scientific history by Herodotus*

As compared with all this, the work of the Greek historians as we possess it in detail in the fifth-century historians, Herodotus and Thucydides, takes us into a new world. The Greeks quite

[1] Ibid., p. 364.

clearly and consciously recognized both that history is, or can be, a science, and that it has to do with human actions. Greek history is not legend, it is research; it is an attempt to get answers to definite questions about matters of which one recognizes oneself as ignorant. It is not theocratic, it is humanistic; the matters inquired into are not τὰ θεῖα, they are τὰ ἀνθρώπινα. Moreover, it is not mythical. The events inquired into are not events in a dateless past, at the beginning of things: they are events in a dated past, a certain number of years ago.

This is not to say that legend, either in the form of theocratic history or in the form of myth, was a thing foreign to the Greek mind. The work of Homer is not research, it is legend; and to a great extent it is theocratic legend. The gods appear in Homer as intervening in human affairs in a way not very different from the way in which they appear in the theocratic histories of the Near East. Similarly, Hesiod has given us an example of myth. Nor is it to say that these legendary elements, theocratic or mythical as the case may be, are entirely absent even from the classical works of the fifth-century historians. F. M. Cornford in his *Thucydides Mythistoricus* (London, 1907) drew attention to the existence of such elements even in the hard-headed and scientific Thucydides. He was of course perfectly right; and similar legendary elements are notoriously frequent in Herodotus. But what is remarkable about the Greeks was not the fact that their historical thought contained a certain residue of elements which we should call non-historical, but the fact that, side by side with these, it contained elements of what we call history.

The four characteristics of history which I enumerated in the Introduction were (a) that it is scientific, or begins by asking questions, whereas the writer of legends begins by knowing something and tells what he knows; (b) that it is humanistic, or asks questions about things done by men at determinate times in the past; (c) that it is rational, or bases the answers which it gives to its questions on grounds, namely appeal to evidence; (d) that it is self-revelatory, or exists in order to tell man what man is by telling him what man has done. Now the first, second, and fourth of these characteristics clearly appear in Herodotus: (1) The fact that history as a science was a Greek invention is recorded to this day by its very name. History is a Greek word, meaning simply an investigation or inquiry. Herodotus, who uses it in the title of his work, thereby 'marks a literary revolution' (as Croiset, an historian of Greek literature, says[1]). Previous writers had been λογογράφοι, writers-down of current stories: 'the historian', say How and Wells, 'sets out to "find" the truth.' It is the use of this word, and its implications, that make Herodotus the father of history. The conversion of legend-writing into the science of history was not native to the Greek mind, it was a fifth-century invention, and Herodotus was the man who invented it. (ii) It is equally clear that history for Herodotus is humanistic as distinct from either mythical or theocratic. As he says in his preface, his purpose is to describe the deeds of men. (iii) His end, as he describes it himself, is that these deeds shall not be forgotten by posterity. Here we have my fourth characteristic of history, namely that it ministers to man's knowledge of man. In particular, Herodotus points out, it reveals man as a rational agent: that is, its function is partly to discover what men have done and partly to discover why they have done it (δι' ἣν αἰτίην ἐπολέμησαν). Herodotus does not confine his attention to bare events; he considers these events in a thoroughly humanistic manner as actions of human beings who had reasons for acting as they did: and the historian is concerned with these reasons.

These three points reappear in the preface of Thucydides, which was obviously written with an eye on that of Herodotus. Thucydides, writing Attic and not Ionic, does not of course use the word ἱστορίη, but he refers to it in other terms: to make it clear that he is no logographer but a scientific student, asking questions instead of repeating legends, he defends his choice of subject by saying that events earlier than those of the Peloponnesian War cannot be accurately ascertained—σαφῶς μὲν εὑρεῖν ἀδύνατα ἦν. He emphasizes the humanistic purpose and the self-revelatory function of history, in words modelled on those of his predecessor. And in one way he improves on Herodotus, for Herodotus makes no mention of evidence (the third of the characteristics mentioned above), and one is left to gather from the body of his work what his idea of evidence was; but Thucydides does say explicitly that historical inquiry rests on

[1] *Histoire de la littérature grecque*, vol. ii, p. 589, *apud* How and Wells, *Commentary on Herodotus* (Oxford, 1912), vol. i, p. 53.

evidence, ἐκ τεκμηρίων σκοποῦντί μοι, 'when I consider in the light of the evidence'. What they thought about the nature of evidence, and the way in which an historian interprets it, is a subject to which I shall return in § 5.

§ 3. *Anti-historical tendency of Greek thought*

In the meantime, I should like to point out how remarkable a thing is this creation of scientific history by Herodotus, for he was an ancient Greek, and ancient Greek thought as a whole has a very definite prevailing tendency not only uncongenial to the growth of historical thought but actually based, one might say, on a rigorously anti-historical metaphysics. History is a science of humar action: what the historian puts before himself is things that men have done in the past, and these belong to a world of change, a world where things come to be and cease to be. Such things, according to the prevalent Greek metaphysical view, ought not to be knowable, and therefore history ought to be impossible.

For the Greeks, the same difficulty arose with the world of nature since it too was a world of this kind. If everything in the world changes, they asked, what is there in such a world for the mind to grasp? They were quite sure that anything which can be an object of genuine knowledge must be permanent; for it must have some definite character of its own, and therefore cannot contain in itself the seeds of its own destruction. If it is to be knowable it must be determinate; if it is determinate, it must be so completely and exclusively what it is that no internal change and no external force can ever set about making it into something else. Greek thought achieved its first triumph when it discovered in the objects of mathematical knowledge something that satisfied these conditions. A straight bar of iron may be bent into a curve, a flat surface of water may be broken into waves, but the straight line and the plane surface, as the mathematician thinks of them, are eternal objects that cannot change their characteristics.

Following the line of argument thus opened up, Greek thought worked out a distinction between two types of thought, know-ledge proper (ἐπιστήμη) and what we translate by 'opinion', δόξα. Opinion is the empirical semi-knowledge we have of matters of fact, which are always changing. It is our fleeting acquaintance with the fleeting actualities of the world; it thus only holds good for its own proper duration, for the here and now; and it is immediate, ungrounded in reasons, incapable of demonstration. True knowledge, on the contrary, holds good not only here and now but everywhere and always, and it is based on demonstrative reasoning and thus capable of meeting and overthrowing error by the weapon of dialectical criticism.

Thus, for the Greeks, process could be known only so far as it was perceived, and the knowledge of it could never be demonstrative. An exaggerated statement of this view, as we get it in the Eleatics, would misuse the weapon of dialectic, which is really valid only against error in the sphere of knowledge strictly so called, to prove that change does not exist and that the 'opinions' we have about the changing are really not even opinions but sheer illusions. Plato rejects that doctrine and sees in the world of change something not indeed intelligible but real to the extent of being perceptible, something intermediate between the nullity with which the Eleatics had identified it and the complete reality and intelligibility of the eternal. On such a theory, history ought to be impossible. For history must have these two characteristics: first it must be about what is transitory, and secondly it must be scientific or demonstrative. But on this theory what is transitory cannot be demonstratively known; it cannot be the object of science; it can only be a matter of αἴσθησις, perception, whereby human sensibility catches the fleeting moment as it flies. And it is essential to the Greek point of view that this momentary sensuous perception of momentary changing things cannot be a science or the basis of a science.

§ 4. *Greek conception of history's nature and value*

The ardour with which the Greeks pursued the ideal of an unchanging and eternal object of knowledge might easily mislead us as to their historical interests. It might, if we read them carelessly, make us think them uninterested in history, somewhat as Plato's attack on the poets might make an unintelligent reader fancy that Plato cared little for poetry. In order to interpret such things correctly we must remember that no competent thinker or writer wastes his time attacking a man of straw. An intense polemic against a certain doctrine is an infallible sign that the doctrine in question figures largely in the writer's environment and even has a strong attraction for himself. The Greek pursuit of the eternal was as eager as it was, precisely because the Greeks themselves had an unusually vivid sense of the temporal. They lived in a time when history was moving with extraordinary rapidity, and in a country where earthquake and erosion change the face of the land with a violence hardly to be seen elsewhere. They saw all nature as a spectacle of incessant change, and human life as changing more violently than anything else. Unlike the Chinese, or the medieval civilization of Europe, whose conception of human society was anchored in the hope of retaining the chief features of its structure unchanged, they made it their first aim to face and reconcile themselves to the fact that such permanence is impossible. This recognition of the necessity of change in human affairs gave to the Greeks a peculiar sensitiveness to history.

Knowing that nothing in life can persist unchanged, they came habitually to ask themselves what exactly the changes had been which, they knew, must have come about in order to bring the present into existence. Their historical consciousness was thus not a consciousness of agelong tradition moulding the life of one generation after another into a uniform pattern; it was a consciousness of violent περιπέτειαι, catastrophic changes from one state of things to its opposite, from smallness to greatness, from pride to abasement, from happiness to misery. This was how they interpreted the general character of human life in their dramas, and this was how they narrated the particular parts of it in their history. The only thing that a shrewd and critical Greek like Herodotus would say about the divine power that ordains the course of history is that it is φθονερὸν καὶ ταραχῶδες: it rejoices in upsetting and disturbing things. He was only repeating (i. 32) what every Greek knew: that the power of Zeus is manifested in the thunderbolt, that of Poseidon in the earthquake, that of Apollo in the pestilence, and that of Aphrodite in the passion that destroyed at once the pride of Phaedra and the chastity of Hippolytus.

It is true that these catastrophic changes in the condition of human life, which to the Greeks were the proper theme of history, were unintelligible. There could be no ἐπιστήμη of them, no demonstrative scientific knowledge. But all the same history

had for the Greeks a definite value. Plato himself laid it down[1]
that right opinion (which is the sort of pseudo-knowledge that
perception gives us of what changes) was no less useful for the
conduct of life than scientific knowledge, and the poets maintained their traditional place in Greek life as the teachers of
sound principles by showing that in the general pattern of these
changes certain antecedents normally led to certain consequents.
Notably, an excess in any one direction led to a violent change
into its own opposite. Why this was so they could not tell; but
they thought it a matter of observation that it was so; that
people who became extremely rich or extremely powerful were
thereby brought into special danger of being reduced to a condition of extreme poverty or weakness. There is here no theory of
causation; the thought does not resemble that of seventeenth-
century inductive science with its metaphysical basis in the
axiom of cause and effect; the riches of Croesus are not the
cause of his downfall, they are merely a symptom, to the intelligent observer, that something is happening in the rhythm of
his life which is likely to lead to a downfall. Still less is the
downfall a punishment for anything that, in an intelligible
moral sense, could be called wrongdoing. When Amasis in
Herodotus (iii. 43) broke off his alliance with Polycrates, he did
it simply on the ground that Polycrates was too prosperous: the
pendulum had swung too far one way and was likely to swing
as far in the other. Such examples have their value to the person
who can make use of them; for he can use his own will to arrest
these rhythms in his life before they reach the danger-point, and
check the thirst for power and wealth instead of allowing it to
drive him to excess. Thus history has a value; its teachings are
useful for human life; simply because the rhythm of its changes
is likely to repeat itself, similar antecedents leading to similar
consequents; the history of notable events is worth remembering
in order to serve as a basis for prognostic judgements, not
demonstrable but probable, laying down not what will happen
but what is likely to happen, indicating the points of danger in
rhythms now going on. Divinas palabras

This conception of history was the very opposite of determi-
nistic, because the Greeks regarded the course of history as
flexible and open to salutary modification by the well-instructed

[1] *Meno*, 97 a–b.

human will. Nothing that happens is inevitable. The person who is about to be involved in a tragedy is actually overwhelmed by it only because he is too blind to see his danger. If he saw it, he could guard against it. Thus the Greeks had a lively and indeed a naïve sense of the power of man to control his own destiny, and thought of this power as limited only by the limitations of his knowledge. The fate that broods over human life is, from this Greek point of view, a destructive power only because man is blind to its workings. Granted that he cannot understand these workings, he can yet have right opinions about them, and in so far as he acquires such opinions he becomes able to put himself in a position where the blows of fate will miss him.

On the other hand, valuable as the teachings of history are, their value is limited by the unintelligibility of its subject-matter; and that is why Aristotle said[1] that poetry is more scientific than history, for history is a mere collection of empirical facts, whereas poetry extracts from such facts a universal judgement. History tells us that Croesus fell and that Polycrates fell; poetry, according to Aristotle's idea of it, makes not these singular judgements but the universal judgement that very rich men, as such, fall. Even this is, in Aristotle's view, only a partially scientific judgement, for no one can see why rich men should fall; the universal cannot be syllogistically demonstrated; but it approaches the status of a true universal because we can use it as the major premiss for a new syllogism applying this generalization to fresh cases. Thus poetry is for Aristotle the distilled essence of the teaching of history. In poetry the lessons of history do not become any more intelligible and they remain undemonstrated and therefore merely probable, but they become more compendious and therefore more useful.

Such was the way in which the Greeks conceived the nature and value of history. They could not, consistently with their general philosophical attitude, regard it as scientific. They had to consider it as, at bottom, not a science but a mere aggregate of perceptions. What, then, was their conception of historical evidence? The answer is that, conformably with this view, they identified historical evidence with the reports of facts given by eyewitnesses of those facts. Evidence consists of

[1] *Poetics*, 1451^{b}5 ff.

eyewitnesses' narratives, and historical method consists of eliciting these.

§ 5. *Greek historical method and its limitations*

Quite clearly, it was in this way that Herodotus conceived of evidence and method. This does not mean that he uncritically believed whatever eyewitnesses told him. On the contrary, he is in practice highly critical of their narratives. And here again he is typically Greek. The Greeks as a whole were skilled in the practice of the law courts, and a Greek would find no difficulty in applying to historical testimony the same kind of criticism which he was accustomed to direct upon witnesses in court. The work of Herodotus or Thucydides depends in the main on the testimony of eyewitnesses with whom the historian had personal contact. And his skill as a researcher consisted in the fact that he must have cross-questioned an eyewitness of past events until he had called up in the informant's own mind an historical picture of those events far fuller and more coherent than any he could have volunteered for himself. The result of this process was to create in the informant's mind for the first time a genuine knowledge of the past events which he had perceived but of which up till then he had δόξα only, not ἐπιστήμη.

This conception of the way in which a Greek historian collected his material makes it a very different thing from the way in which a modern historian may use printed memoirs. Instead of the easy-going belief on the informant's part that his prima facie recollection was adequate to the facts, there could grow up in his mind a chastened and criticized recollection which had stood the fire of such questions as 'Are you quite sure that you remember it just like that? Have you not now contradicted what you were saying yesterday? How do you reconcile your account of that event with the very different account given by so-and-so?' This method of using the testimony of eyewitnesses is undoubtedly the method which underlies the extraordinary solidity and consistency of the narratives which Herodotus and Thucydides finally wrote about fifth-century Greece.

No other method deserving the name scientific was available to the fifth-century historians, but it had three limitations:

First, it inevitably imposed on its users a shortness of historical perspective. The modern historian knows that if only he had the capacity he could become the interpreter of the whole past of mankind; but whatever Greek historians might have thought of Plato's description of the philosopher as the spectator of all time, they would never have ventured to claim Plato's words as a description of themselves. Their method tied them on a tether whose length was the length of living memory: the only source they could criticize was an eyewitness with whom they could converse face to face. It is true that they relate events from a remoter past, but as soon as Greek historical writing tries to go beyond its tether, it becomes a far weaker and more precarious thing. For instance, we must not deceive ourselves into thinking that any scientific value attaches to what Herodotus tells us about the sixth century or to what Thucydides tells us about events before the Pentecontaetia. From our twentieth-century point of view, these early stories in Herodotus and Thucydides are very interesting, but they are mere logography and not scientific. They are traditions which the author who hands them down to us has not been able to raise to the level of history because he has not been able to pass them through the crucible of the only critical method he knew. Nevertheless, this contrast in Herodotus and Thucydides between the unreliability of everything farther back than living memory and the critical precision of what comes within living memory is a mark not of the failure of fifth-century historiography but of its success. The point about Herodotus and Thucydides is not that the remote past is for them still outside the scope of scientific history but that the recent past is within that scope. Scientific history has been invented. Its field is still narrow; but within that field it is secure. Moreover, this narrowness of field did not matter much to the Greeks, because the extreme rapidity with which their own civilization was developing and changing afforded plenty of first-class historical material within the confines set by their method, and for the same reason they could produce first-rate historical work without developing what in fact they never did develop, any lively curiosity concerning the remote past.

Secondly, the Greek historian's method precludes him from choosing his subject. He cannot, like Gibbon, begin by wishing to write a great historical work and go on to ask himself what he shall write about. The only thing he can write about is the

events which have happened within living memory to people
with whom he can have personal contact. Instead of the historian choosing the subject, the subject chooses the historian;
I mean that history is written only because memorable things
have happened which call for a chronicler among the contemporaries of the people who have seen them. One might almost
say that in ancient Greece there were no historians in the sense
in which there were artists and philosophers; there were no
people who devoted their lives to the study of history; the
historian was only the autobiographer of his generation and
autobiography is not a profession.

Thirdly, Greek historical method made it impossible for the
various particular histories to be gathered up into one all-
embracing history. Nowadays we think of monographs on
various subjects as ideally forming parts of a universal history,
so that if their subjects are carefully chosen and their scale and
treatment carefully controlled they might serve as chapters in
a single historical work; and this is the way in which a writer
like Grote actually treated Herodotus' account of the Persian
War and Thucydides' of the Peloponnesian. But if any given
history is the autobiography of a generation, it cannot be rewritten when that generation has passed away, because the
evidence on which it was based will have perished. The work
that a contemporary based on that evidence can thus never be
improved upon or criticized, and it can never be absorbed into
a larger whole, because it is like a work of art, something having
the uniqueness and individuality of a statue or a poem. Thucydides' work is a κτῆμα ἐς αἰεί, that of Herodotus was written
to rescue glorious deeds from the oblivion of time, precisely
because when their generation was dead and gone the work
could never be done again. The rewriting of their histories, or
their incorporation into the history of a longer period, would
have seemed to them an absurdity. To the Greek historians,
therefore, there could never be any such thing as a history of
Greece. There could be a history of a fairly extensive complex
of events, like the Persian War or the Peloponnesian War; but
only on two conditions. First, this complex of events must be
complete in itself: it must have a beginning, a middle, and an
end, like the plot of an Aristotelian tragedy. Secondly, it must
be εὐσύνοπτος, like an Aristotelian city-state. As Aristotle

thought[1] that no community of civilized men under a single government could exceed in size the number of citizens that could be within earshot of a single herald, the dimensions of the political organism being thus limited by a purely physical fact, so the Greek theory of history implies that no historical narrative could exceed in length the years of a man's lifetime, within which alone the critical methods at its disposal could be applied.

§ 6. *Herodotus and Thucydides*

The greatness of Herodotus stands out in the sharpest relief when, as the father of history, he is set against a background consisting of the general tendencies of Greek thought. The most dominant of these was anti-historical, as I have argued, because it involved the position that only what is unchanging can be known. Therefore history is a forlorn hope, an attempt to know what, being transitory, is unknowable. But we have already seen that, by skilful questioning, Herodotus was able to elicit ἐπιστήμη from his informant's δόξα and thus to attain knowledge in a field where Greeks had thought it impossible.

His success must remind us of one of his contemporaries, a man who was not afraid, either in war or in philosophy, to embark on forlorn hopes. Socrates brought philosophy down from heaven to earth by insisting that he himself knew nothing, and inventing a technique whereby, through skilful questioning, knowledge could be generated in the minds of others as ignorant as himself. Knowledge of what? Knowledge of human affairs: in particular, of the moral ideas that guide human conduct.

The parallel between the work of the two men is so striking that I put Herodotus side by side with Socrates as one of the great innovating geniuses of the fifth century. But his achievement ran so strongly counter to the current of Greek thought that it did not long survive its creator. Socrates was after all in the direct line of the Greek intellectual tradition, and that is why his work was taken up and developed by Plato and many other disciples. Not so Herodotus. Herodotus had no successors.

Even if I conceded to an objector that Thucydides worthily carried on the Herodotean tradition, the question would still remain: Who carried it on when Thucydides had finished with it? And the only answer is: Nobody carried it on. These fifth-

[1] *Politics*, 1326ᵇ2–26.

century giants had no fourth-century successors anything like equal in stature to themselves. The decay of Greek art from the late fifth century onwards is undeniable; but it did not entail a decay of Greek science. Greek philosophy still had Plato and Aristotle to come. The natural sciences were still to have a long and brilliant life. If history is a science, why did history share the fate of the arts and not the fate of the other sciences? Why does Plato write as if Herodotus had never lived?

The answer is that the Greek mind tended to harden and narrow itself in its anti-historical tendency. The genius of Herodotus triumphed over that tendency, but after him the search for unchangeable and eternal objects of knowledge gradually stifled the historical consciousness, and forced men to abandon the Herodotean hope of achieving a scientific knowledge of past human actions.

This is not a mere conjecture. We can see the thing happening. The man in whom it happened was Thucydides.

The difference between the scientific outlook of Herodotus and that of Thucydides is hardly less remarkable than the difference between their literary styles. The style of Herodotus is easy, spontaneous, convincing. That of Thucydides is harsh, artificial, repellent. In reading Thucydides I ask myself, What is the matter with the man, that he writes like that? I answer: he has a bad conscience. He is trying to justify himself for writing history at all by turning it into something that is not history. Mr. C. N. Cochrane, in his *Thucydides and the Science of History* (London, 1929), has argued, I think rightly, that the dominant influence on Thucydides is the influence of Hippocratic medicine. Hippocrates was not only the father of medicine, he was also the father of psychology, and his influence is evident not only in such things as the Thucydidean description of the plague, but in such studies in morbid psychology as the description of war-neurosis in general and the special instances of it in the Corcyrean revolution and the Melian dialogue. Herodotus may be the father of history, but Thucydides is the father of psychological history.

Now what is psychological history? It is not history at all, but natural science of a special kind. It does not narrate facts for the sake of narrating facts. Its chief purpose is to affirm laws, psychological laws. A psychological law is not an event nor yet a complex of events: it is an unchanging rule which governs the relations between events. I think that every one who knows both authors will agree with me when I say that what chiefly interests Herodotus is the events themselves; what chiefly interests Thucydides is the laws according to which they happen. But these laws are precisely such eternal and unchanging forms as, according to the main trend of Greek thought, are the only knowable things.

Thucydides is not the successor of Herodotus in historical thought but the man in whom the historical thought of Herodotus was overlaid and smothered beneath anti-historical motives. This is a thesis which may be illustrated by mentioning one familiar feature of Thucydides' method. Consider his speeches. Custom has dulled our susceptibilities; but let us ask ourselves for a moment: could a just man who had a really historical mind have permitted himself the use of such a convention? Think first of their style. Is it not, historically speaking, an outrage to make all these very different characters talk in one and the same fashion, and that a fashion in which no one can ever have spoken when addressing troops before a battle or when pleading for the lives of the conquered? Is it not clear that the style betrays a lack of interest in the question what such and such a man really said on such and such an occasion? Secondly, think of their contents. Can we say that, however unhistorical their style may be, their substance is historical? The question has been variously answered. Thucydides does say (i. 22) that he kept 'as closely as possible' to the general sense of what was actually said; but how close was this? He does not claim that it was very close, because he adds that he has given the speeches roughly as he thought the speakers would have said what was appropriate to the occasion; and when we consider the speeches themselves in their context, it is difficult to resist the conclusion that the judge of 'what was appropriate' was Thucydides himself. Grote argued long ago[1] that the Melian dialogue contains more imagination than history, and I have seen no convincing refutation of his argument. The speeches seem to me to be in substance not history but Thucydidean comments upon the acts of the speakers, Thucydidean reconstructions of their motives and intentions. Even if this be denied, the very controversy on

[1] *History of Greece* (London, 1862), vol. v, p. 95.

this question may be regarded as evidence that the Thucydidean speech is both in style and in content a convention characteristic of an author whose mind cannot be fully concentrated on the events themselves, but is constantly being drawn away from the events to some lesson that lurks behind them, some unchanging and eternal truth of which the events are, Platonically speaking, παραδείγματα or μιμήματα.

§ 7. *The Hellenistic period*

After the fifth century B.C. the historian's outlook underwent an enlargement in time. When Greek thought, having attained a consciousness of itself and its own worth, set out to conquer the world, it embarked on an adventure whose development was too vast to fall within the view of a single generation, and yet its consciousness of its own mission gave it a conviction of the essential unity of that development. This helped the Greeks to overcome the particularism which had coloured all their historiography before the time of Alexander the Great. In their eyes history had been essentially the history of one particular social unit at one particular time:

(i) They were conscious that this particular social unit was only one among many; and, in so far as it came into contact, friendly or hostile, with others during the given space of time, these others put in an appearance on the stage of history. But although for this reason Herodotus has to say something about the Persians, he is interested in them not for their own sake but only as enemies of the Greeks: worthy and honourable enemies, but still enemies and no more. (ii) They were conscious in the fifth century, and even earlier, that there was such a thing as the human world, the totality of all particular social units; they called it ἡ οἰκουμένη, as distinct from ὁ κόσμος, the natural world. But the unity of this human world was for them only a geographical, not an historical, unity. The consciousness of that unity was not an historical consciousness. The idea of oecumenical history, world-history, was still non-existent. (iii) They were conscious that the history of the particular society in which they were interested had been going on for a long time. But they did not try to trace it back very far. The reason for this I have already explained. The only genuinely historical method hitherto invented depended on cross-questioning eyewitnesses;

consequently the backward limit of any historian's field was dictated by the limits of human memory.

These three limitations were all overcome in what is called the Hellenistic period.

(i) The symbol of the parochial outlook of the fifth-century Greeks is the linguistic distinction between Greeks and Barbarians. The fourth century did not obliterate this distinction, but it abolished its rigidity. This was not a matter of theory, it was a matter of practice. It became a familiar fact about the contemporary world that Barbarians could become Greeks. This graecizing of Barbarians is called in Greek Hellenism (ἑλληνίζειν means to talk Greek, and, in a wider sense, to adopt Greek manners and customs) ; and the Hellenistic period is the period when Greek manners and customs were adopted by Barbarians. Thus the Greek historical consciousness, which for Herodotus had been primarily the consciousness of hostility between Greeks and Barbarians (the Persian Wars), becomes the consciousness of co-operation between Greeks and Barbarians, a co-operation in which Greeks take the lead, and Barbarians, by following that lead, become Greeks, heirs to Greek culture, and thus heirs to the Greek historical consciousness.

(ii) Through the conquests of Alexander the Great, whereby the οἰκουμένη or at least a very large part of it (and a part which included all the non-Greek peoples in whom the Greeks were specially interested) became a single political unit, the 'world' became something more than a geographical expression. It became an historical expression. The whole empire of Alexander now shared a single history of the Greek world. Potentially, the whole οἰκουμένη shared it. Any ordinarily well-informed person knew as a fact that Greek history was a single history that held good from the Adriatic to the Indus and from the Danube to the Sahara. For a philosopher, reflecting on this fact, it was possible to extend the same idea over the whole οἰκουμένη: 'The poet says, Dear city of Cecrops: wilt thou not say, Dear city of Zeus?' That is, of course, from Marcus Aurelius[1] in the second century A.D. ; but the idea, the idea of the whole world as a single historical unit, is a typically Stoic idea, and Stoicism is a typical product of the Hellenistic period. It was Hellenism that created the idea of oecumenical history.

[1] *Meditations*, iv. 23.

(iii) But a world-history could not be written on the strength of testimony from living eyewitnesses, and therefore a new method was required, namely compilation. It was necessary to construct a patchwork history whose materials were drawn from 'authorities', that is, from the works of previous historians who had already written the histories of particular societies at particular times. This is what I call the 'scissors-and-paste' historical method. It consists in excerpting the required material from writers whose work cannot be checked on Herodotean principles, because the eyewitnesses who co-operated in that work are no longer alive. As a method, this is far inferior to the Socratic method of the fifth century. It is not a wholly uncritical method, because judgement can and must be exercised as to whether this or that statement, made by this or that authority, is true. But it cannot be used at all without the assurance that this or that authority is on the whole a good historian. Consequently, the oecumenical history of the Hellenistic age (which includes the Roman age) is based on a high estimate of the work done by the particularistic historians of the Hellenic age.

It was especially the vividness and excellence of the work done by Herodotus and Thucydides that re-created a lively idea of the fifth century in the minds of later generations and increased the backward scope of historical thought. Just as the past achievements of great artists gave people a sense that artistic styles other than that of their own day were valuable, so that a generation of literary and artistic scholars and dilettanti arose for whom the preservation and enjoyment of classical art was an end in itself, so there arose historians of a new type who could feel themselves imaginatively as contemporaries of Herodotus and Thucydides while yet remaining men of their own time and able to compare their own times with the past. This past the Hellenistic historians could feel as their own past, and thus it became possible to write a new kind of history with a dramatic unity of any size, so long as the historian could collect materials for it and could weld them into a single story.

§ 8. *Polybius*

The idea of this new kind of history is full-grown in the work of Polybius. Like all real historians, Polybius has a definite theme; he has a story to tell, a story of notable and memorable things, namely the conquest of the world by Rome; but he begins that story at a point more than 150 years before the time of writing, so that the extent of his field is five generations instead of one. His ability to do this is connected with the fact that he is working in Rome, whose people had a kind of historical consciousness quite different from that of the Greeks. History for them meant continuity: the inheritance from the past of institutions scrupulously preserved in the form in which they were received; the moulding of life according to the pattern of ancestral custom. The Romans, acutely conscious of their own continuity with their past, were careful to preserve memorials of that past; they not only kept their ancestral portraits in the house, as a visible symbol of the continuing and watchful presence of their forefathers directing their own life, but they preserved ancient traditions of their own corporate history to an extent unknown to the Greeks. These traditions were no doubt affected by the inevitable tendency to project the characteristics of late Republican Rome into the history of her earliest days; but Polybius, with his critical and philosophical mind, guarded against the historical dangers of that distortion by only beginning his narrative where his authorities became, in his own opinion, trustworthy: and in using these sources he never allowed his critical faculty to go to sleep. It is to the Romans, acting as always under the tuition of the Hellenistic mind, that we owe the conception of a history both oecumenical and national, a history in which the hero of the story is the continuing and corporate spirit of a people and in which the plot of the story is the unification of the world under that people's leadership. Even here, we have not arrived at the conception of national history as we understand it: national history as the complete biography, so to speak, of a people from its very beginnings. For Polybius, the history of Rome begins with Rome already fully formed, adult, ready to go forth on her mission of conquest. The difficult problem of how a national spirit comes into existence is not yet tackled. For Polybius, the given, ready-made national spirit is the ὑποκείμενον of history, the unchanging substance that underlies all change. Just as the Greeks could not even contemplate the possibility of raising the problem which we should call the problem of the origin of the Hellenic people, so even for Polybius there is no problem of

the origin of the Roman people ; if he knew the traditions about
the foundation of Rome, as he doubtless did, he silently cut
them out of his field of vision as lying behind the point at which
historical science, as he conceived it, could begin.

With this larger conception of the field of history comes a
more precise conception of history itself. Polybius uses the
word ἱστορία not in its original and quite general sense as
meaning any kind of inquiry, but in its modern sense of history :
the thing is now conceived as a special type of research needing
a special name of its own. He is an advocate of the claims of this
science to universal study for its own sake, and points out in
the first sentence of his work that this is a thing not hitherto
done ; he thinks of himself as the first person to conceive of
history as such as a form of thought having a universal value.
But he expresses this value in a way which shows that he has
come to terms with the anti-historical or substantialistic tendency which, as I said before, dominated the Greek mind.
History, according to this tendency, cannot be a science, for
there can be no science of transitory things. Its value is not
a theoretical or scientific value, it can only be a practical value—
the kind of value which Plato had ascribed to δόξα, the quasi-
knowledge of what is not eternal and intelligible but temporal
and perceptible. Polybius accepts and emphasizes this notion.
History, for him, is worth studying not because it is scientifically
true or demonstrative, but because it is a school and training-
ground for political life.

But a person who had accepted this notion in the fifth century
(as no one did, because Herodotus still thought of history as a
science and Thucydides, so far as I can see, did not raise the
question of the value of history at all) would have inferred
that the value of history lies in its power of training individual
statesmen, a Pericles or the like, to conduct the affairs of their
own community with skill and success. This view was held by
Isocrates in the fourth century, but it had become impossible
by the time of Polybius. The naïve self-confidence of the
Hellenic age has disappeared with the disappearance of the
city-state. Polybius does not think that the study of history
will enable men to avoid the mistakes of their predecessors and
surpass them in worldly success ; the success to which the study
of history can lead is for him an inner success, a victory not over

circumstance but over self. What we learn from the tragedies
of its heroes is not to avoid such tragedies in our own lives, but
to bear them bravely when fortune brings them. The idea of
fortune, $\tau\acute{\upsilon}\chi\eta$, bulks largely in this conception of history, and
imports into it a new element of determinism. As the canvas on
which the historian paints his picture grows larger, the power
attributed to the individual will grows less. Man finds himself
no longer master of his fate in the sense that what he tries to do
succeeds or fails in proportion to his own intelligence or lack of
it; his fate is master of him, and the freedom of his will is shown
not in controlling the outward events of his life but in controlling
the inward temper in which he faces these events. Here Polybius
is applying to history the same Hellenistic conceptions which
the Stoics and Epicureans applied to ethics. Both these schools
agreed in thinking that the problem of moral life was not how
to control events in the world around us, as the classical Greek
moralists had thought, but how to preserve a purely inward
integrity and balance of mind when the attempt to control outward events had been abandoned. For Hellenistic thought,
self-consciousness is no longer, as it was for Hellenic thought,
a power to conquer the world; it is a citadel providing a safe
retreat from a world both hostile and intractable.

§ 9. *Livy and Tacitus*

With Polybius the Hellenistic tradition of historical thought
passes into the hands of Rome. The only original development
it received there was from Livy, who conceived the magnificent
idea of a complete history of Rome from her very beginning.
A great part of Polybius' work had been done on the fifth-
century method, in collaboration with his friends of the Scipionic
circle who had achieved the culminating stages in the construction of the new Roman world. It was only the introductory
phases of Polybius' narrative that had to depend by scissors-
and-paste means on the work of earlier authorities. In Livy the
centre of gravity is changed. It is no mere introduction, it is
the whole body of his work, that is constructed by scissors and
paste. Livy's whole task is to assemble the traditional records
of early Roman history and weld them together into a single
continuous narrative, the history of Rome. It was the first time
anything of the sort had been done. The Romans, serenely

confident in their own superiority to all other peoples and their
monopoly of the only virtues deserving the name, thought their
own history the only one worth narrating; and hence the history
of Rome as narrated by Livy was to the Roman mind not one
out of a number of possible particular histories but universal
history, the history of the only genuinely historical reality:
oecumenical history, because Rome had now, like Alexander's
Empire, become the world.

Livy was a philosophical historian; less philosophical no
doubt than Polybius, but far more philosophical than any later
Roman historian. His preface therefore deserves the closest study.
I shall comment briefly on a few points in it. First, he pitches
the scientific claims of his work very low. He makes no claim to
original research or original method. He writes as if his chance of
standing out from the ruck of historical writers depended chiefly
on his literary qualities; and certainly these qualities are, as all
his readers have agreed, outstanding. I need not quote the praise
of such qualified critics as Quintilian.[1] Secondly, he emphasizes
his moral purpose. He says that his readers will doubtless prefer
to be told about the recent past; but he wants them to read
about the remote past, because he wishes to hold up before them
the moral example of the early days when Roman society was
simple and uncorrupted, and to show them how the foundations
of Roman greatness were laid in this primitive morality.
Thirdly, he is clear that history is humanistic. It flatters our
conceit, he says, to think of our origins as divine; but the
historian's business is not to flatter his reader's conceit but to
paint the doings and manners of men.

Livy's attitude towards his authorities is sometimes misrepresented. Like Herodotus, he is often charged with the
grossest credulity; but, like Herodotus, wrongly. He does his
best to be critical; but the methodical criticism practised by
every modern historian was still not invented. Here was a mass
of legends; all he could do with them was to decide, as best he
could, whether or not they were trustworthy. Three courses
were open to him: to repeat them, accepting their substantial
accuracy; to reject them; or to repeat them with the caution that
he was not sure of their truth. Thus, at the outset of his history,
Livy says that the traditions referring to events before the

[1] *Inst. or.* x. i. 101.

foundation of Rome, or rather to events before those immediately leading up to that foundation, are fables rather than sound
traditions and can neither be affirmed nor criticized. He therefore repeats them with a caution, merely remarking that they
show a tendency to magnify the origins of the city by mingling
divine agencies with human; but once he comes to the foundation of Rome he accepts the tradition pretty much as he finds it.
There is here only the very crudest attempt at historical criticism. Presented with a great wealth of traditional material, the
historian takes it all at its face value; he makes no attempt to
discover how the tradition has grown up and through what
various distorting media it has reached him; he therefore cannot reinterpret a tradition, that is, explain it as meaning something other than it explicitly says. He has to take it or leave it,
and, on the whole, Livy's tendency is to accept his tradition and
repeat it in good faith.

The Roman Empire was not an age of vigorous and progressive thought. It did singularly little to advance knowledge on
any of the paths that the Greeks had opened up. It kept alive
for a time the Stoic and Epicurean philosophies without developing them; only in Neoplatonism did it show any philosophical originality. In natural science it did nothing to surpass
the achievements of the Hellenistic Age. Even in applied natural
science it was extemely weak. It used Hellenistic fortification,
Hellenistic artillery, and arts and crafts partly Hellenistic and
partly Celtic. In history its interest survived but its vigour
failed. No one ever took up Livy's task again and tried to do it
better. After him, historians either copied him or drew in their
horns and confined themselves to a narrative of the recent past.
So far as method goes, Tacitus already represents a decline.

As a contributor to historical literature, Tacitus is a gigantic
figure; but it is permissible to wonder whether he was an
historian at all. He imitates the parochial outlook of the fifth-
century Greeks without imitating their virtues. He is obsessed
with the history of affairs at Rome, neglecting the Empire, or
seeing it only as refracted through the spectacles of a home-
keeping Roman; and his outlook on these purely Roman affairs
is narrow in the extreme. He is flagrantly biased in favour of
the senatorial opposition; he couples a contempt for peaceful
administration with an admiration for conquest and military

glory, an admiration blinded by his remarkable ignorance of
the actualities of warfare. All these defects make him curiously
unfitted to be the historian of the early Principate, but at
bottom they are only symptoms of a graver and more general
defect. What is really wrong with Tacitus is that he has never
thought out the fundamental problems of his enterprise. His
attitude towards the philosophical groundwork of history is
frivolous, and he takes over the current pragmatic view of
its purpose in the spirit of a rhetorician rather than that of a
serious thinker.

'His professed purpose in writing is to hold up signal examples of
political vice and virtue for posterity to execrate or to admire, and
to teach his readers, even through a narrative which he fears may
weary them by its monotonous horrors, that good citizens may live
under bad rulers; and that it is not mere destiny or the chapter of
accidents, but personal character and discretion, dignified moderation and reserve, that best guard a senator of rank unharmed through
time of peril, in which not only the defiant on one side, but almost as
often the sycophant on the other, are struck down as the course of
events or even the changing humours of the prince may prompt.'[1]

This attitude leads Tacitus to distort history systematically
by representing it as essentially a clash of characters, exaggeratedly good with exaggeratedly bad. History cannot be scientifically written unless the historian can re-enact in his own mind
the experience of the people whose actions he is narrating. Tacitus
never tried to do this: his characters are seen not from inside,
with understanding and sympathy, but from outside, as mere
spectacles of virtue or vice. One can hardly read his descriptions
of an Agricola or a Domitian without being reminded of Socrates'
laugh at Glaucon's imaginary portraits of the perfectly good
and the perfectly bad man: 'My word, Glaucon, how energeti-
cally you are polishing them up like statues for a prize
competition!'[2]

Tacitus has been praised for his character-drawing; but the
principles on which he draws character are fundamentally
vicious and make his character-drawing an outrage on historical
truth. He found warrant for it, no doubt, in the Stoic and Epicurean philosophies of his age, to which I have already referred:

[1] Furneaux in *Cornelii Taciti Annalium Libri I–IV*, edited . . . for the use
of schools (Oxford, 1886), pp. 3–4.   [2] Plato, *Republic*, 361 d.

the defeatist philosophies which, starting from the assumption that the good man cannot conquer or control a wicked world, taught him how to preserve himself unspotted from its wickedness. This false antithesis between the individual man's character and his social environment justifies, in a sense, Tacitus' method of exhibiting the actions of an historical figure as flowing simply from his own personal character, and making no allowance either for the way in which a man's actions may be determined partly by his environment and only in part by his character, or for the way in which character itself may be moulded by the forces to which a man is subjected by his environment. Actually, as Socrates urged against Glaucon, the individual character considered in isolation from its environment is an abstraction, not a really existing thing. What a man does depends only to a limited extent on what kind of man he is. No one can resist the forces of his environment. Either he conquers the world or the world will conquer him.

Thus Livy and Tacitus stand side by side as the two great monuments to the barrenness of Roman historical thought. Livy has attempted a really great task, but he has failed in it because his method is too simple to cope with the complexity of his material, and his story of the ancient history of Rome is too deeply permeated with fabulous elements to be ranked with the greatest works of historical thought. Tacitus has attempted a new approach, the psychological-didactic; but instead of being an enrichment of historical method this is really an impoverishment, and indicates a declining standard of historical honesty. Subsequent historians under the Roman Empire, instead of overcoming the obstacles by which Livy and Tacitus were baffled, never even equalled their achievement. As the Empire went on, historians began more and more to content themselves with the wretched business of compilation, amassing in an uncritical spirit what they found in earlier works and arranging it with no end in view except, at best, edification or some other kind of propaganda.

§ 10. *Character of Greco-Roman historiography: (i) Humanism*

Greco-Roman historiography as a whole has firmly grasped one at least of the four characteristics enumerated in the Introduction (§ ii): it is humanistic. It is a narrative of human history, the history of man's deeds, man's purposes, man's successes and failures. It admits, no doubt, a divine agency; but the function of this agency is strictly limited. The will of the gods as manifested in history only appears rarely; in the best historians hardly at all and then only as a will supporting and seconding the will of man and enabling him to succeed where otherwise he would have failed. The gods have no plan of their own for the development of human affairs; they only grant success or decree failure for the plans of men. This is why a more searching analysis of human actions themselves, discovering in them alone the grounds for their success or failure, tends to eliminate the gods altogether, and to substitute for them mere personifications of human activity, like the genius of the Emperor, the goddess Rome, or the virtues represented on Roman Imperial coins. The ultimate development of this tendency is to find the cause of all historical events in the personality, whether individual or corporate, of human agents. The philosophical idea underlying it is the idea of the human will as freely choosing its own ends and limited in the success it achieves in their pursuit only by its own force and by the power of the intellect which apprehends them and works out means to their achievement. This implies that whatever happens in history happens as a direct result of human will; that some one is directly responsible for it, to be praised or blamed according as it is a good thing or a bad.

Greco-Roman humanism, however, had a special weakness of its own because of its inadequate moral or psychological insight. It was based on the idea of man as essentially a rational animal, by which I mean the doctrine that every individual human being is an animal capable of reason. So far as any given man develops that capacity and becomes actually, and not potentially, reasonable, he makes a success of his life: according to the Hellenic idea, he becomes a force in political life and a maker of history; according to the Hellenistic-Roman idea, he becomes capable of living wisely, sheltered behind his own rationality, in a wild and wicked world. Now the idea that every agent is wholly and directly responsible for everything that he does is a naïve idea which takes no account of certain important regions in moral experience. On the one hand, there is no getting away from the fact that men's characters are formed by their actions and experiences: the man himself undergoes change as his activities develop. On the other hand, there is the fact that to a very great extent people do not know what they are doing until they have done it, if then. The extent to which people act with a clear idea of their ends, knowing what effects they are aiming at, is easily exaggerated. Most human action is tentative, experimental, directed not by a knowledge of what it will lead to but rather by a desire to know what will come of it. Looking back over our actions, or over any stretch of past history, we see that something has taken shape as the actions went on which certainly was not present to our minds, or to the mind of any one, when the actions which brought it into existence began. The ethical thought of the Greco-Roman world attributed far too much to the deliberate plan or policy of the agent, far too little to the force of a blind activity embarking on a course of action without foreseeing its end and being led to that end only through the necessary development of that course itself

§ 11. *Character of Greco-Roman historiography:*
(ii) Substantialism

If its humanism, however weak, is the chief merit of Greco-Roman historiography, its chief defect is substantialism. By this I mean that it is constructed on the basis of a metaphysical system whose chief category is the category of substance. Substance does not mean matter or physical substance; indeed many Greek metaphysicians thought that no substance could be material. For Plato, it would seem, substances are immaterial though not mental; they are objective forms. For Aristotle, in the last resort, the only ultimately real substance is mind. Now a substantialistic metaphysics implies a theory of knowledge according to which only what is unchanging is knowable. But what is unchanging is not historical. What is historical is the transitory event. The substance to which an event happens, or from whose nature it proceeds, is nothing to the historian. Hence the attempt to think historically and the attempt to think in terms of substance were incompatible.

In Herodotus we have an attempt at a really historical point of view. For him events are important in themselves and knowable by themselves. But already in Thucydides the historical point of view is being dimmed by substantialism. For Thucydides the events are important chiefly for the light they throw on eternal and substantial entities of which they are mere accidents. The stream of historical thought which flowed so freely in Herodotus is beginning to freeze up.

As time goes on this freezing process continues, and by the time of Livy history is frozen solid. A distinction is now taken for granted between act and agent, regarded as a special case of substance and accident. It is taken for granted that the historian's proper business is with acts, which come into being in time, develop in time through their phases, and terminate in time. The agent from which they flow, being a substance, is eternal and unchanging and consequently stands outside history. In order that acts may flow from it, the agent itself must exist unchanged throughout the series of its acts: for it has to exist before this series begins and nothing that happens as the series goes on can add anything to it or take away anything from it. History cannot explain how any agent came into being or underwent any change of nature; for it is metaphysically axiomatic that an agent, being a substance, can never have come into being and can never undergo any change of nature. We have already seen how these ideas affected the work of Polybius.

We have sometimes been taught to contrast the unphilosophical Romans with the philosophical Greeks, and we may thus have been led to think that if the Romans were as unphilosophical as all that they would not allow metaphysical considerations to affect their historical work. Nevertheless it was so. And the completeness with which the practical and hard-headed Romans adopted the substantialistic metaphysics of the Greeks does not appear in the Roman historians alone. It appears with equal clarity in the Roman lawyers. Roman law, from beginning to end, is constructed on a framework of substantialistic metaphysical principles which influence its every detail.

I will give two examples of how this influence appears in the two greatest Roman historians.

First, in Livy. Livy set himself the task of writing a history of Rome. Now, a modern historian would have interpreted this as meaning a history of how Rome came to be what it is, a history of the process which brought into existence the characteristic Roman institutions and moulded the typical Roman character. It never occurs to Livy to adopt any such interpretation.

Rome is the heroine of his narrative. Rome is the agent whose actions he is describing. Therefore Rome is a substance, changeless and eternal. From the beginning of the narrative Rome is ready-made and complete. To the end of the narrative she has undergone no spiritual change. The traditions on which Livy relied projected such institutions as augury, the legion, the Senate, and so forth, into the very first years of the city, with the assumption that they remained thereafter unchanged; hence the origin of Rome, as he describes it, was a kind of miraculous leap into existence of the complete city as it existed at a later date. For a parallel, we should have to imagine an historian of England assuming that Hengist created a parliament of Lords and Commons. Rome is described as 'the eternal city'. Why is Rome so called? Because people still think of Rome, as Livy thought of her: substantialistically, non-historically.

Secondly, in Tacitus. Furneaux pointed out long ago[1] that when Tacitus describes the way in which the character of a man like Tiberius broke down beneath the strain of empire, he represents the process not as a change in the structure or conformation of a personality but as the revelation of features in it which had hitherto been hypocritically concealed. Why does Tacitus so misrepresent facts? Is it simply out of spite, in order to blacken the characters of the men whom he has cast for the part of villains? Is it in pursuance of a rhetorical purpose, to hold up awful examples to point his moral and adorn his tale? Not at all. It is because the idea of development in a character, an idea so familiar to ourselves, is to him a metaphysical impossibility. A 'character' is an agent, not an action; actions come and go, but the 'characters' (as we call them), the agents from whom they proceed, are substances, and therefore eternal and unchanging. Features in the character of a Tiberius or a Nero which only appeared comparatively late in life must have been there all the time. A good man cannot become bad. A man who shows himself bad when old must have been equally bad when young, and his vices concealed by hypocrisy. As the Greeks put it, ἀρχὴ ἄνδρα δείξει.[2] Power does not alter a man's character; it only shows what kind of man he already was.

Greco-Roman historiography can therefore never show how

---

[1] *The Annals of Tacitus* (Oxford, 1896), vol. i, p. 158.
[2] Quoted from Bias in Aristotle, *Nic. Eth.* 1130ª1.

anything comes into existence; all the agencies that appear on the stage of history have to be assumed ready-made before history begins, and they are related to historical events exactly as a machine is related to its own movements. The scope of history is limited to describing what people and things do, the nature of these people and things remaining outside its field of vision. The nemesis of this substantialistic attitude was historical scepticism: events, as mere transitory accidents, were regarded as unknowable; the agent, as a substance, was knowable indeed, but not to the historian. But what, then, was the use of history? For Platonism history could have a pragmatic value, and the idea of this as the sole value of history intensifies from Isocrates to Tacitus. And as this process goes on it produces a kind of defeatism about historical accuracy and an unconscientiousness in the historical mind as such.

PART II

THE INFLUENCE OF CHRISTIANITY

§ 1. *The leaven of Christian ideas*

THREE great crises have occurred in the history of European historiography. The first was the crisis of the fifth century B.C. when the idea of history as a science, a form of research, an ἱστορίη, came into being. The second was the crisis of the fourth and fifth centuries A.D. when the idea of history was remodelled by the revolutionary effect of Christian thought. I have now to describe this process and to show how Christianity jettisoned two of the leading ideas in Greco-Roman historiography, namely (i) the optimistic idea of human nature and (ii) the substantialistic idea of eternal entities underlying the process of historical change.

(i) The moral experience which Christianity expressed contained as one of its most important elements a sense of human blindness in action: not a fortuitous blindness due to individual failure of insight, but a necessary blindness inherent in action itself. According to Christian doctrine, it is inevitable that man should act in the dark without knowing what will come of his action. That inability to achieve ends clearly conceived in advance, which in Greek is called ἁμαρτία, missing one's mark, is no longer regarded as accidental but as a permanent element in human nature, arising out of the condition of man as man. This is the original sin upon which St. Augustine laid such stress, and which he connected psychologically with the force of natural desire. Human action, on this view, is not designed in view of preconceived ends by the intellect; it is actuated *a tergo* by immediate and blind desire. It is not only the uninstructed vulgar, it is man as such, that does what he wants to do instead of thinking out a reasonable course of action. Desire is not the tamed horse of Plato's metaphor, it is a runaway horse, and the 'sin' (to use the technical term of theology) into which it leads us is not a sin which we deliberately choose to commit, it is an inherent and original sin proper to our nature. From this it follows that the achievements of man are due not to his own proper forces of will and intellect, but to something other than himself, causing him to desire ends that are worth pursuing. He therefore behaves, from the point of view of the historian, as if he were the wise architect of his own fortunes; but the wisdom displayed in his action is not his, it is the wisdom of God, by whose grace man's desires are directed to worthy ends. Thus the plans which are realized by human action (such plans, I mean, as the conquest of the world by Rome) come about not because men have conceived them, decided on their goodness, and devised means to execute them, but because men, doing from time to time what at the moment they wanted to do, have executed the purposes of God. This conception of grace is the correlative of the conception of original sin.

(ii) The metaphysical doctrine of substance in Greco-Roman philosophy was challenged by the Christian doctrine of creation. According to this doctrine nothing is eternal except God, and all else has been created by God. The human soul is no longer regarded as a past existence *ab aeterno*, and its immortality in that sense is denied; each soul is believed to be a fresh creation. Similarly, peoples and nations considered collectively are not eternal substances but have been created by God. And what God has created He can modify by a reorientation of its nature towards fresh ends: thus by the operation of His grace He can bring about development in the character of a person or a people already created. Even the substances, so called, which were still tolerated by early Christian thought were not really substances as substances had been conceived by the thinkers of antiquity. The human soul is still called a substance, but it is now conceived as a substance created by God at a certain time and depending on God for its continued existence. The natural world is still called a substance, but with the same qualification. God Himself is still called a substance, but His character as substance is now regarded as unknowable: not only undiscoverable by unaided human reason, but not even capable of being revealed. All we can know about God is His activities. By degrees, as the leaven of Christianity worked, even these quasi-substances disappeared. It was in the thirteenth century that St. Thomas Aquinas threw overboard the conception of divine substance and defined God in terms of activity, as *actus purus*. In the eighteenth, Berkeley jettisoned the conception of material substance, and Hume the conception of spiritual substance. The stage was then set for the third crisis in the history of European historiography and for the long-delayed entrance of history as, at last, a science.

The introduction of Christian ideas had a threefold effect on the way in which history was conceived:

(a) A new attitude towards history grew up, according to which the historical process is the working out not of man's purposes but of God's; God's purpose being a purpose for man, a purpose to be embodied in human life and through the activity of human wills, God's part in this working-out being limited to predetermining the end and to determining from time to time the objects which human beings desire. Thus each human agent knows what he wants and pursues it, but he does not know why he wants it: the reason why he wants it is that God has caused him to want it in order to advance the process of realizing His purpose. In one sense man is the agent throughout history, for everything that happens in history happens by his will; in another sense God is the sole agent, for it is only by the working of God's providence that the operation of man's will at any given moment leads to *this* result, and not to a different one. In one sense, again, man is the end for whose sake historical events happen, for God's purpose is man's well-being; in another sense man exists merely as a means to the accomplishment of God's ends, for God has created him only in order to work out His purpose in terms of human life. By this new attitude to human action history gained enormously, because the recognition that what happens in history need not happen through anyone's deliberately wishing it to happen is an indispensable precondition of understanding any historical process.

(b) This new view of history makes it possible to see not only the actions of historical agents, but the existence and nature of those agents themselves, as vehicles of God's purposes and therefore as historically important. Just as the individual soul is a thing created in the fullness of time to have just those characteristics which the time requires if God's purpose is to be fulfilled, so a thing like Rome is not an eternal entity but a transient thing that has come into existence at the appropriate time in history to fulfil a certain definite function and to pass away when that function has been fulfilled. This was a profound revolution in historical thinking; it meant that the process of historical change was no longer conceived as flowing, so to speak, over the surface of things, and affecting their accidents only, but as involving their very substance and thus entailing a real creation and a real destruction. It is the application to history of the Christian conception of God as no mere workman fashioning the world out of a pre-existing matter but as a creator, calling it into existence out of nothing. Here, too, the gain to history is immense, because the recognition that the historical process creates its own vehicles, so that entities like Rome or England are not the presuppositions but the products of that process, is the first step towards grasping the peculiar characteristics of history.

(c) These two modifications in the conception of history were derived, as we have seen, from the Christian doctrines of original sin, grace, and creation. A third was based on the universalism of the Christian attitude. For the Christian, all men are equal in the sight of God: there is no chosen people, no privileged race or class, no one community whose fortunes are more important than those of another. All persons and all peoples are involved in the working out of God's purpose, and therefore the historical process is everywhere and always of the same kind, and every part of it is a part of the same whole. The Christian cannot be content with Roman history or Jewish history or any other partial and particularistic history: he demands a history of the world, a universal history whose theme shall be the general development of God's purposes for human iife. The infusion of Christian ideas overcomes not only the characteristic humanism and the substantialism of Greco-Roman history, but also its particularism.

§ 2. *Characteristics of Christian historiography*

Any history written on Christian principles will be of necessity universal, providential, apocalyptic, and periodized.

(i) It will be a *universal* history, or history of the world, going back to the origin of man. It will describe how the various races of men came into existence and peopled the various habitable parts of the earth. It will describe the rise and fall of civilizations and powers. Greco-Roman oecumenical history is not universal in this sense, because it has a particularistic centre of gravity. Greece or Rome is the centre round which it revolves. Christian universal history has undergone a Copernican revolution, whereby the very idea of such a centre of gravity is destroyed.

(ii) It will ascribe events not to the wisdom of their human agents but to the workings of *Providence* preordaining their course. The theocratic history of the Near East is not providential in this sense, because it is not universal but particularistic. The theocratic historian is interested in the doings of a particular society, and the God who presides over these doings is a God for whom that particular society is a chosen people. Providential history, on the other hand, treats history indeed as a play written by God, but a play wherein no character is the author's favourite character.

(iii) It will set itself to detect an intelligible pattern in this general course of events, and in particular it will attach a central importance in this pattern to the historical life of Christ, which is clearly one of the chief preordained features of the pattern. It will make its narrative crystallize itself round that event, and treat earlier events as leading up to it or preparing for it, and subsequent events as developing its consequences. It will therefore divide history at the birth of Christ into two parts, each having a peculiar and unique character of its own: the first, a forward-looking character, consisting in blind preparation for an event not yet revealed; the second a backward-looking character depending on the fact that the revelation has now been made. A history thus divided into two periods, a period of darkness and a period of light, I shall call *apocalyptic* history.

(iv) Having divided the past into two, it will then naturally tend to subdivide it again: and thus to distinguish other events, not so important as the birth of Christ but important in their way, which make everything after them different in quality from what went before. Thus history is divided into epochs or *periods*, each with peculiar characteristics of its own, and each marked off from the one before it by an event which in the technical language of this kind of historiography is called epoch-making.

All these four elements were in fact consciously imported into historical thought by the early Christians. We may take Eusebius of Caesarea, in the third and early fourth century, as an example. In his *Chronicle* he set himself to compose a universal history where all events were brought within a single chronological framework instead of having events in Greece dated by Olympiads, events in Rome dated by consuls, and so on. This was compilation; but it was a very different thing from the compilations of pagan scholars under the late Empire, because it was inspired by a new purpose, the purpose of showing that the events thus chronicled formed a pattern with the birth of Christ in its centre. It was with this end in view that Eusebius composed another work, the so-called *Praeparatio Evangelica*, in which he showed that the history of the pre-Christian world could be regarded as a process designed to culminate in the Incarnation. Jewish religion, Greek philosophy, Roman law, combined to build up a matrix in which it was possible for the Christian revelation to take root and grow to maturity; if Christ had been born into the world at any other time, the world would not have been able to receive Him.

Eusebius was only one of a large number of men who were struggling to work out in detail the consequences of the Christian conception of man; and when we find many of the Fathers like Jerome, Ambrose, and even Augustine speaking of pagan learning and literature with contempt and hostility it is necessary to remind ourselves that this contempt arises not from lack of education or a barbarous indifference towards knowledge as such, but from the vigour with which these men were pursuing a new ideal of knowledge, working in the teeth of opposition for a reorientation of the entire structure of human thought. In the case of history, the only thing with which we are here concerned, the reorientation not only succeeded at the time, but left its heritage as a permanent enrichment of historical thought.

The conception of history as in principle the history of the world, where struggles like that between Greece and Persia or between Rome and Carthage are looked at impartially with an eye not to the success of one combatant but to the upshot of the struggle from the standpoint of posterity, became a commonplace. The symbol of this universalism is the adoption of a single chronological framework for all historical events. The single universal chronology, invented by Isidore of Seville in the seventh century and popularized by the Venerable Bede in the eighth, dating everything forward and backward from the birth of Christ, still shows where the idea came from.

The providential idea became a commonplace. We are taught

in our school text-books, for example, that in the eighteenth century the English conquered an empire in a fit of absence of mind: that is, they carried out what to us looking back on it appears as a plan, though no such plan was present in their minds at the time.

The apocalyptic idea became a commonplace, although historians have placed their apocalyptic moment at all sorts of times: the Renaissance, the invention of printing, the scientific movement of the seventeenth century, the Enlightenment of the eighteenth, the French Revolution, the Liberal movement of the nineteenth century, or even, as with Marxist historians, in the future.

And the idea of epoch-making events has become a commonplace, and with it the division of history into periods each with its own peculiar character.

All these elements, so familiar in modern historical thought, are totally absent from Greco-Roman historiography and were consciously and laboriously worked out by the early Christians.

§ 3. *Medieval historiography*

The medieval historiography which devoted itself to the working out of these conceptions is in one way a continuation of Hellenistic and Roman historiography. The method remains unchanged. The medieval historian still depends for his facts on tradition, and has no effective weapons for criticizing that tradition. Here he is on a par with Livy, and retains both the weakness of Livy and his strength. He has no means of studying the growth of the traditions that have come down to him or analysing them into their various components. His only criticism is a personal, unscientific, unsystematic criticism, which often betrays him into what, to us, seems foolish credulity. And on the other side of the account he often displays remarkable stylistic merit and imaginative power. For example, the humble monk of St. Albans who has left us the *Flores Historiarum* ascribed to Matthew of Westminster has told stories about King Alfred and the cakes, Lady Godiva, King Canute on the shore at Bosham, and so on, which may be fabulous but are imperishable gems of literature and deserve no less than the history of Thucydides to be cherished as κτήματα ἐς αἰεί.

But unlike Livy the medieval historian treats this material

from a universalistic point of view. Even in the Middle Ages nationalism was a real thing; but an historian who flattered national rivalries and national pride knew that he was doing wrong. His business was not to praise England or France but to narrate the *gesta Dei*. He saw history not as a mere play of human purposes, in which he took the side of his own friends, but as a process, having an objective necessity of its own, wherein even the most intelligent and powerful human agent finds himself involved, not because God is destructive and mischievous, as in Herodotus, but because God is provident and constructive, has a plan of his own with which he will allow no man to interfere; so the human agent finds himself caught up in the stream of the divine purpose, and carried along in it with or without his consent. History, as the will of God, orders itself, and does not depend for its orderliness on the human agent's will to order it. Plans emerge, and get themselves carried into effect, which no human being has planned; and even men who think they are working against the emergence of these plans are in fact contributing to them. They may assassinate Caesar but they cannot arrest the downfall of the Republic; the very assassination adds a new feature to that downfall. Hence the total course of historical events is a criterion which serves to judge the individuals taking part in it.[1] The duty of the individual is to become a willing instrument for furthering its objective purposes. If he sets himself against it, he cannot arrest or alter it, all he can do is to secure his own condemnation by it, frustrating himself and reducing his own life to futility. This is a Patristic doctrine: the Devil is defined by the early Christian writer Hippolytus as ὁ ἀντιτάττων τοῖς κοσμικοῖς.

The great task of medieval historiography was the task of discovering and expounding this objective or divine plan. It was a plan developed in time and therefore through a definite series of stages, and it was reflection on this fact which produced the conception of historical ages each initiated by an epoch-making event. Now, the attempt to distinguish periods in history is a mark of advanced and mature historical thought, not afraid to interpret facts instead of merely ascertaining them;

---

[1] Schiller's famous aphorism *Die Weltgeschichte ist das Weltgericht* is a familiar medieval maxim revived in the late eighteenth century and typical of the medievalism which in many ways characterized the Romantics.

but here as elsewhere medieval thought, though never deficient in boldness and originality, showed itself unable to make good its promises. To illustrate this, I will take a single example of medieval periodizing. In the twelfth century Joachim of Floris divided history into three periods: the reign of the Father or unincarnate God, that is, the pre-Christian age; the reign of the Son or the Christian age; and the reign of the Holy Ghost which was to begin in the future. This reference to a future age betrays an important characteristic of medieval historiography. If challenged to explain how he knew that there was in history any objective plan at all, the medieval historian would have replied that he knew it by revelation; it was part of what Christ had revealed to man concerning God. And this revelation not only gave the key to what God had done in the past, it showed us what God was going to do in the future. The Christian revelation thus gave us a view of the entire history of the world, from its creation in the past to its end in the future, as seen in the timeless and eternal vision of God. Thus medieval historiography looked forward to the end of history as something foreordained by God and through revelation foreknown to man: it thus contained in itself an eschatology.

Eschatology is always an intrusive element in history. The historian's business is to know the past, not to know the future; and whenever historians claim to be able to determine the future in advance of its happening, we may know with certainty that something has gone wrong with their fundamental conception of history. Further, we may know exactly what it is that has gone wrong. What has happened is that they have split up the single reality of the historical process into two separate things, one which determines and one which is determined: the abstract law and the mere fact, the universal and the particular. They have hypostatized the universal into a false particular supposed to exist by itself and for itself, and yet in that isolation they still conceive it as determining the course of particular events. The universal, being thus isolated from the temporal process, does not work in that process, it only works upon it. The temporal process is something passive, shaped by a timeless force working upon it from without. Hence, because the force works in exactly the same way at all times, the knowledge of how it works now is also a knowledge of how it will work in the future, and if we know how it has determined the flow of events at any one time, we thereby know how it would determine it at any other, and therefore we can foretell the future. Thus, in medieval thought, the complete opposition between the objective purpose of God and the subjective purpose of man, so conceived that God's purpose appears as the imposition of a certain objective plan upon history quite irrespective of man's subjective purposes, leads inevitably to the idea that man's purposes make no difference to the course of history and that the only force which determines it is the divine nature. Hence, the divine nature being revealed, those to whom it is revealed by faith can see by faith what the future must be. This may seem to have affinities with substantialism, but it is something quite different, namely transcendence. God in medieval theology is not substance but pure act; and transcendence means that the divine activity is conceived not as working in and through human activity but as working outside it and overruling it, not immanent in the world of human action but transcending that world.

What has happened here is that the pendulum of thought has swung from an abstract and one-sided humanism in Greco-Roman historiography to an equally abstract and one-sided theocentric view in medieval. The work of providence in history is recognized, but recognized in a way which leaves nothing for man to do. One result of this is that historians, as we have seen, fell into the error of thinking that they could forecast the future. Another result is that in their anxiety to detect the general plan of history, and their belief that this plan was God's and not man's, they tended to look for the essence of history outside history itself, by looking away from man's actions in order to detect the plan of God; and consequently the actual detail of human actions became for them relatively unimportant, and they neglected that prime duty of the historian, a willingness to bestow infinite pains on discovering what actually happened. This is why medieval historiography is so weak in critical method. That weakness was not an accident. It did not depend on the limitation of the sources and materials at the disposal of scholars. It depended on a limitation not of what they could do but of what they wanted to do. They did not want an accurate and scientific study of the actual facts of history; what they

wanted was an accurate and scientific study of the divine attributes, a theology based securely on the double foundation of
faith and reason, which should enable them to determine *a priori*
what must have happened and what must be going to happen
in the historical process.

The consequence of this is that when medieval historiography
is looked at from the point of view of a merely scholarly historian, the kind of historian who cares for nothing except accuracy in facts, it seems not only unsatisfactory but deliberately
and repulsively wrong-headed; and the nineteenth-century historians, who did in general take a merely scholarly view of the
nature of history, regarded it with extreme lack of sympathy.
Nowadays, when we are less obsessed by the demand for critical
accuracy and more interested in interpreting facts, we can look
at it with a more friendly eye. We have so far gone back to the
medieval view of history that we think of nations and civilizations as rising and falling in obedience to a law that has little
to do with the purposes of the human beings that compose them,
and we are perhaps not altogether ill-disposed to theories which
teach that large-scale historical changes are due to some kind
of dialectic working objectively and shaping the historical process by a necessity that does not depend on the human will.
This brings us into somewhat close contact with the medieval
historians, and if we are to avoid the errors to which ideas of
their kind are liable, it is useful for us to study medieval historiography and to see how that antithesis between objective necessity and subjective will led to neglect of historical accuracy, and
betrayed historians into an unscholarly credulity and a blind
acceptance of tradition. The medieval historian had every
excuse for being in that sense unscholarly; no one had yet discovered how to criticize sources and to ascertain facts in a
scholarly manner, for this was the work of historical thought
in the centuries that followed the close of the Middle Ages; but
for us, now that that work has been done, there is no excuse;
and if we went back to the medieval conception of history with
all its errors, we should be exemplifying and hastening that
downfall of civilization which some historians are, perhaps pre-
maturely, proclaiming.

§ 4. *The Renaissance historians*

At the close of the Middle Ages one of the main tasks of
European thought was to bring about a fresh reorientation
of historical studies. The great theological and philosophical
systems which had provided a basis for determining the general
plan of history *a priori* had ceased to command assent, and
with the Renaissance a return was made to a humanistic view
of history based on that of the ancients. Accurate scholarship
became important, because human actions were no longer felt
to be dwarfed into insignificance in comparison with a divine
plan. Historical thought once more placed man in the centre
of its picture. But in spite of the new interest in Greco-Roman
thought, the Renaissance conception of man was profoundly
different from the Greco-Roman; and when a writer like
Machiavelli, in the early sixteenth century, expressed his ideas
about history in the shape of a commentary on the first ten
books of Livy he was not reinstating Livy's own view of history.
Man, for the Renaissance historian, was not man as depicted
by ancient philosophy, controlling his actions and creating his
destiny by the work of his intellect, but man as depicted by
Christian thought, a creature of passion and impulse. History
thus became the history of human passions, regarded as necessary manifestations of human nature.

The positive fruits of this new movement were found first of
all in a great clearing away of what had been fanciful and ill-
founded medieval historiography. It was shown, for example,
by Jean Bodin[1] in the mid-sixteenth century that the accepted
scheme of periods, the Four Empires, was based not on accurate
interpretation of the facts but on an arbitrary scheme borrowed
from the Book of Daniel;[2] and numerous scholars, mostly of

---

[1] *Methodus ad facilem historiarum cognitionem* (1566), Cap. vii: 'Confutatio
eorum qui quatuor monarchias . . . statuunt.'

[2] It is significant of the medievalist tendencies of late-eighteenth-century
romanticism, to which I have already called attention in the case of Schiller,
that Hegel reaffirms the long-exploded scheme of the Four Empires in his
passage about world history at the end of the *Philosophie des Rechts*. Readers
of Hegel, accustomed to his inveterate habit of dividing every subject, according to the pattern of his dialectic, into triads, are startled to find that his outline
of world history in the concluding pages of that book is divided into four
sections headed: 'The Oriental Empire, the Greek Empire, the Roman Empire,
the Germanic Empire.' Such readers are apt to think that, for once, facts

Italian origin, set themselves to overthrow the legends in which various countries had concealed their ignorance of their own origins; Polydore Virgil, for example, in the early sixteenth century, destroyed the old story about the foundation of Britain by Brutus the Trojan and laid the foundations of a critical history of England.

By the beginning of the seventeenth century Bacon was able to sum up the situation by dividing his map of knowledge into the three great realms of poetry, history, and philosophy, ruled over by the three faculties of imagination, memory, and understanding. To say that memory presides over history is to say that the essential work of history is to recall and record the past in its actual facts as they actually happened. What Bacon is doing here is to insist that history should be, above all, an interest in the past for its own sake. This is a negation of the claim that historians can foreknow the future, and at the same time it negates the idea that the historian's main function is to detect a divine plan running through the facts. His interest is in the facts themselves.

But the position of history as thus defined was precarious. It had freed itself from the errors of medieval thought, but it had still to find its own proper function. It had a definite programme, the rediscovery of the past, but it had no methods or principles by which this programme could be carried out. Actually, Bacon's definition of history as the realm of memory was wrong, because the past only requires historical investigation so far as it is not and cannot be remembered. If it could be remembered, there would be no need of historians. Bacon's own contemporary Camden was already at work in the best Renaissance tradition on the topography and archaeology of Britain, showing how unremembered history could be reconstructed from data somewhat as, at the same time, natural scientists were using data as the basis of scientific theories. The question how the historian's understanding works to supplement the deficiencies of his memory was a question that Bacon never asked.

have been too strong for the Hegelian dialectic. But it is not facts that have broken through the dialectical scheme; it is a recrudescence of medieval periodizing.

§ 5. *Descartes*

The constructive movement of seventeenth-century thought concentrated itself on the problems of natural science and left those of history on one side. Descartes, like Bacon, distinguished poetry, history, and philosophy, and added a fourth term, divinity; but of these four things he applied his new method to philosophy alone, with its three main divisions of mathematics, physics, and metaphysics, for it was only here that he hoped to attain secure and certain knowledge. Poetry, he said, was more a gift of nature than a discipline; divinity depended on faith in revelation; history, however interesting and instructive, however valuable towards the formation of a practical attitude in life, could not claim truth, for the events which it described never happened exactly as it described them. Thus the reformation of knowledge which Descartes envisaged, and actually did bring about, was designed to contribute nothing to historical thought, because he did not believe history to be, strictly speaking, a branch of knowledge at all.

It is worth while to look more closely at the paragraph on history in the first part of the *Discourse on Method*:

'I thought by now that I had spent enough labour on the study of ancient languages, on the reading of ancient authors, and on their histories and narratives. To live with men of an earlier age is like travelling in foreign lands. It is useful to know something of the manners of other peoples in order to judge more impartially of our own, and not despise and ridicule whatever differs from them, like men who have never been outside their native country. But those who travel too long end by being strangers in their own homes, and those who study too curiously the actions of antiquity are ignorant of what is done among ourselves to-day. Moreover these narratives tell of things which cannot have happened as if they had really taken place, and thus invite us to attempt what is beyond our powers or to hope for what is beyond our fate. And even histories, true though they be, and neither exaggerating nor altering the value of things, omit circumstances of a meaner and less dignified kind in order to become more worthy of a reader's attention; hence the things which they describe never happened exactly as they describe them, and men who try to model their own acts upon them are prone to the madness of romantic paladins and meditate hyperbolical deeds.'

Descartes here makes four points which it is well to distinguish: (1) Historical escapism: the historian is a traveller who by living away from home becomes a stranger to his own age. (2) Historical pyrrhonism: historical narratives are not trustworthy accounts of the past. (3) Anti-utilitarian idea of history: untrustworthy narratives cannot really assist us to understand what is possible and thus to act effectively in the present. (4) History as fantasy-building: the way in which historians, even at best, distort the past is by making it appear more splendid than it really was.

(1) One answer to the 'escapist' view of history would be to show that the historian can genuinely see into the past only so far as he stands firmly rooted in the present; that is, his business is not to leap clean out of his own period of history but to be in every respect a man of his age and to see the past as it appears from the standpoint of that age. This is actually the true answer; but in order that it should be given it was necessary for the theory of knowledge to advance farther than Descartes took it. It was not until the time of Kant that philosphers conceived the idea of knowledge as directed to an object relative to the knower's own point of view. The Kantian 'Copernican revolution' contained implicitly, though Kant himself did not work it out, a theory of how historical knowledge is possible not only without the historian's abandoning the standpoint of his own age, but precisely because he does not abandon that standpoint.

(2) To say that historical narratives relate events that cannot have happened is to say that we have some criterion, other than the narratives which reach us, by which to judge what could have happened. Descartes is here adumbrating a genuinely critical attitude in history which if fully developed would be the answer to his own objection.

(3) The Renaissance scholars, in reviving many elements of the Greco-Roman conception of history, had revived the idea that its value was a practical value, instructing men in the art of politics and practical life. This idea was inevitable so long as people could find no theoretical basis for the alternative belief that its value was theoretical and consisted in truth. Descartes was quite right to reject it; he was in fact anticipating Hegel's remark, in the introduction to his *Philosophy of History*, that the practical lesson of history is that no one ever learns anything

from history; but he did not see that the historical work of his own day, in the hands of men like Buchanan and Grotius, and still more of others in the generation then beginning, like Tillemont and the Bollandist scholars, was actuated by a sheer desire for truth, and that the pragmatic conception which he was criticizing was dead by the time he wrote.

(4) In saying that historical narratives exaggerate the grandeur and splendour of the past, Descartes was actually propounding a criterion by which they could be criticized and by which the truth they concealed or distorted could be rediscovered. If he had continued in that vein, he might have laid down a method or code of rules for historical criticism; actually this is one of the rules laid down at the beginning of the next century by Vico. But Descartes did not realize this, because his intellectual interests were so definitely orientated towards mathematics and physics that when writing about history he could mistake a fertile suggestion towards the improvement of historical method for a demonstration that no such improvement was possible.

Thus the attitude of Descartes towards history was curiously ambiguous. So far as his intention went, his work tended to throw doubt on its value, however that value was conceived, because he meant to direct people away from it and towards exact science. In the nineteenth century science went on its own way independently of philosophy, because the post-Kantian idealists had taken up an increasingly sceptical attitude towards it; and the breach has only begun to be healed in our own time. This estrangement was exactly paralleled by that between history and philosophy in the seventeenth century, which was due to a parallel cause, the historical scepticism of Descartes.

§ 6. *Cartesian historiography*

In point of fact, Descartes's scepticism by no means discouraged the historians. Rather they behaved as if they had taken it as a challenge, an invitation to go away and work out their own methods for themselves, satisfying themselves that critical history was possible, and then come back to the philosophers with a new world of knowledge in their hands. During the latter half of the seventeenth century a new school of historical thought arose which, in spite of the paradox contained in the phrase, might be called Cartesian historiography, somewhat as the classical French drama of the same period has been called a school of Cartesian poetry. I call it Cartesian historiography because it was based, like the Cartesian philosophy, on systematic scepticism and thoroughgoing recognition of critical principles. The main idea of this new school was that the testimony of written authorities must not be accepted without submitting it to a process of criticism based on at least three rules of method: (1) Descartes's own implicit rule, that no authority must induce us to believe what we know cannot have happened; (2) the rule that different authorities must be confronted with each other and harmonized; (3) the rule that written authorities must be checked by the use of non-literary evidence. History thus conceived was still based on written authorities, or what Bacon would have called memory; but historians were now learning to treat their authorities in a thoroughly critical spirit.

As examples of this school I have already mentioned Tillemont and the Bollandists. Tillemont's *History of the Roman Emperors* was.the first attempt to write Roman history with systematic attention to reconciling the statements of different authorities; the Bollandists, a school of Benedictine scholars, set themselves to rewrite the lives of the saints on a critical basis, purging away all exaggeratedly miraculous elements and going more deeply than any one had hitherto done into the problem of sources and the way in which traditions had grown up. It is to this period and especially to the Bollandists that we owe the idea of dissecting a tradition, allowing for the distortion of the medium through which it has reached us, and thus getting rid once for all of the old dilemma between either accepting it *en bloc* as true or rejecting it as false. At the same time, detailed studies were being made of the possibilities of coins, inscriptions, charters, and other non-literary documents, used to check and illustrate the narratives and descriptions of literary historians. It was during this period, for example, that John Horsley of Morpeth in Northumberland made the first systematic collection of Roman inscriptions in Britain, following the lead of Italian, French, and German scholars.

This movement was very little noticed by philosophers. The only one of leading rank who was much affected by it was Leibniz, who applied the new methods of historical scholarship to the history of philosophy with momentous results. We can even call him the modern founder of that study. He never wrote on it at length, but his work is everywhere permeated with knowledge of ancient and medieval philosophical thought, and we owe to him the conception of philosophy as a continuous historical tradition in which new progress comes about not by propounding completely new and revolutionary ideas but by preserving and developing what he calls the *philosophia perennis*, the permanent and unchanging truths which have always been known. This conception, of course, lays too much stress on the idea of permanence and too little on that of change; philosophical truth is conceived too much as an unchanging deposit of external and eternally known verities and too little as something always needing to be re-created by an effort of thought that transcends the past; but that is only a way of saying that Leibniz's conception of history characteristically belonged to a period when the relations between the permanent and the changing, between truths of reason and truths of fact, had not yet been clearly thought out. Leibniz marks a *rapprochement* between the alienated spheres of philosophy and history, not yet an effective contact between them.

In spite of this strongly historical bent in Leibniz, and in spite of the brilliant work which made Spinoza the founder of Biblical criticism, the general tendency of the Cartesian school was sharply anti-historical. And it was precisely this fact that led to the general downfall and discredit of Cartesianism. The powerful new movement of historical thought, growing up as it were under the ban of Cartesian philosophy, constituted by its very existence a refutation of that philosophy; and when the time came for a definite attack upon its principles, the persons who led that attack were quite naturally persons whose main constructive interest was in history. I shall give some account of two such attacks.

§ 7. *Anti-Cartesianism:* (i) *Vico*

The first is that of Vico, who was working in Naples in the early eighteenth century. The interest of Vico's work lies in the fact that he was in the first place a trained and brilliant historian, who set himself the task of formulating the principles of historical method as Bacon had formulated those of scientific;

and in the course of this constructive work he found himself confronted by the Cartesian philosophy as something against which a polemic had to be undertaken. He did not impugn the validity of mathematical knowledge, but he did impugn the Cartesian theory of knowledge with its implication that no other kind of knowledge was possible. Hence he attacked the Cartesian principle that the criterion of truth is the clear and distinct idea. He pointed out that in effect this was only a subjective or psychological criterion. The fact that I think my ideas clear and distinct only proves that I believe them, not that they are true. In saying this, Vico is substantially agreeing with Hume, that belief is nothing but the vivacity of our perceptions. Any idea, says Vico, however false, may convince us by its seeming self-evidence, and nothing is easier than to think our beliefs self-evident when in fact they are baseless fictions reached by sophistical argument: once more, a Humian point. What we need, Vico contends, is a principle by which to distinguish what can be known from what cannot; a doctrine of the necessary limits of human knowledge. This, of course, brings Vico into line with Locke, whose critical empiricism was to supply a starting-point for the other main attack on Cartesianism.

Vico finds this principle in the doctrine that *verum et factum convertuntur*: that is, the condition of being able to know anything truly, to understand it as opposed to merely perceiving it, is that the knower himself should have made it. On this principle nature is intelligible only to God, but mathematics is intelligible to man, because the objects of mathematical thought are fictions or hypotheses which the mathematician has constructed. Any piece of mathematical thinking begins with a *fiat: let* ABC be a triangle and *let* AB = AC. It is because by this act of will the mathematician makes the triangle, because it is his *factum*, that he can have true knowledge of it. This is not, in the ordinary sense of the word, 'idealism'. The existence of the triangle does not depend on its being known : to know things is not to create them; on the contrary, nothing can be known unless it has already been created, and whether a given mind can know it depends on how it has been created.

It follows from the *verum-factum* principle that history, which is emphatically something made by the human mind, is especially adapted to be an object of human knowledge. Vico regards the historical process as a process whereby human beings build up systems of language, custom, law, government, &c.: i.e. he thinks of history as the history of the genesis and development of human societies and their institutions. Here we reach for the first time a completely modern idea of what the subject-matter of history is. There is no antithesis between the isolated actions of men and the divine plan that holds them together, as there was for the Middle Ages; and, on the other hand, there is no suggestion that primitive man (in whom Vico was peculiarly interested) foresaw what was going to come of the developments he was initiating; the plan of history is a wholly human plan, but it does not pre-exist in the shape of an unrealized intention to its own gradual realization. Man is no mere demiurge, fashioning human society as Plato's God fashions the world on an ideal model; like God Himself, he is a real creator, bringing into existence both form and matter together in the corporate work of his own historical development. The fabric of human society is created by man out of nothing, and every detail of this fabric is therefore a human *factum*, eminently knowable to the human mind as such.

Vico is here giving us the results of his long and fruitful researches into the history of such things as law and language. He has found these researches capable of yielding knowledge just as certain as the knowledge Descartes had ascribed to the results of mathematical and physical research; and he expresses the way in which this knowledge has arisen by saying in effect that the historian can reconstruct in his own mind the process by which these things have been created by men in the past. There is a kind of pre-established harmony between the historian's mind and the object which he sets out to study; but this pre-established harmony, unlike that of Leibniz, is not based on a miracle—it is based on the common human nature uniting the historian with the men whose work he is studying.

This new attitude towards history is profoundly anti-Cartesian because the whole structure of the Cartesian system was conditioned by a problem which in the world of history does not arise: the problem of scepticism, the problem of the relation between ideas and things. Descartes, starting his researches into the method of natural science from the sceptical point of view which

then prevailed in France, had to begin by assuring himself that
there really was such a thing as the material world. For history
as conceived by Vico no such problem could exist. The sceptical
point of view is impossible. History, for Vico, is not concerned
with the past as past. It is concerned, in the first instance, with
the actual structure of the society in which we live; the manners
and customs which we share with the people around us. In
order to study these we need not ask whether they really exist.
The question has no meaning. Descartes, looking at the fire,
asked himself whether in addition to his own idea of a fire there
was also a real fire. For Vico, looking at such a thing as the
Italian language of his own day, no parallel question could arise.
The distinction between the idea of such an historical reality
and the reality itself would be meaningless. The Italian language is exactly what the people who use it think it is. For the
historian, the human point of view is final. What God thinks
about the Italian language is a question which he need not ask,
and which he knows he could not answer. Search for the thing
in itself is for him as pointless as it is futile. And Descartes
himself half recognized this when he said[1] that in matters of
morality his rule was to accept the laws and institutions of the
country in which he lived, and to govern his conduct according
to the best opinions which he found commonly received around
him: thus admitting that the individual could not construct
these things for himself *a priori* but must recognize them as
historical facts pertaining to the society in which he lives. It
is true that Descartes only adopted these rules provisionally,
hoping that the time would come when he would be able to
construct his own system of conduct on a metaphysical basis;
but the time never did come, and in the nature of the case never
could; Descartes's hope was only one example of the exaggerated
views he held about the possibilities of *a priori* speculation.
History is a kind of knowledge in which questions about ideas
and questions about facts are not distinguishable; and the whole
point of Descartes's philosophy consists in distinguishing those
two types of question.

With Vico's conception of history as a philosophically justi-
fiable form of knowledge went a conception of historical knowledge as capable of far wider development. Once the historian

---

[1] *Discourse on Method*, part iii.

answers the question how historical knowledge in general is possible, he can proceed to the solution of historical problems hitherto insoluble. This is done by forming a clear conception of historical method and working out the rules which it obeys. Vico was peculiarly interested in what he called the history of remote and obscure periods, that is, in the extension of historical knowledge; and in this connexion he laid down certain rules of method.

First, he held that certain periods of history had a general character, colouring every detail, which reappeared in other periods, so that two different periods might have the same general character, and it was possible to argue analogically from one to the other. He instanced the general resemblance between the Homeric period of Greek history and the European Middle Ages, both of which he called by the generic name of heroic periods. Their common features were such things as government by a warrior-aristocracy, an agricultural economy, a ballad-literature, a morality based on the idea of personal prowess and loyalty, and so forth. To learn more than Homer can tell us about the Homeric age, therefore, we should study the Middle Ages and then see how far we can apply what we have learnt there to early Greece.

Secondly, he showed that these similar periods tended to recur in the same order. Every heroic period is followed by a classical period, where thought prevails over imagination, prose over poetry, industry over agriculture, and a morality based on peace over one based on war. This in turn is followed by a decline into a new barbarism, but a barbarism quite different from the heroic barbarism of the imagination; it is what he calls a barbarism of reflection, where thought still rules, but a thought which has exhausted its creative power and only constructs meaningless networks of artificial and pedantic distinctions. Vico sometimes puts his cycle in the following way: first, the guiding principle of history is brute strength; then valiant or heroic strength; then valiant justice; then brilliant originality; then constructive reflection; and lastly a kind of spendthrift and wasteful opulence which destroys what has been constructed. But he is quite aware that any such scheme is too rigid not to admit of countless exceptions.

Thirdly, this cyclical movement is not a mere rotation of

history through a cycle of fixed phases; it is not a circle but a spiral; for history never repeats itself but comes round to each new phase in a form differentiated by what has gone before. Thus the Christian barbarism of the Middle Ages is differentiated from the pagan barbarism of the Homeric age by everything that makes it distinctively an expression of the Christian mind. For this reason, because history is always creating novelties, the cyclical law does not permit us to forecast the future, and this distinguishes Vico's use of it from the old Greco-Roman idea of a strictly circular movement in history (found for example in Plato, Polybius, and Renaissance historians like Machiavelli and Campanella) and brings it into line with the principle, to whose fundamental importance I have already referred, that the true historian never prophesies.

Vico then goes on to enumerate certain prejudices against which historians have always to be on their guard, like the 'idols' in Bacon's *Novum Organum*. He distinguishes five of these sources of error:

1. Magnificent opinions concerning antiquity, i.e. the prejudice in favour of exaggerating the wealth, power, grandeur, &c., of the period which the historian is studying. The principle which Vico is here expressing negatively is the principle that what makes a past period of history worth studying is not the intrinsic worth of its achievements taken by themselves but its relation to the general course of history. The prejudice is a very real one; e.g. I find that people who are interested in Roman provincial civilization have a strong reluctance to believe (as I have proved from archaeological evidence) that Roman London had only about 10,000–15,000 inhabitants. They would rather it had 50,000–100,000, because they have magnificent opinions concerning antiquity.

2. The conceit of nations. Every nation in dealing with its own past history has a prejudice in favour of painting it in the most favourable colours. Histories of England written by and for English people do not enlarge on military failures, and so forth.

3. The conceit of the learned. This, as Vico interprets it, takes the special form of a prejudice on the part of the historian which makes him suppose that the people about whom he is thinking were like himself in being scholars and students and

in general people of reflective intellect. The academic mind fancies that the persons in whom it is interested must have been academic persons themselves. Actually, Vico held, the most effective men in history have been the least academically minded. Historical greatness and reflective intellect are very rarely combined. The scale of values which governs the historian's own life is very different from that which governed the lives of his chief characters.

4. The fallacy of sources, or what Vico calls the scholastic succession of nations. This error consists in thinking that when two nations have a similar idea or institution one must have learnt it from the other, and Vico shows that it depends on denying the original creative power of the human mind, which can rediscover ideas for itself without learning them from another. He is quite right to warn historians against this fallacy. In point of fact, even where it is certain that one nation has taught another, as China has taught Japan, Greece Rome, Rome Gaul, and so on, the learner invariably learns not what the other has to teach but only the lessons for which its previous historical development has prepared it.

5. Lastly, there is the prejudice of thinking the ancients better informed than ourselves about the times that lay nearer to them. Actually, to take an example that is not one of Vico's, the scholars of King Alfred's time knew much less about Anglo-Saxon origins than we do. Vico's warning against this prejudice is of great importance because, when developed on its positive side, it becomes the principle that the historian does not depend on an unbroken tradition for his knowledge but can reconstruct by scientific methods a picture of a past age which he has not derived from any tradition whatever. This is the explicit denial that history depends on what Bacon called memory, or in other words the statements of authorities.

Vico is not content with negative warnings; he goes on positively to indicate certain methods by which the historian can transcend mere reliance on the statements of authorities. His observations here are commonplaces to the historian of to-day, but in his own time they were revolutionary.

1. He shows how linguistic study can throw light on history. Etymology can show what kind of life a people was leading while its language was coming into existence. The historian is aiming

at a reconstruction of the mental life, the ideas, of the people he is studying; their stock of words shows what their stock of ideas was; and the way in which they use an old word metaphorically in a new sense, when they want to express a new idea, shows what their stock of ideas was before that new one came into existence. Thus, Latin words like *intellegere* and *disserere* show how, when Romans needed words for understanding and discussing, they borrowed from an agricultural vocabulary the words for gleaning and sowing.

2. He makes a similar use of mythology. The gods of primitive religion represent a semi-poetical way of expressing the social structure of the people who invented them. Thus, in Greco-Roman mythology, Vico saw a representation of the domestic, economic, and political life of the ancients. These myths were the way in which a primitive and imaginative mind expressed to itself what a more reflective mind would have stated in codes of law and morality.

3. He propounds a new method (strange as its novelty may appear to us) of using tradition: by taking it not as literally true but as a confused memory of facts distorted through a medium whose refractive index we can to a certain extent define. All traditions are true, but none of them mean what they say; in order to discover what they mean, we must know what kind of people invented them and what such a kind of people would mean by saying that kind of thing.

4. In order to find the key to this reinterpretation we must remember that minds at a given stage of development will tend to create the same kind of products. Savages, at all times and in all places, are savages in mind; by studying modern savages we can learn what ancient savages were like, and thus find out how to interpret the savage myths and legends that conceal the facts of remotest ancient history. Children are savages of a kind, and children's fairy-tales may help in the same direction. Modern peasants are unreflective and imaginative persons, and their ideas throw light on the ideas of primitive society; and so forth.

To sum up: Vico has done two things. First, he has used to the full the advance in critical method which had been achieved by historians of the late seventeenth century and carried this process a stage farther by showing how historical thought can be

constructive as well as critical, cutting it loose from its dependence on written authorities and making it genuinely original
or self-dependent, able to recover by scientific analysis of data
truths which have been completely forgotten. Secondly, he has
developed the philosophical principles implicit in his historical
work up to a point where he can deliver a counter-attack on the
scientific and metaphysical philosophy of Cartesianism, demanding a broader basis for the theory of knowledge and criticizing
the narrowness and abstractness of the prevailing philosophical
creed. Actually he was too far ahead of his time to have very
much immediate influence. The extraordinary merit of his
work was not recognized until, two generations later, German
thought had reached on its own account a point much akin to his
own, through the great blossoming of historical studies which
took place in Germany in the late eighteenth century. When
that happened, German scholars rediscovered Vico and attached
a great value to him, thus exemplifying his own doctrine that
ideas are propagated not by 'diffusion', like articles of commerce,
but by the independent discovery by each nation of what it
needs at any given stage in its own development.

§ 8. *Anti-Cartesianism*: (ii) *Locke, Berkeley, and Hume*

The second and, so far as its historical consequences went,
by far the more effective attack on Cartesianism was that
delivered by the Lockian school culminating in Hume. At first,
the empiricism of this school, though already in conscious
opposition to Descartes, had no conscious relation to the problems of historical thought. But as the school developed it
gradually became clear that the point of view which it was
working out could be used in the interests of history, if only
in a negative sense, that is, in order to destroy the Cartesianism
which had banished history from a place on the map of knowledge. Locke and Berkeley show in their philosophical writings
no special preoccupation with the problems of historical thought
(though Locke's description of his own method as the 'historical
plain method' shows that he was not unaware of the relation
between his own anti-Cartesianism and the study of history.
In his *Essay*, Introduction, § 2, he says that by this he means
that he aims at giving an 'account of the ways whereby our
understandings come to attain those notions of things we have'.

Our 'notions of things' are thus treated by Locke exactly as manners and customs are treated by Vico; the Cartesian problem of the relation between ideas and things being in each case ruled out as a problem that does not arise). But in France the eagerness with which a Lockian philosophy was adopted by the men of the Enlightenment, Voltaire and the Encyclopaedists, whose interests were definitely orientated towards history, shows that this philosophy was in some way peculiarly adapted to serve as a weapon for historical thought first in its defence and then in its counter-attack against the tradition of Descartes. The revolt against Cartesianism is in fact the chief negative feature of French thought in the eighteenth century: its chief positive features are, first, its increasingly historical tone and, secondly, its adoption of a Lockian type of philosophy; and it is obvious that these three features were mutually interdependent.

The main points of the Lockian philosophy are easily enumerated. In each case I think it will be clear that the point is, negatively, anti-Cartesian and, positively, a contribution towards a reorientation of philosophy in the direction of history.

1. The denial of innate ideas and the insistence that knowledge comes through experience.—The conception of innate ideas is an anti-historical conception. If all knowledge consists in making explicit our innate ideas, and if all such ideas are present as potentialities in every human mind, all possible knowledge can theoretically be produced afresh by every human being for himself by his own unaided efforts, and there is no need for that corporate building-up of the body of knowledge which is the special work of history. If all knowledge is based on experience, it is an historical product; truth, as Bacon had already reasserted,[1] is the daughter of time; the best knowledge is a fruit of the ripest and richest experience. Thus an historical view of knowledge is already implicit in the first book of Locke's *Essay*.

2. The denial of any argument intended to bridge an alleged gulf between ideas and things, the denial being grounded on the doctrine that knowledge is concerned not with a reality distinct from our ideas but with the agreement and disagreement of our ideas themselves.—As applied to physical science this doctrine is obviously paradoxical, for in physical science we seem

---

[1] *Novum Organum*, bk. i, § lxxxiv, quoting Aulus Gellius, *Noctes Atticae*, xii. 11.

to aim at knowledge of something incapable of being reduced to ideas; but as applied to our historical knowledge of human institutions like morality, language, law, and politics it is not only devoid of paradox, it is the most natural way of looking at these things, as we have already seen.

3. The denial of abstract ideas and the insistence that all ideas are concrete.—This, which Berkeley showed to be implicit in Locke, is paradoxical as applied to mathematics and physics, but once more is obviously the natural way of thinking about history, where knowledge consists not of abstract generalizations but of concrete ideas.

4. The conception of human knowledge as falling necessarily short of absolute truth and certainty, but capable of attaining (in Locke's words) such certainty as our condition needs; or (as Hume puts it) that reason is incapable of dispelling the clouds of doubt, but that Nature herself (our human nature) suffices for that purpose and lays upon us in our practical life an abso-lute necessity to live and talk and act like other people.—This is cold comfort for a Cartesian intent upon the problems of mathematics and physics, but it is a solid basis for historical knowledge, that being precisely concerned with what Locke calls our condition, the actual state of human affairs, or the way in which men live and talk and act.

The English school, then, is reorientating philosophy in the direction of history, though as a whole it is not clearly aware that it is doing so. Nevertheless, Hume is less blind to the situation than his predecessors were. There must be some significance, in the case of so determined and profound a thinker, in the fact that he deserted philosophical studies in favour of historical at about the age of thirty-five. If in the light of his later interests we look through his philosophical works in search of references to history, we find a few such references; not very many, but quite enough to show that history already interested him, that he was thinking about it philosophically, and that he was curiously confident in the power of his own philosophical theories to explain the problems to which they gave rise.

Of these references I shall consider two. In the first we find Hume applying the principles of his philosophy to the case of historical knowledge conceived in the spirit of the methods worked out by the scholars of the late seventeenth century:

'We believe that Caesar was killed in the senate-house on the Ides of March; and that because this fact is established on the unanimous testimony of historians, who agree to assign this precise time and place to that event. Here are certain characters and letters present either to our memory or senses; which characters we likewise remember to have been used as the signs of certain ideas; and these ideas were either in the minds of such as were immediately present at that action, and received the ideas directly from its existence; or they were derived from the testimony of others, and that again from another testimony, by a visible gradation, till we arrive at those who were eye-witnesses and spectators of the event. 'Tis obvious all this chain of argument or connexion of causes and effects, is at first founded on those characters or letters, which are seen or remembered, and that without the authority either of the memory or senses our whole reasoning would be chimerical and without foundation.'[1]

Here the historian's data are given him by direct perception, they are what Hume calls impressions; he actually sees certain documents in front of him. The question is, Why do those impressions cause him to believe that Caesar was killed at a certain time and place? Hume's answer is easy: the association of these visible signs with certain ideas is a matter of fact, attested by our memory; the association being constant, we believe that the people who originally committed those words to paper meant by them what we should ourselves mean; and thus we believe, assuming their veracity, that they believed what they said, viz. that they actually saw Caesar die at that time and place. This is a quite satisfactory solution for the problem of history as it appeared to an historian of the early eighteenth century who could be content if he had shown historical knowledge to be a system of reasonable beliefs based on testimony. And if the philosopher could go on to show, as Hume did, that no other kind of knowledge was more than a system of reasonable beliefs, the claim of history to a place on the map of knowledge was vindicated.

Secondly, Hume was quite aware that contemporary philosophical thought had cast doubt on the validity of historical knowledge, and he goes out of his way to rebut the stock argument, especially because that argument might claim (unjustly, as he thinks) to be supported by his own principles:

[1] *Treatise of Human Nature*, bk. i, pt. iii, § 4.

' 'Tis evident there is no point of ancient history, of which we can have any assurance, but by passing through many millions of causes and effects, and through a chain of arguments of almost an immeasurable length. Before the knowledge of the fact could come to the first historian, it must be conveyed through many mouths; and after it is committed to writing, each new copy is a new object, of which the connexion with the foregoing is known only by experience and observation. Perhaps therefore it may be concluded, from the precedent reasoning, that the evidence of all ancient history must now be lost, as the chain of causes increases and runs on to a greater length.

Hume goes on to argue that this is contrary to common sense: the evidence of ancient history does not thus decay with mere length. The solution is that

'though the links are innumerable . . . yet they are all of the same kind, and depend on the fidelity of printers and copists. . . . There is no variation in the steps. After we know one, we know all of them; and after we have made one, we can have no scruple as to the rest.'[1]

Thus we see that already in his twenties, when he wrote the *Treatise*, Hume had reflected on the problems of historical thought, had decided that the Cartesian objections to it were invalid, and had arrived at a philosophical system which in his own opinion rebutted those objections and placed history on a footing at least as sound as that of any other science. I would not go so far as to call his entire philosophy a reasoned defence of historical thought, but that was undoubtedly one of the things which it implicitly undertook; and it seems to me that when he had finished his philosophical work and asked himself what he had accomplished in it, he could have said with justice that one thing at any rate was the demonstration that history was a legitimate and valid type of knowledge, more legitimate in fact than most others because not promising more than it could perform and not depending on any questionable metaphysical hypotheses. In the general scepticism to which he was led, the sciences which suffered most were those whose claims were most dogmatic and absolute; the whirlwind of his philosophical criticism, levelling all thought to the position of natural

---

[1] Ibid., § 13.

and reasonable belief, left undamaged the fabric of history, as a type of thought which alone could be satisfied with that condition. Nevertheless, Hume remained unconscious of the full impact of his philosophy upon history, and as a writer of history he ranks with the men of the Enlightenment, barred like them from scientific history by a substantialistic view of human nature which was really quite inconsistent with his philosophical principles.

§ 9. *The Enlightenment*

Hume, in his historical work, and his slightly older contemporary Voltaire stand at the head of a new school of historical thought. Their work and that of their followers may be defined as the historiography of the Enlightenment. By the Enlightenment, *Aufklärung*, is meant that endeavour, so characteristic of the early eighteenth century, to secularize every department of human life and thought. It was a revolt not only against the power of institutional religion but against religion as such. Voltaire regarded himself as the leader of a crusade against Christianity, fighting under the motto *Écrasez l'infâme*, where *l'infâme* meant superstition, religion considered as a function of what was backward and barbarous in human life. The philosophical theory underlying this movement was that certain forms of mental activity are primitive forms, destined to perish when mind arrives at maturity. According to Vico, poetry is the natural mode in which the savage or childish mind expresses itself; the sublimest poetry, he maintains, is the poetry of barbarous or heroic ages, the poetry of Homer or Dante; as man develops, reason prevails over imagination and passion, and poetry is displaced by prose. Intermediately between the poetic or purely imaginative way of presenting its experience to itself, and the prosaic or purely rational, Vico placed a third, the mythical or semi-imaginative. This is the stage of development which puts upon the whole of experience a religious interpretation. Thus Vico thinks of art, religion, and philosophy as three different ways in which the human mind expresses or formulates to itself its whole experience. They cannot live peaceably side by side; their relation to each other is one of dialectical succession in a definite order. It follows that a religious attitude towards life is destined to be superseded by a rational or philosophical one.

No such theory was consciously formulated either by Voltaire or by Hume. But had such a theory been brought to their notice, they might have accepted it, and identified themselves and their colleagues with the agency which was actually bringing the religious era of human history to an end and inaugurating a non-religious rational era. Actually, however, their polemical attitude towards religion was too violent and one-sided to have received support from any such theory of its place in human history. For them it was a thing devoid of all positive value whatever, it was just sheer error, due to the unscrupulous and calculating hypocrisy of a class of beings called priests, who, they seem to have thought, invented it to serve as an instrument of domination over the mass of men. Terms like religion, priest, Middle Ages, barbarism, were for such persons not historical or philosophical or sociological terms with a definite scientific meaning, as they were for Vico, but simply terms of abuse: they had an emotional, not a conceptual, significance. As soon as a term like 'religion' or 'barbarism' has a conceptual significance, the thing that goes by such a name has to be regarded as something with a positive function in human history, and therefore not a mere evil or error but a thing with its own proper value in its own proper place. A truly historical view of human history sees everything in that history as having its own *raison d'être* and coming into existence in order to serve the needs of the men whose minds have corporately created it. To think of any phase in history as altogether irrational is to look at it not as an historian but as a publicist, a polemical writer of tracts for the times. Thus the historical outlook of the Enlightenment was not genuinely historical; in its main motive it was polemical and anti-historical.

For this reason writers like Voltaire and Hume did very little to improve the methods of historical research. They took over the methods devised in the preceding generation by men like Mabillon and Tillemont and the Bollandists, and even these methods they did not use in a really scholarly spirit. They were not sufficiently interested in history for its own sake to persevere in the task of reconstructing the history of obscure and remote periods. Voltaire openly proclaimed that no securely

based historical knowledge was attainable for events earlier than
the close of the fifteenth century; Hume's *History of England*
is a very slight and sketchy piece of work until he comes to the
same period, the age of the Tudors. The real cause of this
restriction of interest to the modern period was that with their
narrow conception of reason they had no sympathy for, and
therefore no insight into, what from their point of view were
non-rational periods of human history; they only began to be
interested in history at the point where it began to be the history
of a modern spirit akin to their own, a scientific spirit. In
economic terms this meant the spirit of modern industry and
commerce. In political terms it meant the spirit of enlightened
despotism. They had no conception of institutions as created
by the spirit of a people in its historical development; they
conceived them as inventions, artifices devised by ingenious
thinkers, and imposed by them on the mass of the people. Their
idea of religion as due to priestcraft was merely an application
of this same principle, the only one they understood, to a phase
of history where it did not apply.

The Enlightenment in its narrower sense, as an essentially
polemical and negative movement, a crusade against religion,
never rose higher than its source, and Voltaire remained its best
and most characteristic expression. But it developed in various
directions without losing its original character. Based as it was
on the idea that human life is and has always been in the main a
blind, irrational business, but is capable of being converted into
something rational, it contained in itself the germs of two immediate developments: a backward-looking or more strictly historical development which should exhibit past history as the play
of irrational forces, and a forward-looking or more practical or
political development, forecasting and endeavouring to bring
about a millennium in which the rule of reason shall have been
established.

(a) As examples of the first tendency we may quote Montesquieu and Gibbon. Montesquieu had the merit of seizing upon
the differences between different nations and different cultures,
but he misunderstood the essential character of these differences.
Instead of explaining their history by reference to human reason,
he thought of it as due to differences in climate and geography.
Man, in other words, is regarded as a part of nature, and the

explanation of historical events is sought in the facts of the natural world. History so conceived would become a kind of natural history of man, or anthropology, where institutions appear not as free inventions of human reason in the course of its development, but as the necessary effects of natural causes. Montesquieu in fact conceived human life as a reflection of geographical and climatic conditions, not otherwise than the life of plants, and this implies that historical changes are simply different ways in which one single and unchangeable thing, human nature, reacts to different stimuli. This misconception of human nature and human action is the real flaw in any theory which, like Montesquieu's, attempts to explain the features of a civilization by reference to geographical facts. To be sure, there is an intimate relation between any culture and its natural environment; but what determines its character is not the facts of that environment, in themselves, but what man is able to get out of them; and that depends on what kind of man he is. As an historian, Montesquieu was uncritical in the extreme; but his insistence on the relation of man to his environment (even though he misconceived the character of that relation) and on the economic factors which in his view underlay political institutions was important not only in itself but for the future development of historical thought.

Gibbon, a typical Enlightenment historian, agreed with all this to the extent of conceiving history as anything but an exhibition of human wisdom; but instead of finding its positive principle in the laws of nature which, as it were, replace for Montesquieu the wisdom of man and create for him social organizations which he could not create for himself, Gibbon finds the motive force of history in human irrationality itself, and his narrative displays what he calls the triumph of barbarism and religion. But in order that there may be such a triumph there must first be something for this irrationality to triumph over; and thus Gibbon places the beginning of his narrative in a golden age when human reason ruled over a happy world, the Antonine period. This conception of a golden age in the past gives Gibbon a rather special place among Enlightenment historians and assimilates him on the one hand to his predecessors, the humanists of the Renaissance, and on the other to his successors, the Romantics at the close of the eighteenth century.

(b) In its forward-looking aspect, where the golden age is conceived as lying in the near future, this movement may be represented by Condorcet, whose *Esquisse d'un tableau des progrès de l'esprit humain*, written during the French Revolution when he was in prison awaiting execution, looks forward to a Utopian future where tyrants and their slaves, priests and their dupes, will have disappeared, and people will behave rationally in the enjoyment of life, liberty, and the pursuit of happiness.

It will be plain from the examples that have been given that the historiography of the Enlightenment is apocalyptic to an extreme degree, as indeed the very word 'enlightenment' suggests. The central point of history, for these writers, is the sunrise of the modern scientific spirit. Before that, everything was superstition and darkness, error and imposture. And of these things there can be no history, not only because they are unworthy of historical study, but because there is in them no rational or necessary development: the story of them is a tale told by an idiot, full of sound and fury, signifying nothing.

Thus in the crucial case, namely the origin of the modern scientific spirit, these writers could have no conception of historical origins or processes. Pure reason cannot come into existence out of pure unreason. There can be no development leading from the one to the other. The sunrise of the scientific spirit was, from the point of view of the Enlightenment, a sheer miracle, unprepared in the previous course of events and uncaused by any cause that could be adequate to such an effect. This inability to explain or expound historically what they regarded as the most important event in history was of course symptomatic; it meant that in a general way they had no satisfactory theory of historical causation and could not seriously believe in the origin or genesis of anything whatever. Consequently, throughout their historical work, their account of causes is superficial to absurdity. It was these historians, for example, who invented the grotesque idea that the Renaissance in Europe was due to the fall of Constantinople and the consequent expulsion of scholars in search of new homes; and a typical expression of this attitude is the remark of Pascal that if Cleopatra's nose had been longer the whole history of the world would have been different—typical, that is, of a bankruptcy of historical method which in despair of genuine explanation acquiesces in the most trivial causes for the vastest effects. Such inability to discover genuine historical causes is, no doubt, connected with the Humian theory of causation according to which we can never perceive any connexion between any two events.

Perhaps the best short way of describing the historiography of the Enlightenment is to say that it took over the conception of historical research which had been devised by the Church historians of the late seventeenth century, and turned it against its authors, using it in a deliberately anti-clerical spirit instead of a deliberately clerical one. No attempt was made to lift history above the level of propaganda; on the contrary, that aspect of it was intensified, for the crusade in favour of reason was still a holy war; and Montesquieu hit the nail on the head when he remarked[1] that in spirit Voltaire was a monastic historian writing for monks. At the same time, the historians of this period did achieve certain definite advances. Intolerant and unreasonable though they were, they were fighting for tolerance. Unable though they were to appreciate the creative power of a popular spirit, they were writing from the point of view of the subject, not the government, and were therefore bringing into an altogether new prominence the history of the arts and sciences, industry, trade, and culture in general. Superficial though they were in their search for causes, they did at least search for them, and thus implicitly conceived history as (in spite of Hume) a process in which one event led necessarily to the next. There was thus a leaven at work in their own thought which was tending to disrupt their own dogmas and transcend their own limitations. Deep down beneath the surface of their work lay a conception of the historical process as a process developing neither by the will of enlightened despots nor by the rigid plans of a transcendent God, but by a necessity of its own, an immanent necessity in which unreason itself is only a disguised form of reason.

§ 10. *The science of human nature*

In § 1 of this Part, I pointed out that Hume's attack on spiritual substance was the philosophical forerunner of scientific history because it destroyed the last vestiges of the substan-

---

[1] 'Voltaire ... est comme les moines, qui n'écrivent pas pour le sujet qu'ils traitent, mais pour la gloire de leur ordre. Voltaire écrit pour son couvent' (*Pensées diverses* in *Œuvres*, Paris, 1866, vol. ii, p. 427).

tialism in Greco-Roman thought. In § 8 I showed how Locke and his followers were reorientating philosophy in the direction of history, although of this they were not fully conscious. What prevented eighteenth-century history from becoming scientific by reaping the full fruits of the philosophical revolution was an unnoticed relic of substantialism implicit in the Enlightenment's quest for a science of human nature. Just as the ancient historians conceived the Roman character, for example, as a thing that had never really come into existence but had always existed and had always been the same, so the eighteenth-century historians, who recognized that all true history is the history of mankind, assumed that human nature had existed ever since the creation of the world exactly as it existed among themselves. Human nature was conceived substantialistically as something static and permanent, an unvarying substratum underlying the course of historical changes and all human activities. History never repeated itself but human nature remained eternally unaltered.

This assumption is present, as we have seen, in Montesquieu, but it also lies at the back of all the philosophical work of the eighteenth century, not to mention earlier periods. The Cartesian innate ideas are the ways of thinking which are natural to the human mind as such, everywhere and always. The Lockian human understanding is something assumed to be everywhere the same, though imperfectly developed in children, idiots, and savages. The Kantian mind which as intuition is the source of space and time, as understanding the source of the categories, and as reason the source of the Ideas of God, freedom, and immortality, is a purely human mind, but Kant unquestioningly assumes it to be the only kind of human mind that exists or ever has existed. Even so sceptical a thinker as Hume accepts this assumption, as I have already hinted. In the Introduction to his *Treatise of Human Nature* he explains the project of his work by saying that 'all the sciences have a relation, greater or less, to human nature, and however wide any of them may seem to run from it, they still return back by one passage or another. Even *Mathematics*, *Natural Philosophy*, and *Natural Religion*' (i.e. the three Cartesian sciences, mathematics, physics, and metaphysics) 'are in some measure dependent on the science of MAN : since they lie under the cognizance of men, and are judged of by their powers and faculties'. Consequently the 'science of man', that is, the science which investigates the 'principles and operations of our reasoning faculty', 'our tastes and sentiments', and 'men as united in society', is 'the only solid foundation for all the other sciences'.

In all this, Hume never shows the slightest suspicion that the human nature he is analysing in his philosophical work is the nature of a western European in the early eighteenth century, and that the very same enterprise if undertaken at a widely different time or place might have yielded widely different results. He always assumes that *our* reasoning faculty, *our* tastes and sentiments, and so forth, are something perfectly uniform and invariable, underlying and conditioning all historical changes. As I have already suggested, his attack on the idea of spiritual substance should, if successful, have demolished this conception of human nature as something solid and permanent and uniform; but it did nothing of the kind, because Hume substituted for the idea of spiritual substance the idea of constant tendencies to associate ideas in particular ways, and these laws of association were just as uniform and unchanging as any substance.

Hume's abolition of spiritual substance amounted to laying down the principle that we must never separate what a mind is from what it does, and that therefore a mind's nature is nothing but the ways in which it thinks and acts. The concept of mental substance was thus resolved into the concept of mental process. But this did not in itself necessitate an historical conception of mind, because all process is not historical process. A process is historical only when it creates its own laws; and according to Hume's theory of mind the laws of mental process are ready-made and unchanging from their beginning. He did not think of mind as learning to think and act in new ways as the process of its activity developed. He certainly thought that his new science of human nature, if successfully achieved, would lead to further progress in the arts and sciences; but not by altering human nature itself—that, he never suggests to be possible—only by improving our understanding of it.

Philosophically, this conception was self-contradictory. If that which we come to understand better is something other than ourselves, for example the chemical properties of matter our improved understanding of it in no way improves the thing itself. If, on the other hand, that which we understand better is our own understanding, an improvement in *that* science is an improvement not only in its subject but in its object also. By coming to think more truly about the human understanding we are coming to improve our own understanding. Hence the historical development of the science of human nature entails an historical development in human nature itself.

This was concealed from eighteenth-century philosophers, because they based their programme for a science of mind on the analogy of the established sciences of nature and failed to notice the lack of complete parallelism between the two cases. Men like Bacon had pointed out that improved knowledge of nature would give us improved power over nature, and this was quite true. Coal tar, for example, once its chemistry is understood, ceases to be refuse and becomes the raw material of dyes, resins, and other products, but the fact that these chemical discoveries have been made in no way alters the nature of coal tar or its by-products. Nature stays put, and is the same whether we understand it or not. To put this in Berkeleian language, it is God's thought, not our thought, that makes nature what it is; in coming to know nature we are not creating anything new, we are only rethinking God's thoughts for ourselves. The eighteenth-century philosophers assumed that exactly the same principles applied to the knowledge of our own mind, which they called human nature in order to express their conception of its resemblance to nature properly so called. They thought of human nature as something which stayed put, however much or however little one knew about it, exactly as nature stays put. They assumed without question a fallacious principle which may be put in the form of a rule-of-three sum: knowledge of nature: nature : : knowledge of mind : mind. This assumption fatally distorted their conception of history in two ways:

(1) Assuming human nature to be constant, they made it impossible for themselves to arrive at the conception of a history of human nature itself; for such a conception implies that human nature is not a constant but a variable. The eighteenth century wished for a universal history, a history of man: but a genuine history of man would have to be a history of how man came to be what he is, and this would imply thinking of

human nature, the human nature actually existing in eighteenth-century Europe, as the product of an historical process, whereas it was regarded as the unchanging presupposition of any such process.

(2) The same error gave them a false view not only of the past but of the future, because it made them look forward to a Utopia in which all the problems of human life should have been solved. For if human nature itself undergoes no change when we come to understand it better, every new discovery we make about it will solve the problems which now perplex us because of our ignorance, and no new problems will be created. Our advancing knowledge of human nature will therefore gradually relieve us of the various difficulties under which we now labour, and human life will consequently become better and better, happier and happier. And if the advance in the science of human nature extends to the discovery of the fundamental laws governing its manifestations, which thinkers of that age thought quite possible on the analogy of the way in which the seventeenth-century scientists had discovered the fundamental laws of physics, the millennium will be achieved. Thus the eighteenth-century conception of progress was based on the same false analogy between knowledge of nature and knowledge of mind. The truth is that if the human mind comes to understand itself better, it thereby comes to operate in new and different ways. A race of men that has acquired the kind of self-knowledge at which the eighteenth-century thinkers were aiming would act in ways not hitherto known, and these new ways of acting would give rise to new moral and social and political problems, and the millennium would be as far away as ever.

PART III

THE THRESHOLD OF SCIENTIFIC HISTORY

§ 1. *Romanticism*

BEFORE any further progress could be made in historical thought, two things were necessary: first, the horizon of history had to be widened through a more sympathetic investigation of those past ages which the Enlightenment had treated as unenlightened or barbaric and left in obscurity; and secondly, the conception of human nature as something uniform and unchanging had to be attacked. It was Herder who first made substantial advances in both of these directions, but he was assisted, so far as the first of them is concerned, by the work of Rousseau.

Rousseau was a child of the Enlightenment, but through his reinterpretation of its principles he became the father of the Romantic movement. He realized that rulers could give their people nothing except what the people themselves were ready to accept, and consequently he argued that the enlightened despot of Voltaire's conception was powerless unless there were an enlightened people. For the idea of a despotic will, imposing on a passive people what the despot knew to be good for it, Rousseau substituted the idea of a general will on the part of the people itself, a will on the part of the people as a whole to pursue its interest as a whole.

In the sphere of practical politics this involved an optimism or Utopianism not greatly different from that of people like Condorcet, though it was differently based: where the Enlightenment based its Utopian expectations on the hope of obtaining enlightened rulers, the Romanticists based theirs on the hope of obtaining an enlightened people by means of popular education. But in the sphere of history the results were very different and indeed revolutionary. The general will as Rousseau conceived it, although it might be more or less enlightened, had always existed and had always been operative. Unlike reason in the Enlightenment theory, it had not come into the world at a comparatively recent date. The principle on which Rousseau explained history, therefore, was a principle which could be applied not only to the recent history of the civilized world but to the history of all races and all times. Ages of barbarism and superstition became at least in principle intelligible and it was possible to see the whole of human history, if not as the history of human reason, at least as the history of human will.

Further, Rousseau's conception of education depends on the doctrine that the child, undeveloped though he may be, has a life of his own, with his own ideals and conceptions, and that the teacher must understand and sympathize with this life, treat it with respect, and help it to develop in a way proper and natural to itself. This conception, applied to history, means that the historian must never do what the Enlightenment historians were always doing, that is, regard past ages with contempt and disgust, but must look at them sympathetically and find in them the expression of genuine and valuable human achievements. Rousseau was so much carried away by this idea as to assert (in his *Discourse on the Arts and Sciences*) that primitive savagery is superior to civilized life; but that exaggeration he later withdrew,[1] and the only part of it that survived as a permanent possession of the Romantic school was the habit of looking back to primitive times as representing a form of society with a value of its own, a value which the development of civilization had lost. When one compares, for example, the complete lack of any sympathy for the Middle Ages shown by Hume with the intense sympathy for the same thing which is found in Sir Walter Scott, one can see how this tendency of Romanticism had enriched its historical outlook.

On this side of its thought Romanticism represents a new tendency to see a positive value and interest in civilizations very different from its own. This, by itself, might develop into a futile nostalgia for the past, a desire, for example, to bring back the Middle Ages; but actually that development was checked by the presence in Romanticism of another conception, viz., the conception of history as a progress, a development of human reason or the education of mankind. According to this conception, past stages in history led necessarily to the present; a given form of civilization can exist only when the time is ripe for it, and has its value just because those are the conditions of its existing; if therefore we could bring back the Middle Ages we should only be going back to a stage in the process which has led

[1] e.g. by implication in *Contrat Social*, I. viii.

to the present, and the process would go on as before. Thus the Romanticists conceived the value of a past stage of history like the Middle Ages in a double way: partly as something of permanent value in itself, as a unique achievement of the human mind, and partly as taking its place in a course of development leading on to things of still greater value.

Thus the Romanticists tended to look upon the past as such with an admiration and sympathy resembling that felt by the humanists for Greco-Roman antiquity; but in spite of the resemblance the difference was very great.[1] The difference in principle is that the humanists despised the past as such, but regarded certain past facts as lifted, so to speak, clean out of the time-process by their own intrinsic excellence, thus becoming classics or permanent models for imitation; whereas the Romantics admired and sympathized with these or other past achievements because in them they recognized the spirit of their own past, valuable to them because it was their own.

This Romantic sympathy with the past, instanced for example in Bishop Percy with his collection of medieval English ballad literature, did not disguise the gulf separating it from the present but actually presupposed that gulf, consciously insisting on the vast dissimilarity between present-day life and that of the past. Thus the tendency of the Enlightenment to care only for the present and the most recent past was counteracted, and people were led to think of the past as all worthy of study and all of a piece. The scope of historical thought was vastly widened, and historians began to think of the entire history of man as a single process of development from a beginning in savagery to an end in a perfectly rational and civilized society.

§ 2. Herder

The first and in some ways the most important expression of

---

[1] For this reason it was a blunder on the part of Walter Pater to include a chapter on Winckelmann in his work on the Renaissance. Winckelmann's study of Greek art was not at all like that of Renaissance scholars. He conceived a profoundly original idea, the idea that there is a history of art, not to be confused with the biographies of artists: a history of art itself, developing through the work of successive artists, without their conscious awareness of any such development. The artist, for this conception, is merely the unconscious vehicle of a particular stage in the development of art. Similar ideas were applied afterwards by Hegel and others to the history of politics, philosophy, and other achievements of the human mind.

this new attitude to the past was Herder's *Ideen zur Philosophie der Menschengeschichte*, written in four volumes published between 1784 and 1791. Herder sees human life as closely related to its setting in the natural world. The general character of this world as he conceived it is that of an organism so designed as to develop within itself higher organisms. The physical universe is a kind of matrix within which, at a specially favoured region which from this point of view may be regarded as its centre, there crystallizes out a peculiar structure, the solar system. This again is a matrix within which its own special conditions give rise to the earth, which is, so far as we know, peculiar among the planets in being a fit theatre for life and in that sense, as the seat of the next stage in evolution, the centre of the solar system. Within the material fabric of the earth there arise special mineral formations, special geographical organisms (the continents), and so forth. Life, in its primitive form as vegetable life, is a further elaboration or crystallization of a highly complex kind. Animal life is a further specialization of vegetable life, human life a further specialization of animal. In each case the new specialization exists in an environment consisting of the unspecialized matrix from which it has emerged, and is itself nothing but a focal point at which the inner nature of this matrix emerges into complete realization. Thus man is the perfect or typical animal; animals are perfect plants, and so on. And in the same way, at two removes, human nature is the perfection of plant nature: thus, Herder explains, sexual love in man is really the same thing as the flowering and fruiting of plants, raised to a higher power.

Herder's general view of nature is frankly teleological. He thinks of each stage in evolution as designed by nature to prepare for the next. None is an end in itself. But with man the process reaches a culmination, because man *is* an end in himself: for man, in his rational and moral life, justifies his own existence. Since the purpose of nature in creating man is to create a rational being, human nature develops itself as a system of spiritual powers whose full development still lies in the future. Man is thus a link between two worlds, the natural world out of which he has grown and the spiritual world which through him is not indeed coming into existence, for it exists eternally in the shape of spiritual laws, but is realizing itself on the earth.

As a natural being, man is divided into the various races of mankind, each closely related to its geographical environment and having its original physical and mental characteristics moulded by that environment; but each race, once formed, is a specific type of humanity which has permanent characteristics of its own depending not on its immediate relation to its environment but on its own inbred peculiarities (as a plant formed in one environment remains the same when transplanted into another). The sensuous and imaginative faculties of different races are thus genuinely differentiated; each race has its own conception of happiness and its own ideal of life. But this racially differentiated humanity is, once more, a matrix in which there arises a higher type of human organism, namely the historical organism, that is, a race whose life instead of remaining static develops in time into higher and higher forms. The favoured centre in which this historical life arises is Europe, owing to its geographical and climatic peculiarities; so that in Europe alone human life is genuinely historical, whereas in China or India or among the natives of America there is no true historical progress but only a static unchanging civilization or a series of changes in which old forms of life are replaced by new forms without that steady cumulative development which is the peculiarity of historical progress. Europe is thus a privileged region of human life, as man is privileged among the animals, the animals among living organisms, and organisms among earthly existents.

Herder's book contains a marvellous quantity of fertile and valuable thoughts. It is one of the richest and most stimulating books on its subject in existence. But the development of thought in it is often loose and hasty. Herder was not a cautious thinker; he jumped to conclusions by analogical methods without testing them, and he was not critical of his own ideas. For instance, it is not really true that Europe is the only country that has a history, though doubtless it was the only country about which in Herder's time Europeans had much historical knowledge. And his doctrine of the differentiation of races, a crucial step in his whole argument, should not be accepted without scrutiny.

Herder, so far as I know, was the first thinker to recognize in a systematic way that there are differences between different

kinds of men, and that human nature is not uniform but diversi-
fied. He pointed out that what makes Chinese civilization, for
example, what it is cannot be the geography and climate of
China but only the peculiar nature of the Chinese. If different
kinds of men are placed in the same environment, they will
exploit the resources of that environment in different ways and
thus create different kinds of civilization. The determining fact
in history, therefore, is the special peculiarities not of man in
general but of this or that kind of man. These special peculiarities Herder regarded as racial peculiarities: that is, the inherited
psychological characteristics of the varieties of the human
species. Herder is thus the father of anthropology, meaning by
that the science which (*a*) distinguishes various physical types
of human beings, and (*b*) studies the manners and customs of
these various types as expressions of psychological peculiarities
going with physical ones.

This was an important new step in the conception of human
nature, because it recognized that human nature was not a
datum but a problem: not something everywhere uniform,
whose fundamental characteristics could be discovered once for
all, but something variable, whose special characteristics called
for separate investigation in special cases. But even so, the conception was not a genuinely historical one. The psychological
characteristics of each race were regarded as fixed and uniform,
so that instead of the Enlightenment's conception of a single
fixed human nature we now have the conception of several fixed
human natures. Each of these is regarded not as an historical
product but as a presupposition of history. There is still no
conception of a people's character as having been made what it
is by that people's historical experience; on the contrary, its
historical experience is regarded as a mere result of its fixed
character.

At the present time, we have seen enough of the evil consequences of this theory to be on our guard against it. The racial
theory of civilization has ceased to be scientifically respectable.
To-day we only know it as a sophistical excuse for national pride
and national hatred. The idea that there is a European race
whose peculiar virtues render it fit to dominate the rest of the
world, or an English race whose innate qualities make imperial-
ism a duty, or a Nordic race whose predominance in America

is the necessary condition of American greatness, and whose purity in Germany is indispensable to the purity of German culture, we know to be scientifically baseless and politically disastrous. We know that physical anthropology and cultural anthropology are different studies, and we find it difficult to see how any one can have confused them. Consequently we are not inclined to be grateful to Herder for having started so pernicious a doctrine.

It would be possible to defend him by arguing that his theory of racial differences does not in itself give any ground for believing in the superiority of one race over another. One might argue that it only implies each type of man to have its own form of life, its own conception of happiness, and its own rhythm of historical development. On this showing, the social institutions and political forms of different peoples can differ without being intrinsically better or worse than one another, and the goodness of a certain political form is never an absolute goodness but only a goodness relative to the people that has created it.

But this would not be a legitimate interpretation of Herder's thought. It is essential to his whole point of view that the differences between the social and political institutions of different races are derived not from the historical experience of each race but from its innate psychological peculiarities, and this is fatal to a true understanding of history. The differentiations between different cultures which can be explained on these lines are not historical differentiations, like that between, say, medieval and Renaissance culture, but non-historical differentiations like that between a community of bees and a community of ants. Human nature has been divided up, but it is still human nature, still nature and not mind; and in terms of practical politics this means that the task of creating or improving a culture is assimilated to that of creating or improving a breed of domestic animals. Once Herder's theory of race is accepted, there is no escaping the Nazi marriage laws.

The problem which Herder bequeathed to his successors, therefore, was the problem of thinking out clearly the distinction between nature and man: nature as a process or sum of processes governed by laws which are blindly obeyed, man as a process or sum of processes governed (as Kant was to put it) not by law simply but by consciousness of law. It had to be shown that history is a process of this second type: that is to say, that the life of man is an historical life because it is a mental or spiritual life.

§ 3. *Kant*

Herder's first volume was published in the spring of 1784 when he was forty. Kant, whose pupil he had been, evidently read the book as soon as it appeared, and although he dissented from many of its doctrines, as his somewhat acid review was to show a year later, it did stimulate him to think for himself about the problems it raised and to write an essay of his own which constitutes his chief work on the philosophy of history. Influenced by his pupil though he was, Kant was already sixty when he read the first part of the *Ideen*, and his mind had been formed by the Enlightenment as it took root in Germany under the aegis of Frederick the Great and of Voltaire, whom Frederick brought to the Prussian court. Hence Kant represents, as compared with Herder, a certain astringent tendency towards anti-Romanticism. In the true style of the Enlightenment, he regards past history as a spectacle of human irrationality and looks forward to a Utopia of rational life. What is really remarkable in him is the way in which he combines the Enlightenment point of view with the Romanticist, very much as in his theory of knowledge he combines rationalism and empiricism.

The essay to which I have referred was published in November 1784, and is called *An Idea for a Universal History from the Cosmopolitan Point of View* (*Idee zu einer allgemeinen Geschichte in weltbürgerlicher Absicht*). Historical study was not one of Kant's main interests, but his exceptional power of picking up the threads of a philosophical discussion even on a subject of which he knew comparatively little enabled him to develop lines of thought which he had found in writers like Voltaire, Rousseau, and Herder and produce something new and valuable, just as his study of Baumgarten enabled him to write a most important work on aesthetics although his artistic culture was of the slightest.

Kant begins his essay by saying that although as noumena, or things in themselves, human acts are determined by moral laws, yet as phenomena, from the point of view of a spectator, they are determined according to natural laws as the effects of causes. History, narrating the course of human actions, deals with them as phenomena, and therefore sees them as subject to natural laws. To detect these laws is certainly difficult, if not impossible; but it is at any rate worth considering whether the general course of history may not show a development in mankind similar to that which biography reveals in a single individual. Here Kant is using the Romanticist idea of the education of mankind not as a dogma or accepted principle but as what he calls in his own technical language an Idea, that is, a guiding principle of interpretation in the light of which we look at facts in order to see whether it improves our understanding of them. As an example of what he means, he points out that every marriage in itself, as it actually happens, is a perfectly free moral act on the part of certain persons; but marriage statistics actually show a surprising uniformity, and from the historian's point of view therefore the statistics can be looked at as if there were some cause determining, under a law of nature, how many marriages there shall be in each year. Just as the statistician deals with these free acts as if they were thus determined, so the historian may look at human history as if it were a process determined in the same way according to a law. If so, what kind of law would this be? It would certainly not be due to human wisdom: for if we review history we find it on the whole not a record of human wisdom but far more a record of human folly, vanity, and wickedness. Even philosophers, Kant observes, wise though they are believed to be, are not wise enough to plan out their own lives and live according to the rules they have made for themselves. Thus, if there is a general progress in the life of mankind, that progress is certainly not due to a plan made for his own guidance by man. But none the less there might be such a plan, namely a plan of nature, which man fulfils without understanding it. To detect such a plan in human history would be a proper task for a new Kepler, and to explain its necessity would require another Newton.

Kant does not say what he means by a plan of nature. In order to interpret the phrase we must turn to the second half of the *Critique of Judgement*, in which the conception of teleology in nature is expounded. Here we find that, according to Kant, the idea that nature has purposes is an idea which we cannot indeed prove or disprove by scientific inquiry, but it is an idea without which we cannot understand nature at all. We do not actually believe it in the way in which we believe a scientific law, but we adopt it as a point of view, admittedly a subjective point of view, from which it is not only possible but profitable, and not only profitable but necessary, to look at the facts of nature. A species of plants or animals looks to us as if it had been ingeniously designed to maintain itself individually by nutrition and self-defence and collectively by reproduction. For example, we see a hedgehog when frightened roll itself into a prickly ball. We do not think this is due to the individual cleverness of this particular hedgehog; all hedgehogs do it, and do it by nature; it is as if nature had endowed the hedgehog with that particular defensive mechanism in order to protect it against carnivorous enemies. In calling it a defensive mechanism we are using the language of metaphor; for a mechanism means a device, and a device implies an inventor; but Kant's point is that without using metaphors of this type we cannot talk or think about nature at all. Likewise, he maintains, we cannot think about history without using similarly teleological metaphors. We use phrases like the conquest of the Mediterranean world by Rome; but actually what we mean by Rome is only this and that individual Roman, and what we mean by the conquest of the Mediterranean world is only the sum of this and that individual piece of warfare or administration which these men carried out. None of them actually said 'I am playing my part in a great movement, the conquest of the Mediterranean world by Rome', but they acted as if they did say that, and we, in looking at the history of their actions, find that these actions can only be envisaged as if they were controlled by a purpose to achieve that conquest, which, as it certainly was not the purpose of this or that individual Roman, we metaphorically describe as a purpose of nature.

It may further be observed that from Kant's point of view it was just as legitimate to talk about a plan of nature revealed in the phenomena studied by the historian as to talk about laws of nature revealed in those studied by the scientist. What laws of nature are to the scientist, plans of nature are to the historian. When the scientist describes himself as discovering laws of nature, he does not mean that there is a legislator called nature; what he means is that phenomena show a regularity and orderliness which not only can be but must be described in some such metaphor. Similarly when the historian speaks of a plan of nature developing itself in history he does not mean that there is an actual mind called nature which consciously makes a plan to be carried out in history, he means that history proceeds as if there were such a mind. Nevertheless this parallelism between plan of nature and law of nature has implications which betray a serious weakness in Kant's philosophy of history.

We have seen that the eighteenth-century philosophers in general misrepresented mind by assimilating it to nature. In particular they talked about human nature as if it were merely one special kind of nature; when what they were really talking about was mind, or something radically different from nature. Kant attempted to avoid this error by his distinction, based on Leibniz, between phenomena and things in themselves. He thought that what makes nature nature, what gives it the peculiarities by which we recognize it as nature, is the fact of its being phenomenon, that is, the fact of its being looked at from outside, from the point of view of a spectator. If we could get inside the phenomena, and relive their inner life in our own minds, their natural characteristics would, he thought, disappear: we should now be apprehending them as things in themselves, and in doing so we should discover that their inner reality is mind. Everything is really and in itself mind; everything is phenomenally, or seen from a spectator's point of view, nature. Thus human action, as we experience it in our own inner life, is mind, that is to say, free self-determining moral activity; but human action as seen from outside, as the historian sees it, is just as much nature as anything is, and for the same reason, namely, because it is being looked at, and thus converted into phenomenon.

Granted this principle, Kant is certainly justified in calling the plan of history a plan of nature, for the parallelism between laws of nature in science and plans of nature in history is complete. But the principle itself is open to grave doubts because it distorts both science and history. (*a*) It distorts science because it implies that behind the phenomena of nature as studied by the scientist there is a reality, nature as it is in itself, which is nothing else than mind; and this is the foundation of that mystical view of nature, so prevalent in the late eighteenth and early nineteenth centuries, which instead of treating natural phenomena as things deserving of study for their own sake treated them as a kind of veil concealing a spiritual reality somehow akin to ourselves. (*b*) It distorts history because it implies that the historian is a mere spectator of the events he describes. This implication is explicitly avowed by Hume in his essay on *The Study of History*: 'To see all the human race, from the beginning of time, pass, as it were, in review before us, . . . what spectacle can be imagined so magnificent, so various, so interesting?'[1] This view of history Kant took for granted, and for him it could have only one meaning. If history is a spectacle, it is a phenomenon; if a phenomenon, it is nature, because nature, for Kant, is an epistemological term and means things seen as a spectacle. No doubt Kant was only adopting a commonplace of his age; nevertheless, he was wrong, because history is not a spectacle. The events of history do not 'pass in review' before the historian. They have finished happening before he begins thinking about them. He has to re-create them inside his own mind, re-enacting for himself so much of the experience of the men who took part in them as he wishes to understand. It is because the eighteenth century did not know this, but falsely regarded history as a spectacle, that it reduced history to nature, subordinating historical processes to laws of geography and climatology, as in Montesquieu, or to laws of human biology, as in Herder.

Kant's parallel between the laws of nature and the plan of nature thus has its roots in the erroneous view of history characteristic of his age. And yet, by his special conception of what the plan of nature was, he took an important step towards overcoming the error. His own ethical work was avowedly (in his own sense of this word) 'metaphysical' in character, that is, it was an attempt to discuss mind not in its phenomenal aspect as a kind of nature, but as a thing in itself; and here he identified the essence of mind as freedom, that is, in his own sense of the word 'freedom', not as mere liberty of choice but as autonomy, the power to make laws for oneself. This enabled him to put forward a new interpretation of the idea of history as the education of the human race. For him, it meant the development of humanity into the state of being fully mind, that is, fully free. The plan of nature in history was therefore understood by Kant

[1] *Philosophical Works* (Edinburgh, 1826), iv. 531.

as a plan for the development of human freedom. In the first section of his *Fundamental Principles of the Metaphysic of Morals* he asks, What is the purpose of nature in endowing man with reason? and he answers, It cannot be to make man happy; it can only be to give him the power of becoming a moral agent. The purpose of nature in creating man is therefore the development of moral freedom; and the course of human history can therefore be conceived as the working-out of this development. It is thus Kant's analysis of human nature as essentially moral nature or freedom that gives him the final key to his conception of history.

We can now return to the summary of Kant's argument. Nature's purpose in creating any of her creatures is, of course, the existence of that creature, the realization of its essence. The teleology of nature is an internal teleology, not an external: she does not make grass to feed cows, and cows to feed men; she makes grass in order that there should be grass, and so on. Man's essence is his reason; therefore she makes men in order that they should be rational. Now it is a peculiarity of reason that it cannot be completely developed in the lifetime of a single individual. No one, for example, can invent the whole of mathematics out of his own head. He has to profit by the work already done by others. Man is an animal that has the peculiar faculty of profiting by the experience of others; and he has this faculty because he is rational, for reason is a kind of experience in which this is possible. If what you want is food, the fact that another cow has eaten a certain blade of grass only prevents you from eating that blade; but if what you want is knowledge, the fact that Pythagoras has discovered the theorem about the square on the hypotenuse gives that piece of knowledge to you more easily than you could have got it for yourself. Consequently the purpose of nature for the development of man's reason is a purpose that can be fully realized only in the history of the human race and not in an individual life.

Kant has here achieved the remarkable feat of showing why there should be such a thing as history; it is, he shows, because man is a rational being, and the full development of his potentialities therefore requires an historical process. It is an argument parallel to that by which Plato shows in the second book of the *Republic* why there must be a community. As against the Sophists, who held that the State is artificial, Plato showed that it was natural because it was based on the fact that the individual man is not self-dependent; he needs the economic services of others in order to satisfy his own desires. As an economic being, he must have a state to live in; similarly, Kant shows that, as a rational being, he must have an historical process to live in.

History, then, is a progress towards rationality, which is at the same time an advance in rationality. This, of course, was by Kant's time a commonplace both of Enlightenment and Romantic thought. We must be careful not to confuse it with the apparently similar but really very different late-nineteenth-century identification of history with progress. The evolutionary metaphysics of the late nineteenth century held that all time-processes were, as such, progressive in character, and that history is a progress merely because it is a sequence of events in time: thus the progressiveness of history was by these thinkers merely one case of evolution or the progressiveness of nature. But the eighteenth century regarded nature as unprogressive, and thought of the progressiveness of history as something differentiating history from nature. There might even, it was thought, be a human society in which there was no progress in rationality; this would be a society without a history, like the non-historical or merely natural societies of bees or ants. Outside the state of nature, however, Kant thought that there was progress, and he therefore asks, Why does human society progress instead of stagnating, and how does this progress come about?

The question is an urgent one because he thinks that a non-historical or stagnant society would be the happiest kind; one in which people lived peaceably in a friendly and easy style, as in the state of nature depicted by Locke, where men 'order their actions and dispose of their possessions and persons as they think fit, within the bounds of the Law of Nature', 'a state also of equality, wherein the power and jurisdiction is reciprocal, no one having more than another', because every man has an equal right to punish transgressions of the law of nature, 'thereby to preserve the innocent and restrain offenders'.[1] As Locke freely admits, there are inconveniences in a state of nature arising

[1] *Of Civil Government*, bk. ii, chap. 2.

from the fact that, there, every man is judge in his own cause; or, as Kant puts it,[1] such a state, in which all men allow their talents to rust unused, is not one that can be regarded as morally desirable, possible though it is, and in many ways attractive. Indeed, neither Locke nor Kant, nor I think any one else of their age, regarded the state of nature as only an abstract possibility, still less as a downright fiction. Hobbes, when this point was raised, replied,[2] first, that 'the savage people in many places of America, except the government of small families the concord whereof dependeth on naturall lust, have no government at all', and secondly that 'in all times kings and persons of soveraigne authority' are in a state of nature with regard to one another. Locke[3] replies similarly that all sovereign states are mutually in a state of nature. And a perfect example of the state of nature as understood by these philosophers is afforded by the life of the early Norwegian colonists of Iceland, as described in the sagas.

Kant's question, therefore, is this: Since such a state of nature is possible, and is in the main a happy state, though from the point of view of moral and intellectual development a low one, what is the force which drives men to leave it behind and embark on the difficult voyage of progress? To this question there had hitherto been a choice of two answers. According to the Greco-Roman view, which was revised by the Renaissance and reaffirmed by the Enlightenment, the force making for progress in human history was human wisdom, human virtue, human merit in general. According to the Christian view, which prevailed from the late Roman Empire to the close of the Middle Ages, it was the providential wisdom and care of God, working in despite of human folly and wickedness. Kant has left both these views so far behind that he never even mentions either of them.

His own answer is: this force is nothing else than the evil in human nature; the irrational and immoral elements of pride, ambition, and greed. These evil elements in human nature make the continuance of a stagnant and peaceful society impossible. They give rise to an antagonism between man and man, and a

---

[1] *Kant's Theory of Ethics*, tr. T. K. Abbott (London, 1923), pp. 40–1.
[2] *Leviathan*, part I, chap. 13.
[3] Loc. cit.

conflict between two motives that sway each man's conduct:
one a social motive, desire for a peaceful and friendly life, the
other an anti-social motive, a desire to domineer over and exploit
his neighbours. The resulting discontent with his own position
in life, whatever that position may be, is the spring which drives
man to overthrow the social system in which he lives, and this
restlessness is the means which nature uses to bring·about the
advancement of human life. This discontent is not a divine discontent which refuses to acquiesce in the existing state of things
because it cannot satisfy the moral demands of a good will; it is
not the discontent of the philanthropist or reformer of society;
it is a purely selfish discontent which, in view of the happiness
of a stagnant life, is not even based on an enlightened view of the
individual's own advantage. To quote Kant:[1] 'Man desires concord; but nature knows better what is good for his species' (not,
observe, for man as an individual; nor even for man corporately
as a society or historical totality; but for man corporately as a
species or biological abstraction); 'she desires discord. Man
wants to live easy and content; but nature compels him to leave
ease and inactive contentment behind, and throw himself into
toils and labours in order that these may drive him to use his
wits in the discovery of means to rise above them.' Nature, that
is to say, does not care for human happiness; she has implanted
in man propensities to sacrifice his own happiness and destroy
that of others, and in following these propensities blindly he is
making himself the tool of nature in her plan, which is certainly
not his, for the moral and intellectual advancement of his
species.

Kant is here whole-heartedly adopting the view, a pessimistic
view if you like so to call it, that the spectacle of human history
is in the main a spectacle of human folly, ambition, greed, and
wickedness, and that any one who goes to it for examples of
wisdom and virtue will be disappointed. This is the point of
view of Voltaire's *Candide* as against the Leibnitian confidence
that all is for the best in the best of all possible worlds. But he
has raised this view to the level of a philosophical doctrine by
arguing that if history is the process in which man *becomes*
rational, he cannot *be* rational at the beginning of it; therefore
the force which serves as mainspring of the process cannot be

[1] *Idee zu einer a. Gesch.*, vierter Satz.

human reason but must be the opposite of reason, that is, passion: intellectual ignorance and moral baseness. Here again the Kantian theory of history is an application of the Kantian ethics, according to which inclination, desire, passion is the opposite of reason or the good will and is therefore in itself evil, the force against which the good will has to fight.

This doctrine is not unworthy of its great author. It is inspiring and stimulating, like Herder's, and far more clearly thought out. Yet it is not well founded. It is based on a rhetorical pessimism about the folly, wickedness, and misery that have characterized the past history of man. This is not a just or sane view of the facts. At all times in the past about which anything is known, there have been occasions when men were wise enough to think successfully what they had to think, good enough to do efficiently what they had to do, and happy enough to find life not only tolerable but attractive. And if anybody objects: 'Occasions, yes, but how few!' the answer is: 'More numerous, at any rate, than those of the opposite kind; for otherwise all human life would long ago have disappeared.'

And the consequences of this exaggerated gloom about the past are seen in Kant's exaggerated hopes for the future. In the last section of his essay he looks forward to a time when man shall have become rational, when the blind forces of evil which have hitherto driven him along the path of progress shall have been conquered. There will then be a reign of peace, when the problem of working out a sound and reasonable political system shall have been solved and a political millennium achieved through the creation of a rational system both of national life and international relations. He half realizes that in human affairs a millennium like this is a contradiction in terms; but yet the prediction is no mere excrescence on his doctrine; it is a logical consequence of it, an exaggerated optimism on one side balancing, and due to, an exaggerated pessimism on the other. This exaggerated division of history into a wholly irrational past and a wholly rational future is the legacy which Kant inherits from the Enlightenment. A profounder knowledge of history would have taught him that what has brought progress about has not been the sheer ignorance or the sheer badness but the concrete actuality of human effort itself, with all its good and bad elements commingled.

In spite of his exaggerations, Kant has made a great contribution to historical thought. At the end of his essay he outlines a programme for a kind of historical inquiry which, he says, has not yet been undertaken, and, he modestly adds, could not be undertaken by one so little learned in history as himself: a universal history which shall show how the human race has gradually become more and more rational, and therefore more and more free: a history of the self-development of the spirit of man. Such a task, he says, will need two qualifications: historical learning and a philosophical head. Mere scholarship will not do it, and mere philosophy will not do it; the two must be combined into a new form of thought owing something to both of them. Similarly, Vico, at the beginning of the century, demanded what he described as a union of philology and philosophy, a scholarly attention to detail and a philosophical attention to principles. I think we may say that in the next hundred years a serious and sustained attempt was made, certainly not always successful, to carry out Kant's programme, and to consider history as the process by which the spirit of man has come to the fuller and fuller development of its original potentialities.

Kant's 'idea', as he calls it, may be summarized in four points: (i) *Universal history* is a feasible ideal, but demands a union of historical and philosophical thought: the facts must be understood as well as narrated, seen from within and not only from outside. (ii) It presupposes a *plan*, i.e. it exhibits a *progress*, or shows something as coming progressively into being. (iii) That which is thus coming into existence is *human rationality*, i.e. intelligence, moral freedom. (iv) The means by which it is being brought into existence is *human irrationality*, i.e. passion, ignorance, selfishness.

I will summarize my criticisms of Kant in a few brief comments on these points. The essence of these comments is that throughout, as in other parts of his philosophical work, he has drawn his antitheses too rigidly.

i (*a*) Universal history and particular history. The antithesis is too rigid. If universal history means a history of everything that has happened, it is impossible. If particular history means a particular study which does not involve a definite conception of the nature and significance of history as a whole, that too is impossible. Particular history is only a name for history itself in its detail; universal history is only a name for the historian's conception of history as such.

i (*b*) Historical thought and philosophical thought. Again the antithesis is too rigid. The union of the two which Kant desiderates is just historical thought itself, seeing the events it describes not as mere observed phenomena but from within.

ii (*a*) All history certainly shows progress, i.e. it is the development of something; but to call this progress a plan of nature as Kant does is to use mythological language.

ii (*b*) The goal of this progress is not, as Kant thought, in the future. History terminates not in the future but in the present. The historian's task is to show how the present has come into existence; he cannot show how the future will have come into existence, for he does not know what the future will be.

iii. That which is coming into existence is certainly human rationality, but this does not mean the disappearance of human irrationality. Once more, the antithesis is too rigid.

iv. Passion and ignorance have certainly done their work, and an important work, in past history, but they have never been mere passion and mere ignorance; they have been rather a blind and blundering will for good and a dim and deluded wisdom.

§ 4. *Schiller*

The most direct follower of Kant, in the theory of history as in the theory of art, was the poet Schiller. He was a keen and gifted thinker, in philosophy a brilliant amateur rather than a persevering worker like Kant; but he had the advantage of Kant in being himself a poet of distinction and for some time, when he occupied the chair of history at Jena, a professional historian. Consequently, just as he reinterprets Kant's philosophy of art by bringing to it the experience of a working poet, so he reinterprets Kant's philosophy of history by bringing to it the experience of a working historian. It is very interesting to see, in his inaugural lecture given at Jena in 1789, how this experience enables him to overcome certain errors in Kant's theory.

The lecture is entitled *The Nature and Value of Universal History (Was heißt und zu welchem Ende studiert man Universal-*

geschichte?). Schiller follows Kant in advocating the study of universal history and in recognizing that it requires a philosophical mind as well as historical scholarship. He paints a lively picture of the contrast between the *Brotgelehrte* or daily-bread scholar (the professional researcher with his dry-as-dust attitude towards the bare facts which are the dry bones of history, a man whose ambition is to become as narrow a specialist as possible and go on knowing more and more about less and less) and the philosophical historian who takes all history for his province and makes it his business to see the connexions between the facts and detect the large-scale rhythms of the historical process. The philosophical historian achieves these results by entering sympathetically into the actions which he describes; unlike the scientist who studies nature, he does not stand over against the facts as mere objects for cognition; on the contrary, he throws himself into them and feels them imaginatively as experiences of his own. This is really the historical method of the Romantic school; and what Schiller is doing, in effect, is to agree with Kant as to the need for a philosophical as opposed to a merely scholarly attitude towards history and to maintain that this philosophical attitude is nothing else than the Romanticist attitude, for which sympathy becomes an integral element in historical knowledge, the element which enables the historian to get inside the facts he is studying.

Universal history, so conceived, is the history of progress from savage beginnings to modern civilization. So far Schiller agrees with Kant, but with two important differences. (i) Whereas Kant places the goal of progress in a future millennium, Schiller places it in the present, and asserts that the ultimate aim of universal history is to show how the present, with such things as modern language, modern law, modern social institutions, modern clothing, and so forth, came to be what it is. Here Schiller definitely improves on Kant, owing no doubt to his actual experience of historical work, which has shown him that history throws no light on the future and that the historical series cannot be extrapolated beyond the present. (ii) Whereas Kant restricts the task of history to the study of political evolution, Schiller includes in it the history of art, of religion, of economics and so forth, and here again he improves on his predecessor.

§ 5. *Fichte*

Another pupil of Kant who developed his ideas on history in a fertile manner was Fichte, who published his Berlin lectures on *The Characteristics of the Present Age* (*Grundzüge des gegenwärtigen Zeitalters*) in 1806. Fichte agrees with Schiller and disagrees with Kant in conceiving the present as the focal point in which the lines of historical development converge: consequently, for him, the fundamental task of the historian is to understand the period of history in which he lives. Every period of history has a peculiar character of its own, penetrating into every detail of its life; and the task Fichte sets himself in these lectures is to analyse the peculiar character of his own age, to show what its central features are and how the others are derived from them. He puts this by saying that every age is the concrete embodiment of a single idea or concept; and accepting as he does the Kantian doctrine that history as a whole is the unfolding of a plan, the development of something akin to the plot of a drama, he holds that the fundamental ideas or concepts of various successive ages form a sequence which, because it is a sequence of concepts, is a logical sequence, one concept leading necessarily to the next. Thus Fichte's theory of the logical structure of the concept serves him as a clue to the periodizing of history.

Every concept, he thinks, has a logical structure involving three phases: thesis, antithesis, synthesis. The concept is first embodied in a pure or abstract form; then it generates its own opposite and realizes itself in the shape of an antithesis between itself and this opposite; then the antithesis is overcome by the negation of the opposite. Now the fundamental concept of history (here Fichte again follows Kant) is rational freedom, and freedom, like any concept, must develop through these necessary stages. Hence the beginning of history is an age in which rational freedom is exemplified in an absolutely simple or immediate shape without any opposition: here freedom exists in the form of blind instinct, freedom to do as one likes, and the society which is the concrete embodiment of this concept is the state of nature, primitive society where there is no government, no authority, but only people doing, so far as conditions permit, what seems good to them. According to the general principles of Fichte's philosophy, however, a freedom of this crude or immediate kind can only develop into a more genuine freedom by generating its own opposite: so, by a logical necessity, there arises a second stage in which the freedom of the individual freely limits itself by the creation of an authority over against itself, the authority of a ruler imposing upon him laws not of his own making. This is the period of authoritarian government, where freedom itself seems to have disappeared, but it has not really disappeared, it has developed into a new stage in which it has created its own opposite (the ruler, as Hobbes showed, is freely created by the common act of the people who thus voluntarily become his subjects) in order to become freedom of a new and better type, i.e. to become what Rousseau called civil freedom as distinct from natural freedom. But Hobbes was wrong in thinking that the process of the growth of freedom ends here. The opposition must be cancelled by a third stage, a revolutionary stage in which authority is rejected and destroyed not because it is a misused authority but simply because it is authority; the subject has come to feel that he can do without authority and take the work of government into his own hands, so as to be both subject and sovereign at once. It is therefore not authority that is destroyed; what is destroyed is the merely external relation between authority and that over which authority is exercised. Revolution is not anarchy, it is the seizure of government by the subjects. Henceforth the distinction between governing and being governed still exists as a real distinction, but it is a distinction without a difference: the same persons govern and are governed.

But Fichte does not stop here. He does not identify his own age with the age of revolution. He thinks that his contemporaries have got beyond that. The conception of the individual as possessing within himself an authority over himself is, in its first and crudest form, the revolutionary idea. But this concept too must generate its own opposite, namely, the idea of an objective reality, a self-existing body of truth which is the criterion of thought and the guide of conduct. This stage of development is science, where the objective truth is that which stands over against thought and where acting rightly means acting in conformity with scientific knowledge. The scientific frame of mind is (as it were) counter-revolutionary: we can destroy human tyrants, but we cannot destroy the facts; things are what they are and their consequences will be what they will be, and if we flout the laws of man we cannot flout the laws of nature. But, once more, the antagonism between mind and nature can be and must be overcome, and its overcoming is the rise of a new kind of rational freedom, the freedom of art, where mind and nature are reunited, mind recognizing in nature its own counterpart and related to it not by way of obedience but by way of sympathy and love. The agent identifies himself with that for whose sake he acts, and thus achieves the highest degree of freedom. This Fichte regards as the characteristic feature of his own age: the free self-devotion of the individual to an end which, though objective, he regards as his own end.

The chief difficulty which a reader finds in dealing with Fichte's view of history is the difficulty of being patient with what appears so silly. In particular, there seem to be two specially flagrant errors at work in his mind: (1) the idea that the present state of the world is perfect, a complete and final achievement of all that history has been working to bring about, and (2) the idea that the historical succession of ages can be determined *a priori* by reference to abstract logical considerations. I think it can be shown that in spite of their apparent silliness there is some truth in both these ideas.

(1) The historian (and for that matter the philosopher) is not God, looking at the world from above and outside. He is a man, and a man of his own time and place. He looks at the past from the point of view of the present: he looks at other countries and civilizations from the point of view of his own. This point of view is valid only for him and people situated like him, but for him it *is* valid. He must stand firm in it, because it is the only one accessible to him, and unless he *has* a point of view he can see nothing at all. For example, the judgement passed on the achievements of the Middle Ages will necessarily differ according as the historian is a man of the eighteenth, nineteenth, or twentieth century. We, in the twentieth century, know how the eighteenth and nineteenth centuries looked at these things, and we know that their views are not views that we can share. We call them historical errors, and we can show reasons for rejecting them. We can easily conceive the work of medieval history as being done better than it was done in the eighteenth century; but we cannot conceive it as being done better than it is in our own times, because if we had a clear idea of how it could be done

better we should be in a position to do it better, and this better way of doing it would be an accomplished fact. The present is our own activities; we are carrying out these activities as well as we know how; and consequently, from the point of view of the present, there must always be a coincidence between what is and what ought to be, the actual and the ideal. The Greeks were trying to be Greeks; the Middle Ages were trying to be medieval; the aim of every age is to be itself; and thus the present is always perfect in the sense that it always succeeds in being what it is trying to be. This does not imply that the historical process has nothing more to do; it only implies that, so far, it has done what it meant to do, and that we cannot tell what it is going to do next.

(2) The idea of constructing history *a priori* seems very foolish; but Fichte was here following up Kant's discovery that in all knowledge, of whatever kind, there are *a priori* elements. In every field of knowledge there are certain fundamental concepts or categories, and corresponding to them certain fundamental principles or axioms, which belong to the form or structure of that type of knowledge and are derived (according to the Kantian philosophy) not from the empirical subject-matter but from the point of view of the knower. Now in history the general conditions of knowledge are derived from the fundamental principle that the knower is placed in the present, and from the point of view of the present is looking at the past. The first axiom of intuition for history (to adopt Kant's terminology) is that every historical event is situated somewhere in past time. This is not a generalization empirically discovered by the historian in the course of his inquiry, it is an *a priori* condition of historical knowledge. But according to the Kantian doctrine of the schematism of the categories, time-relations are schemata or factual representations of conceptual relations: thus the time-relation of before and after is a schema of the conceptual relation of logical antecedent and logical consequent. The whole world of events in time is thus a schematized representation of the world of logical or conceptual relations. Fichte's attempt to detect a conceptual scheme underlying the temporal succession of historical periods is thus a perfectly legitimate application to history of the Kantian doctrine of the schematism of the categories.

This is, no doubt, a somewhat weak defence of Fichte. It comes to saying that if he made a silly mistake about history he was only following a silly mistake of a more general kind made by Kant. But anybody who calls these notions silly mistakes is claiming to understand better than Kant or Fichte the relation between logical sequence and temporal sequence. Ever since Plato in the *Timaeus* said that time is the moving image of eternity, philosophers have for the most part agreed that there was some relation between these two things and that the necessary sequence by which one event leads to another in time was in some way identical in character with the necessary sequence by which one thing leads to another in a non-temporal logical series. If this is denied, and if it is maintained that temporal sequence and logical implication have nothing to do with each other, historical knowledge becomes impossible, for it follows that we can never say about any event 'this *must* have happened'; the past can never appear as the conclusion of a logical inference. If the temporal series is a mere aggregate of disconnected events, we can never argue back from the present to the past. But historical thinking consists precisely of arguing back in this way; and it is therefore based on the assumption (or, as Kant and Fichte would have said, on the *a priori* principle) that there is an internal or necessary connexion between the events of a time-series such that one event leads necessarily to another and we can argue back from the second to the first. On this principle there is only one way in which the present state of things can have come into existence, and history is the analysis of the present in order to see what this process must have been. I am not defending the particular way in which Fichte reconstructed the past history of his own age; I think it was very faulty, and its faults (so far as they are faults of principle) were due to his following Kant in separating too sharply the *a priori* elements in knowledge from the empirical. This made him think that history can be reconstructed on a purely *a priori* basis without reliance on the empirical evidence of documents; but in so far as he insisted that all historical knowledge contains *a priori* concepts and principles he was right, and he understood the nature of history better than the people who ridicule him because they think that history is purely empirical.

In one way, Fichte's philosophy of history makes an important advance on Kant's. In Kant's there are two conceptions presupposed by history itself: (1) a plan of nature, conceived as something formed in advance of its own execution; (2) human nature, with its passions, conceived as the matter in which this form is to be carried out. History itself is the result of imposing this pre-existing form on this pre-existing matter. Thus, the historical process is not conceived as really creative: it is merely a putting together of two abstractions, and there is no attempt to show why the two should ever come together, or indeed why either, let alone both, should exist. Kant's theory, in fact, rests on a number of disconnected assumptions, none of which it attempts to justify. Fichte's theory is logically much simpler and much less exposed to the charge of multiplying entities unnecessarily. The only thing which it presupposes as required before history begins is the concept itself, with its own proper logical structure, and the dynamic relation between the elements in that structure. The driving force in history is just this dynamic movement of the concept, so that instead of two things, a plan and a driving force, in Fichte there is only one, the plan being a dynamic plan (the logical structure of the concept) which supplies its own motive force. The fruits of this Fichtean discovery ripened in Hegel.

§ 6. *Schelling*

Schelling was Hegel's junior, and it may be open to dispute whether the doctrines which Hegel shared with Schelling were reached by independent thinking or under Schelling's influence. But since Schelling published a system of philosophy (perhaps more than one) including his views on history long before Hegel wrote the first sketch of his philosophy of history in the Heidelberg *Encyclopaedia*, it will be convenient to say something of Schelling's views first.

Schelling gave a more systematic development to the ideas of Kant and Fichte, and his thought turned on two principles: first, the idea that whatever exists is knowable, i.e. an embodiment of rationality or, in his own language, a manifestation of the Absolute; secondly, the idea of a relation between two terms which though opposites are both in this way embodiments of the Absolute: the Absolute itself being an identity in which their differences disappear. This two-term pattern reappears all through his philosophy.

There are, according to Schelling,[1] two great realms of the knowable: Nature and History. Each, as intelligible, is a manifestation of the Absolute, but they embody it in opposite ways. Nature consists of things distributed in space, whose intelligibility consists merely in the way in which they are distributed, or in the regular and determinate relations between them. History consists of the thoughts and actions of minds, which are not only intelligible but intelligent, intelligible to themselves, not merely to something other than themselves: hence they are a more adequate embodiment of the Absolute because they contain in themselves both sides of the knowledge-relation, they are subject as well as object. As objectively intelligible, the activity of mind in history is necessary: as subjectively intelligent, it is free. The course of historical development is thus the complete genesis of mind's self-awareness as at once free and under law, that is, morally and politically autonomous (here Schelling follows Kant). The stages through which this development passes are determined by the logical structure of the concept itself (here he follows Fichte): it is therefore in its largest features divisible into two: first a phase where man conceives the Absolute as nature, where reality is conceived as broken up and dispersed into separate realities (polytheism), and where political forms come into existence and perish like natural organisms leaving nothing behind them; and secondly a phase where the Absolute is conceived as history, that is, as a continuous development where man freely works out the purposes of the Absolute, co-operating with providence in its plan for the development of human rationality. This is the modern age, where human life is controlled by scientific, historical, and philosophical thought.

The most important of the conceptions which Schelling is here trying to work out is the conception that in history the Absolute itself is coming into full and complete existence. Even Fichte thought that the logical structure of the concept was complete before history began and served as a presupposition of the process; in Schelling the dynamic structure of the Absolute is not

[1] *System of Transcendental Idealism*, 1800. *Werke* (Stuttgart and Augsburg, 1858), part I, vol. iii, pp. 587–604.

the ground of the dynamic element in history, it is that element itself. The material universe has always been intelligible in so far as it has always been a manifestation of the Absolute; but the Absolute cannot be identical with the barely intelligible, for mere intelligibility is a mere potentiality, which must be actualized by becoming actually understood. Nature *qua* intelligible demands a knower to understand it, and exhibits its full essence only when there is a mind that knows it. Then for the first time is there an actual knower and an actual known, and rationality, which is the Absolute, has advanced to a higher and more complete manifestation of itself. But there now arises a new kind of intelligibility: mind itself is not only a knower but a knowable, and consequently the Absolute cannot be satisfied with a situation in which mind knows nature, there must be a further stage in which mind knows itself. As the process of self-knowledge advances, new stages in self-knowledge enrich the knowing mind and thus create new things for it to know. History is a temporal process in which both knowledge and the knowable are progressively coming into existence, and this is expressed by calling history the self-realization of the Absolute, where the Absolute means both reason as the knowable and reason as the knower.

§ 7. *Hegel*

The culmination of the historical movement which began in 1784 with Herder came with Hegel, whose lectures on the philosophy of history were first delivered in 1822–3. Any one who reads his *Philosophy of History* by itself cannot but think it a profoundly original and revolutionary work, wherein history for the first time steps out full-grown on the stage of philosophical thought. But when consideration is given to the work of his predecessors, his book becomes far less startling and far less original.

He proposes a new kind of history, to be called the philosophy of history (the proposal and the terminology being as old as Voltaire); but the philosophy of history is for him not a philosophical reflection on history but history itself raised to a higher power and become philosophical as distinct from merely empirical, that is, history not merely *ascertained* as so much fact but *understood* by apprehending the reasons why the facts happened as they did. This philosophical history will be a universal history of mankind (here Hegel follows Herder) and will exhibit a progress from primitive times to the civilization of to-day. The plot of this story is the development of freedom, which is identical with the moral reason of man as exhibited in an external system of social relations, so that the question which philosophical history has to answer is the question how the State came into existence (all this is taken from Kant). But the historian knows nothing of the future; history culminates not in a future Utopia but in the actual present (this is Schiller). Man's freedom is the same thing as his consciousness of his freedom, so the development of freedom is a development of consciousness, a process of thought or logical development, in which the various necessary phases or moments of the concept are successively achieved (this is Fichte). Lastly, philosophical history exhibits no merely human process but a cosmic process, a process in which the world comes to realize itself in self-consciousness as spirit (this is Schelling). Thus, every one of the characteristic features of Hegel's philosophy of history is drawn by him from his predecessors, but he has combined their views with extraordinary skill into a theory so coherent and so unified that it deserves independent consideration as a whole, and I propose, therefore, to draw attention to some of its distinctive features.

First, Hegel refuses to approach history by way of nature. He insists that nature and history are different things. Each is a process or congeries of processes; but the processes of nature are not historical: nature has no history. The processes of nature are cyclical; nature goes round and round, and nothing is constructed or built up by the repetition of such revolutions. Each sunrise, each spring, each high tide, is like the last; the law governing the cycle does not change as the cycle repeats itself. Nature is a system of higher and lower organisms, the higher depending on the lower; logically, the higher organisms are posterior to the lower, but not temporally; Hegel flatly denies the evolutionary theory which makes the higher develop in time out of the lower, asserting that people who believe this are mistaking a logical succession for a temporal one. History, on the contrary, never repeats itself; its movements travel not in circles but in spirals, and apparent repetitions are always differentiated by having acquired something new. Thus wars reappear from time to time in history, but every new war is in some ways a new kind of war, owing to the lessons learnt by human beings in the last one.

Hegel must be given credit for having stated an important distinction; but he has stated it wrongly. He is right to distinguish the non-historical processes of nature from the historical processes of human life, but wrong to reinforce this distinction by denying the doctrine of evolution. Since Darwin we have found ourselves obliged to accept that doctrine and to conceive the process of nature as resembling the process of history in a way in which Hegel thought it did not resemble it, namely, by producing increments of itself as it goes on. But it remains true that the process of nature is different from the process of history —that, for example, the succession of geological periods is not a truly historical succession—because it is peculiar to history that the historian re-enacts in his own mind the thoughts and motives of the agents whose actions he is narrating, and no succession of events is an historical succession unless it consists of acts whose motives can, in principle at least, be thus re-enacted. Geology presents us with a series of *events*, but history is not history unless it presents us with a series of *acts*. Thus Hegel's conclusion is right, that there is no history except the history of human life, and that, not merely as life, but as rational life, the life of thinking beings.

Secondly, and following immediately from this, all history is the history of thought. In so far as human actions are mere events, the historian cannot understand them; strictly, he cannot even ascertain that they have happened. They are only knowable to him as the outward expression of thoughts. For example, to reconstruct the history of a political struggle like that between the Roman emperors of the first century and the senatorial opposition, what the historian has to do is to see how the two parties conceived the political situation as it stood, and how they proposed to develop that situation: he must grasp their political ideas both concerning their actual present and concerning their possible future. Here again Hegel was certainly right; it is not knowing what people did but understanding what they thought that is the proper definition of the historian's task.

Thirdly, the force which is the mainspring of the historical process (to use Kant's phrase) is reason. This is a very important and difficult doctrine. What Hegel means by it is that everything which happens in history happens by the will of man, for the historical process consists of human actions; and the will of man is nothing but man's thought expressing itself outwardly in action. If it is said that human thought is often or generally far from reasonable, Hegel will reply that this is an error which comes of failing to apprehend the historical situation in which a given piece of thinking is done. Thinking is never done *in vacuo*; it is always done by a determinate person in a determinate situation; and every historical character in every historical situation thinks and acts as rationally as that person in that situation *can* think and act, and nobody can do more. This is a very fertile and valuable principle, which Hegel worked out with important consequences. He held that the abstractly rational man conceived by the Enlightenment is nothing real; the reality is always a man who is both rational and passionate, never purely one or the other, his passions being those of a rational being and his thoughts those of a passionate being; and, further, without passion there is no reason and no action. To prove, therefore, that someone acted in a certain way from passion—e.g. a judge sentencing a criminal in a fit of anger or a statesman overriding opposition from motives of ambition—is not to prove that he did not act rationally; for the judge's sentence or the statesman's policy may be a just or a wise one notwithstanding this passionate element in its execution. Hence, Hegel maintains, the admitted fact that human history exhibits itself as a display of passions does not prove that it is not controlled by reason. He thinks of passion as the stuff, so to speak, out of which history is made: it is, from one point of view, a display of passions and nothing else; but all the same it is a display of reason, for reason uses passion itself as its tool in bringing about its ends.

This conception of the *cunning of reason*, the conception of reason as tricking the passions into the position of its agents, is a famous difficulty of Hegel's theory. He seems to personify reason into something outside human life, which brings about through the agency of blind and passionate men purposes which are its purposes and not theirs. Sometimes, perhaps, Hegel falls into a view like the theological view of the Middle Ages, where the plans that are executed in history are the plans of God and in no sense the plans of man; or (if it is possible to distinguish the two) the crypto-theological view of the Enlightenment historians and Kant, where the plans that are executed in history are the plans not of man but of nature. On the whole, however, it is clear that what Hegel wanted to do was to get away from this view. The reason whose plans are executed in history is, for Hegel, neither an abstract natural reason nor a transcendent divine reason, but human reason, the reason of finite persons. And the relation which he asserts between reason and passion is not a relation between God or nature as rational and man as passionate, but a relation between human reason and human passion. This must be remembered when it is said that Hegel's view of history is a rationalistic view; his rationalism is of a very curious kind because it conceives irrational elements as essential to reason itself. This conception of the intimate relation between reason and unreason in human life and in mind as such really heralds a new conception of man, a dynamic instead of a static conception, and signifies that Hegel is working away from the abstract and static theory of human nature which prevailed in the eighteenth century.

Fourthly, since all history is the history of thought and exhibits the self-development of reason, the historical process is at bottom a logical process. Historical transitions are, so to speak, logical transitions set out on a time-scale. History is nothing but a kind of logic where the relation of logical priority and posteriority is not so much replaced as enriched or consolidated by becoming a relation of temporal priority and posteriority. Hence the developments that take place in history are never accidental, they are necessary; and our knowledge of an historical process is not merely empirical, it is *a priori*, we can *see* the necessity of it.

Nothing in Hegel's philosophy has aroused more protest and hostility than this idea of history as a logical process developed in time and of our knowledge of it as *a priori*, but I have already argued in connexion with Fichte that this idea is not so absurd as at first sight it may seem; and indeed most of the objections to it are mere misunderstandings. Fichte's error, as I pointed out in § 5, was to think that history could be reconstructed on a purely *a priori* basis without reliance on empirical evidence.

Hegel's critics, on the other hand, commonly fall into the opposite error of believing that historical knowledge is purely empirical; that this is an error I also argued in § 5. Hegel himself avoided both those errors. Like Kant he distinguished pure *a priori* knowledge from knowledge containing *a priori* elements, and he regarded history as an instance not of the former but of the latter. History in his view consisted of empirical events which were the outward expressions of thought, and the thoughts behind the events—not the events themselves—formed a chain of logically connected concepts. When you only look at the events and not at the thoughts behind them you see no necessary connexion at all, and the people who blame Hegel for thinking that there are necessary connexions in history are looking at history empirically, as mere outward facts, and assure us quite rightly that when they look at it in that way they see no logical connexions. Quite right, Hegel would have answered; between the mere events, there *are* none. But history consists of actions, and actions have an inside and an outside; on the outside they are mere events, related in space and time but not otherwise; on the inside they are thoughts, bound to each other by logical connexions. What Hegel is doing is to insist that the historian must first work empirically by studying documents and other evidence; it is only in this way that he can establish what the facts are. But he must then look at the facts from the inside, and tell us what they look like from that point of view. It is no reply to him to say that they look different from the outside.

This retort, I think, applies even to the most serious and systematic of all Hegel's critics, namely Croce. He maintains that Hegel's whole philosophy of history is a gigantic blunder, produced by confusing two quite different things: namely opposition and distinction. Concepts, Croce says, are related by opposition: good and bad, true and false, freedom and necessity, and so forth; and the theory of their relation, he admits, has been well expounded by Hegel in his theory of dialectic, which describes the way in which any concept stands in a necessary relation to its own opposite, generating it at first and then negating it, so that the way in which the concept lives is by creating and overcoming oppositions. But the individual things which are the instances of concepts are never related to each other by way of opposition, only by way of distinction: consequently the relations between them are not dialectical, and in history, which is the history of individual actions and persons and civilizations, there is consequently no dialectic, whereas Hegel's whole philosophy of history turns on the principle that every historical process is a dialectical process in which one form of life, for example Greece, generates its own opposite, in this case Rome, and out of this thesis and antithesis there arises a synthesis, in this case the Christian world.

Plausible though Croce's view is, it does not really get to the heart of the problem. It implies that in talking of history we should never use words like opposition or antagonism, and synthesis or reconciliation: we ought not for example to say that despotism and liberalism are opposite political doctrines, we ought only to say that they are different: we ought not to speak of an opposition, but only of a difference, between Whigs and Tories, or Catholics and Protestants. Now, it is true that we do not need to use terms like opposition (let me call them *dialectical* terms) when we are talking only of the outward events of history; but when we are talking of the inward thoughts which underlie these events it seems to me that we cannot avoid them. For example, we can describe the mere outward events of the colonization of New England without using any dialectical language; but when we try to see these events as a deliberate attempt on the part of the Pilgrim Fathers to carry out in terms of practice a Protestant idea of life, we are talking about thoughts and we must describe them in dialectical terms; we must for example speak of the opposition between the congregational idea of religious institutions and the episcopal idea, and admit that the relation between the idea of a priesthood based on apostolic succession and the idea of one not so based is a dialectical relation. From this point of view Greek civilization is the realizing of the Greek idea of life, that is, the Greek conception of man; Roman civilization is the realizing of the Roman conception of man; and between these two conceptions the relation, on Croce's own showing, is a dialectical relation. But this is all that Hegel ever maintained.

A fifth point, and another on which Hegel has been bitterly criticized, is his doctrine that history ends not in the future but in the present. For example, the very able and sympathetic

Swiss writer Eduard Fueter says[1] that a philosophy of history which traces the course of human life from its beginning to the end of the world and the last judgement, as medieval thinkers did, is a respectable and dignified thing: but Hegel's philosophy of history, which makes history end not with the last judgement but with the present day, only ends in glorifying and idealizing the present, denying that any further progress is possible, and providing a pseudo-philosophical justification for a policy of rigid and unintelligent conservatism.

But here again Hegel, like Fichte, is surely in the right. The philosophy of history is, according to his idea of it, history itself philosophically considered, that is, seen from the inside. But the historian has no knowledge of the future; what documents, what evidence, has he from which to ascertain facts that have not yet happened? And the more philosophically he looks at history the more clearly he recognizes that the future is and always must be a closed book to him. History *must* end with the present, because nothing else has happened. But this does not mean glorifying the present or thinking that future progress is impossible. It only means recognizing the present as a fact and realizing that we do not know what future progress will be. As Hegel put it, the future is an object not of knowledge but of hopes and fears; and hopes and fears are not history. If Hegel in the practical politics of his later life was an unintelligent conservative, that was the fault of Hegel as a man; there is no reason to regard it as the fault of his philosophy of history.

But although on these points Hegel seems to be in the right as against his critics, it is impossible to read his *Philosophy of History* without feeling that, magnificent work though it is, it has great faults. I do not refer merely to Hegel's ignorance of the many historical facts that have been discovered since his time; I refer to something deeper in the very method and fabric of his work. It is a striking fact, and one which many readers have noticed, that as an historian Hegel was at his best in his lectures on the history of philosophy, which are a genuine triumph of historical method and have been the model for all subsequent histories of thought. This means that his method, based as it was on the principle that all history is the history of thought, was not only legitimate but brilliantly successful when

[1] *Geschichte der neueren Historiographie* (Munich and Berlin, 1911), p. 433.

the subject-matter with which he was dealing was thought at its purest, i.e. philosophical thought; but this is not the subject-matter of his *Philosophy of History*.

Hegel himself held that there are many kinds of thought, and that they differ in degree as more or less perfect examples of rationality. At the bottom comes what he calls subjective mind, the kind of thought that psychology deals with, where thought is hardly more than the living organism's consciousness of its own sensations. Then, next higher in the scale, comes what he calls objective mind, where thought expresses itself by creating outward manifestations of itself in social and political systems. Then, at the top, comes absolute mind, in its three forms of art, religion, and philosophy. These all transcend the sphere of social and political life and overcome the opposition between subject and object, the thinker and the institution or law which he finds in existence and has to obey: a work of art, a religious belief, or a philosophical system is a perfectly free and at the same time a perfectly objective expression of the mind that conceives it.

Now in the *Philosophy of History*, Hegel is restricting the field of his study to political history. Here he is following Kant; but Kant had a good reason for doing this and Hegel had not. On the strength of his distinction between phenomena and things in themselves Kant, as we have seen, regarded historical events as phenomena, events in a time series of which the historian is a spectator. Human actions as things in themselves are in his view moral actions; and he thought that the same actions which, as things in themselves, were moral actions were, as phenomena, political actions. Hence history must and can only be the history of politics. When Hegel repudiated the Kantian distinction between phenomena and things in themselves, he repudiated by implication the Kantian doctrines that all history is political history and that history is a spectacle. Hence the central position of the State in his *Philosophy of History* is an anachronism, and to be consistent with himself he ought to have held that the historian's business is to study not so much the process of objective mind as the history of absolute mind, i.e. art, religion, and philosophy. And in fact nearly half of Hegel's collected works is devoted to the study of these three things. The *Philosophy of History* is an illogical excrescence on the corpus of Hegel's works. The legitimate fruit of his revolution in historical method, so far

as that fruit is to be found in his own writings, is the eight
volumes entitled *Aesthetics*, *Philosophy of Religion*, and *History
of Philosophy*.

The ordinary criticism of Hegel is therefore mistaken. Beginning with the recognition that his philosophy of history is somehow unsatisfactory, which every one must admit, it argues: 'This
is what comes of treating history as rational. The moral is that
history is not human thought developing itself, it is just brute
fact.' The right criticism would run: 'This is what comes of
treating political history by itself as if it were the whole of
history. The moral is that political developments should be
conceived by the historian as integrated with economic, artistic,
religious, and philosophical developments and that the historian
should not be content with anything short of a history of man in
his concrete actuality.' In point of fact, this second criticism
was the one which would seem consciously or unconsciously to
have influenced certain nineteenth-century historians.

§ 8. *Hegel and Marx*

Nineteenth-century historiography did not abandon Hegel's
belief that history is rational—to do that would have been to
abandon history itself—but rather aimed at achieving a history
of concrete mind by insisting on the elements which in his
formal *Philosophy of History* Hegel had neglected, and working
them into a solid whole. Of his more immediate disciples, Baur
specialized in the history of Christian doctrine, and Marx in the
history of economic activity, while Ranke was later to apply
systematically his conception of historical movements or periods
as the realization of a conception or idea such as Protestantism.
Capitalism in Marx or Protestantism in Ranke is an 'idea' in the
true Hegelian sense: a thought, a conception of man's life held
by man himself, and thus akin to a Kantian category, but a
category historically conditioned: a way in which people come
to think at a certain time, and in accordance with which they
organize their whole life, only to find that the idea changes by
a dialectic of its own into a different idea and that the manner of
life which expressed it will not hold together, but breaks up and
transforms itself into the expression of a second idea which
replaces the first.

Marx's view of history has both the strength and the weakness of Hegel's: its strength, in penetrating behind the facts to the logical nexus of underlying concepts; its weakness, in selecting one aspect of human life (in Hegel the political, in Marx the economic) as in this sense fully rational by itself. Marx, like Hegel, insisted that human history is not a number of different parallel histories, economic, political, artistic, religious, and so on, but one single history. But like Hegel, again, he conceived this unity not as an organic unity in which every thread of the developing process preserved its own continuity as well as its intimate connexion with the others, but as a unity in which there was only one continuous thread (in Hegel the thread of political history, in Marx that of economic history), the other factors having no continuity of their own but being, for Marx, at every point in their development mere reflections of the basic economic fact. This committed Marx to the paradox that if certain people held, for example, certain philosophical views, they had no philosophical reasons for holding them, but only economic reasons. Historical studies of politics, of art, of religion, of philosophy, constructed on this principle, can have no real historical value; they are mere exercises in ingenuity where, for example, the real and important problem of discovering the connexion between Quakerism and banking is burked by saying in effect that Quakerism is only the way in which bankers think about banking. The Marxian paradox, however, is only symptomatic of an anti-historical naturalism which infects much of his thought and which can best be illustrated by reference to his attitude to Hegel's dialectic.

Marx made a famous boast that he had taken Hegel's dialectic and 'stood it on its head'; but he did not mean quite what he said. Hegel's dialectic begins with thought, goes on to nature, and ends with mind. Marx did not invert this order. He referred to the first and second terms only, not the third, and he meant that whereas Hegel's dialectic began with thought and went on to nature, his own dialectic began with nature and went on to thought.

Marx was not a philosophical ignoramus, and he did not for a moment suppose that the priority of thought over nature in Hegel meant that Hegel regarded nature as a product of mind. He knew that Hegel, like himself, regarded mind as a product (a dialectical product) of nature. He knew that the word 'thought', in the sense in which Hegel called logic the 'science of thought', meant not that which thinks but that which it thinks. Logic, for Hegel, is not a science of 'how we think', it is a science of Platonic forms, abstract entities, 'ideas'—if we remember to take seriously Hegel's own warning that we must not suppose ideas to exist only in people's heads. That would be 'subjective idealism', a thing that Hegel abominated. They only got into people's heads, according to him, because people were able to think; and if the 'ideas' had not been independent of people's thinking them, there would not have been any people or, indeed, any world of nature either; because these 'ideas' were the logical framework within which alone a world of nature and men, of unthinking beings and thinking beings, was possible.

These 'ideas' not only made a framework for nature, they also made a framework for history. History, as the actions in which man expressed his thoughts, had the general outlines of its structure laid down for it in advance by the conditions under which the thinking activity, mind, alone can exist. Among these conditions are the two following: first, that mind should arise within and continue to inhabit a world of nature; secondly, that it should work by apprehending those necessities which lie behind nature. Accordingly, the historical activities of man, as activities that take place or go on, take place or go on in a natural environment, and could not go on otherwise; but their 'content', i.e. what in particular people think and what in particular people do by way of expressing this thought, is determined not by nature but by the 'ideas', the necessities studied by logic. Thus logic is the key to history, in the sense that men's thoughts and actions, as studied by history, follow a pattern which is the coloured version of the pattern logic has already drawn in black and white.

This is what Marx was thinking of when he said he had turned Hegel's dialectic upside down. When he made that statement, what he had in mind was history, perhaps the only thing in which Marx was much interested. And the point of his remark was that whereas for Hegel, because logic came before nature, it was for logic to determine the pattern on which history worked, and for nature only to determine the environment in which it worked, for Marx himself nature was more than the environment of history, it was the source from which its pattern was derived. It was no use, he thought, to draw patterns for history out of logic, like the famous Hegelian pattern for the three stages of freedom: 'For the Oriental world, one is free; for the Greco-Roman world, some are free; for the modern world, all are free.' It was better to draw patterns out of the world of nature as Marx did with his no less famous one of 'primitive communism, capitalism, socialism', where the meaning of the terms is professedly derived not from 'ideas' but from natural facts.

What Marx was doing was to reassert the fundamental principle of eighteenth-century historical naturalism, the principle that historical events have natural causes. He reasserted this principle, no doubt, with a difference. The Hegelian side in the pedigree of his thought gave it the right to bear in its arms the term 'dialectical'. The materialism on which he so strongly insisted was not ordinary eighteenth-century materialism, it was 'dialectical materialism'. The difference is not unimportant; but it must not be exaggerated. Dialectical materialism was still materialism. And the whole point of Marx's conjuring-trick with the Hegelian dialectic was accordingly this: that whereas Hegel had broken away from the historical naturalism of the eighteenth century, and had not indeed achieved, except in a partial way, but had at any rate demanded an autonomous history (for a history that recognized no authority except that of logical necessity might not undeservedly claim the title of autonomous), Marx went back on this demand and subjected history once more to that dominion by natural science from which Hegel had proclaimed it free.

The step which Marx took was a retrograde one; but, like so many other retrograde steps, it was more retrograde in appearance than it was in reality; for the territory he was evacuating was territory that had never been effectively occupied. Hegel had demanded an autonomous history, but he had not in fact achieved it. He had seen, as it were prophetically, that history ought on principle to be liberated from its pupilage to natural science; but in his own actual historical thinking that liberation had not been fully achieved. It had not been achieved, that is to say, with regard to what he ordinarily called history, i.e. political and economic history; a field in which Hegel was not a master and in which he mainly contented himself with scissors-

and-paste methods. In his history of philosophy, however, and here alone, he did enter into effective occupation of an historical field, and it was here that he must have convinced himself, as he has convinced many a reader, that his claim of autonomy for historical thought was in principle justified. That is one reason why dialectical materialism has always had its greatest successes with political and economic history, and its greatest failures in the history of philosophy.

If Marx's reversal of the Hegelian dialectic was a backward step, it was also a preliminary to an advance. It was based on the realities of the situation which Hegel bequeathed to his pupils, and, in particular, it led to a great advance in the handling of that particular kind of history, economic history, in which Hegel was weak and in which Marx was exceptionally strong. If all modern treatment of the history of philosophy goes back to Hegel as the great modern master of the subject, all modern treatment of economic history goes back in the same sense to Marx. Nevertheless, the practice of research can no more be left to-day where Hegel left it for the history of philosophy, or where Marx left it for economic history, than the theory of history can be left where Hegel left it with his 'philosophy of history' or where Marx left it with his 'dialectical materialism'. These were expedients whereby a type of history which had not passed beyond the scissors-and-paste stage attempted to conceal the defects inherent in that stage by the adoption of non-historical methods. They belong to the embryology of historical thought. The conditions which justified, and indeed necessitated, them no longer exist.

§ 9. *Positivism*

The historical materialism of Marx and his colleagues exercised little immediate influence on historical practice, which in the nineteenth century came more and more to suspect all philosophies of history as baseless speculations. This was connected with a general tendency in the same century towards positivism. Positivism may be defined as philosophy acting in the service of natural science, as in the Middle Ages philosophy acted in the service of theology. But the positivists had their own notion (rather a superficial notion) of what natural science was. They thought it consisted of two things: first, ascertaining facts;

secondly, framing laws. The facts were immediately ascertained by sensuous perception. The laws were framed through generalizing from these facts by induction. Under this influence a new kind of historiography arose, which may be called positivistic historiography.

Throwing themselves with enthusiasm into the first part of the positivist programme, historians set to work to ascertain all the facts they could. The result was a vast increase of detailed historical knowledge, based to an unprecedented degree on accurate and critical examination of evidence. This was the age which enriched history by the compilation of vast masses of carefully sifted material, like the calendars of close and patent rolls, the corpus of Latin inscriptions, new editions of historical texts and sources of every kind, and the whole apparatus of archaeological research. The best historian, like Mommsen or Maitland, became the greatest master of detail. The historical conscience identified itself with an infinite scrupulosity about any and every isolated matter of fact. The ideal of universal history was swept aside as a vain dream, and the ideal of historical literature became the monograph.

But all through this period there was a certain uneasiness about the ultimate purpose of this detailed research. It had been undertaken in obedience to the spirit of positivism according to which the ascertaining of facts was only the first stage of a process whose second stage was the discovery of laws. The historians themselves for the most part were quite happy going on ascertaining new facts; the field for discovery was inexhaustible, and they asked nothing better than to explore it. But philosophers who understood the positivist programme looked on at this enthusiasm with misgiving. When, they asked, were the historians going to embark on the second stage? And at the same time ordinary people who were not specialists in history became bored; they did not see that it mattered whether this or that fact were discovered or not; and a gulf gradually widened between the historian and the ordinary intelligent man. Positivist philosophers complained that so long as it stuck to mere facts history was not scientific; ordinary men complained that the facts which it was bringing to light were not interesting. These two complaints came to much the same thing. Each implied that the mere ascertaining of facts for their own sake was unsatisfactory, and that its justification lay beyond itself in something further that could or should be done with the facts thus ascertained.

It was in this situation that Auguste Comte demanded that historical facts should be used as the raw material of something more important and more genuinely interesting than themselves. Every natural science, said the positivists, began by ascertaining facts and then went on to discover their causal connexions; accepting this assertion, Comte proposed that there should be a new science called sociology, which was to begin by discovering the facts about human life (this being the work of the historians) and then go on to discover the causal connexions between these facts. The sociologist would thus be a kind of super-historian, raising history to the rank of a science by thinking scientifically about the same facts about which the historian thought only empirically.

This programme was very like the Kantian and post-Kantian programme for reinterpreting hoards of facts into a grandiose philosophy of history. The only difference was that for the idealists this projected super-history was to be based on the conception of mind as something peculiar and different from nature: whereas for the positivists it was based on the conception of mind as in no way fundamentally different from nature. Historical process, for the positivists, was in kind identical with natural process, and that was why the methods of natural science were applicable to the interpretation of history.

This programme appears at first sight to throw away with one single careless gesture all the advances which the eighteenth century had so laboriously made in the understanding of history. But this was not actually the case. The new positivistic denial of a fundamental distinction between nature and history really implied not so much a rejection of the eighteenth-century conception of history as a criticism of the eighteenth-century conception of nature. One indication of this is that nineteenth-century thought in general, hostile though it was to much of Hegel's philosophy of history, was far more fundamentally hostile to his philosophy of nature. Hegel, as we have seen, regarded differences between higher and lower organisms as logical, not as temporal, and he thus rejected the idea of evolution. But in the generation after his death, the life of nature began to be thought of as a progressive life, and to that extent a life resembling the life of history. In 1859, when Darwin published *The Origin of Species*, this conception was not new. In scientific circles the conception of nature as a static system, where all species were (in the old phrase) special creations, had long been superseded by the conception of species as coming into existence in a time-process. The novelty of Darwin's idea was not that he believed in evolution, but that he held it to be brought about by what he called natural selection, a process akin to the artificial selection by which man improves the breeds of domestic animals. But in the popular mind this was not clearly recognized, and Darwin came to stand as the champion and indeed the inventor of the very idea of evolution. In its general effect on thought, *The Origin of Species* thus figures as the book which first informed everybody that the old idea of nature as a static system had been abandoned.

The effect of this discovery was vastly to increase the prestige of historical thought. Hitherto the relation between historical and scientific thought, i.e. thought about history and thought about nature, had been antagonistic. History demanded for itself a subject-matter essentially progressive; science, one essentially static. With Darwin, the scientific point of view capitulated to the historical, and both now agreed in conceiving their subject-matter as progressive. Evolution could now be used as a generic term covering both historical progress and natural progress. The victory of evolution in scientific circles meant that the positivistic reduction of history to nature was qualified by a partial reduction of nature to history.

This *rapprochement* had its dangers. It tended to injure natural science by leading to the assumption that natural evolution was automatically progressive, creative by its own law of better and better forms of life; and it might have injured history through the assumption that historical progress depended on the same so-called law of nature and that the methods of natural science, in its new evolutionary form, were adequate to the study of historical processes. What prevented this injury to history was the fact that historical method had now found itself and become a far more definite, systematic, and self-conscious thing than it had been half a century earlier.

The historians of the early and middle nineteenth century

had worked out a new method of handling sources, the method of philological criticism. This essentially consisted of two operations: first, the analysis of sources (which still meant literary or narrative sources) into their component parts, distinguishing earlier and later elements in them and thus enabling the historian to discriminate between the more and the less trustworthy portions; and secondly, the internal criticism of even the more trustworthy parts, showing how the author's point of view affected his statement of the facts, and so enabling the historian to make allowance for the distortions thus produced. The classical example of this method is Niebuhr's treatment of Livy, where he argues that a great part of what was usually taken for early Roman history is patriotic fiction of a much later period; and that even the earliest stratum is not sober historical fact but something analogous to ballad-literature, a national epic (as he calls it) of the ancient Roman people. Behind that epic, Niebuhr detected the historical reality of early Rome as a society of peasant-farmers. I need not here trace the history of this method back through Herder to Vico; the important point to notice is that by the middle of the nineteenth century it had become the secure possession of all competent historians, at least in Germany.

Now, the result of possessing this method was that historians knew how to do their own work in their own way, and no longer ran much risk of being misled by the attempted assimilation of historical method to scientific. From Germany the new method spread by degrees to France and England, and wherever it spread it taught historians that they had a task of a quite special kind to carry out, a task concerning which positivism had nothing useful to teach them. Their business, they saw, was to ascertain facts by the use of this critical method, and to reject the invitation given them by the positivists to hurry on to a supposed second stage, the discovery of general laws. Consequently the claims of Comtian sociology were quietly set aside by the abler and more conscientious historians, who came to regard it as sufficient for them to discover and state the facts themselves: in the famous words of Ranke, *wie es eigentlich gewesen.*[1] History as the knowledge of individual facts was

---

[1] *Geschichten der romanischen und germanischen Völker*, preface to the 1st edition (*Werke*, Leipzig, 1874, vol. xxxiii–xxxiv, p. vii).

gradually detaching itself as an autonomous study from science as the knowledge of general laws.

But although this growing autonomy of historical thought enabled it to resist to some extent the extremer forms of the positivist spirit, it was nevertheless deeply influenced by that spirit. As I have already explained, nineteenth-century historiography accepted the first part of the positivist programme, the collection of facts, even if it declined the second, the discovery of laws. But it still conceived its facts in a positivistic manner, i.e. as separate or atomic. This led historians to adopt two rules of method in their treatment of facts: (i) Each fact was to be regarded as a thing capable of being ascertained by a separate act of cognition or process of research, and thus the total field of the historically knowable was cut up into an infinity of minute facts each to be separately considered. (ii) Each fact was to be thought of not only as independent of all the rest but as independent of the knower, so that all subjective elements (as they were called) in the historian's point of view had to be eliminated. The historian must pass no judgement on the facts: he must only say what they were.

Both these rules of method had a certain value: the first trained historians to attend accurately to matters of detail, the second trained them to avoid colouring their subject-matter with their own emotional reactions. But both were in principle vicious. The first led to the corollary that nothing was a legitimate problem for history unless it was either a microscopic problem, or else capable of being treated as a group of microscopic problems. Thus Mommsen, by far the greatest historian of the positivistic age, was able to compile a corpus of inscriptions or a handbook of Roman constitutional law with almost incredible accuracy, and was able to show how to use the corpus by, for example, treating military epitaphs statistically and thus finding out where the legions were recruited at different times; but his attempt to write a history of Rome broke down exactly at the point where his own contributions to Roman history began to be important. He devoted his life to the study of the Roman Empire, and his *History of Rome* ends at the battle of Actium. The legacy of positivism to modern historiography on this side of its work, therefore, is a combination of unprecedented mastery over small-scale problems with unprecedented weakness in dealing with large-scale problems.

The second rule, against passing judgements on the facts, had effects no less crippling. Not only did it prevent historians from discussing in a proper and methodical way such questions as: Was this or that policy a wise one? Was this or that economic system sound? Was this or that movement in science or art or religion an advance, and if so why?; it also prevented them from either sharing or criticizing the judgements made by people in the past about events or institutions contemporary with themselves: for example, they could recount all the facts about Emperor-worship in the Roman world, but because they did not allow themselves to form judgements about its value and significance as a religious and spiritual force they could not understand what the people who practised it really felt about it. What did the ancients think about slavery? What was the attitude of ordinary people in the Middle Ages towards the Church and its system of creed and doctrine? In a movement like the rise of nationalism, how much was due to popular emotion, how much to economic forces, how much to deliberate policy? Questions like these, which for Romantic historians had been objects of methodical investigation, were ruled out by the positivist methods as illegitimate. The refusal to judge the facts came to mean that history could only be the history of external events, not the history of the thought out of which these events grew. This was why positivistic historiography bogged itself in the old error of identifying history with political history (e.g. in Ranke and still more in Freeman), and ignored the history of art, religion, science, &c., because these were subjects with which it was incapable of dealing. For example, the history of philosophy was never during that period studied with such success as it had been by Hegel, and a theory actually grew up (which to a Romantic historian, or to us to-day, would seem merely comic) that philosophy or art has properly speaking no history at all.

All these consequences flowed from a certain error in historical theory. The conception of history as dealing with facts and nothing but facts may seem harmless enough, but what is a fact? According to the positivistic theory of knowledge, a fact is something immediately given in perception. When it is said that science consists first in ascertaining facts and then in discovering laws, the facts, here, are facts directly observed by the scientist: for example, the fact that this guinea-pig, after receiving an injection of this culture, develops tetanus. If any one doubts the fact he can repeat the experiment with another guinea-pig, which will do just as well; and consequently, for the scientist, the question whether the facts really are what they are said to be is never a vital question, because he can always reproduce the facts under his own eyes. In science, then, the facts are empirical facts, facts perceived as they occur.

In history, the word 'fact' bears a very different meaning. The fact that in the second century the legions began to be recruited wholly outside Italy is not immediately given. It is arrived at inferentially by a process of interpreting data according to a complicated system of rules and assumptions. A theory of historical knowledge would discover what these rules and assumptions are, and would ask how far they are necessary and legitimate. All this was entirely neglected by the positivistic historians, who thus never asked themselves the difficult question: How is historical knowledge possible? How and under what conditions can the historian know facts which, being now gone beyond recall or repetition, cannot be for him objects of perception? They were precluded from asking this question by their false analogy between scientific facts and historical facts. Owing to this false analogy, they thought such a question could need no answer. But, owing to the same false analogy, they were all the time misconceiving the nature of historical facts, and consequently distorting the actual work of historical research in the ways I have described.

PART IV

SCIENTIFIC HISTORY

§ 1. *England*

(i) *Bradley*

IN European philosophy towards the end of the nineteenth century there was a kind of springtime of new growth after the winter that had set in at Hegel's death. On its negative side this new movement of thought showed itself mainly as a revolt against positivism. But positivism, though it actually was a philosophical system, refused to claim that title. It claimed only to be scientific. It was in fact nothing but the methodology of natural science raised to the level of a universal methodology: natural science identifying itself with knowledge. Consequently an attack on positivism was bound to appear in addition as a revolt against science and also as a revolt against intellect as such. Properly understood it was neither of these things. It was not a revolt against science, it was a revolt against the philosophy which claimed that science was the only kind of knowledge that existed or ever could exist. It was not a revolt against the intellect, it was a revolt against the theory which limited the intellect to the kind of thinking characteristic of natural science. But every revolt against one thing is a revolt in the interests of something else, and on its positive side this new movement of thought was an attempt (becoming clearer and clearer as the movement progressed towards maturity) to vindicate history as a form of knowledge distinct from natural science and yet valid in its own right.

Nevertheless, the early sponsors of these new ideas did their work under the shadow of positivism, and they had great difficulty in disentangling themselves from the positivist point of view. If they succeeded in overcoming this difficulty at certain points of their thought, they relapsed into positivism at others. Consequently when we now look back on the movement we see it as a confused mixture of positivism and various anti-positivist motives; and when we try to criticize its results and reduce them to order we soon realize that the easiest way of doing this would be by eliminating the anti-positivistic elements and regarding it as an incoherent statement of positivism. This, of course, would be a false interpretation; it would imply mistaking the ferment of new growth for the vacillations of a feeble and inconsistent thought, and developing the ideas of these new philosophers in exactly the wrong direction, by backing out of the difficulties they raise instead of facing and overcoming them. In analysing the thought of a philosopher, just as in analysing, say, a political situation, one will always find incoherences and contradictions; these contradictions are always between retrograde and progressive elements; and it is of the utmost importance, if we are to make anything of our analysis, to distinguish correctly which are the progressive elements and which the retrograde. The great merit of studying our subject historically is that it enables us to make this distinction with certainty.

In England the leader of the new movement to which I have referred was F. H. Bradley, and his first published work was specifically concerned with the problems of history. This was *The Presuppositions of Critical History*, written in 1874. The situation out of which this essay grew was the condition of Biblical criticism as developed by the Tübingen school, notably F. C. Baur and David Strauss. These German theologians had applied the new methods of historical criticism to the narratives of the New Testament, and the result was very destructive to belief in the credibility of those narratives. The destructiveness of this result, however, was due not simply to the use of critical methods, but to the positivistic spirit in which those methods were used. The critical historian is one who is no longer content to say 'the authorities say that such and such an event happened, and therefore I believe that it did'. He says 'the authorities say that it happened, and it is for me to decide whether they are telling the truth or not'. Thus, critical historians were bound to ask whether the New Testament narratives, in this or that particular, were reporting historical fact or fictions that grew up as part of the legendary tradition of a new religious sect. Either alternative was theoretically possible. Take for example the story of the Resurrection of Jesus. Thomas Arnold, who was once professor of history at Oxford as well as headmaster of Rugby, described that as the best-attested fact in history. But, replied the critics, its being well attested only proves that a lot of people believed it, not that it happened. So far their argument was soundly based, but their positivistic assumptions began to be evident when they claimed to be able to show: (*a*) that it cannot have happened, (*b*) that the people who believed it had good cause for believing it even though it did not happen. (*a*) It cannot have happened, so they argued, because it was a miracle, and a miracle is a breach of the laws of nature; the laws of nature are discovered by science, and therefore the whole prestige and authority of science is thrown into the scales on the side of denying that the Resurrection really took place. (*b*) But the members of the early Church were not scientifically minded people; they lived in an atmosphere where the distinction between what could and what could not happen meant nothing; everyone in those days believed in miracles; and therefore it is only natural that their imaginations should invent miracles like this, so creditable to their own Church and reflecting such glory on its founder.

The result was that the critics, without the smallest anti-religious or anti-Christian bias but on the contrary wishing to base their own Christian beliefs only on the solid rock of critically ascertained historical fact, set to work to rewrite the New Testament narratives leaving out the miraculous elements. At first they did not realize how far this committed them to scepticism about Christian origins, but very soon the problem arose: If the miracles are omitted together with everything else that is tarred with the same brush, what is left? According to the critical theory, the early Christians only put the miracles in because they were unscientific, imaginative, credulous people; but that fact vitiates not only their testimony to the miracles but all their other testimony as well. Why then should we believe that Jesus ever lived at all? Surely, argued the more extreme critics, all the New Testament can really tell us is that the people who wrote it lived and were the kind of people they show themselves to be in their writings: a sect of Jews with strange beliefs, whom a combination of circumstances raised by degrees to the religious mastery of the Roman world. A radical historical scepticism resulted not from the use of critical methods but from a combination of those methods with uncriticized and unnoticed positivistic assumptions.

This is the background of Bradley's essay. Instead of taking sides with or against the critics in the controversy that raged round their conclusions, he sets himself the task of investigating philosophically their methods and the principles on which they depend. He starts with the fact that critical history exists, and that all history is to some extent critical, since no historian copies out the statements of his authorities just as he finds them. 'Critical history', then, 'must have a criterion'; and it is clear that the criterion can only be the historian himself. The way in which he handles his authorities will and must depend on what he brings to the study of them. Now the historian is a man with an experience of his own; he experiences the world in which he lives; and it is this experience which he brings with him to the interpretation of historical evidence. He cannot be simply a tranquil mirror reflecting what that evidence tells him; until he has exerted himself and laboured to interpret it, it tells him nothing, for in itself it is only 'a host of jarring witnesses, a chaos of disjointed and discrepant narrations'. What he makes out of this welter of material depends on what he is: that is to say, upon the body of experience which he brings with him to the work. But the evidence on which he has to work is itself already composed of testimony, that is, of statements made by various people; and because these are meant to be statements of objective fact, and not mere records of subjective feeling, they contain judgement and inference and are liable to error. What the critical historian has to do is to decide whether the persons whose testimony he is using were, on this or that occasion, judging correctly or erroneously. This decision must be made on the basis of his own experience. This experience tells him what kind of things can happen; and this is the canon by which he criticizes testimony.

The crux arises when our witness alleges a fact wholly without analogy in our own experience. Can we believe him or must we reject that part of his testimony? Bradley's answer is that if in our own experience we encountered a fact unlike anything we had encountered before, we should think ourselves entitled to believe in its reality only when we had verified it by 'the most careful examination often repeated'. These then are the only terms on which I can believe such a fact or testimony: I must be assured that the witness is as conscientious an observer as myself, and that he, too, has verified his observation in the same way: in that case 'his judgement is to me precisely the same as my own'. In other words, he must not be such a man as to allow his beliefs about what has happened to be influenced by a religious or other view of the world in which I do not share; for if so, his judgement cannot be to me the same as my own; and he must have taken the same amount of trouble to ascertain the fact which I should myself take. But in history these conditions cannot possibly be fulfilled; for the witness is always a son of his time, and the mere progress of human knowledge makes it impossible that his point of view and standard of accuracy should be identical with my own. Consequently, no historical testimony can establish the reality of facts that have no analogy in our present experience. All we can do in cases where it tries and fails to do this is to conclude that the witness has made a mistake, and to treat this mistake itself as an historical fact that has to be explained. Sometimes we can infer what the fact was which he thus mistakenly reported; sometimes this cannot be done, and we can only say that the testimony exists but that we have not the data for reconstructing the fact.

Such is Bradley's argument in outline. It is so rich and goes so deep into its subject that no brief commentary can do it justice. But I will try to disentangle the points in it which seem satisfactory from those which are less so.

On the positive side of the account, Bradley is absolutely right in holding that historical knowledge is no mere passive acceptance of testimony, but a critical interpretation of it; that this criticism implies a criterion; and that the criterion is something the historian brings with him to the work of interpretation, that is to say, the criterion is the historian himself. He is right in holding that to accept testimony means making the thought of the witness one's own thought: re-enacting that thought in one's own mind. For example, if a witness says that Caesar was murdered, and I accept his statement, my own statement 'this man was right to say that Caesar was murdered', implies a statement of my own, 'Caesar was murdered', and this is the original statement of the witness. Bradley stops short, however, of taking the next step and realizing that the historian re-enacts in his own mind not only the thought of the witness but the thought of the agent whose action the witness reports.

Where he goes wrong, I think, is in his conception of the

relation between the historian's criterion and that to which he applies it. His view is that the historian brings to his work a ready-made body of experience by which he judges the statements contained in his authorities. Because this body of experience is conceived as ready-made, it cannot be modified by the historian's own work *as* an historian: it has to be there, complete, before he begins his historical work. Consequently this experience is regarded not as consisting of historical knowledge but as knowledge of some other kind, and Bradley in fact conceives it as scientific knowledge, knowledge of the laws of nature. This is where the positivism of his age begins to infect his thought. He regards the historian's scientific knowledge as giving him the means of distinguishing between what can and what cannot happen; and this scientific knowledge he conceives in the positivistic manner, as based on induction from observed facts on the principle that the future will resemble the past and the unknown the known.

The inductive logic of John Stuart Mill is the shadow which broods over all this part of Bradley's essay. But there is an inner inconsistency in this logic itself. On the one side, it claims that scientific thought reveals to us laws of nature to which there cannot be exceptions; on the other, it holds that this revelation is based on induction from experience, and therefore can never give us universal knowledge that is more than probable. Hence in the last resort the attempt to base history on science breaks down; for although there might be facts which are inconsistent with the laws of nature as we conceive them (that is, miracles might happen), the occurrence of these facts is so improbable that no possible testimony would convince us of it. This impasse really wrecks the whole theory; for what is true in the extreme case of miracle is true in principle of any event whatever. And it was Bradley's consciousness of this, no doubt, that led him after composing this essay to devote himself to the searching examination of Mill's *Logic* whose results he published in his *Principles of Logic* nine years later.

Bradley rightly saw that the historian's criterion is something which he brings with him to the study of the evidence, and that this something is simply himself; but it is himself not *qua* scientist, as Bradley thought, but *qua* historian. It is only by practising historical thought that he learns to think historically.

His criterion is therefore never ready-made; the experience from which it is derived is his experience of historical thinking, and it grows with every growth in his historical knowledge. History is its own criterion; it does not depend for its validity on something outside itself, it is an autonomous form of thought with its own principles and its own methods. Its principles are the laws of the historical spirit and no others; and the historical spirit creates itself in the work of historical inquiry. This was too bold a claim on behalf of history for any one to make in an age when natural science was absolute sovereign of the intellectual world; but it is the claim which Bradley's thought logically implies, and in time it was seen to be a necessary and just one.

Although this claim was not explicitly made by Bradley himself, and although in his later philosophical career he did not explicitly return to the problem of history, he did actually proceed to construct, first, a logic orientated (though readers seldom recognize this) towards the epistemology of history, and then a metaphysic in which reality was conceived from a radically historical point of view. I cannot here demonstrate this in detail, but I will briefly illustrate it. In the *Principles of Logic*, Bradley's sustained polemic against positivistic logic has a constructive aspect in its sustained appeal to and analysis of historical knowledge. For example, in dealing with the quantity of judgements he maintains[1] that the abstract universal and the abstract particular do not exist: 'the *concrete* particular and the *concrete* universal both have reality, and they are different names for the individual. What is real is the individual; and this individual, though one and the same, has internal differences. You may hence regard it in two opposite ways. So far as it is one against other individuals, it is particular. So far as it is the same throughout its diversity, it is universal.' Here Bradley is stating the identity of the universal and individual judgement, which, as Croce was to explain twenty years later, is the definition of historical knowledge. And in order to show that history is what he is thinking of, Bradley goes on to illustrate his thesis by saying: 'Thus a man is particular by virtue of his limiting and exclusive relations to all other phenomena. He is universal because he is one throughout all his different

[1] Op. cit., second edition, Oxford 1922, vol. i, p. 188.

attributes. You may call him particular, or again universal, because, being individual, he actually is both. . . . The individual is both a concrete particular and a concrete universal.'

Nothing could be a clearer statement of the doctrine that reality consists neither of isolated particulars nor of abstract universals but of individual facts whose being is historical. And this doctrine is the fundamental thesis of Bradley's *Logic*. When we turn to *Appearance and Reality*, we find the same thought pushed a stage farther. The fundamental thesis there is that reality is not something other than its appearances, hidden behind them, but is these appearances themselves, forming a whole of which we can say that it forms a single system consisting of experience and that all our experiences form part of it. A reality so defined can only be the life of mind itself, that is, history. Even the ultimate problem which Bradley left unsolved betrays at once the fact that history was the thing which he was trying to understand and the precise way in which he stopped short of understanding it. The terms of this problem are as follows. Reality is not only experience it is immediate experience, it has the immediacy of feeling. But thought divides, distinguishes, mediates; therefore, just so far as we think about reality, we deform it by destroying its immediacy, and thus thought can never grasp reality. We enjoy reality in the immediate flow of our mental life, but when we think, we cease to enjoy it, because it ceases to be immediate: we break it up into discrete parts, and this break-up destroys its immediacy and therefore destroys itself. Bradley has thus bequeathed to his successors a dilemma. Either reality is the immediate flow of subjective life, in which case it is subjective but not objective, it is enjoyed but cannot be known, or else it is that which we know, in which case it is objective and not subjective, it is a world of real things outside the subjective life of our mind and outside each other. Bradley himself accepted the first horn of the dilemma; but to accept either horn is to be committed to the fundamental error of conceiving the life of mind as a mere immediate flow of feelings and sensations, devoid of all reflection and self-knowledge. So conceived, mind is itself, but it does not know itself; the being of mind is such as to make self-knowledge impossible.

(ii) *Bradley's successors*

The effect of Bradley's work on subsequent English philosophy was to induce it, in general, to accept this error as an axiomatic truth, and to adopt the second horn of the resulting dilemma. In Oxford, the result was Cook Wilson and Oxford realism; in Cambridge, it was Bertrand Russell and Cambridge realism. Realism in both cases meant the doctrine that what mind knows is something other than itself, and that mind in itself, the activity of knowing, is immediate experience and therefore unknowable. Alexander has expressed the Bradleian dilemma with admirable clearness when he lays it down[1] that knowledge is a relation between two things, a mind and its object, and that the mind therefore does not know itself, it only enjoys itself. Everything that we know is thus placed outside the mind, and constitutes a body of things whose proper collective name is nature; history, which is the mind's knowledge of itself, is ruled out as impossible. This argument is doubtless in fact derived from the empiricist tradition of English thought, but not directly. It is not based on Locke and Hume, for their primary aim was to enrich and develop the mind's knowledge of itself; it is based on the naturalistic empiricism of the nineteenth century, where (true to the principles of positivism) knowledge meant natural science. The reaction against Bradley, due in the last resort to Bradley's own faults, has reinforced and hardened this tradition, so that the English philosophy of the last generation has deliberately orientated itself towards natural science and has turned away from the problem of history with a kind of instinctive repugnance. Its central problem has always been our knowledge of the external world as given in perception and conceived by scientific thought. When one searches its literature for any discussion, however slight, of the problems of history, the result is astonishing in its meagreness. On that topic there seems to be in the main a conspiracy of silence.

A serious attempt to cope with the philosophy of history was made by Robert Flint in a number of volumes between 1874 and 1893, but these were limited to a collection and discussion of views put forward by other writers, and although they are learned and painstaking works they throw little light on the subject, for Flint never properly thought out his own point of

---

[1] *Space, Time, and Deity* (London, 1920), vol. i, pp. 11-13.

view, and consequently his criticism of others is superficial and unsympathetic.

The few other English philosophers who have dealt with the problem of history since Bradley have contributed nothing of value until the last few years. Bosanquet, who was closely associated with Bradley himself, treated history with open contempt as a false form of thought, 'the doubtful story of successive events'.[1] That is to say, he assumed as correct the positivistic view of its subject-matter as consisting of isolated facts separated from one another in time, and he saw that if this was their nature historical knowledge was impossible. In his *Logic*, where great attention is bestowed on the methods of scientific research, nothing is said about those of history. Elsewhere he describes history as 'a hybrid form of experience, incapable of any considerable degree of "being or trueness"',[2] in which reality is misconceived by being treated as contingent.

This complete misunderstanding of history has been restated and emphasized in later times by Dr. Inge,[3] who follows Bosanquet in conceiving the proper object of knowledge Platonically as a timeless world of pure universality. It is reflected, too, in treatises on logic like those of Cook Wilson and Joseph, where the special problems of historical thinking are passed over in silence. More recently still, the kind of logic which professes to be most up to date has inspired a text-book by Miss L. Susan Stebbing (*A Modern Introduction to Logic*, edn. 2, London, 1933). This contains one chapter on historical method (chapter xix, esp. pp. 382–8). Its substance is derived entirely from a well-known French manual written by Langlois and Seignobos (*Introduction aux études historiques*, Paris, 1898) to expound the pre-scientific form of history which I call 'scissors-and-paste history'; it is therefore about as useful to the modern reader as would be a discussion of physics in which no mention was made of relativity.

(iii) *Late nineteenth-century historiography*

Those who pursued historical research in the late nineteenth century were very little interested in the theory of what they

---

[1] *The Principle of Individuality and Value* (London, 1912), p. 79.
[2] Ibid., pp. 78–9.
[3] *God and the Astronomers* (London, 1933), chaps. iii and iv.

were doing. Characteristically of a positivistic age, the historians of that period were more or less openly contemptuous, as a matter of professional convention, of philosophy in general and the philosophy of history in particular. In their contempt for philosophy they were in part echoing the ordinary parrot-cry of positivism that natural science had now finally dethroned philosophical thought; but in part they were reacting against positivism too, for positivism itself was a philosophy, maintaining the doctrine that natural science was the perfect type of knowledge; and even the least reflective historian could see that a blind worship of natural science must be hostile to historical research. Their contempt for the philosophy of history had no reference to Hegel's or any other genuine philosophy of history, of which they knew nothing; it was directed against positivistic fabrications like Buckle's attempt to discover historical laws or Herbert Spencer's identification of history with natural evolution. In the main, English historians of the late nineteenth century thus went on their own way without often pausing to utter general reflections on their work; on the rare occasions when they did so, as for example in Freeman's book on *The Methods of Historical Study* (London, 1886), or here and there in inaugural lectures, nothing worthy of notice came of it.

In spite of this general detachment of English historians from philosophical thought, however, they were influenced very definitely by their intellectual environment. In the later nineteenth century the idea of progress became almost an article of faith. This conception was a piece of sheer metaphysics derived from evolutionary naturalism and foisted upon history by the temper of the age. It had its roots no doubt in the eighteenth-century conception of history as the progress of the human race in and towards rationality; but in the nineteenth, theoretical reason had come to mean the mastery of nature (knowledge being equated with natural science, and natural science, in the popular view, with technology) and practical reason had come to mean the pursuit of pleasure (morality being equated with promoting the greatest happiness of the greatest number, and happiness with quantity of pleasure). The progress of humanity, from the nineteenth-century point of view, meant getting richer and richer and having a better and better time. And the evolutionary philosophy of Spencer seemed to prove that such a process must of necessity go on, and go on indefinitely; while the then economic condition of England appeared to corroborate that doctrine in at least the one most interesting case.

In order to realize the lengths to which this dogma of progress was pushed, it is necessary to go slumming among the most unsavoury relics of third-rate historical work. A certain Robert Mackenzie published in 1880 a book called *The Nineteenth Century—A History*, depicting that century as a time of progress from a state of barbarism, ignorance, and bestiality which can hardly be exaggerated, to a reign of science, enlightenment, and democracy. France before the Revolution was a country in which liberty was wholly extinct, the king one of the meanest and basest of human creatures, the nobility omnipotent to oppress and merciless in using their power. Britain (not England, for the author was a Scot) presents a picture drawn in the same colours except that savage criminal laws and brutalizing industrial conditions play a larger part. A beam of sunshine steals over the scene with the advent of the Reform Bill, the most beneficent event in British history, ushering in a new era when legislation instead of being uniformly selfish in aim was uniformly directed at overthrowing iniquitous preferences. A brilliant period follows when all wrongs were being righted as fast as possible; everybody was rapidly getting happier and happier until a culmination of joy was reached in the dazzling victories of the Crimea. But the victories of peace were no less dazzling; they include the splendours of the cotton trade, the magnificent conception of steam locomotion, which awakened the dormant love of travel and taught people in distant parts of the earth to love one another instead of hating one another as before; the bold conception of stretching an electric pathway in the depths of the Atlantic, which gave every village the inestimable privilege of instantaneous communication with every part of the inhabited globe; newspapers, by which every morning the same topics are presented to all minds, generally with intelligence and moderation, often with consummate skill; breech-loading rifles, ironclads, heavy artillery, and torpedoes (these, too, among the blessings of peace); a vastly increased consumption of tea, sugar, and spirits; lucifer matches, and so forth. I spare the reader any account of the chapters on France, Prussia, Austria, Italy, Russia, Turkey, the United

States, and the Papacy, and pass straight to the author's conclusion:

'Human history is a record of progress—a record of accumulating knowledge and increasing wisdom, of continual advancement from a lower to a higher platform of intelligence and well-being. Each generation passes on to the next the treasures which it inherited, beneficially modified by its own experience, enlarged by the fruits of all the victories which itself has gained. The rate of this progress . . . is irregular and even fitful . . . but the stagnation is only apparent. . . . The nineteenth century has witnessed progress rapid beyond all precedent, for it has witnessed the overthrow of the barriers which prevented progress. . . . Despotism thwarts and frustrates the forces by which providence has provided for the progress of man; liberty secures for these forces their natural scope and exercise. . . . The growth of man's well-being, rescued from the mischievous tampering of self-willed princes, is left now to the beneficent regulation of great providential laws.'

These rhapsodies, if not out of date on their first publication, were certainly outmoded a decade later, when they were still being reprinted. Spencerian evolutionism, with its belief in the inheritance of acquired characteristics and the beneficent kindliness of natural law, had by that time been succeeded by a new naturalism of gloomier cast. Huxley in 1893 delivered his Romanes lecture on *Evolution and Ethics*, in which he maintained that social progress was possible only by flying in the face of natural law: by 'checking the cosmic process at every step and substituting for it another which may be called the ethical process'. The life of man, in so far as it follows the laws of nature, is the life of a brute, differing from other brutes only in being more intelligent. The theory of evolution, he concluded, offered no basis for the hope of a millennium. The result of such reflections was that historians studied the past in a new spirit of detachment. They began to think of it as the proper field for a dispassionate and therefore truly scientific study, from which partisan spirit, praise and blame, should be banished. They began to criticize Gibbon not for having taken sides against Christianity in particular but for having taken sides at all; Macaulay not for being a Whig historian but for being a party historian. This was the period of Stubbs and Maitland, the period when English historians first mastered the objectively scientific critical methods of the great Germans, and learnt to study facts in all their detail with a proper apparatus of scholarship.

(iv) *Bury*

One historian of that period stands out from the rest in having an altogether unusual equipment of philosophical training. J. B. Bury was not a powerful philosophical intellect, but he read a certain amount of philosophy, and realized that there were philosophical problems connected with historical research. His work therefore took on a certain air of self-consciousness. In the preface to his *History of Greece* he makes the unusual admission that the book is written from his own point of view; in the introduction to his edition of Gibbon he explains the principles on which he has edited him, and in a number of scattered essays he discusses points of historical theory. He also undertook such semi-philosophical works as an historical book on *The Idea of Progress* and a shorter one called *A History of Freedom of Thought*.

These writings reveal Bury as a positivist in historical theory, but a perplexed and inconsistent one. History for him, in the true positivistic manner, consists of an assemblage of isolated facts, each capable of being ascertained or investigated without reference to the others. Thus he was able to accomplish the very strange feat of bringing Gibbon up to date by means of footnotes, adding to the aggregate of knowledge already contained in his pages the numerous facts that had been ascertained in the meantime, without suspecting that the very discovery of these facts resulted from an historical mentality so different from Gibbon's own that the result was not unlike adding a saxophone obbligato to an Elizabethan madrigal. He never saw that one new fact added to a mass of old ones involved the complete transformation of the old. This view of history as consisting of detached parts achieved its classical expression, for the English public, in the Cambridge histories, modern, medieval, and ancient, vast compilations where the chapters, sometimes even the subdivisions of a chapter, are written by different hands, the editor being given the task of assembling the fruit of this mass-production into a single whole. Bury was one of the editors, though the original scheme was due to Lord Acton, a generation earlier.

If we follow the development of Bury's thought[1] on the principles and methods of history, we find him in 1900 still content to deal with the survival of the Eastern Empire according to the strict formulae of positivism: the treatment of an event not as unique but as an instance of a certain type, and the explanation of it by discovering a cause applicable not to it alone but to every event of the same general kind. Here the method is exactly that of the empirical sciences of nature as analysed by positivistic logic. By 1903, when he delivered his Cambridge inaugural lecture, Bury had begun to revolt against this method. In that lecture he proclaimed that historical thought as we now understand it is a new thing in the world, barely a century old: not at all the same thing as natural science, but having a special character of its own, offering to mankind a new view of the world and a new armoury of intellectual weapons. What, he asks, might we not make of the human world in which we live, when we realize the possibilities of this new intellectual attitude towards it? Here the uniqueness of historical thought is clearly seen and impressively stated; but when Bury goes on to ask what this new thing is, he replies: 'History is simply a science, no less and no more'. The lecture exhibits a mind torn between two conceptions: one, obscure but powerful, of the difference between history and science, the other, clear and paralysing, of their indistinguishable identity. Bury has made a violent effort to free himself from this latter conception, and failed.

Next year, conscious of his failure, he returned to the attack in a lecture on *The Place of Modern History in the Perspective of Knowledge*. Is history, he asks, a mere reservoir of facts accumulated for the use of sociologists and anthropologists, or is it an independent discipline to be studied for its own sake? He cannot answer this question, for he sees that it is a philosophical one and realizes that it lies, therefore, outside his competence. But he will go so far as to answer it hypothetically. If we adopt a naturalistic philosophy,

'then I think we must conclude that the place of history, within the frame of such a system, is subordinate to sociology or anthropology.

[1] I am here drawing on my review of his posthumous *Selected Essays*, edited by H. W. V. Temperley (Cambridge, 1930) in the *English Historical Review*, 1931, p. 461.

... But on an idealistic interpretation of knowledge it is otherwise. ... If thought is not the result, but the presupposition, of the processes of nature, it follows that history, of which thought is the characteristic and guiding force, belongs to a different order of ideas from the kingdom of nature, and demands a different interpretation.'

There he leaves it. The moment was a dramatic one in the development of his mind. His conviction of the dignity and worth of historical thought had come into open conflict with his own positivistic training and principles. Committed as he was to the service of history, he accepted the consequences.

In 1909 he published an essay on *Darwinism and History*, deliberately attacking the idea that historical events can be explained by reference to general laws. Uniformities, yes; laws, no. What really determines them is 'chance coincidence'. Examples are 'the sudden death of a leader, a marriage without issue', and in general the decisive function of individuality, which sociology falsely eliminates in order to facilitate its task of assimilating history to the uniformity of science. The 'chapter of accidents' everywhere enters as a disturbing element into historical processes. In an essay called *Cleopatra's Nose* (1916) he repeats the same idea. History is determined not by causal sequences such as form the subject-matter of science, but by the fortuitous 'collision of two or more independent chains of causes'. Here the very words of Bury's argument seem to echo those of Cournot in his *Considérations sur la marche des idées et des événements dans les temps modernes* (Paris, 1872), where he expounded a conception of chance, based on the distinction between 'general causes' and 'special causes': chance being defined as 'l'*indépendance* mutuelle de plusieurs séries de causes et d'effets qui concourent *accidentellement*' (his italics; op. cit. i. 1). A note in Bury's *Idea of Progress*,[1] read together with a footnote to *Darwinism and History*,[2] suggests that he may have derived his own doctrine from Cournot, who, however; develops it by pointing out that in so far as anything is merely fortuitous there can be no history of it. The true function of history, he holds, is to distinguish the necessary from the merely accidental. Bury is developing, or rather disintegrating, this theory by adding to it the doctrine that, in so far as history is individual, everything in it is accidental and nothing necessary, but after

[1] London, 1920, p. 368.   [2] *Selected Essays*, p. 37.

illustrating what he means he concludes his essay by suggesting 'that as time goes on contingencies will become less important in human evolution and chance have less power over the course of events'.

The impression made on a reader by the last paragraph of this essay is a painful one. With great toil, Bury had in the preceding dozen years reached a conception of history as knowledge of the individual. He realized, early in that process, that this conception was essential to the dignity and worth of historical thought. But by 1916 he is so dissatisfied with what he has discovered that he is prepared to give it up; to see in this very individuality an irrational, because accidental, element in the world and to hope that, with the march of science, it may one day be eliminated. If he had grasped his own idea firmly, he would have realized both that this hope was vain (for he had really proved, in the preceding pages, that accidents in his sense of the word must necessarily happen) and also that by entertaining it he was turning traitor to his own historical vocation.

This disastrous conclusion, from which he never afterwards deviated, was due to the fact that instead of conceiving individuality as the very substance of the historical process, he had never thought of it as more than a partial and occasional interference with sequences which in their general structure are causal sequences. Individuality for him only meant the unusual, the exceptional, an interruption in the ordinary course of events: where the ordinary course of events means a course of events causally determined and scientifically comprehensible. But Bury himself knew, or had known in 1904, that history does not consist of events causally determined and scientifically comprehensible; these are ideas appropriate to the interpretation of nature, and history, as he then rightly said, 'demands a different interpretation'. If he had logically developed the ideas of his earlier essay he would have concluded that individuality, instead of appearing in history only now and then in the shape of the accidental or contingent, is just that out of which history is made; what prevented him from advancing to this conclusion was his positivistic prejudice that individuality as such is unintelligible, and that in consequence the generalizations of science are the only possible form of knowledge.

Thus, after realizing that an 'idealistic' philosophy was the only one which could account for the possibility of historical knowledge, Bury fell back into the 'naturalistic' one which he had tried to repudiate. The phrase 'contingency of history' expresses this final collapse of his thought. Contingency means unintelligibility; and the contingency of history is simply a name for 'the role of the individual' seen through the spectacles of a positivism for which nothing is intelligible except what is general. Professor Norman H. Baynes, Bury's successor as our leading master of late Roman and Byzantine history, has spoken bitterly of 'the devastating doctrine of contingency in history' which dimmed Bury's historical insight towards the end of his life. The criticism is just. Bury had done his best work under the inspiration of a belief in the autonomy and dignity of historical thought; but the atmosphere of positivism in which his mind had formed itself undermined this belief, and reduced the proper object of historical knowledge to the level of something which, precisely because it was not an object of scientific thought, was unintelligible.

(v) *Oakeshott*

Bury, however, did set historians an example of attempting to think out the philosophical implications of their own work, and this example was not thrown away. In Cambridge, it was followed by at least one historian of the next generation, by an historian armed with a preparation vastly superior to Bury's in philosophical studies. I refer to Mr. Michael B. Oakeshott of Caius College who published a book called *Experience and its Modes* (Cambridge, 1933), in which he dealt at length and in a masterly way with the philosophical problem of history. The general thesis of the book is that experience is a 'concrete whole which analysis divides into experiencing and what is experienced'; and experience is not (as it is for Bradley) immediate consciousness, the mere flow of sensations and feelings, it is also and always thought, judgement, assertion of reality. There is no sensation which is not also thought, no intuition which is not also judgement, no volition which is not also cognition. These distinctions, like that between subject and object, are in no sense arbitrary or unreal; they represent no false dissection of experience itself, they are integral elements in it; but they are distinctions, not divisions, and above all they are distinctions within experience, not distinctions between elements in experience and something foreign to it. Hence thought as such is not, as in Bradley, a falsification of experience involving the break-up of its immediacy; thought is experience itself; and thought, as 'experience without reservation or arrest, without presupposition or postulate, without limit or category', is philosophy.

Here Bradley's dilemma is transcended. Because experience is no longer conceived as immediate, but as containing mediation or thought within itself, the real is no longer divided into that which 'knows' but cannot be known ('knows', because a knowledge where the knower can never say 'I know' is not knowledge at all) and that which is 'known' but cannot know. Mind's right to know itself is re-established.

The question now arises: What is the difference between such forms of thought as history and science? Each is an attempt to envisage reality (that is, experience) from a particular point of view, in terms of a particular category. History is the way in which we conceive the world *sub specie praeteritorum*: its differentia is the attempt to organize the whole world of experience in the shape of past events. Science is the way in which we conceive the world *sub specie quantitatis*: its differentia is the attempt to organize the world of experience as a system of measurements. Such attempts differ radically from that of philosophy, for in philosophy there is no such primary and inviolable postulate. If we ask for a parallel formula applying to philosophy and inquire: 'In terms of what, then, does philosophy seek to conceive the world of experience?', there is no answer to the question. Philosophy is the attempt to conceive reality not in any particular way, but just to conceive it.

Oakeshott states this idea by saying that whereas philosophy is experience itself, history and science and so forth are 'modes' of experience. Experience is 'modified' (the conception, of course, comes from Descartes and Spinoza) by arresting it at a certain point, and there, using the point of arrest as a fixed postulate or category, constructing a 'world of ideas' in terms of that postulate. Such a world of ideas is not a constituent element in experience itself, not, as it were, a reach of its river, but a backwater, a digression from its unreserved flow. It is not, however, a 'world of mere ideas'. It is not only coherent in itself, it is a way of representing experience as a whole. It is not *a* world, a separate sphere of experience in which things of a special kind are known in a special way, but *the* world, as seen from that fixed point in experience, and therefore, subject to that qualification, rightly seen.

History, then, is experience as a whole, conceived as a system of past events. From this point of view Oakeshott develops a brilliant and penetrating account of the aims of historical thought and the character of its object. He begins by showing that history is a whole or a world. It does not consist of isolated events. This involves him in a vigorous and triumphant attack on the positivistic theory of history as a series of events external to one another, each to be apprehended (if indeed anything can be thus apprehended) in isolation from the rest. 'The historical series', he concludes (op. cit., p. 92), 'is a bogy.' History is not a series but a world: which means that its various parts bear upon one another, criticize one another, make one another intelligible. Next, he shows that it is not only a world but a world of ideas. It is not a world of objective events which the historian somehow exhumes from the past and makes the object of a present cognition. It is the historian's world of ideas. 'The distinction between history as it happened (the course of events) and history as it is thought, the distinction between history itself and merely experienced history, must go; it is not merely false, it is meaningless' (p. 93). What the historian is doing, when he fancies he is merely cognizing past events as they actually happened, is in reality organizing his present consciousness; as can be seen when we reflect on the impossibility of separating 'what has come to us' from 'our interpretation of it' (p. 94). This does not mean that it is a world of mere ideas; mere ideas are abstractions and are nowhere found in experience; like all real ideas the historian's ideas are critical ideas, true ideas, thoughts.

Further, history is like every form of experience in that it starts with a given world of ideas and ends by making that world coherent. The data or materials with which the historian starts are not independent of his experience, they are his historical experience itself in its initial form: they are ideas already conceived in the light of his own historical postulates, and the criticism of historical knowledge turns primarily not on the discovery of hitherto unknown materials but on the revision of these initial postulates. The growth of historical knowledge, consequently, comes about not by adding new facts to those already known, but by transforming the old ideas in the light of the new. ' The process in historical thinking is never a process of incorporation ; it is always a process by which a given world of ideas is transformed into a world that is more than a world' (p. 99).

So much for generalities. But what in particular are the postulates in virtue of which historical experience is history, and not experience at large or in some other special form ? The first postulate is the idea of the past. But history is not the past as such. The historical past is a special past: not the merely remembered past, nor the merely fancied past ; not a past that merely might have been or merely must have been ; not the whole past, for although the distinction between an historical and a non-historical past has often been wrongly and arbitrarily drawn, the distinction is a real one ; not the practical past, the past to which we are personally attached, as in the patriotic love of our country's past achievements or the religious value which we attach to the circumstances in which our own creed was born. The historical past is 'the past for its own sake' (p. 106), the past just in so far as it is past, different from the present and independent of it: a fixed and finished past, a dead past. Or rather, this is how the historian thinks of it. But so to think of it is to forget that history is experience. A fixed and finished past is a past divorced from present experience ; and therefore divorced from evidence (since evidence is always present) and therefore unknowable. 'What really happened' is only 'what the evidence obliges us to believe' (p. 107). Thus the facts of history are present facts. The historical past is the world of ideas which the present evidence creates in the present. In historical inference we do not move from our present world to a past world ; the movement in experience is always a movement within a present world of ideas.

The paradoxical result is that the historical past is not past at all ; it is present. It is not a past surviving into the present ; it must *be* the present. But it is not the present as such, the merely contemporary. It is present, because all experience whatever is present ; but not merely present. It is also past, and this pastness involves a modification of its character as experience. The historical past does not stand over against the present world of experience as something different from it; it is a special organization of that world *sub specie praeteritorum*. 'History, because it is experience, is present . . .; but because it is history, the formulation of experience as a whole *sub specie praeteritorum*, it is the continuous assertion of a past which is not past and of a present which is not present' (p. 111). This means, I think, that the historian's thought is a perfectly genuine experience, but what he is experiencing is what is going on in his mind now; in so far as he places it, as it were, at arm's length from him in the past, he is misconceiving it; he is arranging in imaginary pigeon-holes of past time what is actually all present and not past at all. And this does not imply that he is making historical mistakes about the past. There *is* no past, except for a person involved in the historical mode of experience; and for him the past is what he carefully and critically thinks it to be. He makes no mistake *qua* historian: the only mistake he makes is the philosophical mistake of arranging in the past what is actually all present experience.

I shall not analyse the whole of Oakeshott's argument. I have said enough to indicate its general direction and character. The first thing to be said about it is that it entirely vindicates the autonomy of historical thought. The historian is master in his own house; he owes nothing to the scientist or to anyone else. And this house is not built and furnished out of mere ideas of his own, which may or may not correspond with the ideas of other historians or with the real past which they are all alike trying to know; it is a house inhabited by all historians, and it consists not of ideas about history but of history itself. From this double point of view—the autonomy and objectivity of historical thought, which are only two names for its rationality, its character as a genuine form of experience—Oakeshott is able without difficulty to criticize every form of historical positivism, whether as taught by Bury, to whom he makes frequent and penetrating reference, or as practised by the naturalistic anthropologists and their chief, Sir James Frazer. Moreover, though he does not actually do this, he is in a position to make short work of philosophical objections to the idea of history itself, such as are lodged by writers like Bosanquet and Dr. Inge.

This constitutes a new and valuable achievement for English

thought. But there is a further problem which, as I understand him, Oakeshott has failed to solve. History for him is not a necessary phase or element in experience as such; on the contrary, it is a backwater of thought due to an arrest of experience at a certain point. If we ask why there should be such an arrest, there is no answer. If we ask whether such an arrest is justified, that is, whether experience itself is enriched by it, the answer is in the negative. Genuine experience, undistorted by any such arrest, can only be philosophy. The historian is a philosopher who has turned aside from the path of philosophical thought to play a game which is none the less arbitrary for being only one of a potentially infinite number of such games, others being those of science and practical life. The problem which Oakeshott has failed to solve is the question why there is or should be such a thing as history at all. No doubt, he would state this differently: what I call failing to answer this question he would describe as discovering that the question has no answer. For him it is a mere fact that experience is arrested at that point. But I think this belief is inconsistent with his own philosophical principles. A mere fact, divorced from other facts, is for him (as for myself) a monstrosity; in his own words, nothing real, but an abstraction. If philosophy is concrete experience it cannot tolerate such things; it cannot separate the *what* from the *why*. The double question is therefore a legitimate and inevitable one: first, What exactly is the point in experience at which it arrests itself to become history, and how is this point arrived at in the development of experience itself? Secondly, How and why does it happen that when this point is reached an arrest sometimes occurs there? These questions Oakeshott has not answered; and he could only answer them by doing what he has not done, namely giving such an account of experience itself, such a map of the river of experience, as would show the position of this and other points at which arrests may take place.

The reason why he has not done this, I am compelled to think, is because, in spite of his insistence on the conception of experience as no mere immediacy but as containing within itself thought, judgement, assertion of reality, he has not worked out the implications of this conception. It implies that experience is no mere featureless flow of ideas, but understands itself, that is, has features and grasps them. It implies that the modes of

experience arise out of these features and are therefore, in some
sort, not accidental but necessary, not backwaters off the stream
but reaches or currents or eddies in the stream itself, integral
parts of its flow. It implies that such special forms of experience
as history must be somehow conceived as integrated within the
whole of experience.

This failure to explain how and why history arises within
experience as a necessary mode of it results, unless I am mistaken, in a failure to clear up one feature of history itself. We
have seen that Oakeshott states a dilemma: the object of
historical thought is either present or past: the historian thinks
of it as past, but that is where he is wrong; that is in fact the
philosophical error which makes him an historian; it is really
present. And this is connected with another dilemma which he
states at the beginning of his whole argument: either we must
think of historical experience from inside, as it appears to the
historian, or from outside, as it appears to the philosopher; but
obviously our inquiry is a philosophical one, therefore we must
reject the historian's point of view altogether. Now, in the sequel
it appears to me that instead of abiding by this programme he
escapes between the horns of this second dilemma by expounding the nature of historical experience as it appears to one who
is simultaneously historian and philosopher. I say this because
his exposition of the nature of history, as it proceeds, clears up
points of principle where confusion and error would hamper,
and actually have hampered, the historian's own work. Unless
I am mistaken, Oakeshott himself is a more powerful historian
for having cleared up these points. His philosophy has got inside
his history; and instead of resulting in a situation where historical experience, remaining simply what it always was, has
been studied successfully by something quite different, namely,
philosophical thought, historical experience itself has been
revivified and illuminated by that thought.

Now let us return to the first dilemma: either past or present,
but not both. According to Oakeshott, the historian is an historian just because he makes the philosophical mistake of thinking that the present is past. But he himself has exploded that
error. An exploded error, if its refutation is really grasped, has
no more power over the intellect. The explosion of this error,
therefore, should result in the simple disappearance of history

as a mode of experience. But it does not; for Oakeshott, history remains a genuine and legitimate activity of thought. Why is this? I can only suppose it to be because the so-called error was not an error at all. Once more, there is an escape between the horns of the dilemma. The historian, if he thinks his past is a dead past, is certainly making a mistake; but Oakeshott supposes that there is no third alternative to the disjunction that the past is either a dead past or not past at all but simply present. The third alternative is that it should be a living past, a past which, because it was thought and not mere natural event, can be re-enacted in the present and in that re-enactment known as past. If this third alternative could be accepted, we should get the result that history is not based on a philosophical error and is therefore not in his sense a mode of experience, but an integral part of experience itself.

The reason why Oakeshott rules out this third alternative (which he does without any discussion or even mention of it) is, I think, connected with his failure to grasp the consequences of admitting that experience contains in itself an element of mediation, thought, or assertion of reality. Of a merely immediate experience, like that of sheer feeling (if there is such a thing), it is true that what is inside it cannot be also outside it. The subjective is merely subjective and cannot be also objective. But in an experience which is mediation or thought, that which is experienced is real, and is experienced as real. So far as historical experience is thought, therefore, what it experiences or thinks as past really is past. The fact that it is also present does not prevent it from being past, any more than, when I perceive a distant object, where perceiving means not only sensation but thought, the fact that I perceive it here prevents it from being there. If I look at the sun and am dazzled, my being dazzled is here only, in me and not in the sun; but in so far as I perceive the sun, by thinking 'what dazzles me is there in the sky', I perceive it as there, away from me. Similarly the historian thinks of his object as there, or rather then, away from him in time; and, because history is knowledge and not mere immediate experience, he can experience it both as then and as now: now in the immediacy of historical experience, but then in its mediacy.

In spite of this limitation, Oakeshott's work not only represents the high-water mark of English thought upon history, but shows a complete transcendence of the positivism in which that thought has been involved, and from which it has tried in vain to free itself, for at least half a century. It is therefore full of hope for the future of English historiography. True, it has failed to show that history is a necessary form of experience; it has only demonstrated that men are at liberty to be historians, not that they are under any obligation to be so; but, granted they choose to be, it has demonstrated their indefeasible right, and their peremptory duty, to play their game according to its own rules; to tolerate no interference, and listen to no analogies, from any outside quarter.

(vi) *Toynbee*

As a contrast with Oakeshott's work, which represents the transformation of historical thought from a positivistic stage to a new stage which I may perhaps call idealistic, by philosophical criticism of its principles from within, I may here mention Professor Arnold Toynbee's great *Study of History*,[1] which represents a restatement of the positivistic view itself. Toynbee has given us the first three volumes of a much larger projected work; and whatever may appear in the later volumes, these three have no doubt given a sufficient sample of his method and indication of his aims. In its details his work is enormously impressive by virtue of the almost incredible mass of erudition contained in it; but here I am concerned not with details but with principles. The main principle seems to be that the subject-matter of history is the lives of certain unitary divisions of the human species which Toynbee calls societies. One of these is our own, which he calls Western Christendom. Another is Eastern or Byzantine Christendom. A third is Islamic society: a fourth, Hindu society: a fifth, Far Eastern society. All these exist as civilizations at the present day, but we can also detect what appear to be fossilized relics of societies now extinct; one set of such relics including Monophysite and Nestorian Christians in the East, together with the Jews and Parsees, and another including the various branches of Buddhism and the Jains of

[1] Vols. i–iii, London 1934. [Collingwood wrote this passage in 1936 and it was not subsequently revised. Vols. iv–vi of *A Study of History* were published in 1939.]

India. Differences and relations between these societies he calls oecumenical; differences and relations within a single society, such as those between Athens and Sparta, or France and Germany, he regards as quite different in kind, and these he calls parochial. The field of the historian's study offers him an infinite variety of tasks, but among these the most important are concerned with discerning and distinguishing these entities called societies and studying the relations between them.

This study is pursued by means of certain general concepts or categories. One of these categories is *affiliation* and its correlative *apparentation*, exemplified for instance in the relation between our own society and the Hellenic society from which it is historically derived. Some societies are, so to speak, Melchizedek societies, not affiliated to any other; some have no others affiliated to them: some are interrelated through affiliation to the same parent society and so on: thus it is possible to arrange societies according to the concept of affiliation into various classes, exhibiting the concept in these various ways. Another category is that of *civilization*, as distinct from *primitive society*. Every society is either primitive or civilized; the vast majority are primitive, and these are in general relatively small in geographical extent and in population, relatively short-lived, and commonly meeting their end through violence, either at the hands of a civilized society or through destruction by another uncivilized one. Civilizations are rarer in number and individually larger in scale; but the important thing to bear in mind about them is that the unity which they form is the unity not of an individual but of a class. There is no one thing, civilization, except in the sense of the common character 'civilizedness' belonging to the many different civilizations. The unity of civilization is an illusion fostered by the peculiar way in which our own civilization has entangled all others in the meshes of its own economic system, and is at once dispelled if instead of attending to the economic map of the world we look at its cultural map. Another category is that of *interregnum* or *time of troubles*, the chaotic period between the decay of one society and the rise of one affiliated to it, like the European Dark Ages between the death of Hellenism and the rise of Western Christendom. Another is that of the *internal proletariat*, the body of persons within a society which owes nothing to that society except its physical life, although it may very well become the dominant element in the society affiliated to it, e.g. the Christians towards the close of the Hellenic society. Another is that of the *external proletariat*, or barbarian world surrounding a given society, which joins hands with the internal proletariat to break it up when its creative power is exhausted. Others are the *universal State* and *universal Church*, organizations concentrating in themselves the entire political and religious life respectively of the society in which they arise. By studying historical records in the light of these categories we can detect many societies now extinct which have been civilized in their time: a Syriac, a Minoan, a Sumeric, a Hittite, a Babylonic, an Andean, a Yucatec, a Mexic, a Mayan, and an Egyptiac, this last the longest-lived of all, for it lasted from the 4th millennium B.C. to the first century A.D.

With these prolegomena, Toynbee gets to work on his main task, which is the comparative study of civilizations. His first chief question is how and why civilizations arise: his second, how and why they grow; his third, how and why they break down. He then goes on, according to the general plan prefixed to his first volume, to study the nature of universal states and universal churches, heroic ages, and contacts between civilizations in space and time; the whole work is to close with sections on the prospects of Western civilization and on 'the inspirations of historians'.

I began discussing Toynbee's work by saying that it represented a restatement of historical positivism. What I meant was that the principles which constitute its individuality are principles derived from the methodology of natural science. These principles are based on the conception of external relations. The natural scientist finds himself confronted by separate, discrete facts which can be counted: or alternatively he cuts up the phenomena that confront him into such countable discrete facts. He then proceeds to determine the relations between them, these relations being always links connecting one fact with another external to it. A collection of facts thus linked together forms, again, a single fact whose relations to others of the same order are of the same external kind. If the scientist's methods are to work at all, the first thing necessary is that a

clear line should be drawn between one fact and another. There
must be no overlapping.

These are the principles on which Toynbee deals with history.
The first thing he does is to cut up the field of historical study
into a specifiable number of distinct sections, each called a
society. Each society is wholly self-contained. It is for Toynbee
a very important question whether Western Christendom is a
continuation of Hellenic society or a different society related
to it by way of affiliation. The right answer, according to him,
is the second. Anyone who gives the first, or who blurs the
absolute distinction between the two answers, has committed
an unpardonable offence against the first canon of historical
method as he conceives it. We are not allowed to say that
Hellenic civilization has turned into Western Christendom by a
process of development involving the accentuation of some of
its elements, the fading away of others, and the emergence of
certain new elements within itself and the borrowing of others
from external sources. The philosophical principle involved in
saying that would be the principle that a civilization may
develop into new forms while yet remaining itself, whereas
Toynbee's principle is that if a civilization changes it ceases to
be itself and a new civilization comes into being. And this
dilemma as regards development in time holds good equally
with regard to contacts in space. Such contacts are external
contacts between one society and another; they therefore presuppose a clean cut between one society and its neighbours. We
must be able to say exactly where one society leaves off and
another begins. We are not allowed to say that one shades off
into the next.

This is the positivistic conception of individuality, the conception according to which the individual is constituted as such
by being cut off from everything else by a sharp boundary
distinguishing clearly what is within it from what is outside.
The inner and the outer are mutually exclusive. This is the kind
of individuality which is possessed by a stone or any other
material body. It is the primary characteristic of the world
of nature, and distinguishes that world from the world of mind,
where individuality consists not of separateness from environment but of the power to absorb environment into itself. It is
therefore not what individuality means in history, so far as the

world of history is a world of mind. The historian who studies
a civilization other than his own can apprehend the mental life
of that civilization only by re-enacting its experience for himself.
If the Western European of to-day studies Hellenic civilization
historically, he enters into possession of the mental wealth of
that civilization and makes it an integral part of his own. As
a matter of fact, Western civilization has formed itself by doing
exactly this, by reconstructing within its own mind the mind
of the Hellenic world and developing the wealth of that mind
in new directions. Thus Western civilization is not related to
Hellenic in any merely external way. The relation is an internal
one. Western civilization expresses, and indeed achieves, its
individuality not by distinguishing itself from Hellenic civilization but by identifying itself therewith.

Toynbee has failed to see this because his general conception
of history is ultimately naturalistic; he regards the life of a
society as a natural and not a mental life, something at bottom
merely biological and best understood on biological analogies.
And this is connected with the fact that he never reaches the
conception of historical knowledge as the re-enactment of the
past in the historian's mind. He regards history as a mere
spectacle, something consisting of facts observed and recorded
by the historian, phenomena presented externally to his gaze,
not experiences into which he must enter and which he must
make his own. This is merely a way of saying that he has not
undertaken any philosophical analysis of the way in which his
historical knowledge has been attained. He possesses enormous
quantities of it, but he treats it as if it were something he finds
ready-made in books, and the problem that interests him is only
the problem of arranging it when collected. His whole scheme
is really a scheme of pigeon-holes elaborately arranged and
labelled, into which ready-made historical facts can be put.
Such schemes are not in themselves vicious; but they always
entail certain dangers: notably the danger of forgetting that the
facts thus pigeon-holed have to be separated from their context
by an act of dissection. This act, become habitual, leads to an
obsession: one forgets that the historical fact, as it actually exists
and as the historian actually knows it, is always a process in
which something is changing into something else. This element
of process is the life of history. In order to pigeon-hole historical

facts, the living body of history must first be killed (that is, its essential character as process must be denied) so that it may be dissected.

The criticism which must be passed on Toynbee's principles is thus twofold. First, he regards history itself, the historical process, as cut up by sharp lines into mutually exclusive parts, and denies the continuity of the process in virtue of which every part overlaps and interpenetrates others. His distinction between societies or civilizations is really a distinction between focal points in the process: he has misunderstood it as a distinction between chunks or lumps of fact into which the process is divided. Secondly, he misconceives the relation between the historical process and the historian who knows it. He regards the historian as the intelligent spectator of history, in the same way in which the scientist is the intelligent spectator of nature: he fails to see that the historian is an integral element in the process of history itself, reviving in himself the experiences of which he achieves historical knowledge. Just as the various parts of the process are misconceived as placed outside one another, so the process as a whole and the historian are placed outside one another. And these two criticisms come in the last resort to the same thing: namely that history is converted into nature, and the past, instead of living in the present, as it does in history, is conceived as a dead past, as it is in nature. But at the same time I must add that this criticism only affects fundamental principles. In the detail of his work, Toynbee shows a very fine historical sense and only rarely allows his actual historical judgements to be falsified by the errors in his principles. One place where this does happen is in his judgement of the Roman Empire, which he regards as a mere phase in the decline of Hellenism. That is to say, because its relation to Greece is too close to permit of its being regarded as a distinct civilization, and because that is the only condition on which he could allow it a genuine achievement of its own, his dilemma forces him to ignore all that it did achieve and to treat it as a mere phenomenon of decay. But in history as it actually happens there are no mere phenomena of decay: every decline is also a rise, and it is only the historian's personal failures of knowledge or sympathy—partly due to mere ignorance, partly to the preoccupations of his own practical life—that prevent him from seeing this double character, at once creative and destructive, of any historical process whatever.

§ 2. *Germany*

(i) *Windelband*

In Germany, the home of historical criticism, a great deal of interest was taken towards the end of the nineteenth century, and increasingly after it, in the theory of history and, in particular, the nature of the distinction between it and science. Among the heirlooms which Germany inherited from her great philosophical period, the age of Kant and Hegel, was the idea that Nature and History were in some sense two distinct worlds each with a character of its own. Philosophers of the nineteenth century used to repeat the distinction as a commonplace, which passed from hand to mouth so often that its significance was worn quite flat in the process. Lotze, for example, in his *Microcosmus*, published in 1856, asserted that Nature is the realm of necessity and History the realm of freedom: an echo of post-Kantian idealism which, in Lotze, means nothing definite, as the vague and empty chapters on history in that work prove all too clearly. Lotze inherited from the German idealists, and in particular from Kant, the idea that man has a dual nature; a physiologist by early training, he insisted that man's body is nothing but a bundle of mechanisms, but at the same time he held that man's mind is free: thus man as body inhabits the world of nature but as mind he inhabits the world of history. But instead of working out the relation between these two things, as the great idealists had done, Lotze left the whole question in the air and never attempted to think it out at all. His work is characteristic of the woolly and emotional nebulosities which in Germany followed the collapse of the idealist school.

Other German writers used other formulae for characterizing the terms of the same familiar antithesis. In his *Grundriss der Historik* (Jena, 1858) the distinguished historian Droysen defined nature as the coexistence of being (*das Nebeneinander des Seienden*) and history as the succession of becoming (*das Nacheinander des Gewordenen*); a merely rhetorical antithesis which owed any plausibility it might possess to overlooking the fact that in the world of nature too there are events and processes which follow one another in a determinate order, and that in history there are things which coexist, like liberalism and capitalism, and whose coexistence is a problem for historical thought. The triviality of such formulae showed that people were merely presupposing the distinction between nature and history, not trying to understand it.

The first genuine attempt to understand it came with the advent of the neo-Kantian school late in the century. It followed from the general principles of this school that, to understand the difference between nature and history, one must approach the distinction from the subjective side: that is, one must distinguish the ways in which the scientist and the historian do their thinking. It was from this point of view that Windelband, the eminent historian of philosophy, approached the subject in a Rectorial Address,[1] delivered at Strassburg in 1894, which at once became famous.

Here he laid it down that history and science were two different things each with a method of its own. Science, he explained, had as its purpose the formulation of general laws: history, the description of individual facts. This distinction he pompously baptized by saying that there were two kinds of science (*Wissenschaft*): *nomothetic* science, which is science in the common sense of the word, and *idiographic* science, which is history. This distinction between science as knowledge of the universal and history as knowledge of the individual was in itself of very small value. It was not even accurate as a statement of the prima facie difference: for the judgement 'this is a case of typhoid fever' is not history but science, although it is a description of individual fact, and the statement 'all Roman silver of the third century is debased' is not science but history although it is a generalization. Of course, there is a sense in which Windelband's distinction can be defended against this criticism: the generalization about third-century coinage is really a statement about an individual fact, namely the monetary policy of the late Roman Empire; and the diagnosis of this disease as typhoid is not so much an individual judgement as the subsumption of a certain fact under a general formula, namely, the definition of typhoid. The business of the scientist as such is not to diagnose

[1] *Geschichte und Naturwissenschaft.* Reprinted in *Präludien*, vol. ii (5th edn., Tübingen, 1915), pp. 136–60.

typhoid in a particular case (though in a subsidiary way that is his business too) but to define it in its general nature; and the business of the historian as such is to explore the individual features of individual historical events, not to construct generalizations, though that too is a thing that enters into his work as a secondary feature. But when this is said, it is admitted that the formulation of laws and the description of individuals are not two mutually exclusive forms of thought, between which the whole field of reality can be divided by an amicable agreement, as Windelband thinks.

All that Windelband is really doing in his discussion of the relation between science and history is to put forward a claim on the part of historians to do their own work in their own way and be let alone; it represents a kind of secessionist movement of historians from the general body of a civilization in thrall to natural science. But what this work is, and what is the way in which it can or should be done, Windelband cannot tell us. Nor is he conscious of this inability. When he speaks of an 'idiographic science' he is implying that there can be scientific, i.e. rational or non-empirical, knowledge of the individual; but, strange as it may seem in so learned an historian of thought, he does not realize that the whole tradition of European philosophy from the early Greeks to his own day had declared with one voice that this knowledge is an impossibility: the individual, as a fleeting and transient existence, can only be perceived or experienced as it occurs and can never be the object of that stable and logically constructed thing which is called scientific knowledge. The point had been very clearly made by Schopenhauer:[1]

'History lacks the fundamental characteristic of science, namely the subordination of the objects of consciousness; all it can do is to present a simple co-ordination of the facts it has registered. Hence there is no system in history as there is in the other sciences . . . . The sciences, being systems of cognitions, speak always of kinds; history always of individuals. History, therefore, would be a science of individuals, which implies a self-contradiction.'

To this self-contradiction Windelband shows himself strangely blind, especially in such passages as that in which he congratu-

---

[1] *Die Welt als Wille und Vorstellung* (3rd edn., 1859), vol. ii, pp. 499–509, *Über Geschichte*.

lates his modern countrymen on replacing the old-fashioned word 'history', *Geschichte*, by the new and better one *Kulturwissenschaft*, science of culture. The only change really introduced by this word lies in the fact of its verbal similarity to the name of a natural science; that is to say, the sole reason for adopting it is that it enables people to forget how deep is the difference between history and natural science and to slur over the distinction in the positivistic manner, by assimilating history to the general pattern of science.

So far as Windelband dealt at all with the question how there can be a science of the individual, he answered it by saying that the historian's knowledge of historical events consists of judgements of value, that is, pronouncements on the spiritual worth of the actions which he is investigating. Thus the historian's thought is ethical thought, and history is a branch of morals. But this is to answer the question how history can be a science by saying that it is not a science. In his *Introduction to Philosophy*,[1] Windelband divides the whole subject-matter into two parts: the theory of knowledge and the theory of value, and history falls in the second part. Thus history ends by being extruded from the sphere of knowledge altogether, and we are left with the conclusion that what the historian does with the individual is not to know or think it, but somehow to intuit its value; an activity on the whole akin to that of the artist. But, once more, the relation between history and art is not systematically thought out

(ii) *Rickert*

Closely connected with Windelband's thought, but much more systematic, is that of Rickert, whose first work on the subject was published at Freiburg in 1896. Rickert maintains in effect that Windelband was really stating two distinctions between science and history instead of one. The first is the distinction between generalizing and individualizing thought: the second, the distinction between valuing and non-valuing thought. Combining these two, he gets four types of sciences: (1) non-valuing and generalizing, or pure natural science; (2) non-valuing and individualizing, or the quasi-historical sciences of nature like geology, evolutionary biology, &c.; (3) valuing

[1] Eng. tr. London [1921].

and generalizing, or the quasi-scientific sciences of history like sociology, economics, theoretical jurisprudence, and so forth; (4) valuing and individualizing, or history proper. Further, he sees that Windelband's attempt to divide reality into two mutually exclusive spheres of nature and history cannot be defended. Nature as it really exists does not consist of laws; it consists of individual facts, just like history. Consequently Rickert arrives at the formula that reality as a whole is really history. Natural science is a network of generalizations and formulae built up by the human intellect: in the last resort an arbitrary intellectual construction, not corresponding to. any reality. This is the idea expressed in the title of his book, *Die Grenzen der naturwissenschaftlichen Begriffsbildung*, the limits of the formation of scientific concepts. Thus, his four kinds of sciences together form a scale having at one end the extreme case of arbitrary and abstract thought, a mere manipulation of artificial concepts: at the other, the extreme case of concrete and genuine knowledge, the knowledge of reality in its individual existence.

At first sight this seems a conclusive counter-attack on positivism. Natural science, from being held up as the one and only type of genuine knowledge, has been degraded to the position of an arbitrary play of abstractions, constructed in the air and achieving its perfection just so far as it leaves out the actual truth of concrete fact: history is regarded not only as a possible and legitimate form of knowledge but as the only genuine knowledge that exists or can exist. But this *revanche* not only fails in doing justice to natural science, it also misunderstands history. Rickert regards nature, after the positivistic manner, as cut up into separate facts and he goes on to deform history by regarding it in a similar way as an assemblage of individual facts supposed to differ from the facts of nature only in being vehicles of value. But the essence of history lies not in its consisting of individual facts, however valuable these facts may be, but in the process or development leading from one to another. Rickert fails to see that the peculiarity of historical thought is the way in which the historian's mind, as the mind of the present day, apprehends the process by which this mind itself has come into existence through the mental development of the past. He fails to see that what gives value to past facts is the fact that they are not mere past facts, they are not a dead past but a living past, a heritage of past thoughts which by the work of his historical consciousness the historian makes his own. The past cut off from the present, converted into a mere spectacle, can have no value at all; it is history converted into nature. Thus, in the long run, positivism has its revenge on Rickert; historical facts become mere disjointed occurrences, and as such can stand to each other only in the same kind of external relations of time and space, contiguity, resemblance, and causation, as the facts of nature.

(iii) *Simmel*

A third attempt at a philosophy of history, taking shape during the same period, was that of Simmel, whose first essay[1] on the subject dates from 1892. Simmel's was a lively and versatile mind, gifted with a good deal of originality and penetration, but defective in solid thought; and his work on history is full of good observations but of little value as a systematic study of the problem. He realized vividly that for the historian there can be no question of knowing facts in an empirical sense of the word 'know': the historian can never be acquainted with his object, precisely because that object is the past: it consists of events that have finished happening and are no longer there to be observed. Consequently the problem of distinguishing history from science as Windelband and Rickert stated it does not arise. The facts of nature and the facts of history are not facts in the same sense of the word. The facts of nature are what the scientist can perceive or produce in the laboratory under his own eyes; the facts of history are not 'there' at all: all that the historian has before him are documents and relics from which he has somehow to reconstruct the facts. Further, he sees that history is an affair of spirit, of human personalities, and that the only thing that enables the historian to reconstruct it is the fact that he himself is a spirit and a personality. All this is excellent. But now comes Simmel's problem. The historian, beginning from his documents, constructs in his own mind what professes to be a picture of the past. This picture is in his mind and nowhere else; it is a subjective mental construction. But he claims that this subjective construction possesses objective

---

[1] *Die Probleme der Geschichtsphilosophie* (Leipzig).

truth. How can this be? How can the merely subjective picture constructed in the historian's mind be projected into the past and described as something that actually happened?

Once more, it is greatly to Simmel's credit that he sees this problem. But he cannot solve it. He can only say that the historian feels convinced of the objective reality of his subjective constructions: he regards them as something real, irrespectively of his thinking them at this moment. But obviously, this is no solution. The question is not whether the historian feels this conviction, but by what right he feels it. Is it an illusion, or is it based on some solid ground? Simmel cannot answer that question. And the reason seems to be that he has not gone far enough in his criticism of the notion of historical fact. He has rightly seen that past facts, as past, are not present to the historian's perception; but because he has not sufficiently grasped the nature of the historical process he does not realize that the historian's own mind is heir to the past and has come to be what it is through the development of the past into the present, so that in him the past is living in the present. He thinks of the historical past as a dead past, and when he asks how the historian can revive it in his own mind he naturally can give no answer. He has confused the historical process, in which the past lives on in the present, with a natural process, in which the past dies when the present is born. This reduction of the historical process to a natural process is part of the legacy of positivism, so that here once more Simmel's failure to construct a philosophy of history is due to his incomplete escape from a positivistic point of view.

(iv) *Dilthey*

The best work done on the subject during this period was that of the lonely and neglected genius Dilthey, whose first and only book upon it was published as early as 1883 and was called *Introduction to the Sciences of Mind* (*Einleitung in die Geisteswissenschaften*). But he continued until 1910 to publish scattered essays, always interesting and important, partly on the history of thought, notably a series of very able studies on the formation of the modern mind since the Renaissance and Reformation, and partly on the theory of history. It was his intention to write a great *Critique of Historical Reason* on the model of the Kantian critiques, but this intention was never carried out.

In the *Introduction to the Sciences of Mind* he took up the position, eleven years before Windelband, that history deals with concrete individuals and natural science with abstract generalizations. But this never led him to a satisfactory philosophy of history, because the individuals of which he was thinking were conceived as isolated past facts and were not integrated into a genuine process of historical development. We have already seen (Pt. III, § 9) that this way of conceiving history was the characteristic weakness of historical thought itself during that period, and also that the same conception in Windelband and Rickert blocked the way to a true understanding of the philosophical problem of history.

But Dilthey was not satisfied with this position. In later essays[1] he raises the question how the historian actually performs the work of coming to know the past, starting as he does simply from documents and data which do not by themselves reveal it. These data, he replies, offer him only the occasion for reliving in his own mind the spiritual activity which originally produced them. It is in virtue of his own spiritual life, and in proportion to the intrinsic richness of that life, that he can thus infuse life into the dead materials with which he finds himself confronted. Thus genuine historical knowledge is an inward experience (*Erlebnis*) of its own object, whereas scientific knowledge is the attempt to understand (*begreifen*) phenomena presented to him as outward spectacles. This conception of the historian as living in his object, or rather making his object live in him, is a great advance on anything achieved by any of Dilthey's German contemporaries. But a problem still remains, because life for Dilthey means immediate experience, as distinct from reflection or knowledge; and it is not enough for the historian to *be* Julius Caesar or Napoleon, since that does not constitute a knowledge of Julius Caesar or Napoleon any more than the obvious fact that he *is* himself constitutes a knowledge of himself.

This problem Dilthey tries to solve by recourse to psychology. By existing at all, I am myself; but it is only by means of psychological analysis that I come to know myself, that is, to understand the structure of my own personality. Similarly, the

[1] *Gesammelte Schriften*, vol. vii.

historian who relives the past in his own mind must, if he is to be
an historian, understand the past which he is reliving. By simply
reliving it, he is developing and enlarging his own personality,
incorporating in his own experience the experience of others in
the past; but whatever is so incorporated becomes part of the
structure of his personality, and the rule still holds good that
this structure can be understood only in terms of psychology.
What this means in practice may be seen from one of Dilthey's
last works, in which he deals with the history of philosophy
according to his own formula, reducing it to a study in the
psychology of philosophers, on the principle that there are certain fundamental types of mental structure, and that each type
has a certain necessary attitude to, and conception of, the world.[1]
The differences between different philosophies are thus reduced
to mere resultants of differences in psychological structure or
disposition. But this way of treating the subject makes nonsense of it. The only question that matters about a philosophy
is whether it is right or wrong. If a given philosopher thinks as
he does because, being that kind of man, he cannot help thinking
like that, this question does not arise. Philosophy handled
from this psychological point of view ceases to be philosophy
at all.

This shows that something has gone wrong with Dilthey's
argument, and it is not difficult to see what it is. Psychology is
not history but science, a science constructed on naturalistic
principles. To say that history becomes intelligible only when
conceived in terms of psychology is to say that historical knowledge is impossible and that the only kind of knowledge is
scientific knowledge: history by itself is mere life, immediate
experience, and therefore the historian as such merely experiences a life which the psychologist as such and he alone
understands. Dilthey has come up against the question which
Windelband and the rest had not the penetration to recognize:
the question how there can be a knowledge, as distinct from an
immediate experience, of the individual. He has answered that
question by admitting that there cannot be such a knowledge,
and falling back on the positivistic view that the only way in
which the universal (the proper object of knowledge) can be
known is by means of natural science or a science constructed

[1] *Das Wesen der Philosophie* (*Gesammelte Schriften*, vol. v).

on naturalistic principles. Thus in the end he, like the rest of his generation, surrenders to positivism.

The point at which his argument goes wrong is no less easy to identify. Dilthey, as I have explained, argues that to be myself is one thing, namely immediate experience: to understand myself is another, namely psychological science. He assumes that the self-knowledge of mind is identical with psychology. But on his own showing history has a good claim to share that title. I may now be experiencing an immediate feeling of discomfort, and I may ask myself why I have this feeling. I may answer that question by reflecting that this morning I received a letter criticizing my conduct in what seems to me a valid and unanswerable manner. Here I am not making psychological generalizations; I am recognizing in its detail a certain individual event or series of events, which are already present to my consciousness as a feeling of discomfort or dissatisfaction with myself. To understand that feeling is to recognize it as the outcome of a certain historical process. Here the self-understanding of my mind is nothing else than historical knowledge. Push the case a step farther. When, as an historian, I relive in my own mind a certain experience of Julius Caesar, I am not simply being Julius Caesar; on the contrary, I am myself, and know that I am myself; the way in which I incorporate Julius Caesar's experience in my own personality is not by confusing myself with him, but by distinguishing myself from him and at the same time making his experience my own. The living past of history lives in the present; but it lives not in the immediate experience of the present, but only in the self-knowledge of the present. This Dilthey has overlooked; he thinks it lives in the present's immediate experience of itself; but that immediate experience is not historical thought.

Dilthey and Simmel have in fact chosen opposite horns of the same false dilemma. Each realizes that the historical past, that is, the experience and thought of the agents whose acts the historian studies, must become part of the historian's own personal experience. Each then argues that this experience, because his own, is merely private and personal, an immediate experience within his own mind and nothing objective. Each sees that it must be something objective if it is to be an object of historical knowledge. But how can it be objective when it is

purely subjective? How can it be something knowable if it is
merely a state of his own mind? Simmel says, by projecting it
into the past: with the result that history becomes merely the
illusory projection of our own states of mind upon the blank
screen of the unknowable past. Dilthey says, by becoming the
object of psychological analysis: with the result that history
disappears altogether and is replaced by psychology. The
answer to both doctrines is that since the past is not a dead
past but lives on in the present, the historian's knowledge is not
exposed to the dilemma at all: it is not either knowledge of the
past and therefore not knowledge of the present, or else knowledge of the present and therefore not knowledge of the past; it
is knowledge of the past in the present, the self-knowledge of
the historian's own mind as the present revival and reliving of
past experiences.

These four men between them started a vigorous movement
in Germany for the study of the philosophy of history. Wilhelm
Bauer, in his *Introduction to the Study of History*,[1] went so far as
to say that in his own time the philosophy of history was being
much more actively pursued than history itself. But although
books and pamphlets on the subject have poured from the press,
genuinely new ideas have been rare. The general problem bequeathed to posterity by the writers I have analysed may be
stated by saying that it concerns the distinction between history
and natural science, or historical process and natural process.
It starts from the positivistic principle that natural science is the
only true form of knowledge, which implies that all processes
are natural processes; the problem is how to get away from that
principle. Over and over again, as we have seen, the principle
has been denied, but those who denied it have never completely
freed their minds from its influence. However strongly they
have insisted that history is a development and a spiritual development, they have failed to make good the implications of
these phrases and have uniformly, in the last resort, fallen back
on thinking of history as if it were nature. The peculiarity of
an historical or spiritual process is that since the mind is that
which knows itself, the historical process which is the life of the
mind is a self-knowing process: a process which understands
itself, criticizes itself, values itself, and so forth. The German

---

[1] *Einführung in das Studium der Geschichte* (Tübingen, 1921).

school of *Geschichtsphilosophie* has never grasped this. It has always regarded history as an object confronting the historian in the same way in which nature confronts the scientist: the task of understanding, valuing, or criticizing it is not done by itself for itself, it is done to it by the historian standing outside it. The result of this is that the spirituality or subjectivity which properly belongs to the historical life of mind itself is taken away from it and given to the historian. This converts the historical process into a natural process, a process intelligible to an intelligent spectator but not to itself. The life of mind thus conceived remains a life but ceases to be a mental life; it becomes a merely physiological life or at best a life of irrational instinct: a life which, however emphatically it is called a spiritual life, is being conceived as a natural life. The German movement of which I am speaking thus never succeeds in escaping from naturalism, that is, from the conversion of mind into nature.

(v) *Meyer*

At the close of the nineteenth century the extreme form of this naturalism may be seen in the positivistic historians like K. Lamprecht, P. Barth, E. Bernheim, the author of a well-known handbook of historical method,[1] K. Breysig, and other writers, who have conceived the true or highest task of history as the discovery of causal laws connecting certain constant types of historical phenomena. Perversions of history on these lines all share one characteristic in common, namely a distinction between two kinds of history: empirical history, which merely discharges the humble office of ascertaining the facts, and philosophical or scientific history, which has the nobler task of discovering the laws connecting the facts. Wherever this distinction is detected, the cloven hoof of naturalism has betrayed itself. There is no such thing as empirical history, for the facts are not empirically present to the historian's mind: they are past events, to be apprehended not empirically but by a process of inference according to rational principles from data given or rather discovered in the light of these principles; and there is no such thing as the supposed further stage of philosophical or scientific history which discovers their causes or laws or in general explains them, because an historical fact once

[1] *Lehrbuch der historischen Methode* (Leipzig, 1889), 6th edn., 1908.

genuinely ascertained, grasped by the historian's re-enactment
of the agent's thought in his own mind, is already explained.
For the historian there is no difference between discovering
what happened and discovering why it happened.

The best historians everywhere are conscious of this in their
own actual work, and in Germany many of them, partly through
their experience of actual research and partly through the influence of the philosophers already discussed, have now come
to realize enough of it to resist the claims of positivism at
least in its extremer forms. But their realization of it down
to the present has generally been at best partial, and consequently even the strongest opponents of positivism have been
a good deal influenced by it and have taken up a somewhat
confused position on questions of theory and method.

A good example of this is afforded by Eduard Meyer, one of
the most distinguished of recent German historians, whose essay
on *The Theory and Methodology of History* (*Zur Theorie und
Methodik der Geschichte*), published at Halle in 1902 and later
reissued in a revised form,[1] shows how a first-rate historian
of long experience thought about the principles of his own work
at the beginning of the present century. Here, as in Bury but
far more clearly thought out, we find an attempt to disentangle
history from errors and fallacies due to the influence of natural
science: an anti-positivistic view of its task, which in the long
run fails to rise decisively above the atmosphere of positivism.

Meyer begins by a detailed and penetrating criticism of the
positivistic tendency, which was prevalent in the nineties and
to which I have just referred. If the task of history is supposed
to consist in ascertaining general laws governing the course of
historical events, it is expurgated of three factors which are
in reality of high importance: chance or accident, free will, and
ideas or the demands and conceptions of men. The historically
significant is identified with the typical or recurring: thus history becomes the history of groups or societies, and the individual disappears from it except in the guise of a mere instance
of general laws. The task of history, so conceived, is to establish
certain social and psychological types of life, following one
another in a determinate order. Meyer quotes Lamprecht[2] as

---

[1] *Kleine Schriften* (Halle, 1910), pp. 3–67.
[2] In *Zukunft*, 2 Jan. 1897.

the leading exponent of this idea. Lamprecht distinguished[1] six phases of this kind in the life of the German nation, and generalized this result for application to every national history. But by such analysis, says Meyer, the living figures of history are destroyed and their place is taken by vague generalities and unreal phantoms. The result is a reign of empty catchwords. As against all this, Meyer contends that the proper object of historical thought is historical fact in its individuality, and that chance and free will are determining causes that cannot be banished from history without destroying its very essence. Not only is the historian as such uninterested in the so-called laws of this pseudo-science, but there are no historical laws. Breysig[2] has attempted to state twenty-four of them, but every one is either false or so vague that history can find no value in them. They may serve as clues for investigating historical facts, but they lack all necessity. The historian's failure to establish them results not from poverty of material or weakness of intellect, but from the nature of historical knowledge itself, whose business is the discovery and exposition of events in their individuality.

When Meyer leaves polemics and goes on to expound the positive principles of historical thought, he begins by laying down the first principle that its object is past events or rather changes as such. Theoretically, therefore, it deals with any and every change, but by custom it deals only with those in human affairs. This limitation, however, he does not explain or defend. Yet it is of crucial importance, and his failure to explain it is a serious weakness in his theory. The real reason for it is that the historian is not concerned with events as such but with actions, i.e. events brought about by the will and expressing the thought of a free and intelligent agent, and discovers this thought by rethinking it in his own mind: but this Meyer fails to see, and he never gets farther towards answering the question 'What is an historical fact?' than to say: 'An historical fact is a past event.'

The first consequence of this failure is an embarrassment over the distinction between the infinite multiplicity of events that have actually happened and the much smaller number of events which the historian is able or anxious to investigate. Meyer

---

[1] *Deutsche Geschichte* (Berlin, 1892).
[2] *Der Stufenbau und die Gesetze der Weltgeschichte* (Berlin, 1905).

bases this distinction on the fact that the historian can know
only those events for which he has evidence: but even then, the
number of knowable events far exceeds the number of those that
are historically interesting. Many events are knowable and
known, but no historian thinks of them as historical events.
What then constitutes the historicity of an event? For Meyer,
those events are historical which have been efficacious (*wirksam*),
i.e. have produced consequences. For example, the philosophy
of Spinoza was for a long time quite without influence, but later
people became interested in it and it began to influence their
thought. Hence from being a non-historical fact it became an
historical one: it is non-historical for the historian of the seventeenth century but becomes historical for the historian of the
eighteenth. This is surely a quite arbitrary and perverse distinction. For the historian of the seventeenth century Spinoza is
a highly interesting phenomenon, whether or not he was read
and accepted as a leader of thought; because the formation of
his philosophy was in itself a noteworthy achievement of the
seventeenth-century mind. What makes that philosophy an
object of our historical study is not the fact that Novalis or
Hegel studied it but the fact that *we* can study it, reconstruct it
in our own minds, and thus appreciate its philosophical value.

Meyer's false position here is due to a relic in his own thought
of the positivistic spirit against which he was protesting. He
sees that a mere past event taken in isolation cannot be an
object of historical knowledge, but he thinks that it becomes one
in virtue of its connexions with other events, these connexions
being conceived by him in the positivistic manner as external
causal connexions. This, however, begs the question. If the
historical importance of an event is defined as its efficacy in
producing further events, what constitutes the historical importance of those others? For he would hardly hold that an
event becomes historically important through producing consequences themselves devoid of historical importance. If,
however, the historical importance of Spinoza consists in his in-
fluencing the German Romantics, wherein consists the historical
importance of the German Romantics? Pursuing this line of
inquiry we shall ultimately reach the present day, and conclude
that the historical importance of Spinoza is his importance to
us here and now. Further we cannot go; for, as Meyer observes,

it is impossible to judge the historical importance of anything in the present, since we cannot yet tell what is going to come of it.

This reflection deprives of its value a great deal of Meyer's positive theory concerning historical method. The whole conception of the historical past as consisting of events linked together in causal series is fundamental for that theory. On it depends Meyer's conception of historical research, as the search for causes; of historical necessity, as the determination of an event by such causes; of historical contingency or chance, as the intersection of two or more causal series; of historical importance, as the productiveness of further events in series: and so forth. All these conceptions are tainted by positivism and consequently fallacious.

The valuable side of his theory consists in his doctrine of historical interest. Here alone he shows real grasp on a truth of principle. Having realized that even when we confine ourselves to important events in the sense above defined, we are still confronted with an embarrassingly large number of them, he goes on to reduce this number by appeal to a new principle of selection based on the interest of the historian and of the present-day life of which the historian is a representative. It is the historian as a living agent who brings out of himself the problems whose solution he desires to find and thus constructs the clues with which he is to approach his material. This subjective element is an essential factor in all historical knowledge. Yet even here Meyer does not grasp the full import of his own doctrine. He is still worried by the fact that however much information we have concerning a given period we still might obtain more, and this more might modify the results already thought secure. Hence, he argues, all historical knowledge is uncertain. He fails to see that the historian's problem is a present problem, not a future one: it is to interpret the material now available, not to anticipate future discoveries. To quote Oakeshott again, the word 'truth' has no meaning for the historian unless it means 'what the evidence obliges us to believe'.

Meyer's great merit lies in his effective criticism of the openly positivistic sociological pseudo-history fashionable in his time. In details, too, his essay constantly reveals a lively sense of historical reality. But where his theory breaks down is in his failure to press his attack on positivism to its logical conclusion.

He is content to acquiesce in a naïve realism which treats historical fact as one thing and the historian's knowledge of it as another. He thus conceives history in the last resort as a mere spectacle seen from outside, not as a process to which the historian himself is integral as at once part of it and the self-consciousness of it. All intimacy in the relation between the historian and his subject-matter disappears, the conception of historical importance becomes meaningless, and consequently Meyer's principles of historical method, depending as they do on the selection of the important, vanish into thin air.

(vi) *Spengler*

In sharp contrast to Meyer's work, and to the work of the better twentieth-century German historians, is Oswald Spengler's relapse into positivistic naturalism. *Der Untergang des Abendlandes*[1] has had such a vogue in this country and in America, as well as in Germany, that it may be worth while to indicate here again my reasons for regarding it as radically unsound.

According to Spengler, history is a succession of self-contained individual units which he calls cultures. Each culture has a special character of its own; each exists in order to express this character in every detail of its life and development. But each resembles all the others in having an identical life-cycle, resembling that of an organism. It begins with the barbarism of a primitive society; it goes on to develop a political organization, arts and sciences, and so forth, at first in a stiff and archaic manner, then blossoming into its classical period, then congealing into decadence, and finally sinking into a new type of barbarism where everything is commercialized and vulgarized, and here its life ends. Out of this decadent condition nothing new emerges; that culture is dead and its creative power is spent. Further, not only is the cycle of phases fixed, but the time which it takes is fixed; so that if we nowadays, for example, can detect the point at which we stand in the cycle of our own culture, we can accurately foretell what the future phases of it will be.

This conception is openly positivistic. For history itself is substituted a morphology of history, a naturalistic science whose

[1] Eng. tr.: *The Decline of the West*, 2 vols., London, 1926–8. For a fuller consideration of the book see my article in *Antiquity*, vol. i, 1927, pp. 311–25.

value consists in external analysis, the establishment of general laws, and (conclusive mark of non-historical thought) the claim to foretell the future on scientific principles. The facts are positivistically conceived as isolated from each other instead of growing organically out of each other; but the facts are now huge chunks of fact—bigger and better facts, each with a fixed internal structure, but each related to the others non-historically. Their only interrelations are (a) temporal and spatial, (b) morphological, i.e. relations consisting in similarity of structure. This anti-historical and merely naturalistic view of history infects even Spengler's conception of the inner detail of each culture taken by itself; for the succession of phases within a culture, as he conceives it, is no more historical than the succession of the various phases in the life of an insect as egg, larva, pupa, and imago. Thus at every point the idea of historical process as a mental process, where the past is conserved in the present, is elaborately denied. Every phase in a culture turns automatically into the next when its time is ripe, irrespectively of what the individual persons living in it may do. Further, the unique characteristic which marks off any one culture from any other and pervades all its details (the Greekness of Greek culture, the Western-Europeanness of Western European culture, and so on) is conceived not as an ideal of life worked out and achieved by the men of that culture through a spiritual effort, whether conscious or unconscious; it belongs to them as a natural possession, in exactly the same way in which dark skin-pigment belongs to negroes or blue eyes to Scandinavians. The whole groundwork of the theory is thus based on a deliberate and painstaking attempt to extrude from history everything that makes it historical, and to substitute at every point a naturalistic conception of principle for the corresponding historical one.

Spengler's book is loaded with a mass of historical learning, but even this is constantly deformed and perverted to fit his thesis. To take one example out of many, he maintains that as part of its fundamental character the classical or Graeco-Roman culture lacked all sense of time, cared nothing for the past or the future, and therefore (unlike the Egyptian, which had a keen time-sense) did not build tombs for its dead. He seems to have forgotten that in Rome orchestral concerts are held every week in the mausoleum of Augustus; that the tomb

of Hadrian was for centuries the fortress of the Popes; and that
for miles and miles outside the city the ancient roads are lined
with the vastest collection of tombs in the whole world. Even
the positivistic thinkers of the nineteenth century, in their misguided attempts to reduce history to a science, went no farther
in the reckless and unscrupulous falsification of facts.

There are obvious similarities between Spengler and Toynbee. The main difference is that with Spengler the isolation of
the various cultures is as complete as that of the Leibnitian
monads. The relations of time, place, and similarity between
them are only perceptible from the detached point of view of
the historian. For Toynbee, these relations, though external,
form part of the experience of the civilizations themselves. It is
essential to Toynbee's view that some societies should be
affiliated to others; the continuity of history is thus safeguarded,
though only in a form which robs it of its full meaning: in
Spengler's nothing like affiliation is possible. There is no
positive relation whatever between one culture and another.
Thus the triumph of naturalism, which in Toynbee only affects
general principles, in Spengler penetrates into every detail.

§ 3. *France*

(i) *Ravaisson's spiritualism*

It is only right that France, the native land of positivism,
should also be the country in which positivism has been most
tenaciously and brilliantly criticized. And the attack on
positivism to which French thought has devoted its best
energies in the late nineteenth and early twentieth century, like
so many other critical and revolutionary movements in the
same country, has in fact only been another proof of the in-
domitable consistency of the French mind. The Enlightenment
which in the eighteenth century attacked the fortress of established religion was in essence a self-assertion of human reason
and human liberty against dogma and superstition as such.
Positivism converted natural science into a new system of
dogma and superstition; and the reawakening of French philosophy to attack that new fortress might once more have
inscribed on its banners the old motto *Écrasez l'infâme*.

This new movement of French thought, unlike that of German, was not consciously and explicitly orientated towards history. But a close inspection of its main characteristics shows that the idea of history was one of its leading conceptions. If we identify the idea of history with the idea of spiritual life or process, the closeness of the connexion becomes obvious, for notoriously the idea of spiritual process is the guiding idea of modern French philosophy. In one way, paradoxical though it may seem, this movement of French thought has a firmer hold on the problem of history than the parallel movement in Germany. For the German movement, however much it talks about history, is always thinking of it in terms of epistemology: its real interest is in the historian's subjective mental processes; and with its general prejudice against metaphysics (a prejudice partly neo-Kantian and partly positivistic) it evades the task of inquiring into the objective nature of the historical process itself, with the result that, as we have seen, it conceives that process as a mere spectacle for the historian's mind and thus converts it into a natural process. But the French mind, resolutely metaphysical in its tradition of thought, concentrates on grasping the character of spiritual process itself, with the result that it has gone far to solve the problem of the philosophy of history without ever mentioning the word history at all.

All I shall do here is to pick out a few points in this singularly rich and varied movement, and show how they bear on our main question. Two themes are constantly recurring throughout its texture: one negative, a criticism of natural science, the other positive, an exposition of the conception of spiritual life or process. They are the negative and positive sides of one single idea. Natural science, raised by positivism to the rank of metaphysics, conceives reality as a system of processes governed everywhere by the law of causality. Everything is what it is because it is determined by something else. Spiritual life is a world whose reality is its freedom or spontaneity: not a lawless or chaotic world, but a world whose laws are freely made by that same spirit which freely obeys them. If such a world exists at all, the metaphysics of positivism must be fallacious. Consequently it must be shown that this metaphysics is unsound; it must be attacked on its own ground and refuted there. In other words, it must be shown that however much the methods of natural science may be justified in their own sphere, this sphere is something short of reality as a whole; it is a limited and dependent reality, dependent for its very existence on the freedom or spontaneity which positivism denies.

Ravaisson[1] in the sixties took the first step towards such an argument by contending that the conception of reality as mechanical, or governed by efficient causes, cannot stand as a metaphysical doctrine because it fails to give any account of the whole within which these causes operate. In order that this whole should exist and maintain itself there must be in it not only a principle of efficient causation, linking part to part, but also a principle of teleology or final causation, which organizes the parts into a whole. This is Leibniz's conception of a synthesis of efficient and final causes, together with the further doctrine, also derived from Leibniz, that our knowledge of the teleological principle is derived from our consciousness of it as the working principle of our own minds. Our knowledge of ourselves as spirit, as a self-creative and self-organizing life, thus enables us to detect a similar life in nature; and (although positivism fails to see this) it is only because nature is a teleologically living organism that there are causal relations between its parts. Here we see an attempt to establish the reality of spirit by resolving the reality of nature itself into spirit; but we already know, from our analysis of later German thought, that such a resolution not only fails to do justice to natural science, by denying that there is anything genuinely natural, but endangers the conception of spirit by identifying it with something that is to be found in nature. The danger is that a third term, neither mere nature nor genuine spirit, tends to be substituted for both. This third term is life, conceived not as spiritual life or the process of mind, but as biological or physiological life, a fundamental conception in the work of Bergson.

(ii) *Lachelier's idealism*

In order to escape this danger it was necessary to insist that the life of the spirit is not mere life but rationality, that is, the activity of thinking. The man who saw this was Lachelier, one of the greatest of modern French philosophers. During his long life as a teacher, to whom in that capacity French thought owes

[1] *Rapport sur la philosophie en France au XIXme siècle* (Paris, 1867).

an incalculable debt, Lachelier published little, but what he did publish is a model of profound thought and clear expression. His brief essay on *Psychology and Metaphysics*[1] is a masterly exposition of the thesis that psychology, as a naturalistic science, cannot grasp mind as it actually is; it can only study the immediate data of consciousness, our sensations and feelings; but the essence of mind is that it knows, that is, has as its objects not mere states of itself but a real world. What enables it to know is the fact that it thinks; and the activity of thought is a free or self-creative process, which depends on nothing else except itself in order to exist. If then we ask why thought exists, the only possible answer is that existence itself, whatever else it may be, is the activity of thinking. The centre of Lachelier's argument here is the idea that knowledge itself is a function of freedom; it is only because the activity of spirit is absolutely spontaneous that knowledge is possible. Hence natural science, instead of casting doubt on the reality of spirit by failing to discover it in nature, or vindicating it by discovering it there (which it can never do), vindicates it in a quite different way, by being itself a product of spiritual activity in the scientist. This clear conception of the life of spirit as a life that is both freedom and knowledge and also knowledge of its own freedom, a life which no scientific thought can detect or analyse in psychological terms, is just what we found lacking in the German school. It is not yet a theory of history, but it is the basis of such a theory.

If other French thinkers had grasped Lachelier's conception, they would not have needed to pursue the criticisms of natural science which occupied so large a place in the French philosophy of the late nineteenth and early twentieth centuries. Lachelier's argument had in fact cut away the foundations of the structure whose upper works they were attacking: not science itself, but the philosophy which attempted to show that science was the only possible form of knowledge and therefore by implication reduced mind to nature. I need not, therefore, describe the work done by Boutroux and his school, who attempted to vindicate the reality of the spiritual life by throwing doubt on the solidity of scientific knowledge. But in order to show what became of these criticisms when pushed home and erected into a con-

[1] *Œuvres* (Paris, 1933), vol. i, pp. 169–219.

structive philosophy, I must say something of the work of Bergson.

(iii) *Bergson's evolutionism*

The essentially constructive character of Bergson's mind is revealed by the fact that his first book emphasizes the positive side of the double theme which I have described as characteristic of modern French thought. The *Essai sur les Données immédiates de la Conscience* (translated into English in 1913 under the title *Time and Free Will*) is an exposition of the characteristics of our own mental life as present in actual experience. This life is a succession of mental states, but it is a succession in a very special sense of the word. One state does not follow another, for one does not cease to exist when the next begins; they interpenetrate one another, the past living on in the present, fused with it, and present in the sense that it confers upon it a peculiar quality derived from the fact of the fusion. For example, in listening to a tune we do not experience the different notes separately: the way in which we hear each note, the state of mind which is the hearing of that note, is affected by the way in which we heard the last and, indeed, all the previous ones. The total experience of hearing the tune is thus a progressive and irreversible series of experiences which telescope into one another; it is therefore not many experiences, but one experience, organized in a peculiar way. The way in which it is organized is time, and this in fact is just what time is: it is a manifold of parts which, unlike those of space, interpenetrate one another, the present including the past. This temporal organization is peculiar to consciousness, and is the foundation of freedom: for, because the present contains the past in itself the present is not determined by the past as something external to it, a cause of which it is the effect: the present is a free and living activity which embraces and sustains its own past by its own act.

So far Bergson's analysis of consciousness affords a valuable contribution to the theory of history, although he does not use it in that way. We have already seen that an essential element in any such theory must be the conception of mental life as a process in which the past is not a mere spectacle to the present, but actually lives in the present. But the process which Bergson is describing, although it is a mental process, is not a rational process. It is not a succession of thoughts, it is a mere succession of immediate feelings and sensations. These feelings and sensations are not knowledge; our awareness of them is purely subjective, not objective; in experiencing them we are not knowing anything that is independent of the experience. To obtain knowledge, we must look outside ourselves; and when we do this we find ourselves looking at a world of things separated from one another in space, not interpenetrating one another even in their time-aspect, for the time in which they change is quite different from the interpenetrating time of inner consciousness; it is the clock-time of the external world, a spatialized time in which different times exclude one another just like parts of space. Thus the science which is our knowledge of this external world, the work of the intellect, affords a complete contrast with our inner experience: the intellect is a faculty which cuts things up into separate and self-contained parcels. Why should we have a faculty that does anything so strange? The answer Bergson gives is that we need it for the purpose of acting. Thus natural science is not a way of knowing the real world; its value lies not in its truth but in its utility; by scientific thought we do not know nature, we dismember it in order to master it.

In all his later works Bergson never gets beyond this original dualism, though it constantly assumes fresh forms. The life of consciousness always remains for him a life of immediate experience, devoid of all thought, all reflection, all rationality. Its consciousness is only the intuition of its own states. Consequently its process, although it resembles an historical process in the way in which it preserves its past in its present, falls short of being a genuinely historical process because the past which is preserved in the present is not a known past; it is only a past whose reverberations in the present are immediately experienced as the present itself is immediately experienced. These reverberations at last die away; and when they have done so, just because they are no longer immediately experienced and cannot be experienced otherwise, there can be no reviving of them. Consequently there can be no history; for history is not immediate self-enjoyment, it is reflection, mediation, thought. It is an intellectual labour whose purpose is to think the life of the mind instead of merely enjoying it. But according to Berg-

son's philosophy this is impossible: what is inward can only be
enjoyed, not thought; what is thought is always the outward,
and the outward is the unreal, that which has been fabricated
for the purposes of action.

(iv) *Modern French historiography*

Modern French thought, working along these lines (for Bergson has enjoyed and still enjoys a popularity which reveals the
essential correctness of his analysis of the mind of his nation),
possesses a peculiarly vivid consciousness of itself as a living and
active process, and has a wonderful ability to vivify whatever
it can absorb into that process. Whatever is not so absorbed
the French mind conceives as something of a totally different
kind, a mere mechanism, to be reckoned with in action according
as it is a tractable and useful mechanism or an intractable and
hostile one, but never to be entered into or sympathized with
as a spiritual life akin to itself. This is how the French attitude
in international politics develops itself in a manner quite
Bergsonian. And the spirit of modern French historiography
works in the same way. The French historian seeks, following
Bergson's well-known rule, *s'installer dans le mouvement*, to work
himself into the movement of the history he is studying, and to
feel that movement as something that goes on within himself.
Recapturing the rhythm of this movement by an act of imaginative sympathy, he can express it with extraordinary brilliance
and fidelity. For examples I need only refer to one or two
masterpieces of recent French historical literature, such as
Camille Jullian's *Histoire de la Gaule* or Monsieur Élie Halévy's
works on *Philosophical Radicalism* or the *History of the English People*. When once this sympathetic insight has been
achieved, it is easy to state the essential lines of the process in
a few pages; and this is why French historians excel all others
in writing brief and pregnant works, popular in the best sense
of the word, conveying to the general public a vivid feeling of
the character of a period or movement: exactly what German
historians, muscle-bound in their struggle with the facts, cannot
do. But what the French cannot do is what the Germans do so
well: to treat isolated facts with scientific accuracy and detachment. The great scandal of recent French scholarship, the widespread acceptance of the Glozel forgeries, showed both the

weakness of modern French scholars in scientific technique and
the way in which a question which ought to have been a purely
technical one became in their minds a question of national
honour. The Glozel controversy, grotesquely enough, gave rise
to the formation of an international commission to settle it ; and
of course the findings of that commission were not accepted.

Thus in the last resort the modern French movement finds
itself entangled in the same error as the German. Each of them
ultimately confuses mind with nature and fails to distinguish
the historical process from the natural process. But whereas the
German movement tries to find the historical process objectively
existing outside the thinker's mind, and fails to find it there just
because it is not outside, the French movement tries to find it
existing subjectively inside the thinker's mind, and fails to find
it because, being thus enclosed within the subjectivity of the
thinker, it ceases to be a process of knowledge and becomes a
process of immediate experience: it becomes a merely psychological process, a process of sensations, feelings, and sentiments.
The root of the error in both cases is the same. The subjective
and the objective are regarded as two different things, hetero-
geneous in their essence, however intimately related. This conception is right in the case of natural science, where the process
of scientific thought is a spiritual or historical process having
as its object a natural process; but it is wrong in the case of
history, where the process of historical thought is homogeneous
with the process of history itself, both being processes of
thought. The only philosophical movement which has grasped
this peculiarity of historical thought firmly and has used it
as a systematic principle is that which was initiated by Croce
in Italy.

§ 4. *Italy*

(i) *Croce's essay of 1893*

Modern Italian philosophy is far less rich in competent writers
and in varied points of view than either French or German ; and,
in particular, its literature on the theory of history as such,
though more considerable than the French, bulks very small as
compared with the German. But as compared with French
philosophy it is more important for the subject of history,
because it approaches the subject directly and places it in the

centre of its problems; and it starts with an advantage over the German in the fact that the tradition of historical work, which in Germany hardly goes back beyond the eighteenth century, in Italy goes back to Machiavelli and even to Petrarch. Ever since the nineteenth century the leaders of Italian thought have been building up a tradition of serious and sustained historical research; and the length, variety, and richness of this tradition give a peculiar weight to the pronouncements of modern Italians on the subject, as one that has worked itself into the very bones of their civilization.

In 1893, when Benedetto Croce wrote his first essay on the theory of history at the age of twenty-seven, not only was he personally an historian of some distinction, but he had behind him a certain amount of recent Italian philosophical thought on the same subject. This, however, he absorbed into his own work so completely that for our purposes it may be passed over.

This essay was entitled *History subsumed under the Concept of Art*.[1] The question whether history was a science or an art had been lately discussed, especially in Germany, and for the most part the answer had been given that it was a science. One remembers that Windelband's attack on this answer was not made until 1894. Croce's essay may therefore be profitably compared with Windelband's; in many ways they are alike, but even at this early stage of his career it was obvious that Croce was superior to Windelband as a philosophic intelligence, and saw further into the real question at issue.

He began by clearing up the conception of art. He pointed out that art is neither a means of giving and receiving sensuous pleasure, nor a representation of natural fact, nor the construction and enjoyment of systems of formal relations (the three theories of it then most in favour), but the intuitive vision of individuality. The artist sees and represents this individuality: his public sees it as he has represented it. Art is thus not an activity of the emotions, but a cognitive activity: it is knowledge of the individual. Science, on the contrary, is knowledge of the general: its work is to construct general concepts and to work out the relations between them. Now history is altogether concerned with concrete individual facts. 'History', says Croce,

---

[1] *La Storia ridotta sotto il concetto generale dell' Arte.* Reprinted in *Primi Saggi* (Bari, 1919).

'has only one duty: to narrate facts.' What is called seeking for the causes of these facts is only looking closer at the facts themselves and apprehending the individual relations between them. It is useless, because meaningless, to call history 'descriptive science', for the fact that it is descriptive makes it no longer a science. Here Croce gives in advance the right answer to Windelband. The term 'description' may, no doubt, be used as a name for the analytic and generalizing account which empirical science gives of its object; but if it means what it means in history, the phrase 'descriptive science' is a *contradictio in adjecto*. The aim of the scientist is to understand facts in the sense of recognizing them as instances of general laws; but in this sense history does not understand its object; it contemplates it, and that is all. This is exactly what the artist does; so that the comparison between history and art, already made by Dilthey in 1883 and by Simmel in 1892, both of whom Croce quotes, is wholly just. But for him the relation goes farther than a mere comparison: it is an identity. Each is precisely the same thing: the intuition and representation of the individual.

Obviously, the matter could not be left here. If history is art, it is at least a very peculiar kind of art. All the artist does is to state what he sees; the historian has both to do this and also to assure himself that what he sees is the truth. Croce puts this by saying that art in general, in the wide sense, represents or narrates the possible; history represents or narrates that which has really happened. That which has happened is, of course, not impossible; if it were, it would not have happened; the real thus falls inside the sphere of the possible, not outside it, and thus history as narration of the real falls inside art as the narration of the possible.

Such is the argument of Croce's essay. It attracted a good deal of attention and was criticized in many quarters, but in re-reading the criticisms to-day one sees that Croce's answers were on the whole justified; he had penetrated farther into the subject than any of his critics. The real weakness of his argument is the one to which he himself called attention in his preface to a reprint of it twenty-six years later.

'I did not detect', he writes, 'the new problem raised by the conception of history as artistic representation of the real. I did not see that a representation in which the real is dialectically distinguished from the possible is something more than a merely artistic representation or intuition; it comes about by virtue of the concept; not indeed the empirical or abstract concept of science, but the concept which is philosophy and, as such, is both representation and judgement, universal and individual in one.'

In other words: art as such is pure intuition and does not contain thought; but in order to distinguish the real from the merely possible, one must think; consequently, to define history as the intuition of the real is to say in one breath that it is art and also that it is more than art. If the phrase 'descriptive science' is a *contradictio in adjecto*, so is the phrase 'intuition of the real': for intuition, just because it is intuition and not thought, knows nothing of any distinction between the real and the imaginary.

Even with this weakness, Croce's early theory already marks an advance on the German view which it so much resembles. Each seizes upon the distinction between the individual and the universal as the key to the distinction between history and science. Each leaves itself with unsolved problems on its hands. But the difference is that the Germans were content to go on calling history a science, without answering the question how a science of the individual is possible; and the result was that they conceived historical science and natural science as two kinds of science, a conception which left the door open to naturalism, re-insinuating itself into the idea of history along the traditional associations of the word 'science'. Croce, by denying that history was a science at all, cut himself at one blow loose from naturalism, and set his face towards an idea of history as something radically different from nature. We have seen that the problem of philosophy everywhere in the late nineteenth century was the problem of liberating itself from the tyranny of natural science; the boldness of Croce's move was therefore exactly what the situation demanded. It was the clean cut which he made in 1893 between the idea of history and the idea of science that enabled him to develop the conception of history so much farther than any philosopher of his generation.

It took him some time to see wherein his early theory was defective. In his first large-scale philosophical work, the *Aesthetic* of 1902, he still repeats his original view of history: it does not search for laws, he says,[1] nor frame concepts, it does not use induction or deduction, it does not demonstrate, it narrates. Inasmuch as its task is to present the spectacle of a completely determined individual, it is identical with art. And when he goes on to raise the question how history differs from the pure imagination of art, he answers it in the old way, by saying that it distinguishes as art does not between the real and the unreal.

(ii) Croce's second position: the 'Logic'

It was only in his *Logic*, published in 1909, that he faced the question how this distinction was possible. Logic is the theory of thought, and only thought can make the distinction between truth and falsehood which marks history off from art in the strict (and, as Croce would now admit, the only true) sense. To think is to make judgements, and logic traditionally distinguishes two kinds of judgement, the universal and the individual. The universal judgement defines the content of a conception, as when we say that the three angles of any triangle are equal to two right angles. The individual judgement states an individual matter of fact, as when we say that this triangle encloses the property of so-and-so. These are the two kinds of cognition which have been called *a priori* and empirical (Kant), *vérités de raison* and *vérités de fait* (Leibniz), relations between ideas and matters of fact (Hume), and so forth.

Now, Croce argues,[2] the traditional division of truths into these two classes is false. To distinguish the existence of the individual as a mere matter of fact, a *vérité de fait*, from *vérités de raison*, implies that the existence of the individual is irrational. But that is absurd. An individual fact would not be what it is had there not been reasons for it. And on the other hand to distinguish a universal truth as a *vérité de raison* from *vérités de fait* implies that universal truths are not realized in matters of fact. But what is a universal truth, unless it is true universally of the facts to which it applies?

He concludes that necessary or universal truth and contingent or individual truth are not two different kinds of cognition but inseparable elements in every real cognition. A universal

---

[1] Eng. tr., 2nd edn. (London, 1922), pp. 26–8
[2] Eng. tr. (London, 1917), pp. 198 ff.

truth is true only as realized in a particular instance: the universal must, as he puts it, be incarnate in the individual. And he goes on to show that even in judgements which at first sight appear to be utterly and abstractly universal, pure definitions, there is really what he calls an historical element, an element of *this*, *here*, and *now*, inasmuch as the definition has been framed by an individual historical thinker to meet a problem that has arisen in a particular way at a particular time in the history of thought. On the other hand, the individual or historical judgement is no mere intuition of a given fact or apprehension of a sense-datum; it is a judgement with a predicate; this predicate is a concept; and this concept is present to the mind of the person who makes the judgement as a universal idea of which, if he understands his own thought, he must be able to give a definition. Thus, there is only one kind of judgement, and it is both individual and universal: individual in so far as it describes an individual state of things, and universal in so far as it describes it by thinking it under universal concepts.

To illustrate this double argument. First, that the universal judgement is really individual. John Stuart Mill defined a right act as one which procures the greatest happiness of the greatest number. This looks at first sight an utterly non-historical judgement, true of all times and places if indeed it is true at all. But what Mill was doing when he made it was describing what we mean when we call an action 'right'; and here the word *we* means not all human beings everywhere and always, but nineteenth-century Englishmen with the moral and political ideas of their time. Mill is describing, whether well or ill, a particular phase in the history of human morality. He may not know that he is doing this, but this is what he is doing.

Secondly, that the individual judgement of history is universal in the sense that its predicate is a concept of which a definition could and should be forthcoming. I open a history book at random and read the following sentence: 'It must not be forgotten that monarchs such as Louis XI and Ferdinand the Catholic, notwithstanding their crimes, completed the national work of making France and Spain two great and powerful nations.' This sentence implies that the writer and reader understand the terms 'crime', 'nation', 'powerful', and so forth, and understand them in the same sense: it implies that the writer and reader possess in common a certain system of ethical and political ideas. The sentence, as an historical judgement, assumes that these ideas are coherent and logically defensible; that is, it presupposes an ethical and political philosophy. It is through the medium of this ethical and political philosophy that we grasp the historical reality of Louis XI; and conversely, it is because we find the concepts of this philosophy realized in Louis XI that we grasp what those concepts are.

This is Croce's doctrine of the mutual implication of the universal or definitive judgement and the individual or historical judgement, and his solution of the problem how philosophy (i.e. the universal judgement) is related to history. Instead of trying to place philosophy and history outside one another in two mutually exclusive spheres, and thus making an adequate theory of history impossible, he brings them together into a single whole, a judgement whose subject is the individual while its predicate is the universal. History is thus no longer conceived as mere intuition of the individual; it does not simply apprehend the individual, in which case it would be art; it judges the individual; and hence the universality, the *a priori* character, which belongs indefeasibly to all thought, is present in history in the form of the predicate of the historical judgement. What makes the historian a thinker is the fact that he thinks out the meanings of these predicates, and finds these meanings embodied in the individuals he contemplates. But this thinking-out of the meaning of a concept is philosophy; hence philosophy is an integral part of historical thinking itself; the individual judgement of history is a judgement only because it contains in itself, as one of its elements, philosophical thinking.

(iii) *History and philosophy*

This involves a very remarkable and original view of the relation between philosophy and history. Hitherto it had generally been assumed that philosophy was the queen of the sciences, and that history occupied a humble place somewhere among her subjects, or on the outskirts of her realm. But for Croce, in this culminating phase of his thought, the task of philosophy is limited to thinking out the meaning of concepts which as actual functions of thought exist only as predicates of historical judgements. There is only one kind of judgement, the individual judgement of history. In other words, all reality is history and all knowledge is historical knowledge. Philosophy is only a constituent element within history; it is the universal element in a thought whose concrete being is individual.

This may be compared with the German view, found for example in Rickert, that all reality is historical. But Rickert has arrived at his doctrine by way of the nominalistic principle that all concepts are mere fictions of the intellect, which implies that the judgement 'Louis XI committed crimes' is a merely verbal proposition and means 'the word crime is a word which I apply to the actions of Louis XI'. For Croce, 'crime' is not a word but a concept, and the statement that Louis XI committed crimes is therefore a statement not about the historian's arbitrary use of words but about the actions of Louis XI. Rickert and Croce might agree that historical fact is the only reality; but the meanings they would attach to these words are wholly different. Rickert would mean that reality consists of isolated unique events, bare particulars conceived as particulars are conceived, for example, by the logic of Mill; particulars having in them no element of universality: the universal, on such a view, being added to the particular by an arbitrary act of the mind. Croce would mean that reality consists of concepts or universals embodied in particular facts, the particular being nothing but the incarnation of the universal.

(iv) *History and nature*

But what, all this time, has become of natural science, and how is the natural process related on Croce's view to the historical? The answer is that, for him, natural science is not knowledge at all, but action. He draws a sharp distinction between the concepts of science and the concepts of philosophy. The concepts of philosophy are functions of thought, universal and necessary: to affirm them is simply for thought to think itself. It is impossible, for example, to think without thinking that our thought is true: thus the act of thought in affirming itself affirms the distinction between truth and falsehood. The concepts of science, on the contrary, are arbitrary constructions; there is not one of them that need be thought. They are of two kinds, empirical, like the concepts of cat or rose, and abstract, like the concepts of triangle or uniform movement. In the former case the concept is only a way in which we choose to group certain facts which we might with equal truth group otherwise. In the latter, the concept has no instances at all; it cannot be true, because it is true of nothing; all we can do is to posit it and work out its implications hypothetically. These arbitrary constructions are in reality not concepts, therefore, but (we may call them) conceptual fictions; Croce also calls them pseudo-concepts. And the whole of natural science consists of thought about pseudo-concepts. But what is the point of constructing pseudo-concepts? What are they? They are not errors, he insists, any more than they are truths. Their value is a practical value. By making them we are manipulating in ways useful to us realities which we do not thereby understand better, but which thereby become more tractable to our purposes. Here we find Croce adopting the pragmatist theory of natural science which we have already found in Bergson. But there is this important difference: that whereas, for Bergson, the reality which we thus manipulate is in itself nothing but immediate inward experience, which makes it unintelligible how any action of ours or any one else's can turn it into objective spatial facts, for Croce the reality which we convert into nature by applying pseudo-concepts to it is in itself history, sequences of facts that really happen and are knowable to our historical thought as they really are. It is an historical fact that we observe a cat killing a bird; like all historical facts, this is the incarnation of a concept at a particular place and time; and the true and only possible way of knowing it is to know it as an historical fact. As so known, it takes its place in the body of historical knowledge. But we may, instead of knowing it as it really is, fabricate for our own purposes the pseudo-concepts cat and bird, and thus arrive at the general rule not to leave a cat alone with a canary.

Thus nature, for Croce, is in one sense real and in one sense unreal. It is real, if nature means individual events as they happen and are observed to happen; but in that sense nature is only a part of history. It is unreal, if nature means a system of abstract general laws; for these laws are only the pseudo-concepts under which we arrange the historical facts that we observe and remember and expect.

On this view the distinction which I have sometimes drawn

in the preceding chapters between natural processes and historical processes disappears. History is no longer in any special sense knowledge of the human as opposed to the natural world. It is simply the knowledge of facts or events as they actually happen, in their concrete individuality. A distinction remains, but it is not a distinction between man or spirit and nature. It is the distinction between apprehending the individuality of a thing by thinking oneself into it, making its life one's own, and analysing or classifying it from an external point of view. To do the first is to grasp it as an historical fact; to do the second is to make it a subject-matter for science. It is easy to see that either of these two attitudes may be taken up towards human beings and their activities. For example, to study a past philosopher's thought in such a way as to make it one's own, relive it as he lived it, as a thought arising out of certain determinate problems and situations and pursued so far and no farther, is to treat it historically. If a thinker cannot do this, and can only analyse its parts and classify it as belonging to this or that type (as Dilthey handled the history of philosophy in the last stage of his thought) he is treating it as subject-matter for science and making it into mere nature. To quote Croce himself:[1]

'Do you wish to understand the true history of a neolithic Ligurian or Sicilian? Try, if you can, to become a neolithic Ligurian or Sicilian in your mind. If you cannot do that, or do not care to, content yourself with describing and arranging in series the skulls, implements, and drawings which have been found belonging to these neolithic peoples. Do you wish to understand the true history of a blade of grass? Try to become a blade of grass; and, if you cannot do it, satisfy yourself with analysing its parts, and even arranging them in a sort of ideal or fanciful history.'

As concerns neolithic man, the advice is obviously good. If you can enter into his mind and make his thoughts your own, you can write his history, and not otherwise; if you cannot, all you can do is to arrange his relics in some kind of tidy order, and the result is ethnology or archaeology but it is not history. Yet the reality of neolithic man was an historical reality. When he made a certain implement, he had a purpose in mind;

[1] *Teoria e Storia della Storiografia* (Bari, 1917), p. 119; Eng. tr., *Theory and History of Historiography* (London, 1921), pp. 134–5.

the implement came into being as an expression of his spirit, and if you treat it as non-spiritual that is only because of the failure of your historical insight. But is this true of a blade of grass? Is its articulation and growth an expression of its own spiritual life? I am not so sure. And when we come to a crystal, or a stalactite, my scepticism reaches the point of rebellion. The process by which these things form themselves appears to me to be a process in which, through no lack of our own historical sympathy, we look in vain for any expression of thought. It is an event; it has individuality; but it seems to lack that inwardness which, according to this passage of Croce, is made (and, I think, rightly made) the criterion of historicity. The resolution of nature into spirit seems to me incomplete, and not at all proved by the converse fact that spirit, by being handled scientifically instead of historically, can be resolved into nature.

But this raises a problem which is outside my present subject. I shall therefore not pursue it, unless and except so far as the attempted resolution of nature into spirit affects the conception of spirit, that is, of history, itself. And I do not find that in Croce's work there is any such affection. This is because, whether or no there is such a thing as nature, as distinct from spirit, at least it cannot enter as a factor into the world of spirit. When people think that it can, and speak (as we saw that Montesquieu, for example, did) of the influence of geography or climate on history, they are mistaking the effect of a certain person's or people's conception of nature on their actions for an effect of nature itself. The fact that certain people live, for example, on an island has in itself no effect on their history; what has an effect is the way they conceive that insular position; whether for example they regard the sea as a barrier or as a highway to traffic. Had it been otherwise, their insular position, being a constant fact, would have produced a constant effect on their historical life; whereas it will produce one effect if they have not mastered the art of navigation, a different effect if they have mastered it better than their neighbours, a third if they have mastered it worse than their neighbours, and a fourth if every one uses aeroplanes. In itself, it is merely a raw material for historical activity, and the character of historical life depends on how this raw material is used.

(v) *Croce's final view: the autonomy of history*

Croce has thus vindicated the autonomy of history, its right to conduct its own business in its own way, both against philosophy and against science. Philosophy cannot interfere with history according to the Hegelian formula of superimposing a philosophical history on the top of ordinary history, because that distinction is meaningless. Ordinary history is already philosophical history: it contains philosophy inside itself in the shape of predicates to its judgements. Philosophical history is a term synonymous with history. And within the concrete whole which is historical knowledge, philosophical knowledge is a component part: it is the thinking out of predicate-concepts. Croce put this by defining philosophy as the methodology of history.

As against science, the vindication proceeds on opposite lines. History is secured against the encroachments of science not because it already contains science as an element within itself, but because it must be complete before science begins. Science is a cutting-up and rearranging of materials which must be given to it at the start; and these materials are historical facts. When the scientist tells us that his theories are based on facts—observations and experiments—he means that they are based on history, for the idea of fact and the idea of history are synonymous. That a certain guinea-pig has been inoculated in a certain way and has then developed certain symptoms is a matter of history. The pathologist is a person who takes this and certain similar facts and arranges them in a certain way. Consequently history must be kept free from any interference on the part of science, for unless it first established facts by its own independent work there would be no material for the scientist to handle.

It was in Croce's work of 1912 and 1913[1] that these ideas were fully worked out. In that work we find not only a complete expression of the autonomy of history, but also a double demonstration of its necessity: its necessity relatively to philosophy as the concrete thought of which philosophy is only the methodological moment, and its necessity relatively to science

[1] These being the dates of the essays which in 1915 formed the book *Zur Theorie und Geschichte der Historiographie* (Tübingen) published in 1917 at Bari as *Teoria e Storia della Storiografia*.

as the source of all 'scientific facts'—a phrase which only means those historical facts which the scientist arranges into classes.

Let us look in some detail at the conception of history which emerges from this point of view.[1] All history is contemporary history: not in the ordinary sense of the word, where contemporary history means the history of the comparatively recent past, but in the strict sense: the consciousness of one's own activity as one actually performs it. History is thus the self-knowledge of the living mind. For even when the events which the historian studies are events that happened in the distant past, the condition of their being historically known is that they should 'vibrate in the historian's mind', that is to say, that the evidence for them should be here and now before him and intelligible to him. For history is not contained in books or documents; it lives only, as a present interest and pursuit, in the mind of the historian when he criticizes and interprets those documents, and by so doing relives for himself the states of mind into which he inquires.

It follows that the subject-matter of history is not the past as such, but the past for which we possess historical evidence. Much of the past has perished, in the sense that we have no documents for reconstructing it. We believe, for example, on the strength of mere testimony, that there were great painters among the ancient Greeks; but this belief is not historical knowledge, because, their works having perished, we have no means of reliving in our own minds their artistic experience. There were also great sculptors; but this we do not merely believe, we know it; for we possess their works and can make them part of our own present aesthetic life. Our history of Greek sculpture is our present aesthetic experience of these works.

This distinction serves to distinguish two very different things: history and chronicle. The names of the great Greek painters, as handed down to us by tradition, do not form a history of Greek painting: they form a chronicle of Greek painting. Chronicle, then, is the past as merely believed upon testimony but not historically known. And this belief is a mere act of will: the will to preserve certain statements which we do not under-

[1] [The section on Croce was written in 1936 and not subsequently amplified to take account of his *La Storia come Pensiero e come Azione* (Bari, 1938), Eng. tr., *History as the Story of Liberty* (London, 1941).]

stand. If we did understand them, they would be history. Every history becomes chronicle when related by a person who cannot relive the experiences of its characters: the history of philosophy, for example, as written or read by people who do not understand the thoughts of the philosophers in question. In order that there should be chronicle, there must first be history: for chronicle is the body of history from which the spirit has gone; the corpse of history.

History, so far from depending on testimony, has therefore no relation with testimony at all. Testimony is merely chronicle. So far as any one speaks of authorities or of accepting statements or the like, he is talking of chronicle and not of history. History is based on a synthesis of two things which only exist in that synthesis: evidence and criticism. Evidence is only evidence so far as it is used as evidence, that is to say, interpreted on critical principles; and principles are only principles so far as they are put into practice in the work of interpreting evidence.

But the past leaves relics of itself, even when these relics are not used by any one as materials for its history; and these relics are of many kinds, and include the relics of historical thought itself, that is, chronicles. We preserve these relics, hoping that in the future they may become what now they are not, namely historical evidence. What particular parts and aspects of the past we now recall by historical thought depends on our present interests and attitude towards life; but we are always aware that there are other parts and other aspects which there is no need for us to recall at present, and in so far as we recognize that these too will one day interest us we make it our business not to lose or destroy their records. This task of keeping relics against the time when they will become material for history is the task of pure scholars, archivists, and antiquaries. Just as the antiquary keeps implements and pots in his museum without necessarily reconstructing history from them, and as the archivist in the same way keeps public documents, so the pure scholar edits and emends and reprints texts of, for example, ancient philosophy without necessarily understanding the philosophical ideas they express, and therefore without being able to reconstruct the history of philosophy.

This work of scholarship is often taken for history itself; and as so taken it becomes a special type of pseudo-history, which

Croce calls philological history. As thus misconceived, history consists in accepting and preserving testimony, and the writing of history consists in transcribing, translating, and compiling. Such work is useful, but it is not history; there is no criticism, no interpretation, no reliving of past experience in one's own mind. It is mere learning or scholarship. But it is possible, in exaggerated reaction against the claims of learning to be regarded as identical with history, to run to the other extreme. What the mere scholar lacks is living experience. By itself, this living experience is mere feeling or passion; and a one-sided insistence on feeling or passion produces a second type of pseudo-history, romantic or poetical history, whose true purpose is not to discover the truth about the past but to express the author's feelings towards it: patriotic history, partisan history, history inspired by liberal or humanitarian or socialist ideals; in general, all history whose function is to express either the historian's love and admiration for his subject, or else his hatred and contempt for it: 'writing it up' or 'debunking' it. And in this context Croce points out that whenever historians indulge in conjecture or permit themselves to assert mere possibilities they are in fact giving way to the temptation of poeticizing or romanticizing history: they are going beyond what the evidence proves and expressing their own personal feelings by permitting themselves to believe what they would like to believe. Genuine history has no room for the merely probable or the merely possible; all it permits the historian to assert is what the evidence before him obliges him to assert.

PART V

EPILEGOMENA

§ 1. *Human Nature and Human History*

(i) *The science of human nature*

MAN, who desires to know everything, desires to know himself. Nor is he only one (even if, to himself, perhaps the most interesting) among the things he desires to know. Without some knowledge of himself, his knowledge of other things is imperfect: for to know something without knowing that one knows it is only a half-knowing, and to know that one knows is to know oneself. Self-knowledge is desirable and important to man, not only for its own sake, but as a condition without which no other knowledge can be critically justified and securely based.

Self-knowledge, here, means not knowledge of man's bodily nature, his anatomy and physiology; nor even a knowledge of his mind, so far as that consists of feeling, sensation, and emotion; but a knowledge of his knowing faculties, his thought or understanding or reason. How is such knowledge to be attained? It seems an easy matter until we think seriously about it; and then it seems so difficult that we are tempted to think it impossible. Some have even reinforced this temptation by argument, urging that the mind, whose business it is to know other things, has for that very reason no power of knowing itself. But this is open sophistry: first you say what the mind's nature is, and then you say that because it has this nature no one can know that it has it. Actually, the argument is a counsel of despair, based on recognizing that a certain attempted method of studying the mind has broken down, and on failure to envisage the possibility of any other.

It seems a fair enough proposal that, in setting out to understand the nature of our own mind, we should proceed in the same way as when we try to understand the world about us. In studying the world of nature, we begin by getting acquainted with the particular things and particular events that exist and go on there; then we proceed to understand them, by seeing how they fall into general types and how these general types are interrelated. These interrelations we call laws of nature;

and it is by ascertaining such laws that we understand the things
and events to which they apply. The same method, it might
seem, is applicable to the problem of understanding mind. Let
us begin by observing, as carefully as possible, the ways in
which our own minds and those of others behave under given
circumstances; then, having become acquainted with these facts
of the mental world, let us try to establish the laws which
govern them.

Here is a proposal for a 'science of human nature' whose
principles and methods are conceived on the analogy of those
used in the natural sciences. It is an old proposal, put forward
especially in the seventeenth and eighteenth centuries, when the
principles and methods of natural science had been lately per-
fected and were being triumphantly applied to the investigation
of the physical world. When Locke undertook his inquiry into
that faculty of understanding which 'sets Man above the rest of
sensible Beings, and gives him all the Advantage and Dominion
which he has over them', the novelty of his project lay not in
his desire for a knowledge of the human mind, but in his attempt
to gain it by methods analogous to those of natural science: the
collection of observed facts and their arrangement in classifica-
tory schemes. His own description of his method as an 'historical, plain Method' is perhaps ambiguous; but his follower Hume
was at pains to make it clear that the method to be followed by
the science of human nature was identical with the method of
physical science as he conceived it: its 'only solid foundation',
he wrote, 'must be laid on experience and observation'. Reid,
in his *Inquiry into the Human Mind*, was if possible even more
explicit. 'All that we know of the body, is owing to anatomical
dissection and observation, and it must be by an anatomy of the
mind that we can discover its powers and principles.' And from
these pioneers the whole English and Scottish tradition of
a 'philosophy of the human mind' was derived.

Even Kant did not take an essentially different view. He
certainly claimed that his own study of the understanding was
something more than empirical; it was to be a demonstrative
science; but then he held the same view concerning the science
of nature; for that also, according to him, has in it an *a priori*
or demonstrative element, and is not based merely on experience.

It is evident that such a science of human nature, if it could attain even a tolerable approximation to the truth, could hope for results of extreme importance. As applied to the problems of moral and political life, for example, its results would certainly be no less spectacular than were the results of seventeenth-century physics when applied to the mechanical arts in the eighteenth century. This was fully realized by its promoters. Locke thought that by its means he could 'prevail with the busy Mind of Man, to be more cautious in meddling with things exceeding its Comprehension; to stop, when it is at the utmost of its Tether; and to sit down in a quiet Ignorance of those Things, which, upon Examination, are found to be beyond the reach of our Capacities'. At the same time, he was convinced that the powers of our understanding are sufficient for our needs 'in this state', and can give us all the knowledge we require for 'the comfortable provision for this life, and the way that leads to a better'. 'If [he concludes] we can find out those Measures, whereby a Rational creature, put in the state which Man is in this World, may and ought to govern his Opinions and Actions depending thereon, we need not be troubled that some other things escape our knowledge.'

Hume is even bolder. ''Tis evident', he writes, 'that all the sciences have a relation, more or less, to human nature ... since they lie under the cognizance of men, and are judged of by their powers and faculties. 'Tis impossible to tell what changes and improvements we might make in these sciences were we thoroughly acquainted with the extent and force of human understanding.' And in sciences directly concerned with human nature, like morals and politics, his hopes of a beneficent revolution are proportionately higher. 'In pretending, therefore, to explain the principles of human nature, we in effect propose a complete system of the sciences, built on a foundation almost entirely new, and the only one upon which they can stand with any security.' Kant, for all his habitual caution, claimed no less when he said that his new science would put an end to all the debates of the philosophical schools, and make it possible to solve all the problems of metaphysics at once and for ever.

It need not imply any underestimate of what these men actually achieved if we admit that these hopes were in the main unfulfilled, and that the science of human nature, from Locke to the present day, has failed to solve the problem of understanding what understanding is, and thus giving the human mind knowledge of itself. It was not through any lack of sympathy with its objects that so judicious a critic as John Grote found himself obliged to treat the 'philosophy of the human mind' as a blind alley out of which it was the duty of thought to escape.

What was the reason for this failure? Some might say that it was because the undertaking was in principle a mistake: mind cannot know itself. This objection we have already considered. Others, notably the representatives of psychology, would say that the science of these thinkers was not sufficiently scientific: psychology was still in its infancy. But if we ask these same men to produce here and now the practical results for which those early students hoped, they excuse themselves by saying that psychology is still in its infancy. Here I think they wrong themselves and their own science. Claiming for it a sphere which it cannot effectively occupy, they belittle the work it has done and is doing in its proper field. What that field is, I shall suggest in the sequel.

There remains a third explanation: that the 'science of human nature' broke down because its method was distorted by the analogy of the natural sciences. This I believe to be the right one. It was no doubt inevitable that in the seventeenth and eighteenth centuries, dominated as they were by the new birth of physical science, the eternal problem of self-knowledge should take shape as the problem of constructing a science of human nature. To any one reviewing the field of human research, it was evident that physics stood out as a type of inquiry which had discovered the right method of investigating its proper object, and it was right that the experiment should be made of extending this method to every kind of problem. But since then a great change has come over the intellectual atmosphere of our civilization. The dominant factor in this change has not been the development of other natural sciences like chemistry and biology, or the transformation of physics itself since more began to be known about electricity, or the progressive application of all these new ideas to manufacture and industry, important though these have been; for in principle they have done nothing that might not have been foreseen as implicit in seventeenth-century physics itself. The really new element in the thought of to-day as compared with that of three centuries ago is the rise of history. It is true that the same Cartesian spirit which did so much for physics was already laying the foundations of critical method in history before the seventeenth century was out ;[1] but the modern conception of history as a study at once critical and constructive, whose field is the human past in its entirety, and whose method is the reconstruction of that past from documents written and unwritten, critically analysed and interpreted, was not established until the nineteenth, and is even yet not fully worked out in all its implications. Thus history occupies in the world of to-day a position analogous to that occupied by physics in the time of Locke: it is recognized as a special and autonomous form of thought, lately established, whose possibilities have not yet been completely explored. And just as in the seventeenth and eighteenth centuries there were materialists, who argued from the success of physics in its own sphere that all reality was physical, so among ourselves the success of history has led some people to suggest that its methods are applicable to all the problems of knowledge, in other words, that all reality is historical.

This I believe to be an error. I think that those who assert it are making a mistake of the same kind which the materialists made in the seventeenth century. But I believe, and in this essay I shall try to show, that there is at least one important element of truth in what they say. The thesis which I shall maintain is that the science of human nature was a false attempt —falsified by the analogy of natural science—to understand the mind itself, and that, whereas the right way of investigating nature is by the methods called scientific, the right way of investigating mind is by the methods of history. I shall contend that the work which was to be done by the science of human nature is actually done, and can only be done, by history: that history is what the science of human nature professed to be, and that Locke was right when he said (however little he understood what he was saying) that the right method for such an inquiry is the historical, plain method.

[1] 'Historical criticism was born in the seventeenth century from the same intellectual movement as the philosophy of Descartes.' E. Bréhier, in *Philosophy and History: Essays presented to Ernst Cassirer* (Oxford, 1936), p. 160.

(ii) *The field of historical thought*[1]

I must begin by attempting to delimit the proper sphere of historical knowledge as against those who, maintaining the historicity of all things, would resolve all knowledge into historical knowledge. Their argument runs in some such way as this.

The methods of historical research have, no doubt, been developed in application to the history of human affairs: but is that the limit of their applicability? They have already before now undergone important extensions: for example, at one time historians had worked out their methods of critical interpretation only as applied to written sources containing narrative material, and it was a new thing when they learnt to apply them to the unwritten data provided by archaeology. Might not a similar but even more revolutionary extension sweep into the historian's net the entire world of nature? In other words, are not natural processes really historical processes, and is not the being of nature an historical being?

Since the time of Heraclitus and Plato, it has been a commonplace that things natural, no less than things human, are in constant change, and that the entire world of nature is a world of 'process' or 'becoming'. But this is not what is meant by the historicity of things; for change and history are not at all the same. According to this old-established conception, the specific forms of natural things constitute a changeless repertory of fixed types, and the process of nature is a process by which instances of these forms (or quasi-instances of them, things approximating to the embodiment of them) come into existence and pass out of it again. Now in human affairs, as historical research had clearly demonstrated by the eighteenth century, there is no such fixed repertory of specific forms. Here, the process of becoming was already by that time recognized as involving not only the instances or quasi-instances of the forms, but the forms themselves. The political philosophy of Plato and Aristotle teaches in effect that city-states come and go, but the

[1] In the argument of this section I owe much to Mr. Alexander's admirable essay on 'The Historicity of Things', in the volume on *Philosophy and History* already quoted. If I seem to be controverting his main thesis, that is not because I disagree with his argument or any part of it, but only because I mean more than he does by the word 'historicity'. For him, to say that the world is 'a world of events' is to say that 'the world and everything in it is historical'. For me, the two things are not at all the same.

idea of the city-state remains for ever as the one social and political form towards whose realization human intellect, so far as
it is really intelligent, strives. According to modern ideas, the
city-state itself is as transitory a thing as Miletus or Sybaris. It
is not an eternal ideal, it was merely the political ideal of the
ancient Greeks. Other civilizations have had before them other
political ideals, and human history shows a change not only in
the individual cases in which these ideals are realized or partially
realized, but in the ideals themselves. Specific types of human
organization, the city-state, the feudal system, representative
government, capitalistic industry, are characteristic of certain
historical ages.

At first, this transience of specific forms was imagined to be
a peculiarity of human life. When Hegel said that nature has
no history, he meant that whereas the specific forms of human
organization change as time goes on, the forms of natural
organization do not. There is, he grants, a distinction of higher
and lower in the specific forms of nature, and the higher forms
are a development out of the lower; but this development is
only a logical one, not a temporal, and in time all the 'strata'
of nature exist simultaneously.[1] But this view of nature has
been overthrown by the doctrine of evolution. Biology has
decided that living organisms are not divided into kinds each
permanently distinct from the rest, but have developed their
present specific forms through a process of evolution in time.
Nor is this conception limited to the field of biology. It appeared
simultaneously, the two applications being closely connected
through the study of fossils, in geology. To-day even the stars
are divided into kinds which can be described as older and
younger; and the specific forms of matter, no longer conceived
in the Daltonian manner, as elements eternally distinct like the
living species of pre-Darwinian biology, are regarded as subject
to a similar change, so that the chemical constitution of our
present world is only a phase in a process leading from a very
different past to a very different future.

This evolutionary conception of nature, whose implications
have been impressively worked out by philosophers like M. Bergson, Mr. Alexander, and Mr. Whitehead, might seem at first

---

[1] *Naturphilosophie: Einleitung. System der Philosophie*, § 249, *Zusatz* (*Werke*,
Glockner's edition, vol. ix, p. 59).

sight to have abolished the difference between natural process
and historical process, and to have resolved nature into history.
And if a further step in the same resolution were needed, it
might seem to be provided by Mr. Whitehead's doctrine that
the very possession of its attributes by a natural thing takes
time. Just as Aristotle argued that a man cannot be happy at
an instant, but that the possession of happiness takes a lifetime,
so Mr. Whitehead argues that to be an atom of hydrogen takes
time—the time necessary for establishing the peculiar rhythm
of movements which distinguishes it from other atoms—so that
there is no such thing as 'nature at an instant'.

These modern views of nature do, no doubt, 'take time
seriously'. But just as history is not the same thing as change,
so it is not the same thing as 'timefulness', whether that means
evolution or an existence which takes time. Such views have
certainly narrowed the gulf between nature and history of which
early nineteenth-century thinkers were so conscious; they have
made it impossible to state the distinction any longer in the way
in which Hegel stated it; but in order to decide whether the gulf
has been really closed and the distinction annulled, we must
turn to the conception of history and see whether it coincides
in essentials with this modern conception of nature.

If we put this question to the ordinary historian, he will
answer it in the negative. According to him, all history properly
so called is the history of human affairs. His special technique,
depending as it does on the interpretation of documents in which
human beings of the past have expressed or betrayed their
thoughts, cannot be applied just as it stands to the study of
natural processes; and the more this technique is elaborated in
its details, the farther it is from being so applicable. There is
a certain analogy between the archaeologist's interpretation of
a stratified site and the geologist's interpretation of rock-horizons
with their associated fossils; but the difference is no less clear
than the similarity. The archaeologist's use of his stratified relics
depends on his conceiving them as artifacts serving human purposes and thus expressing a particular way in which men have
thought about their own life; and from his point of view the
palaeontologist, arranging his fossils in a time-series, is not
working as an historian, but only as a scientist thinking in a
way which can at most be described as quasi-historical.

Upholders of the doctrine under examination would say that here the historian is making an arbitrary distinction between things that are really the same, and that his conception of history is an unphilosophically narrow one, restricted by the imperfect development of his technique; very much as some historians, because their equipment was inadequate to studying the history of art or science or economic life, have mistakenly restricted the field of historical thought to the history of politics. The question must therefore be raised, why do historians habitually identify history with the history of human affairs? In order to answer this question, it is not enough to consider the characteristics of historical method as it actually exists, for the question at issue is whether, as it actually exists, it covers the whole field which properly belongs to it. We must ask what is the general nature of the problems which this method is designed to solve. When we have done so, it will appear that the special problem of the historian is one which does not arise in the case of natural science.

The historian, investigating any event in the past, makes a distinction between what may be called the outside and the inside of an event. By the outside of the event I mean everything belonging to it which can be described in terms of bodies and their movements: the passage of Caesar, accompanied by certain men, across a river called the Rubicon at one date, or the spilling of his blood on the floor of the senate-house at another. By the inside of the event I mean that in it which can only be described in terms of thought: Caesar's defiance of Republican law, or the clash of constitutional policy between himself and his assassins. The historian is never concerned with either of these to the exclusion of the other. He is investigating not mere events (where by a mere event I mean one which has only an outside and no inside) but actions, and an action is the unity of the outside and inside of an event. He is interested in the crossing of the Rubicon only in its relation to Republican law, and in the spilling of Caesar's blood only in its relation to a constitutional conflict. His work may begin by discovering the outside of an event, but it can never end there; he must always remember that the event was an action, and that his main task is to think himself into this action, to discern the thought of its agent.

In the case of nature, this distinction between the outside and the inside of an event does not arise. The events of nature are mere events, not the acts of agents whose thought the scientist endeavours to trace. It is true that the scientist, like the historian, has to go beyond the mere discovery of events; but the direction in which he moves is very different. Instead of conceiving the event as an action and attempting to rediscover the thought of its agent, penetrating from the outside of the event to its inside, the scientist goes beyond the event, observes its relation to others, and thus brings it under a general formula or law of nature. To the scientist, nature is always and merely a 'phenomenon', not in the sense of being defective in reality, but in the sense of being a spectacle presented to his intelligent observation; whereas the events of history are never mere phenomena, never mere spectacles for contemplation, but things which the historian looks, not at, but through, to discern the thought within them.

In thus penetrating to the inside of events and detecting the thought which they express, the historian is doing something which the scientist need not and cannot do. In this way the task of the historian is more complex than that of the scientist. In another way it is simpler: the historian need not and cannot (without ceasing to be an historian) emulate the scientist in searching <u>for the</u> causes or laws of events. For science, the event is discovered by perceiving it, and the further search for its cause is conducted by assigning it to its class and determining the relation between that class and others. For history, the object to be discovered is not the mere event, but the thought expressed in it. To discover that thought is already to understand it. After the historian has ascertained the facts, there is no further process of inquiring into their causes. When he knows what happened, he already knows why it happened.

This does not mean that words like 'cause' are necessarily out of place in reference to history; it only means that they are used there in a special sense. When a scientist asks 'Why did that piece of litmus paper turn pink?' he means 'On what kinds of occasions do pieces of litmus paper turn pink?' When an historian asks 'Why did Brutus stab Caesar?' he means 'What did Brutus think, which made him decide to stab Caesar?' <u>The</u> cause of the event, for him, means the thought in the mind of the person by whose agency the event came about: and this is not something other than the event, it is the inside of the event itself.

The processes of nature can therefore be properly described as sequences of mere events, but those of history cannot. They are not processes of mere events but processes of actions, which have an inner side, consisting of processes of thought; and what the historian is looking for is these processes of thought. All history is the history of thought.

But how does the historian discern the thoughts which he is trying to discover? There is only one way in which it can be done: by re-thinking them in his own mind. The historian of philosophy, reading Plato, is trying to know what Plato thought when he expressed himself in certain words. The only way in which he can do this is by thinking it for himself. This, in fact, is what we mean when we speak of 'understanding' the words. So the historian of politics or warfare, presented with an account of certain actions done by Julius Caesar, tries to understand these actions, that is, to discover what thoughts in Caesar's mind determined him to do them. This implies envisaging for himself the situation in which Caesar stood, and thinking for himself what Caesar thought about the situation and the possible ways of dealing with it. The history of thought, and therefore all history, is the re-enactment of past thought in the historian's own mind.

But oh, the problems involved here!

This re-enactment is only accomplished, in the case of Plato and Caesar respectively, so far as the historian brings to bear on the problem all the powers of his own mind and all his knowledge of philosophy and politics. It is not a passive surrender to the spell of another's mind; it is a labour of active and therefore critical thinking. The historian not only re-enacts past thought, he re-enacts it in the context of his own knowledge and therefore, in re-enacting it, criticizes it, forms his own judgement of its value, corrects whatever errors he can discern in it. This criticism of the thought whose history he traces is not something secondary to tracing the history of it. It is an indispensable condition of the historical knowledge itself. Nothing could be a completer error concerning the history of thought than to suppose that the historian as such merely ascertains 'what so-and-so thought', leaving it to some one else to decide 'whether it was true'. All thinking is critical thinking; the thought which re-enacts past thoughts, therefore, criticizes them in re-enacting them.

It is now clear why historians habitually restrict the field of historical knowledge to human affairs. A natural process is a process of events, an historical process is a process of thoughts. Man is regarded as the only subject of historical process, because man is regarded as the only animal that thinks, or thinks enough, and clearly enough, to render his actions the expressions of his thoughts. The belief that man is the only animal that thinks at all is no doubt a superstition; but the belief that man thinks more, and more continuously and effectively, than any other animal, and is the only animal whose conduct is to any great extent determined by thought instead of by mere impulse and appetite, is probably well enough founded to justify the historian's rule of thumb.

It does not follow that all human actions are subject-matter for history; and indeed historians are agreed that they are not. But when they are asked how the distinction is to be made between historical and non-historical human actions, they are somewhat at a loss how to reply. From our present point of view we can offer an answer: so far as man's conduct is determined by what may be called his animal nature, his impulses and appetites, it is non-historical; the process of those activities is a natural process. Thus, the historian is not interested in the fact that men eat and sleep and make love and thus satisfy their natural appetites; but he is interested in the social customs which they create by their thought as a framework within which these appetites find satisfaction in ways sanctioned by convention and morality.

Consequently, although the conception of evolution has revolutionized our idea of nature by substituting for the old conception of natural process as a change within the limits of a fixed system of specific forms the new conception of that process as involving a change in these forms themselves, it has by no means identified the idea of natural process with that of historical process; and the fashion, current not long ago, of using the word 'evolution' in an historical context, and talking of the evolution of parliament or the like, though natural in an age when the science of nature was regarded as the only true form of

knowledge, and when other forms of knowledge, in order to
justify their existence, felt bound to assimilate themselves to
that model, was the result of confused thinking and a source
of further confusions.

There is only one hypothesis on which natural processes could
be regarded as ultimately historical in character: namely, that
these processes are in reality processes of action determined by
a thought which is their own inner side. This would imply that
natural events are expressions of thoughts, whether the thoughts
of God, or of angelic or demonic finite intelligences, or of minds
somewhat like our own inhabiting the organic and inorganic
bodies of nature as our minds inhabit our bodies. Setting aside
mere flights of metaphysical fancy, such an hypothesis could
claim our serious attention only if it led to a better understanding of the natural world. In fact, however, the scientist can
reasonably say of it 'je n'ai pas eu besoin de cette hypothèse',
and the theologian will recoil from any suggestion that God's
action in the natural world resembles the action of a finite
human mind under the conditions of historical life. This at least
is certain: that, so far as our scientific and historical knowledge
goes, the processes of events which constitute the world of
nature are altogether different in kind from the processes of
thought which constitute the world of history.

(iii) *History as knowledge of mind*

History, then, is not, as it has so often been mis-described,
a story of successive events or an account of change. Unlike
the natural scientist, the historian is not concerned with events
as such at all. He is only concerned with those events which
are the outward expression of thoughts, and is only concerned
with these in so far as they express thoughts. At bottom, he is
concerned with thoughts alone; with their outward expression
in events he is concerned only by the way, in so far as these
reveal to him the thoughts of which he is in search.

In a sense, these thoughts are no doubt themselves events
happening in time; but since the only way in which the historian can discern them is by re-thinking them for himself, there
is another sense, and one very important to the historian, in
which they are not in time at all. If the discovery of Pythagoras
concerning the square on the hypotenuse is a thought which we

to-day can think for ourselves, a thought that constitutes a permanent addition to mathematical knowledge, the discovery of Augustus, that a monarchy could be grafted upon the Republican constitution of Rome by developing the implications of *proconsulare imperium* and *tribunicia potestas*, is equally a thought which the student of Roman history can think for himself, a permanent addition to political ideas. If Mr. Whitehead is justified in calling the right-angled triangle an eternal object, the same phrase is applicable to the Roman constitution and the Augustan modification of it. This is an eternal object because it can be apprehended by historical thought at any time; time makes no difference to it in this respect, just as it makes no difference to the triangle. The peculiarity which makes it historical is not the fact of its happening in time, but the fact of its becoming known to us by our re-thinking the same thought which created the situation we are investigating, and thus coming to understand that situation.

Historical knowledge is the knowledge of what mind has done in the past, and at the same time it is the redoing of this, the perpetuation of past acts in the present. Its object is therefore not a mere object, something outside the mind which knows it; it is an activity of thought, which can be known only in so far as the knowing mind re-enacts it and knows itself as so doing. To the historian, the activities whose history he is studying are not spectacles to be watched, but experiences to be lived through in his own mind; they are objective, or known to him, only because they are also subjective, or activities of his own.

It may thus be said that historical inquiry reveals to the historian the powers of his own mind. Since all he can know historically is thoughts that he can re-think for himself, the fact of his coming to know them shows him that his mind is able (or by the very effort of studying them has become able) to think in these ways. And conversely, whenever he finds certain historical matters unintelligible, he has discovered a limitation of his own mind; he has discovered that there are certain ways in which he is not, or no longer, or not yet, able to think. Certain historians, sometimes whole generations of historians, find in certain periods of history nothing intelligible, and call them dark ages; but such phrases tell us nothing about those ages themselves, though they tell us a great deal about the persons who use them, namely that they are unable to re-think the thoughts which were fundamental to their life. It has been said that *die Weltgeschichte ist das Weltgericht*; and it is true, but in a sense not always recognized. It is the historian himself who stands at the bar of judgement, and there reveals his own mind in its strength and weakness, its virtues and its vices.

But historical knowledge is not concerned only with a remote past. If it is by historical thinking that we re-think and so rediscover the thought of Hammurabi or Solon, it is in the same way that we discover the thought of a friend who writes us a letter, or a stranger who crosses the street. Nor is it necessary that the historian should be one person and the subject of his inquiry another. It is only by historical thinking that I can discover what I thought ten years ago, by reading what I then wrote, or what I thought five minutes ago, by reflecting on an action that I then did, which surprised me when I realized what I had done. In this sense, all knowledge of mind is historical. The only way in which I can know my own mind is by performing some mental act or other and then considering what the act is that I have performed. If I want to know what I think about a certain subject, I try to put my ideas about it in order, on paper or otherwise; and then, having thus arranged and formulated them, I can study the result as an historical document and see what my ideas were when I did that piece of thinking: if I am dissatisfied with them, I can do it over again. If I want to know what powers my mind possesses as yet unexplored, for example, whether I can write poetry, I must try to write some, and see whether it strikes me and others as being the real thing. If I want to know whether I am as good a man as I hope, or as bad as I fear, I must examine acts that I have done, and understand what they really were: or else go and do some fresh acts and then examine those. All these inquiries are historical. They proceed by studying accomplished facts, ideas that I have thought out and expressed, acts that I have done. On what I have only begun and am still doing, no judgement can as yet be passed.

The same historical method is the only one by which I can know the mind of another, or the corporate mind (whatever exactly that phrase means) of a community or an age. To study the mind of the Victorian age or the English political spirit is simply to study the history of Victorian thought or English political activity. Here we come back to Locke and his 'historical, plain Method'. Mind not only declares, but also enjoys or possesses, its nature, both as mind in general and as this particular sort of mind with these particular dispositions and faculties, by thinking and acting, doing individual actions which express individual thoughts. If historical thinking is the way in which these thoughts are detected as expressed in these actions, it would seem that Locke's phrase hits the truth, and that historical knowledge is the only knowledge that the human mind can have of itself. The so-called science of human nature or of the human mind resolves itself into history.

It will certainly be thought (if those who think in this way have had patience to follow me thus far) that in saying this I am claiming more for history than it can ever give. The false view of history as a story of successive events or a spectacle of changes has been so often and so authoritatively taught in late years, especially in this country, that the very meaning of the word has become debauched through the assimilation of historical process to natural process. Against misunderstandings arising from this source I am bound to protest, even if I protest in vain. But there is one sense in which I should agree that the resolution of a science of mind into history means renouncing part of what a science of mind commonly claims, and, I think, claims falsely. The mental scientist, believing in the universal and therefore unalterable truth of his conclusions, thinks that the account he gives of mind holds good of all future stages in mind's history: he thinks that his science shows what mind will always be, not only what it has been in the past and is now. The historian has no gift of prophecy, and knows it; the historical study of mind, therefore, can neither foretell the future developments of human thought nor legislate for them, except so far as they must proceed—though in what direction we cannot tell—from the present as their starting-point. Not the least of the errors contained in the science of human nature is its claim to establish a framework to which all future history must conform, to close the gates of the future and bind posterity within limits due not to the nature of things (limits of that kind are real, and are easily accepted) but to the supposed laws of the mind itself.

Another type of objection deserves longer consideration. It may be granted that mind is the proper and only object of historical knowledge, but it may still be contended that historical knowledge is not the only way in which mind can be known. There might be a distinction between two ways of knowing mind. Historical thought studies mind as acting in certain determinate ways in certain determinate situations. Might there not be another way of studying mind, investigating its general characteristics in abstraction from any particular situation or particular action? If so, this would be a scientific, as opposed to an historical, knowledge of mind: not history, but mental science, psychology, or the philosophy of mind.

If such a science of mind is to be distinguished from history, how is the relation between the two to be conceived? It seems to me that two alternative views of this relation are possible.

One way of conceiving it would be to distinguish between what mind is and what it does: and to entrust the study of what it does, its particular actions, to history, and reserve the study of what it is for mental science. To use a familiar distinction, its functions depend on its structure, and behind its functions or particular activities as revealed in history there lies a structure which determines these functions, and must be studied not by history but by another kind of thought.

This conception, however, is very confused. In the case of a machine, we distinguish structure from function, and think of the latter as depending on the former. But we can do this only because the machine is equally perceptible to us in motion or at rest, and we can therefore study it in either state indifferently. But any study of mind is a study of its activities; if we try to think of a mind absolutely at rest, we are compelled to admit that if it existed at all (which is more than doubtful) at least we should be quite unable to study it. Psychologists speak of mental mechanisms; but they are speaking not of structures but of functions. They do not profess ability to observe these so-called mechanisms when they are not functioning. And if we look closer at the original distinction we shall see that it does not mean quite what it seems to mean. In the case of a machine, what we call function is really only that part of the machine's total functioning which serves the purpose of its maker or user. Bicycles are made not in order that there may be bicycles, but in order that people may travel in a certain way. Relatively to that purpose, a bicycle is functioning only when some one is riding it. But a bicycle at rest in a shed is not ceasing to function: its parts are not inactive, they are holding themselves together in a particular order; and what we call possession of its structure is nothing but this function of holding itself thus together. In this sense, whatever is called structure is in reality a way of functioning. In any other sense, mind has no function at all; it has no value, to itself or to any one else, except to be a mind, to perform those activities which constitute it a mind. Hume was therefore right to maintain that there is no such thing as 'spiritual substance', nothing that a mind is, distinct from and underlying what it does.

This idea of a mental science would be, to use Comte's famous distinction, 'metaphysical', depending on the conception of an occult substance underlying the facts of historical activity; the alternative idea would be 'positive', depending on the conception of similarities or uniformities among those facts themselves. According to this idea, the task of mental science would be to detect types or patterns of activity, repeated over and over again in history itself.

That such a science is possible is beyond question. But two observations must be made about it.

First, any estimate of the value of such a science, based on the analogy of natural science, is wholly misleading. The value of generalization in natural science depends on the fact that the data of physical science are given by perception, and perceiving is not understanding. The raw material of natural science is therefore 'mere particulars', observed but not understood, and, taken in their perceived particularity, unintelligible. It is therefore a genuine advance in knowledge to discover something intelligible in the relations between general types of them. What they are in themselves, as scientists are never tired of reminding us, remains unknown: but we can at least know something about the patterns of facts into which they enter.

A science which generalizes from historical facts is in a very different position. Here the facts, in order to serve as data, must first be historically known; and historical knowledge is not perception, it is the discerning of the thought which is the inner side of the event. The historian, when he is ready to hand over such a fact to the mental scientist as a datum for generalization, has already understood it in this way from within. If he has not done so, the fact is being used as a datum for generalization before it has been properly 'ascertained'. But if he has done so, nothing of value is left for generalization to do. If, by historical thinking, we already understand how and why Napoleon established his ascendancy in revolutionary France, nothing is added to our understanding of that process by the statement (however true) that similar things have happened elsewhere. It is only when the particular fact cannot be understood by itself that such statements are of value.

Hence the idea that such a science is valuable depends on a tacit and false assumption that the 'historical data', 'phenomena of consciousness', or the like upon which it is based are merely perceived and not historically known. To think that they can be thus merely perceived is to think of them not as mind but as nature; and consequently sciences of this type tend systematically to dementalize mind and convert it into nature. Modern examples are the pseudo-history of Spengler, where the individual historical facts which he calls 'cultures' are frankly conceived as natural products, growing and perishing 'with the same superb aimlessness as the flowers of the field', and the many psychological theories now fashionable, which conceive virtues and vices, knowledge and illusion, in the same way.

Secondly, if we ask how far the generalizations of such a science hold good, we shall see that its claim to transcend the sphere of history is baseless. Types of behaviour do, no doubt, recur, so long as minds of the same kind are placed in the same kind of situations. The behaviour-patterns characteristic of a feudal baron were no doubt fairly constant so long as there were feudal barons living in a feudal society. But they will be sought in vain (except by an inquirer content with the loosest and most fanciful analogies) in a world whose social structure is of another kind. In order that behaviour-patterns may be constant, there must be in existence a social order which recurrently produces situations of a certain kind. But social orders are historical facts, and subject to inevitable changes, fast or slow. A positive science of mind will, no doubt, be able to establish uniformities and recurrences, but it can have no guarantee that the laws it establishes will hold good beyond the historical period from which its facts are drawn. Such a science (as we have lately been taught with regard to what is called classical economics) can do no more than describe in a general way certain characteristics of the historical age in which it is constructed. If it tries to overcome this limitation by drawing on a wider field, relying on ancient history, modern anthropology, and so on, for a larger basis of facts, it will still never be more than a generalized description of certain phases in human history. It will never be a non-historical science of mind.

To regard such a positive mental science as rising above the sphere of history, and establishing the permanent and unchanging laws of human nature, is therefore possible only to a person who mistakes the transient conditions of a certain historical age for the permanent conditions of human life. It was easy for men of the eighteenth century to make this mistake, because their historical perspective was so short, and their knowledge of cultures other than their own so limited, that they could cheerfully identify the intellectual habits of a western European in their own day with the intellectual faculties bestowed by God upon Adam and all his progeny. Hume, in his account of human nature, never attempted to go beyond observing that in point of fact 'we' think in certain ways, and left undiscussed the question what he meant by the word 'we'. Even Kant, in his attempt to go beyond the 'question of fact' and settle the 'question of right', only showed that we must think in these ways if we are to possess the kind of science which we actually possess. When he asks how experience is possible, he means by experience the kind of experience enjoyed by men of his own age and civilization. He was, of course, not aware of this. No one in his time had done enough work on the history of thought to know that both the science and the experience of an eighteenth-century European were highly peculiar historical facts, very different from those of other peoples and other times. Nor was it yet realized that, even apart from the evidence of history, men must have thought in very different ways when as yet they were hardly emerged from the ape. The idea of a science of human nature, as entertained in the eighteenth century, belonged to a time when it was still believed that the human species, like every other, was a special creation with unalterable characteristics.

The fallacy inherent in the very idea of a science of human

nature is not removed by pointing out that human nature, like every kind of nature, must according to the principles of modern thought be conceived as subject to evolution. Indeed, such a modification of the idea only leads to worse consequences. Evolution, after all, is a natural process, a process of change; and as such it abolishes one specific form in creating another. The trilobites of the Silurian age may be the ancestors of the mammals of to-day, including ourselves; but a human being is not a kind of wood-louse. The past, in a natural process, is a past superseded and dead. Now suppose the historical process of human thought were in this sense an evolutionary process. It would follow that the ways of thinking characteristic of any given historical period are ways in which people must think then, but in which others, cast at different times in a different mental mould, cannot think at all. If that were the case, there would be no such thing as truth: according to the inference correctly drawn by Herbert Spencer, what we take for knowledge is merely the fashion of present-day thought, not true but at the most useful in our struggle for existence. The same evolutionary view of the history of thought is implied by Mr. Santayana, when he denounces history as fostering 'the learned illusion of living again the life of the dead', a subject fit only for 'minds fundamentally without loyalties and incapable or fearful of knowing themselves'; persons interested not in 'the rediscovery of an essence formerly discovered or prized', but only in 'the fact that people once entertained some such idea'.[1]

The fallacy common to these views is the confusion between a natural process, in which the past dies in being replaced by the present, and an historical process, in which the past, so far as it is historically known, survives in the present. Oswald Spengler, vividly realizing the difference between modern mathematics and that of the Greeks, and knowing that each is a function of its own historical age, correctly argues from his false identification of historical with natural process that to us Greek mathematics must be not only strange but unintelligible. But in fact, not only do we understand Greek mathematics easily enough, it is actually the foundation of our own. It is not the dead past of a mathematical thought once entertained by persons whose names and dates we can give, it is the living past

Danger of evolutionary thesis

[1] *The Realm of Essence*, p. 69.

of our own present mathematical inquiries, a past which, so far as we take any interest in mathematics, we still enjoy as an actual possession. Because the historical past, unlike the natural past, is a living past, kept alive by the act of historical thinking itself, the historical change from one way of thinking to another is not the death of the first, but its survival integrated in a new context involving the development and criticism of its own ideas. Mr. Santayana, like so many others, first wrongly identifies historical process with natural process, and then blames history for being what he falsely thinks it to be. Spencer's theory of the evolution of human ideas embodies the error in its crudest form.

Man has been defined as an animal capable of profiting by the experience of others. Of his bodily life this would be wholly untrue: he is not nourished because another has eaten, or refreshed because another has slept. But as regards his mental life it is true; and the way in which this profit is realized is by historical knowledge. The body of human thought or mental activity is a corporate possession, and almost all the operations which our minds perform are operations which we learned to perform from others who have performed them already. Since mind is what it does, and human nature, if it is a name for anything real, is only a name for human activities, this acquisition of ability to perform determinate operations is the acquisition of a determinate human nature. Thus the historical process is a process in which man creates for himself this or that kind of human nature by re-creating in his own thought the past to which he is heir.

This inheritance is not transmitted by any natural process. To be possessed, it must be grasped by the mind that possesses it, and historical knowledge is the way in which we enter upon the possession of it. There is not, first, a special kind of process, the historical process, and then a special way of knowing this, namely historical thought. The historical process is itself a process of thought, and it exists only in so far as the minds which are parts of it know themselves for parts of it. By historical thinking, the mind whose self-knowledge is history not only discovers within itself those powers of which historical thought reveals the possession, but actually develops those powers from a latent to an actual state, brings them into effective existence.

It would therefore be sophistical to argue that, since the historical process is a process of thought, there must be thought already present, as its presupposition, at the beginning of it, and that an account of what thought is, originally and in itself, must be a non-historical account. History does not presuppose mind; it is the life of mind itself, which is not mind except so far as it both lives in historical process and knows itself as so living.

The idea that man, apart from his self-conscious historical life, is different from the rest of creation in being a rational animal is a mere superstition. It is only by fits and starts, in a flickering and dubious manner, that human beings are rational at all. In quality, as well as in amount, their rationality is a matter of degree: some are oftener rational than others, some rational in a more intense way. But a flickering and dubious rationality can certainly not be denied to animals other than men. Their minds may be inferior in range and power to those of the lowest savages, but by the same standards the lowest savages are inferior to civilized men, and those whom we call civilized differ among themselves hardly less. There are even among non-human animals the beginnings of historical life: for example, among cats, which do not wash by instinct but are taught by their mothers. Such rudiments of education are something not essentially different from an historic culture.

Historicity, too, is a matter of degree. The historicity of very primitive societies is not easily distinguishable from the merely instinctive life of societies in which rationality is at vanishing-point. When the occasions on which thinking is done, and the kinds of things about which it is done, become more frequent and more essential to the life of society, the historic inheritance of thought, preserved by historical knowledge of what has been thought before, becomes more considerable, and with its development the development of a specifically rational life begins.

Thought is therefore not the presupposition of an historical process which is in turn the presupposition of historical knowledge. It is only in the historical process, the process of thoughts, that thought exists at all; and it is only in so far as this process is known for a process of thoughts that it is one. The self-knowledge of reason is not an accident; it belongs to its essence. This is why historical knowledge is no luxury, or mere amusement of a mind at leisure from more pressing occupations, but a prime duty, whose discharge is essential to the maintenance, not only of any particular form or type of reason, but of reason itself.

(iv) *Conclusions*

It remains to draw a few conclusions from the thesis I have tried to maintain.

First, as regards history itself. The methods of modern historical inquiry have grown up under the shadow of their elder sister, the method of natural science; in some ways helped by its example, in other ways hindered. Throughout this essay it has been necessary to engage in a running fight with what may be called a positivistic conception, or rather misconception, of history, as the study of successive events lying in a dead past, events to be understood as the scientist understands natural events, by classifying them and establishing relations between the classes thus defined. This misconception is not only an endemic error in modern philosophical thought about history, it is also a constant peril to historical thought itself. So far as historians yield to it, they neglect their proper task of penetrating to the thought of the agents whose acts they are studying, and content themselves with determining the externals of these acts, the kind of things about them which can be studied statistically. Statistical research is for the historian a good servant but a bad master. It profits him nothing to make statistical generalizations, unless he can thereby detect the thought behind the facts about which he is generalizing. At the present day, historical thought is almost everywhere disentangling itself from the toils of the positivistic fallacy, and recognizing that in itself history is nothing but the re-enactment of past thought in the historian's mind; but much still needs to be done if the full fruits of this recognition are to be reaped. All kinds of historical fallacies are still current, due to confusion between historical process and natural process: not only the cruder fallacies of mistaking historical facts of culture and tradition for functions of biological facts like race and pedigree, but subtler fallacies affecting methods of research and the organization of historical inquiry, which it would take too long to enumerate here. It is not until these have been eradicated that we can see how far historical thought, attaining at last its proper shape and stature, is able to make good the claims long ago put forward on behalf of the science of human nature.

Secondly, with regard to past attempts to construct such a science.

The positive function of so-called sciences of the human mind, whether total or partial (I refer to such studies as those on the theory of knowledge, of morals, of politics, of economics, and so forth), has always tended to be misconceived. Ideally, they are designed as accounts of one unchanging subject-matter, the mind of man as it always has been and always will be. Little acquaintance with them is demanded in order to see that they are nothing of the sort, but only inventories of the wealth achieved by the human mind at a certain stage in its history. The *Republic* of Plato is an account, not of the unchanging ideal of political life, but of the Greek ideal as Plato received it and re-interpreted it. The *Ethics* of Aristotle describes not an eternal morality but the morality of the Greek gentleman. Hobbes's *Leviathan* expounds the political ideas of seventeenth-century absolutism in their English form. Kant's ethical theory expresses the moral convictions of German pietism; his *Critique of Pure Reason* analyses the conceptions and principles of Newtonian science, in their relation to the philosophical problems of the day. These limitations are often taken for defects, as if a more powerful thinker than Plato would have lifted himself clean out of the atmosphere of Greek politics, or as if Aristotle ought to have anticipated the moral conceptions of Christianity or the modern world. So far from being a defect, they are a sign of merit; they are most clearly to be seen in those works whose quality is of the best. The reason is that in those works the authors are doing best the only thing that can be done when an attempt is made to construct a science of the human mind. They are expounding the position reached by the human mind in its historical development down to their own time.

When they try to justify that position, all they can do is to exhibit it as a logical one, a coherent whole of ideas. If, realizing that any such justification is circular, they try to make the whole depend on something outside itself, they fail, as indeed they must; for since the historical present includes in itself its own past, the real ground on which the whole rests, namely the past out of which it has grown, is not outside it but is included within it.

If these systems remain valuable to posterity, that is not in spite of their strictly historical character but because of it. To us, the ideas expressed in them are ideas belonging to the past; but it is not a dead past; by understanding it historically we incorporate it into our present thought, and enable ourselves by developing and criticizing it to use that heritage for our own advancement.

But a mere inventory of our intellectual possessions at the present time can never show by what right we enjoy them. To do this there is only one way: by analysing them instead of merely describing them, and showing how they have been built up in the historical development of thought. What Kant, for example, wanted to do when he set out to justify our use of a category like causation, can in a sense be done; but it cannot be done on Kant's method, which yields a merely circular argument, proving that such a category can be used, and must be used if we are to have Newtonian science; it can be done by research into the history of scientific thought. All Kant could show was that eighteenth-century scientists did think in terms of that category; the question why they so thought can be answered by investigating the history of the idea of causation. If more than this is required; if a proof is needed that the idea is true, that people are right to think in that way; then a demand is being made which in the nature of things can never be satisfied. How can we ever satisfy ourselves that the principles on which we think are true, except by going on thinking according to those principles, and seeing whether unanswerable criticisms of them emerge as we work? To criticize the conceptions of science is the work of science itself as it proceeds; to demand that such criticism should be anticipated by the theory of knowledge is to demand that such a theory should anticipate the history of thought.

Finally, there is the question what function can be assigned to the science of psychology. At first sight its position appears equivocal. On the one hand, it claims to be a science of mind; but if so, its apparatus of scientific method is merely the fruit of a false analogy, and it must pass over into history and, as such, disappear. And this is certainly what ought to happen so far as psychology claims to deal with the functions of reason itself. To speak of the psychology of reasoning, or the psychology of the moral self (to quote the titles of two well-known books), is to misuse words and confuse issues, ascribing to a quasi-naturalistic science a subject-matter whose being and development are not natural but historical. But if psychology avoids this danger and renounces interference with what is properly the subject-matter of history, it is likely to fall back into a pure science of nature and to become a mere branch of physiology, dealing with muscular and nervous movements.

But there is a third alternative. In realizing its own rationality, mind also realizes the presence in itself of elements that are not rational. They are not body; they are mind, but not rational mind or thought. To use an old distinction, they are psyche or soul as distinct from spirit. These irrational elements are the subject-matter of psychology. They are the blind forces and activities in us which are part of human life as it consciously experiences itself, but are not parts of the historical process: sensation as distinct from thought, feelings as distinct from conceptions, appetite as distinct from will. Their importance to us consists in the fact that they form the proximate environment in which our reason lives, as our physiological organism is the proximate environment in which they live. They are the basis of our rational life, though no part of it. Our reason discovers them, but in studying them it is not studying itself. By learning to know them, it finds out how it can help them to live in health, so that they can feed and support it while it pursues its own proper task, the self-conscious creation of its own historical life.

§ 2. The Historical Imagination

An inquiry into the nature of historical thinking is among the tasks which philosophy may legitimately undertake; and at the present time [1935] there are reasons, as it seems to me, for thinking such an inquiry not only legitimate but necessary. For there is a sense in which, at particular periods of history, particular philosophical problems are, as it were, in season, and claim the special attention of a philosopher anxious to be of service to his age. In part, the problems of philosophy are unchanging; in part, they vary from age to age, according to the special characteristics of human life and thought at the time; and in the best philosophers of every age these two parts are so interwoven that the permanent problems appear *sub specie saeculi*, and the special problems of the age *sub specie aeternitatis*. Whenever human thought has been dominated by some special interest, the most fruitful philosophy of the age has reflected that domination; not passively, by mere submission to its influence, but actively, by making a special attempt to understand it and placing it in the focus of philosophical inquiry.

In the Middle Ages theology was the interest that served in this way to focus philosophical speculation. In the seventeenth century it was physical science. To-day, when we conventionally date the beginnings of modern philosophy to the seventeenth century, we mean, I think, that the scientific interest which then began to dominate human life still dominates it. But if we compare the seventeenth-century mind, in its general orientation, with that of to-day, by comparing the subjects dealt with in their literature, we can hardly fail to be struck by one important difference. Since the time of Descartes, and even since the time of Kant, mankind has acquired a new habit of thinking historically. I do not mean that there were no historians worthy of the name until a century and a half ago; that would be untrue: I do not even mean that since then the bulk of historical knowledge and the output of historical books have enormously increased; that would be true but relatively unimportant. What I mean is that during this time historical thought has worked out a technique of its own, no less definite in its character and certain in its results than its elder sister, the technique of natural science; and that, in thus entering upon the *sichere Gang einer Wissenschaft*, it has taken a place in human life from which its influence has permeated and to some extent transformed every department of thought and action.

Among others, it has profoundly influenced philosophy; but on the whole the attitude of philosophy towards this influence has been more passive than active. Some philosophers are inclined to welcome it; others to resent it; comparatively few have thought philosophically about it. Attempts have been made, chiefly in Germany and Italy, to answer the questions: What is historical thinking? and What light does it throw on the traditional problems of philosophy? and by answering these questions to do for the historical consciousness of to-day what Kant's transcendental analytic did for the scientific consciousness of the eighteenth century. But for the most part, and especially in this country, it has been usual to ignore all such questions, and to discuss the problems of knowledge in seeming unawareness that there is such a thing as history. This custom can of course be defended. It may be argued that history is not knowledge at all, but only opinion, and unworthy of philosophical study. Or it may be argued that, so far as it is knowledge, its problems are those of knowledge in general, and call for no special treatment. For myself, I cannot accept either defence. If history is opinion, why should philosophy on that account ignore it? If it is knowledge, why should philosophers not study its methods with the same attention that they give to the very different methods of science? And when I read the works of even the greatest contemporary and recent English philosophers, admiring them deeply and learning from them more than I can hope to acknowledge, I find myself constantly haunted by the thought that their accounts of knowledge, based as they seem to be primarily on the study of perception and of scientific thinking, not only ignore historical thinking but are actually inconsistent with there being such a thing.

No doubt, historical thought is in one way like perception. Each has for its proper object something individual. What I perceive is this room, this table, this paper. What the historian thinks about is Elizabeth or Marlborough, the Peloponnesian War or the policy of Ferdinand and Isabella. But what we perceive is always the this, the here, the now. Even when we hear a distant explosion or see a stellar conflagration long after it has happened, there is still a moment at which it is here and now perceptible, when it is this explosion, this new star. Historical thought is of something which can never be a this, because it is never a here and now. Its objects are events which have finished happening, and conditions no longer in existence. Only when they are no longer perceptible do they become objects for historical thought. Hence all theories of knowledge that conceive it as a transaction or relation between a subject and an object both actually existing, and confronting or compresent to one another, theories that take acquaintance as the essence of knowledge, make history impossible.

In another way history resembles science: for in each of them knowledge is inferential or reasoned. But whereas science lives in a world of abstract universals, which are in one sense everywhere and in another nowhere, in one sense at all times and in another at no time, the things about which the historian reasons are not abstract but concrete, not universal but individual, not indifferent to space and time but having a where and a when of their own, though the where need not be here and the when cannot be now. History, therefore, cannot be made to square with theories according to which the object of knowledge is abstract and changeless, a logical entity towards which the mind may take up various attitudes.

Nor is it possible to give an account of knowledge by combining theories of these two types. Current philosophy is full of such combinations. Knowledge by acquaintance and knowledge by description; eternal objects and the transient situations into which they are ingredient; realm of essence and realm of matter; in these and other such dichotomies, as in the older dichotomies of matters of fact and relations between ideas, or truths of fact and truths of reason, provision is made for the peculiarities both of a perception which grasps the here and now, and of the abstract thought that apprehends the everywhere and always: the αἴσθησις and νόησις of philosophical tradition. But just as history is neither αἴσθησις nor νόησις, so it is not a combination of the two. It is a third thing, having some of the characteristics of each, but combining them in a way impossible to either. It is not partly acquaintance with transient situations and partly reasoned knowledge of abstract entities. It is wholly a reasoned knowledge of what is transient and concrete.

My purpose here is to offer a brief account of this third thing which is history; and I will begin by stating what may be called the common-sense theory of it, the theory which most people believe, or imagine themselves to believe, when first they reflect on the matter.

According to this theory, the essential things in history are memory and authority. If an event or a state of things is to be historically known, first of all some one must be acquainted with it; then he must remember it; then he must state his recollection of it in terms intelligible to another; and finally that other must accept the statement as true. History is thus the believing some one else when he says that he remembers something. The believer is the historian; the person believed is called his authority.

This doctrine implies that historical truth, so far as it is at all accessible to the historian, is accessible to him only because it exists ready made in the ready-made statements of his authorities. These statements are to him a sacred text, whose value depends wholly on the unbrokenness of the tradition they represent. He must therefore on no account tamper with them. He must not mutilate them; he must not add to them; and, above all, he must not contradict them. For if he takes it upon himself to pick and choose, to decide that some of his authority's statements are important and others not, he is going behind his authority's back and appealing to some other criterion; and this, on the theory, is exactly what he cannot do. If he adds to them, interpolating in them constructions of his own devising, and accepting these constructions as additions to his knowledge, he is believing something for a reason other than the fact that his authority has said it; and this again he has no right to do. Worst of all, if he contradicts them, presuming to decide that his authority has misrepresented the facts, and rejecting his statements as incredible, he is believing the opposite of what he has been told, and committing the worst possible offence against the rules of his craft. The authority may be garrulous, discursive, a gossip and a scandal-monger; he may have overlooked or forgotten or omitted facts; he may have ignorantly or wilfully mis-stated them; but against these defects the historian has no remedy. For him, on the theory, what his authorities tell him is the truth, the whole accessible truth, and nothing but the truth.

These consequences of the common-sense theory have only to be stated in order to be repudiated. Every historian is aware that on occasion he does tamper in all these three ways with what he finds in his authorities. He selects from them what he thinks important, and omits the rest; he interpolates in them things which they do not explicitly say; and he criticizes them by rejecting or amending what he regards as due to misinformation or mendacity. But I am not sure whether we historians always realize the consequences of what we are doing. In general, when we reflect on our own work, we seem to accept

what I have called the common-sense theory, while claiming
our own rights of selection, construction, and criticism. No
doubt these rights are inconsistent with the theory; but we
attempt to soften the contradiction by minimizing the extent
to which they are exercised, thinking of them as emergency
measures, a kind of revolt into which the historian may be driven
at times by the exceptional incompetence of his authorities, but
which does not fundamentally disturb the normal peaceful
régime in which he placidly believes what he is told because he
is told to believe it. Yet these things, however seldom they are
done, are either historical crimes or facts fatal to the theory:
for on the theory they ought to be done, not rarely, but never.
And in fact they are neither criminal nor exceptional. Throughout the course of his work the historian is selecting, constructing,
and criticizing; it is only by doing these things that he maintains
his thought upon the *sichere Gang einer Wissenschaft*. By
explicitly recognizing this fact it is possible to effect what, again
borrowing a Kantian phrase, one might call a Copernican revolution in the theory of history: the discovery that, so far from
relying on an authority other than himself, to whose statements
his thought must conform, the historian is his own authority
and his thought autonomous, self-authorizing, possessed of a
criterion to which his so-called authorities must conform and
by reference to which they are criticized.

The autonomy of historical thought is seen at its simplest in
the work of selection. The historian who tries to work on the
common-sense theory, and accurately reproduce what he finds
in his authorities, resembles a landscape-painter who tries to
work on that theory of art which bids the artist copy nature.
He may fancy that he is reproducing in his own medium the
actual shapes and colours of natural things; but however hard
he tries to do this he is always selecting, simplifying, schematiz-
ing, leaving out what he thinks unimportant and putting in what
he regards as essential. It is the artist, and not nature, that is
responsible for what goes into the picture. In the same way, no
historian, not even the worst, merely copies out his authorities;
even if he puts in nothing of his own (which is never really
possible), he is always leaving out things which, for one reason
or another, he decides that his own work does not need or
cannot use. It is he, therefore, and not his authority, that is

responsible for what goes in. On that question he is his own master: his thought is to that extent autonomous.

An even clearer exhibition of this autonomy is found in what I have called historical construction. The historian's authorities tell him of this or that phase in a process whose intermediate phases they leave undescribed; he then interpolates these phases for himself. His picture of his subject, though it may consist in part of statements directly drawn from his authorities, consists also, and increasingly with every increase in his competence as an historian, of statements reached inferentially from those according to his own criteria, his own rules of method, and his own canons of relevance. In this part of his work he is never depending on his authorities in the sense of repeating what they tell him; he is relying on his own powers and constituting himself his own authority; while his so-called authorities are now not authorities at all but only evidence.

The clearest demonstration of the historian's autonomy, however, is provided by historical criticism. As natural science finds its proper method when the scientist, in Bacon's metaphor, puts Nature to the question, tortures her by experiment in order to wring from her answers to his own questions, so history finds its proper method when the historian puts his authorities in the witness-box, and by cross-questioning extorts from them information which in their original statements they have withheld, either because they did not wish to give it or because they did not possess it. Thus, a commander's dispatches may claim a victory; the historian, reading them in a critical spirit, will ask: 'If it was a victory, why was it not followed up in this or that way?' and may thus convict the writer of concealing the truth. Or, by using the same method, he may convict of ignorance a less critical predecessor who has accepted the version of the battle given him by the same dispatches.

The historian's autonomy is here manifested in its extremest form, because it is here evident that somehow, in virtue of his activity as an historian, he has it in his power to reject something explicitly told him by his authorities and to substitute something else. If that is possible, the criterion of historical truth cannot be the fact that a statement is made by an authority. It is the truthfulness and the information of the so-called authority that are in question; and this question the historian has to answer for himself, on his own authority. Even if he accepts what his authorities tell him, therefore, he accepts it not on their authority but on his own; not because they say it, but because it satisfies his criterion of historical truth.

The common-sense theory which bases history upon memory and authority needs no further refutation. Its bankruptcy is evident. For the historian there can never be authorities, because the so-called authorities abide a verdict which only he can give. Yet the common-sense theory may claim a qualified and relative truth. The historian, generally speaking, works at a subject which others have studied before him. In proportion as he is more of a novice, either in this particular subject or in history as a whole, his forerunners are, relatively to his incompetence, authoritative; and in the limiting case where his incompetence and ignorance were absolute, they could be called authorities without qualification. As he becomes more and more master of his craft and his subject, they become less and less his authorities, more and more his fellow students, to be treated with respect or contempt according to their deserts.

And as history does not depend on authority, so it does not depend upon memory. The historian can rediscover what has been completely forgotten, in the sense that no statement of it has reached him by an unbroken tradition from eyewitnesses. He can even discover what, until he discovered it, no one ever knew to have happened at all. This he does partly by the critical treatment of statements contained in his sources, partly by the use of what are called unwritten sources, which are increasingly employed as history becomes increasingly sure of its own proper methods and its own proper criterion.

I have spoken of the criterion of historical truth. What is this criterion? According to the common-sense theory, it is the agreement of the statements made by the historian with those which he finds in his authorities. This answer we now know to be false, and we must seek another. We cannot renounce the search. Some answer to the question there must be, for without a criterion there can be no criticism. One answer to this question was offered by the greatest English philosopher of our time in his pamphlet on *The Presuppositions of Critical History*. Bradley's essay was an early work with which in his maturity he was dissatisfied; but, unsatisfactory though it cer-

tainly is, it bears the stamp of his genius. In it Bradley faces
the question how it is possible for the historian, in defiance of
the common-sense theory, to turn the tables on his so-called
authorities and to say 'This is what our authorities record, but
what really happened must have been not this but that'.

His answer to this question was that our experience of the
world teaches us that some kinds of things happen and others
do not; this experience, then, is the criterion which the historian
brings to bear on the statements of his authorities. If they tell
him that things happened of a kind which, according to his
experience, does not happen, he is obliged to disbelieve them; if
the things which they report are of a kind which according to his
experience does happen, he is free to accept their statements.

There are many obvious objections to this idea, on which I
shall not insist. It is deeply tinged with the empiricist philosophy against which Bradley was soon so effectively to rebel.
But apart from this there are certain special points in which
the argument appears to me defective.

First, the proposed criterion is a criterion not of what did
happen but of what could happen. It is in fact nothing but
Aristotle's criterion of what is admissible in poetry; and hence
it does not serve to discriminate history from fiction. It would
no doubt be satisfied by the statements of an historian, but it
would be satisfied no less adequately by those of an historical
novelist. It cannot therefore be the criterion of critical history.

Secondly, because it can never tell us what did happen, we
are left to rely for that on the sheer authority of our informant.
We undertake, when we apply it, to believe everything our
informant tells us so long as it satisfies the merely negative
criterion of being possible. This is not to turn the tables on our
authorities; it is blindly to accept what they tell us. The critical
attitude has not been achieved.

Thirdly, the historian's experience of the world in which he
lives can only help him to check, even negatively, the statements
of his authorities in so far as they are concerned not with history
but with nature, which has no history. The laws of nature have
always been the same, and what is against nature now was
against nature two thousand years ago; but the historical as
distinct from the natural conditions of man's life differ so much
at different times that no argument from analogy will hold.

That the Greeks and Romans exposed their new-born children in order to control the numbers of their population is no less true for being unlike anything that happens in the experience of contributors to the *Cambridge Ancient History*. In point of fact Bradley's treatment of the subject grew not out of the ordinary course of historical study but out of his interest in the credibility of the New Testament narratives, and in particular their miraculous element; but a criterion which only serves in the case of miracle is of sadly little use to the weekday historian.

Bradley's essay, inconclusive though it is, remains memorable for the fact that in it the Copernican revolution in the theory of historical knowledge has been in principle accomplished. For the common-sense theory, historical truth consists in the historian's beliefs conforming to the statements of his authorities; Bradley has seen that the historian brings with him to the study of his authorities a criterion of his own by reference to which the authorities themselves are judged. What it is, Bradley failed to discover. It remains to be seen whether, sixty years later, his problem, which in the meantime I believe no English-speaking philosopher has discussed in print, can be advanced beyond the point at which he left it.

I have already remarked that, in addition to selecting from among his authorities' statements those which he regards as important, the historian must in two ways go beyond what his authorities tell him. One is the critical way, and this is what Bradley has attempted to analyse. The other is the constructive way. Of this he has said nothing, and to this I now propose to return. I described constructive history as interpolating, between the statements borrowed from our authorities, other statements implied by them. Thus our authorities tell us that on one day Caesar was in Rome and on a later day in Gaul; they tell us nothing about his journey from one place to the other, but we interpolate this with a perfectly good conscience.

This act of interpolation has two significant characteristics. First, it is in no way arbitrary or merely fanciful: it is necessary or, in Kantian language, *a priori*. If we filled up the narrative of Caesar's doings with fanciful details such as the names of the persons he met on the way, and what he said to them, the construction would be arbitrary: it would be in fact the kind of construction which is done by an historical novelist. But if our construction involves nothing that is not necessitated by the evidence, it is a legitimate historical construction of a kind without which there can be no history at all.

Secondly, what is in this way inferred is essentially something imagined. If we look out over the sea and perceive a ship, and five minutes later look again and perceive it in a different place, we find ourselves obliged to imagine it as having occupied intermediate positions when we were not looking. That is already an example of historical thinking; and it is not otherwise that we find ourselves obliged to imagine Caesar as having travelled from Rome to Gaul when we are told that he was in these different places at these successive times.

This activity, with this double character, I shall call *a priori* imagination; and, though I shall have more to say of it hereafter, for the present I shall be content to remark that, however unconscious we may be of its operation, it is this activity which, bridging the gaps between what our authorities tell us, gives the historical narrative or description its continuity. That the historian must use his imagination is a commonplace; to quote Macaulay's *Essay on History*, 'a perfect historian must possess an imagination sufficiently powerful to make his narrative affecting and picturesque'; but this is to underestimate the part played by the historical imagination, which is properly not ornamental but structural. Without it the historian would have no narrative to adorn. The imagination, that 'blind but indispensable faculty' without which, as Kant has shown, we could never perceive the world around us, is indispensable in the same way to history: it is this which, operating not capriciously as fancy but in its *a priori* form, does the entire work of historical construction.

Two misunderstandings may here be forestalled. First, it may be thought that by imagining we çan present to ourselves only what is imaginary in the sense of being fictitious or unreal. This prejudice need only be mentioned in order to be dispelled. If I imagine the friend who lately left my house now entering his own, the fact that I imagine this event gives me no reason to believe it unreal. The imaginary, simply as such, is neither unreal nor real.

Secondly, to speak of *a priori* imagination may seem a paradox, for it may be thought that imagination is essentially capricious, arbitrary, merely fanciful. But in addition to its historical function there are two other functions of *a priori* imagination which are, or ought to be, familiar to all. One is the pure or free, but by no means arbitrary, imagination of the artist. A man writing a novel composes a story where parts are played by various characters. Characters and incidents are all alike imaginary; yet the whole aim of the novelist is to show the characters acting and the incidents developing in a manner determined by a necessity internal to themselves. The story, if it is a good story, cannot develop otherwise than as it does; the novelist in imagining it cannot imagine it developing except as it does develop. Here, and equally in all other kinds of art, the *a priori* imagination is at work. Its other familiar function is what may be called the perceptual imagination, supplementing and consolidating the data of perception in the way so well analysed by Kant, by presenting to us objects of possible perception which are not actually perceived: the under side of this table, the inside of an unopened egg, the back of the moon. Here again the imagination is *a priori*: we cannot but imagine what cannot but be there. The historical imagination differs from these not in being *a priori*, but in having as its special task to imagine the past: not an object of possible perception, since it does not now exist, but able through this activity to become an object of our thought.

The historian's picture of his subject, whether that subject be a sequence of events or a past state of things, thus appears as a web of imaginative construction stretched between certain fixed points provided by the statements of his authorities; and if these points are frequent enough and the threads spun from each to the next are constructed with due care, always by the *a priori* imagination and never by merely arbitrary fancy, the whole picture is constantly verified by appeal to these data, and runs little risk of losing touch with the reality which it represents.

Actually, this is very much how we do think of historical work, when the common-sense theory has ceased to satisfy us, and we have become aware of the part played in it by the constructive imagination. But such a conception is in one way seriously at fault: it overlooks the no less important part played by criticism. We think of our web of construction as pegged down, so to speak, to the facts by the statements of authorities, which we regard as data or fixed points for the work of construction. But in so thinking we have slipped back into the theory, which we now know to be false, that truth is given us ready made in these statements. We know that truth is to be had, not by swallowing what our authorities tell us, but by criticizing it; and thus the supposedly fixed points between which the historical imagination spins its web are not given to us ready made, they must be achieved by critical thinking.

There is nothing other than historical thought itself, by appeal to which its conclusions may be verified. The hero of a detective novel is thinking exactly like an historian when, from indications of the most varied kinds, he constructs an imaginary picture of how a crime was committed, and by whom. At first, this is a mere theory, awaiting verification, which must come to it from without. Happily for the detective, the conventions of that literary form dictate that when his construction is complete it shall be neatly pegged down by a confession from the criminal, given in such circumstances that its genuineness is beyond question. The historian is less fortunate. If, after convincing himself by a study of the evidence already available that Bacon wrote the plays of Shakespeare or that Henry VII murdered the Princes in the Tower, he were to find an autograph document confessing the fact, he would by no means have verified his conclusions; the new document, so far from closing the inquiry, would only have complicated it by raising a new problem, the problem of its own authenticity.

I began by considering a theory according to which everything is given: according to which all truth, so far as any truth is accessible to the historian, is provided for him ready made in the ready-made statements of his authorities. I then saw that much of what he takes for true is not given in this way but constructed by his *a priori* imagination; but I still fancied that this imagination worked inferentially from fixed points given in the same sense. I am now driven to confess that there are for historical thought no fixed points thus given: in other words, that in history, just as there are properly speaking no authorities, so there are properly speaking no data.

Historians certainly think of themselves as working from data; where by data they mean historical facts possessed by them ready made at the beginning of a certain piece of historical research. Such a datum, if the research concerns the Peloponnesian War, would be, for example, a certain statement of Thucydides, accepted as substantially true. But when we ask what gives historical thought this datum, the answer is obvious: historical thought gives it to itself, and therefore in relation to historical thought at large it is not a datum but a result or achievement. It is only our historical knowledge which tells us that these curious marks on paper are Greek letters; that the words which they form have certain meanings in the Attic dialect; that the passage is authentic Thucydides, not an interpolation or corruption; and that on this occasion Thucydides knew what he was talking about and was trying to tell the truth. Apart from all this, the passage is merely a pattern of black marks on white paper: not any historical fact at all, but something existing here and now, and perceived by the historian. All that the historian means, when he describes certain historical facts as his data, is that for the purposes of a particular piece of work there are certain historical problems relevant to that work which for the present he proposes to treat as settled; though, if they are settled, it is only because historical thinking has settled them in the past, and they remain settled only until he or some one else decides to reopen them.

His web of imaginative construction, therefore, cannot derive its validity from being pegged down, as at first I described it, to certain given facts. That description represented an attempt to relieve him of the responsibility for the nodal points of his fabric, while admitting his responsibility for what he constructs between them. In point of fact, he is just as responsible for the one as for the other. Whether he accepts or rejects or modifies or reinterprets what his so-called authorities tell him, it is he that is responsible for the statement which, after duly criticizing them, he makes. The criterion that justifies him in making it can never be the fact that it has been given him by an authority.

This brings me back to the question what this criterion is. And at this point a partial and provisional answer can be given. The web of imaginative construction is something far more solid and powerful than we have hitherto realized. So far from relying for its validity upon the support of given facts, it actually serves as the touchstone by which we decide whether alleged facts are genuine. Suetonius tells me that Nero at one time intended to evacuate Britain. I reject his statement, not because any better authority flatly contradicts it, for of course none does; but because my reconstruction of Nero's policy based on Tacitus will not allow me to think that Suetonius is right. And if I am told that this is merely to say I prefer Tacitus to Suetonius, I confess that I do: but I do so just because I find myself able to incorporate what Tacitus tells me into a coherent and continuous picture of my own, and cannot do this for Suetonius.

It is thus the historian's picture of the past, the product of his own *a priori* imagination, that has to justify the sources used in its construction. These sources are sources, that is to say, credence is given to them, only because they are in this way justified. For any source may be tainted: this writer prejudiced, that misinformed; this inscription misread by a bad epigraphist, that blundered by a careless stonemason; this potsherd placed out of its context by an incompetent excavator, that by a blameless rabbit. The critical historian has to discover and correct all these and many other kinds of falsification. He does it, and can only do it, by considering whether the picture of the past to which the evidence leads him is a coherent and continuous picture, one which makes sense. The *a priori* imagination which does the work of historical construction supplies the means of historical criticism as well.

Freed from its dependence on fixed points supplied from without, the historian's picture of the past is thus in every detail an imaginary picture, and its necessity is at every point the necessity of the *a priori* imagination. Whatever goes into it, goes into it not because his imagination passively accepts it, but because it actively demands it.

The resemblance between the historian and the novelist, to which I have already referred, here reaches its culmination. Each of them makes it his business to construct a picture which is partly a narrative of events, partly a description of situations, exhibition of motives, analysis of characters. Each aims at making his picture a coherent whole, where every character and every situation is so bound up with the rest that this character in this situation cannot but act in this way, and we cannot imagine him as acting otherwise. The novel and the history must both of them make sense; nothing is admissible in either except what is necessary, and the judge of this necessity is in both cases the imagination. Both the novel and the history are self-explanatory, self-justifying, the product of an autonomous or self-authorizing activity; and in both cases this activity is the *a priori* imagination.

As works of imagination, the historian's work and the novelist's do not differ. Where they do differ is that the historian's picture is meant to be true. The novelist has a single task only: to construct a coherent picture, one that makes sense. The historian has a double task: he has both to do this, and to construct a picture of things as they really were and of events as they really happened. This further necessity imposes upon him obedience to three rules of method, from which the novelist or artist in general is free.

First, his picture must be localized in space and time. The artist's need not; essentially, the things that he imagines are imagined as happening at no place and at no date. Of *Wuthering Heights* it has been well said that the scene is laid in Hell, though the place-names are English; and it was a sure instinct that led another great novelist to replace Oxford by Christminster, Wantage by Alfredston, and Fawley by Marychurch, recoiling against the discord of topographical fact in what should be a purely imaginary world.

Secondly, all history must be consistent with itself. Purely imaginary worlds cannot clash and need not agree; each is a world to itself. But there is only one historical world, and everything in it must stand in some relation to everything else, even if that relation is only topographical and chronological.

Thirdly, and most important, the historian's picture stands in a peculiar relation to something called evidence. The only way in which the historian or any one else can judge, even tentatively, of its truth is by considering this relation; and, in practice, what we mean by asking whether an historical statement is true is whether it can be justified by an appeal to the evidence: for a truth unable to be so justified is to the historian a thing of no interest. What is this thing called evidence, and what is its relation to the finished historical work?

We already know what evidence is not. It is not ready-made historical knowledge, to be swallowed and regurgitated by the historian's mind. Everything is evidence which the historian can use as evidence. But what can he so use? It must be some-thing here and now perceptible to him: this written page, this spoken utterance, this building, this finger-print. And of all the things perceptible to him there is not one which he might not conceivably use as evidence on some question, if he came to it with the right question in mind. The enlargement of historical knowledge comes about mainly through finding how to use as evidence this or that kind of perceived fact which historians have hitherto thought useless to them.

The whole perceptible world, then, is potentially and in principle evidence to the historian. It becomes actual evidence in so far as he can use it. And he cannot use it unless he comes to it with the right kind of historical knowledge. The more historical knowledge we have, the more we can learn from any given piece of evidence; if we had none, we could learn nothing. Evidence is evidence only when some one contemplates it historically. Otherwise it is merely perceived fact, historically dumb. It follows that historical knowledge can only grow out of historical knowledge; in other words, that historical thinking is an original and fundamental activity of the human mind, or, as Descartes might have said, that the idea of the past is an 'innate' idea.

Historical thinking is that activity of the imagination by which we endeavour to provide this innate idea with detailed content. And this we do by using the present as evidence for its own past. Every present has a past of its own, and any imaginative reconstruction of the past aims at reconstructing the past of this present, the present in which the act of imagina-tion is going on, as here and now perceived. In principle the aim of any such act is to use the entire perceptible here-and-now as evidence for the entire past through whose process it has come into being. In practice, this aim can never be achieved. The perceptible here-and-now can never be perceived, still less inter-preted, in its entirety; and the infinite process of past time can never be envisaged as a whole. But this separation between what is attempted in principle and what is achieved in practice is the lot of mankind, not a peculiarity of historical thinking. The fact that it is found there only shows that herein history is like art, science, philosophy, the pursuit of virtue, and the search for happiness.

It is for the same reason that in history, as in all serious matters, no achievement is final. The evidence available for solving any given problem changes with every change of historical method and with every variation in the competence of historians. The principles by which this evidence is interpreted change too; since the interpreting of evidence is a task to which a man must bring everything he knows: historical knowledge, knowledge of nature and man, mathematical knowledge, philosophical knowledge; and not knowledge only, but mental habits and possessions of every kind: and none of these is unchanging. Because of these changes, which never cease, however slow they may appear to observers who take a short view, every new generation must rewrite history in its own way; every new historian, not content with giving new answers to old questions, must revise the questions themselves; and—since historical thought is a river into which none can step twice—even a single historian, working at a single subject for a certain length of time, finds when he tries to reopen an old question that the question has changed.

This is not an argument for historical scepticism. It is only the discovery of a second dimension of historical thought, the history of history: the discovery that the historian himself, together with the here-and-now which forms the total body of evidence available to him, is a part of the process he is studying, has his own place in that process, and can see it only from the point of view which at this present moment he occupies within it.

But neither the raw material of historical knowledge, the detail of the here-and-now as given him in perception, nor the various endowments that serve him as aids to interpreting this evidence, can give the historian his criterion of historical truth. That criterion is the idea of history itself: the idea of an imaginary picture of the past. That idea is, in Cartesian language, innate; in Kantian language, *a priori*. It is not a chance product of psychological causes; it is an idea which every man possesses as part of the furniture of his mind, and discovers himself to possess in so far as he becomes conscious of what it is to have a mind. Like other ideas of the same sort, it is one to which no fact of experience exactly corresponds. The historian, however long and faithfully he works, can never say that his work, even in crudest outline or in this or that smallest detail, is done once for all. He can never say that his picture of the past is at any point adequate to his idea of what it ought to be. But, however fragmentary and faulty the results of his work may be, the idea which governed its course is clear, rational, and universal. It is the idea of the historical imagination as a self-dependent, self-determining, and self-justifying form of thought.

§ 3. *Historical Evidence*

Introduction

'History,' said Bury, 'is a science; no less, and no more.'

Perhaps it is no less: that depends on what you mean by a science. There is a slang usage, like that for which 'hall' means a music-hall or 'pictures' moving pictures, according to which 'science' means natural science. Whether history is a science in that sense of the word, however, need not be asked; for in the tradition of European speech, going back to the time when Latin speakers translated the Greek ἐπιστήμη by their own word *scientia*, and continuing unbroken down to the present day, the word 'science' means any organized body of knowledge. If that is what the word means Bury is so far incontestably right, that history is a science, nothing less.

But if it is no less, it is certainly more. For anything that is a science at all must be more than merely a science, it must be a science of some special kind. A body of knowledge is never merely organized, it is always organized in some particular way. Some bodies of knowledge, like meteorology, are organized by collecting observations concerned with events of a certain kind which the scientist can watch as they happen, though he cannot produce them at will. Others, like chemistry, are organized not only by observing events as they happen, but by making them happen under strictly controlled conditions. Others again are organized not by observing events at all, but by making certain assumptions and proceeding with the utmost exactitude to argue out their consequences.

History is organized in none of these ways. Wars and revolutions, and the other events with which it deals, are not deliberately produced by historians under laboratory conditions in order to be studied with scientific precision. Nor are they even observed by historians, in the sense in which events are observed by natural scientists. Meteorologists and astronomers will make

arduous and expensive journeys in order to observe for themselves events of the kinds in which they are interested, because
their standard of observation is such that they cannot be satisfied
with descriptions by inexpert witnesses; but historians do not
fit out expeditions to countries where wars and revolutions are
going on. And this is not because historians are less energetic or
courageous than natural scientists, or less able to obtain the
money such expeditions would cost. It is because the facts which
might be learned through such expeditions, like the facts
which might be learned through the deliberate fomenting of a
war or a revolution at home, would not teach historians anything they want to know.

The sciences of observation and experiment are alike in this,
that their aim is to detect the constant or recurring features in
all events of a certain kind. A meteorologist studies one cyclone
in order to compare it with others; and by studying a number
of them he hopes to find out what features in them are constant,
that is, to find out what cyclones as such are like. But the
historian has no such aim. If you find him on a certain occasion
studying the Hundred Years War or the Revolution of 1688,
you cannot infer that he is in the preliminary stages of an
inquiry whose ultimate aim is to reach conclusions about wars
or revolutions as such. If he is in the preliminary stages of any
inquiry, it is more likely to be a general study of the Middle
Ages or the seventeenth century. This is because the sciences of
observation and experiment are organized in one way and
history is organized in another. In the organization of meteorology, the ulterior value of what has been observed about one
cyclone is conditioned by its relation to what has been observed
about other cyclones. In the organization of history, the ulterior
value of what is known about the Hundred Years War is conditioned, not by its relation to what is known about other wars,
but by its relation to what is known about other things that
people did in the Middle Ages.

Equally obvious is the difference between the organization
of history and that of the 'exact' sciences. It is true that in
history, as in exact science, the normal process of thought is
inferential; that is to say, it begins by asserting this or that, and
goes on to ask what it proves. But the starting-points are of very
different kinds. In exact science they are assumptions, and the

traditional way of expressing them is in sentences beginning with a word of command prescribing that a certain assumption be made: 'Let ABC be a triangle, and let AB = AC.' In history they are not assumptions, they are facts, and facts coming under the historian's observation, such as, that on the page open before him there is printed what purports to be a charter by which a certain king grants certain lands to a certain monastery. The conclusions, too, are of different kinds. In exact science, they are conclusions about things which have no special habitation in space or time: if they are anywhere, they are everywhere, and if they are at any time they are at all times. In history, they are conclusions about events, each having a place and date of its own. The exactitude with which place and date are known to the historian is variable; but he always knows that there were both a place and a date, and within limits he always knows what they were; this knowledge being part of the conclusion to which he is led by arguing from the facts before him.

These differences in starting-point and conclusion imply a difference in the entire organization of the respective sciences. When a mathematician has made up his mind what the problem is which he desires to solve, the next step before him is to make assumptions which will enable him to solve it; and this involves an appeal to his powers of invention. When an historian has similarly made up his mind, his next business is to place himself in a position where he can say: 'The facts which I am now observing are the facts from which I can infer the solution of my problem.' His business is not to invent anything, it is to discover something. And the finished products, too, are differently organized. The scheme upon which exact sciences have been traditionally arranged depends on relations of logical priority and posteriority: one proposition is placed before a second, if understanding of the first is needed in order that the second should be understood; the traditional scheme of arrangement in history is a chronological scheme, in which one event is placed before a second if it happened at an earlier time.

History, then, is a science, but a science of a special kind. It is a science whose business is to study events not accessible to our observation, and to study these events inferentially, arguing to them from something else which is accessible to our observation, and which the historian calls 'evidence' for the events in which he is interested.

(i) *History as inferential*

History has this in common with every other science: that the historian is not allowed to claim any single piece of knowledge, except where he can justify his claim by exhibiting to himself in the first place, and secondly to any one else who is both able and willing to follow his demonstration, the grounds upon which it is based. This is what was meant, above, by describing history as inferential. The knowledge in virtue of which a man is an historian is a knowledge of what the evidence at his disposal proves about certain events. If he or somebody else could have the very same knowledge of the very same events by way of memory, or second sight, or some Wellsian machine for looking backwards through time, this would not be historical knowledge; and the proof would be that he could not produce, either to himself or to any other critic of his claims, the evidence from which he had derived it. Critic, not sceptic; for a critic is a person able and willing to go over somebody else's thoughts for himself to see if they have been well done; whereas a sceptic is a person who will not do this; and because you cannot make a man think, any more than you can make a horse drink, there is no way of proving to a sceptic that a certain piece of thinking is sound, and no reason for taking his denials to heart. It is only by his peers that any claimant to knowledge is judged.

This necessity of justifying any claim to knowledge by exhibiting the grounds upon which it is based is a universal characteristic of science because it arises from the fact that a science is an organized body of knowledge. To say that knowledge is inferential is only another way of saying that it is organized. What memory is, and whether it is a kind of knowledge or not, are questions that need not be considered in a book about history: for this at least is clear, in spite of what Bacon and others have said, that memory is not history, because history is a certain kind of organized or inferential knowledge, and memory is not organized, not inferential, at all. If I say 'I remember writing a letter to So-and-so last week', that is a statement of memory, but it is not an historical statement. But if I can add 'and my memory is not deceiving me; because here is his reply', then I am basing a statement about the past on evidence; I am talking history. For the same reason, there is no need in an essay like this to consider the claims of people who say that when they are in a place where a certain event has recurred they can in some way see the event going on before their eyes. What actually happens on occasions like this, and whether the people to whom it happens thereby obtain knowledge of the past, are certainly interesting questions, but this is not the right place to discuss them; for even if these people do obtain knowledge of the past, it is not organized or inferential knowledge; not scientific knowledge; not history.

(ii) *Different kinds of inference*

Different kinds of science are organized in different ways; and it should follow (indeed, this would seem to be only the same thing in other words) that different kinds of science are characterized by different kinds of inference. The way in which knowledge is related to the grounds upon which it is based is in fact not one and the same for all kinds of knowledge. That this is so, and that therefore a person who has studied the nature of inference as such—let us call him a logician—can correctly judge the validity of an inference purely by attending to its form, although he has no special knowledge of its subject-matter, is a doctrine of Aristotle; but it is a delusion, although it is still believed by many very able persons who have been trained too exclusively in the Aristotelian logic and the logics that depend upon it for their chief doctrines.[1]

The main scientific achievement of the ancient Greeks lay in mathematics; their main work on the logic of inference was naturally, therefore, devoted to that form of inference which occurs in exact science. When at the end of the Middle Ages the modern natural sciences of observation and experiment began

[1] The reader will perhaps forgive me a personal reminiscence here. I was still a young man when a very distinguished visitor addressed an academic society on an archaeological subject that came within my special field of studies. The point he made was new and revolutionary, and it was easy for me to see that he had proved it up to the hilt. I imagined, foolishly enough, that so lucid and cogent a piece of reasoning must convince any hearer, even one who previously knew nothing about its subject-matter. I was at first much disconcerted, but in the long run greatly instructed, by finding that the demonstration had quite failed to convince the (very learned and acute) logicians in the audience.

to take shape, a revolt against Aristotelian logic was inevitable; in particular, a revolt against the Aristotelian theory of demonstration, which could by no manner of means be made to cover the technique actually used in the new sciences. Thus, by degrees, there came into existence a new logic of inference, based on analysis of the procedure used in the new natural sciences. The text-books of logic in use to-day still bear the marks of this revolt in the distinction they draw between two kinds of inference, 'deductive' and 'inductive'. It was not until late in the nineteenth century that historical thought reached a stage of development comparable with that reached by natural science about the beginning of the seventeenth; but this event has not yet begun to interest those philosophers who write text-books of logic.

The chief characteristic of inference in the exact sciences, the characteristic of which Greek logicians tried to give a theoretical account when they formulated the rules of the syllogism, is a kind of logical compulsion whereby a person who makes certain assumptions is forced, simply by so doing, to make others. He has freedom of choice in two ways: he is not compelled to make the initial assumption (a fact technically expressed by saying that 'the starting-points of demonstrative reasoning are not themselves demonstrable'), and when once he has done so he is still at liberty, whenever he likes, to stop thinking. What he cannot do is to make the initial assumption, to go on thinking, and to arrive at a conclusion different from that which is scientifically correct.

In what is called 'inductive' thinking there is no such compulsion. The essence of the process, here, is that having put certain observations together, and having found that they make a pattern, we extrapolate this pattern indefinitely, just as a man who has plotted a few points on squared paper and says to himself 'the points I have plotted suggest a parabola', proceeds to draw as much of the parabola as he likes in either direction. This is technically described as 'proceeding from the known to the unknown', or 'from the particular to the universal'. It is essential to 'inductive' thinking, though the logicians who have tried to construct a theory of such thinking have not always realized this, that the step so described is never taken under any kind of logical compulsion. The thinker who takes it is logically free to take it or not to take it, just as he pleases. There is nothing in the pattern formed by the observations he or some-one else has actually made which can oblige him to extrapolate in that particular way, or indeed to extrapolate at all. The reason why this very obvious truth has been so often overlooked is that people have been hypnotized by the prestige of Aristote-lian logic into thinking that they see a closer resemblance than actually exists between 'deductive' and 'inductive' thinking, that is, between exact science and the sciences of observation and experiment. In both cases there are, for any given piece of thinking, certain starting-points, traditionally called premisses, and a certain terminal point, traditionally called a conclusion; and in both cases the premisses 'prove' the conclusion. But whereas in exact science this means that they enforce the con-clusion, or make it logically obligatory, in the sciences of observation and experiment it means only that they justify it, that is, authorize anybody to think it who wishes to do so. What they provide, when they are said to 'prove' a certain conclusion, is not compulsion to embrace it, but only permission; a perfectly legitimate sense of the word 'prove' (*approuver, probare*), as there should be no need to show.

If in practice this permission, like so many permissions, amounts to virtual compulsion, that is only because the thinker who avails himself of it does not regard himself as free to extra-polate or not, just as he pleases. He regards himself as under an obligation to do so, and to do it in certain ways: obligations which, when we inquire into their history, we find to have their roots in certain religious beliefs about nature and its creator God. It would be out of place to develop this statement more fully here; but not, perhaps, to add that if to-day it seems to some readers paradoxical, that is only because the facts have been obscured by a smoke-screen of propagandist literature, beginning with the 'illuminist' movement of the eighteenth century and prolonged by the 'conflict between religion and science' in the nineteenth, whose purpose was to attack Christian theology in the supposed interests of a 'scientific view of the world' which in fact is based upon it and could not for a moment survive its destruction. Take away Christian theology, and the scientist has no longer any motive for doing what inductive thought gives him permission to do. If he goes on doing it at all, that is only because he is blindly following the conventions of the professional society to which he belongs.

(iii) *Testimony*

Before trying to describe the special characteristics of historical inference positively, we shall find it useful to describe them negatively: to describe something that is very often, but mistakenly, identified with it. Like every science, history is autonomous. The historian has the right, and is under an obligation, to make up his own mind by the methods proper to his own science as to the correct solution of every problem that arises for him in the pursuit of that science. He can never be under any obligation, or have any right, to let someone else make up his mind for him. If anyone else, no matter who, even a very learned historian, or an eyewitness, or a person in the confidence of the man who did the thing he is inquiring into, or even the man who did it himself, hands him on a plate a ready-made answer to his question, all he can do is to reject it: not because he thinks his informant is trying to deceive him, or is himself deceived, but because if he accepts it he is giving up his autonomy as an historian and allowing someone else to do for him what, if he is a scientific thinker, he can only do for himself. There is no need for me to offer the reader any proof of this statement. If he knows anything of historical work, he already knows of his own experience that it is true. If he does not already know that it is true, he does not know enough about history to read this essay with any profit, and the best thing he can do is to stop here and now.

When the historian accepts a ready-made answer to some question he has asked, given him by another person, this other person is called his 'authority', and the statement made by such an authority and accepted by the historian is called 'testimony'. In so far as an historian accepts the testimony of an authority and treats it as historical truth, he obviously forfeits the name of historian; but we have no other name by which to call him.

Now, I am not for a moment suggesting that testimony ought never to be accepted. In the practical life of every day, we constantly and rightly accept the information that other people offer us, believing them to be both well informed and truthful, and having, sometimes, grounds for this belief. I do not even deny, though I do not assert it, that there may be cases in which, as perhaps in some cases of memory, our acceptance of such testimony may go beyond mere belief and deserve the name of knowledge. What I assert is that it can never be historical knowledge, because it can never be scientific knowledge. It is not scientific knowledge because it cannot be vindicated by appeal to the grounds on which it is based. As soon as there are such grounds, the case is no longer one of testimony. When testimony is reinforced by evidence, our acceptance of it is no longer the acceptance of testimony as such; it is the affirmation of something based upon evidence, that is, historical knowledge.

(iv) *Scissors and paste*

There is a kind of history which depends altogether upon the testimony of authorities. As I have already said, it is not really history at all, but we have no other name for it. The method by which it proceeds is first to decide what we want to know about, and then to go in search of statements about it, oral or written, purporting to be made by actors in the events concerned, or by eyewitnesses of them, or by persons repeating what actors or eyewitnesses have told them, or have told their informants, or those who informed their informants, and so on. Having found in such a statement something relevant to his purpose, the historian excerpts it and incorporates it, translated if necessary and recast into what he considers a suitable style, in his own history. As a rule, where he has many statements to draw upon, he will find that one of them tells him what another does not; so both or all of them will be incorporated. Sometimes he will find that one of them contradicts another; then, unless he can find a way of reconciling them, he must decide to leave one out; and this, if he is conscientious, will involve him in a critical consideration of the contradictory authorities' relative degree of trustworthiness. And sometimes one of them, or possibly even all of them, will tell him a story which he simply cannot believe, a story characteristic, perhaps, of the superstitions or prejudices of the author's time or the circle in which he lived, but not credible to a more enlightened age, and therefore to be omitted.

History constructed by excerpting and combining the testimonies of different authorities I call scissors-and-paste history. I repeat that it is not really history at all, because it does not satisfy the necessary conditions of science; but until lately it was the only kind of history in existence, and a great deal of the history people are still reading to-day, and even a good deal of what people are still writing, belongs to this type. Consequently people who know little about history (some of whom, in spite of my recent farewell, may still be reading these pages) will say with some impatience: 'Why, this thing that you say is not history, is just history itself; scissors and paste, that is what history is; and that is why history is not a science, which is a fact that everybody knows, in spite of groundless claims by professional historians magnifying their office'. I shall therefore say a little more about the vicissitudes of scissors-and-paste history.

Scissors and paste was the only historical method known to the later Greco-Roman world or the Middle Ages. It existed in its simplest form. An historian collected testimony, spoken or written, using his own judgement as to its trustworthiness, and put it together for publication: the work which he did on it being partly literary—the presentation of his material as a connected, homogeneous, and convincing narrative—and partly rhetorical, if I may use that word to indicate the fact that most ancient and medieval historians aimed at proving a thesis, in particular some philosophical or political or theological thesis.

It was only in the seventeenth century, when the post-medieval reform of natural science had attained completion, that historians began to think their house also needed to be set in order. Two new movements in historical method now began. One was a systematic examination of authorities, in order to determine their relative credibility, and in particular to establish principles according to which this determination should be carried out. The other was a movement to broaden the basis of history by making use of non-literary sources, such as coins and inscriptions and suchlike relics of antiquity which hitherto had been of interest not to historians but only to collectors of curiosities.

The first of these movements did not overstep the limits of scissors-and-paste history, but it permanently altered its character. As soon as it became understood that a given statement, made by a given author, must never be accepted for historical truth until the credibility of the author in general and of this statement in particular had been systematically inquired into, the word 'authority' disappeared from the vocabulary of historical method, except as an archaistic survival; for the man who makes the statement came henceforth to be regarded not as someone whose word must be taken for the truth of what he says, which is what was meant by calling him an authority, but as someone who has voluntarily placed himself in the witness-box for cross-examination. The·document hitherto called an authority now acquired a new status, properly described by calling it a 'source', a word indicating simply that it contains the statement, without any implications as to its value. That is *sub judice*; and it is the historian who judges.

This is 'critical history', as it was worked out from the seventeenth century onwards, and officially acclaimed in the nineteenth as the apotheosis of the historical consciousness. There are two things to observe about it: that it was still only a form of scissors and paste; and that it had already, in principle, been superseded by something very different.

(1) The problem of which historical criticism offers a solution is a problem interesting to nobody but the practitioner of scissors-and-paste history. The presupposition of the problem is that in a certain source we have found a certain statement which bears on our subject. The problem is: Shall we incorporate this statement in our own narrative or not? The methods of historical criticism are intended to solve this problem in one or other of two ways: affirmatively or negatively. In the first case, the excerpt is passed as fit for the scrap-book; in the second, it is consigned to the waste-paper basket.

(2) But many historians in the nineteenth century, and even in the eighteenth, were aware that this dilemma was fallacious. It was by now a commonplace that if in some source you found a statement which for some reason could not be accepted as literally true, you must not on that account reject it as worthless. It might be a way, perhaps a well-established way according to the custom of the time when it was written, of saying something which you, through ignorance of that custom, did not recognize as its meaning.

The first person to make this point was Vico, at the beginning of the eighteenth century. It is true that in Germany, the home of 'critical history' in the late eighteenth and early nineteenth centuries, the importance of Vico's work was not as widely recognized as it ought to have been; but he was not entirely unknown there; indeed, some very famous German scholars, like F. A. Wolf, actually borrowed some of his ideas. Now, anyone who had read Vico, or even a second-hand version of some of his ideas, must have known that the important question about any statement contained in a source is not whether it is true or false, but what it means. And to ask what it means is to step right outside the world of scissors-and-paste history into a world where history is not written by copying out the testimony of the best sources, but by coming to your own conclusions.

Critical history is of interest to the student of historical method to-day only as the final form taken by scissors-and-paste history on the eve of its dissolution. I will not venture to name any historian, or even any historical work, as one from which the last traces of it have disappeared. But I will venture to say that any historian (if there is any) who practises it consistently, or any historical work written entirely on this method, is at least a century out of date.

So much for one of the two movements which gave new life to history in the seventeenth century. The other, the archaeological movement, was totally hostile to the principles of scissors-and-paste history, and could have arisen only when those principles were moribund. No very profound knowledge of coins and inscriptions is needed in order to realize that the assertions they make are by no means uniformly trustworthy, and indeed are to be judged more as propaganda than as statements of fact. Yet this gives them an historical value of their own; for propaganda, too, has its history.

If any reader still thinks that history as practised to-day is a scissors-and-paste affair, and is willing to go to a little trouble in order to settle the question, let him take the history of Greece down to the end of the Peloponnesian War, which I mention as an example peculiarly favourable to himself because Herodotus and Thucydides have there maintained the position of 'authorities' to a quite peculiar degree, and compare in detail the account of it given by Grote with that given in the *Cambridge Ancient History*. Let him mark in each book every sentence of which he can find the original in Herodotus or Thucydides; and by the time he is through with the job he will have learnt something about how historical method has changed in the last hundred years.

(v) *Historical inference*

In (ii) it was pointed out that proof might be either compulsive, as in exact science, where the nature of inference is such that nobody can affirm the premisses without being obliged to affirm the conclusion also, or permissive, as in 'inductive' science, where all a proof can do is to justify the thinker in affirming its conclusion, granted that he wishes to do so. An inductive argument with a negative conclusion is compulsive, that is to say it absolutely forbids the thinker from affirming what he wishes to affirm; with a positive conclusion, it is never more than permissive.

If history means scissors-and-paste history, the only kind of proof known to the historian is of this latter kind. For the scissors-and-paste historian, there is only one kind of problem which is capable of being settled by any sort of argument. This is the problem whether to accept or reject a certain piece of testimony bearing upon the question in which he is interested. The sort of argument by which he settles a problem of this kind is, of course, historical criticism. If criticism leads him to a negative conclusion, viz. that the statement or its author is untrustworthy, this forbids him to accept it, just as a negative result in an 'inductive' argument (for example, a result showing that events of the kind in which he is interested happen in the absence of that kind of event which he hopes to identify as their cause) forbids the inductive scientist to affirm the view he hoped to affirm. If criticism leads him to a positive conclusion, the most it gives him is a *nihil obstat*. For the positive conclusion is in effect that the man who made the statement is not known to be either ignorant or mendacious, and that the statement itself bears upon it no recognizable marks of being untrue. But it may be untrue for all that: and the man who made it, though in general he bears a good name for being well informed and honest, may on this one occasion have fallen a victim to misinformation about his facts, misunderstanding of them, or a desire to suppress or distort what he knew or believed to be the truth.

To avert a possible misunderstanding, it may be added here

that one might think there was another kind of problem for the scissors-and-paste historian, beside the kind which consists in whether to accept or reject a given piece of testimony, which therefore has to be settled by methods other than those of historical criticism: the problem, namely, of what implications follow from a piece of testimony that he has accepted, or would follow if he did accept it. But this is not a problem specially belonging to scissors-and-paste history; it is a problem which arises in history or pseudo-history of any kind whatever, and indeed in any kind of science or pseudo-science. It is simply the general problem of implication. When it occurs in scissors-and-paste history, however, it presents one peculiar feature. If a certain statement coming to the historian by way of testimony has a certain implication, and if this implicational relation is a compulsive one, nevertheless if the inference which leads him to accept the testimony is only permissive the same permissive character attaches to his assertion of its implication. If he has only borrowed his neighbour's cow, and she has a calf in his field, he cannot claim the calf as his own property. Any answer to the question whether the scissors-and-paste historian is obliged or only permitted to accept certain testimony carries with it a corresponding answer to the question whether he is obliged or only permitted to accept the implications of that testimony.

One hears it said that history is 'not an exact science'. The meaning of this I take to be that no historical argument ever proves its conclusion with that compulsive force which is characteristic of exact science. Historical inference, the saying seems to mean, is never compulsive, it is at best permissive; or, as people sometimes rather ambiguously say, it never leads to certainty, only to probability. Many historians of the present writer's generation, brought up at a time when this proverb was accepted by the general opinion of intelligent persons (I say nothing of the few who were a generation ahead of their time), must be able to recollect their excitement on first discovering that it was wholly untrue, and that they were actually holding in their hands an historical argument which left nothing to caprice, and admitted of no alternative conclusion, but proved its point as conclusively as a demonstration in mathematics. Many of these, again, must be able to recollect the shock of discovering on reflection that the proverb was not, strictly speaking, an error about history, history as they were practising it, the science of history, but a truth about something else, namely scissors-and-paste history.

If any reader wishes to rise here on a point of order and protest that a philosophical question, which ought therefore to be settled by reasoning, is being illegitimately disposed of by reference to the authority of historians, and quote against me the good old story about the man who said 'I'm not arguing, I'm telling you', I can only admit that the cap fits. I am not arguing; I am telling him.

Is this wrong of me? The question I want settled is whether an inference of the kind used in scientific history, as distinct from scissors-and-paste history, yields compulsion or only permission to embrace its conclusion. Suppose the question had been not about history but about mathematics. Suppose somebody had wanted to know whether Euclid's proof of what is called Pythagoras' theorem compels or merely permits a man to adopt the view that the square on the hypotenuse is equal to the sum of the squares on the other two sides. I speak with submission; but for myself I can think of only one thing that a sensible man in that situation would do. He would try to find somebody whose mathematical education had got as far as Euclid I. 47, and ask him. And if he did not like his answer, he would look for other people similarly qualified to give one, and ask them. If all else failed to convince him, he would have to get down to it and study the elements of plane geometry for himself.

The one thing that he will not do, if he is a man of any intelligence, is to say 'This is a philosophical question, and the only answer I will be satisfied with is a philosophical answer'. He can call it anything he pleases; he cannot alter the fact that the only way of knowing whether a given type of argument is cogent or not is to learn how to argue that way, and find out. Meanwhile, the second best thing is to take the word of people who have done so for themselves.

(vi) *Pigeon-holing*

Scissors-and-paste historians who have become disgusted with the work of copying out other people's statements, and, conscious of having brains, feel a laudable desire to use them, are often found satisfying this desire by inventing a system of pigeon-holes in which to arrange their learning. This is the origin of all those schemes and patterns into which history has again and again, with surprising docility, allowed itself to be forced by such men as Vico, with his pattern of historical cycles based on Greco-Roman speculations; Kant, with his proposal for a 'universal history from a cosmopolitan point of view'; Hegel, who followed Kant in conceiving universal history as the progressive realization of human freedom; Comte and Marx, two very great men who followed Hegel's lead each in his own way; and so on down to Flinders Petrie, Oswald Spengler, and Arnold Toynbee in our own time, whose affinities are less with Hegel than with Vico.

Although we find it as late as the twentieth century and as early as the eighteenth, not to mention isolated occurrences even earlier, this impulse towards arranging the whole of history in a single scheme (not a chronological scheme merely, but a qualitative scheme, in which 'periods' each with its own pervasive character follow one another in time, according to a pattern which may be necessary *a priori* on logical grounds, or may be forced upon our minds by the fact of its frequent repetition, or may be a bit of both) is in the main a nineteenth-century phenomenon. It belongs to the period when scissors-and-paste history was on its last legs; when people were becoming dissatisfied with it but had not yet broken away from it. This is why the people who have indulged it have been, in general, men with a high degree of intelligence and a real talent for history, but a talent which has been to some extent thwarted and baffled by the limitations of scissors and paste.

It is typical of this condition that some of them described their pigeon-holing enterprise as 'raising history to the rank of a science'. History as they found it meant scissors-and-paste history; that, obviously, was no science, because there was nothing autonomous, nothing creative, about it; it was merely the transhipment of ready-made information from one mind into another. They were conscious that history might be something more than this. It might have, and it ought to have, the characteristics of a science. But how was this to be brought about? At this point the analogy of the natural sciences came,

they thought, to their aid. It had been a commonplace ever
since Bacon that a natural science began by collecting facts,
and then went on to construct theories, that is, to extrapolate
the patterns discernible in the facts already collected. Very
well: let us put together all the facts that are known to historians, look for patterns in them, and then extrapolate these
patterns into a theory of universal history.

It proved to be not at all a difficult task for anybody with an
active mind and a taste for hard work. For there was no need to
collect all the facts known to historians. Any large collection of
facts, it was found, revealed patterns in plenty; and extrapolat-
ing such patterns into the remote past, about which there was
very little information, and into the future, about which there
was none, gave the 'scientific' historian just that sense of power
which scissors-and-paste history denied him. After being taught
to believe that he, as an historian, could never know anything
except what his authorities told him, he found himself discovering, as he fancied, that this lesson had been a fraud; that by
converting history into a science he could ascertain, entirely for
himself, things that his authorities had concealed from him or
did not know.

This was a delusion. The value of each and all of these pigeon-
holing schemes, if that means their value as means for discovering historical truths not ascertainable by the interpretation of
evidence, was exactly nil. And in fact none of them ever had
any scientific value at all; for it is not enough that science
should be autonomous or creative, it must also be cogent
or objective; it must impress itself as inevitable on anyone
who is able and willing to consider the grounds upon which it
is based, and to think for himself what the conclusions are to
which they point. That is what none of these schemes can do.
They are the offspring of caprice. If any of them has ever been
accepted by any considerable body of persons beside the one
who invented it, that is not because it has struck them as
scientifically cogent, but because it has become the orthodoxy
of what is in fact, though not necessarily in name, a religious
community. This was to some extent achieved by Comtism,
and to a much greater extent by Marxism. In these cases, or at
any rate in the case of Marxism, historical schemes of the kind
in question proved to have an important magical value, as

providing a focus for emotions and in consequence an incentive to action. In other cases they have had an amusement value, not without its function in the life of a jaded scissors-and-paste man.

And the delusion was not complete. The hope that scissors-and-paste history would one day be replaced by a new kind of history that should be genuinely scientific was a well-grounded hope, which has in fact been realized. The hope that this new kind of history would enable the historian to know things that his authorities could not or would not tell him was also well grounded, and has also been fulfilled. How these things have happened, we shall very soon see.

(vii) *Who killed John Doe?*

When John Doe was found, early one Sunday morning, lying across his desk with a dagger through his back, no one expected that the question who did it would be settled by means of testimony. It was not likely that anyone saw the murder being done. It was even less likely that someone in the murderer's confidence would give him away. It was least likely of all that the murderer would walk into the village police-station and denounce himself. In spite of this, the public demanded that he should be brought to justice, and the police had hopes of doing it; though the only clue was a little fresh green paint on the handle of the dagger, like the fresh green paint on the iron gate between John Doe's garden and the rector's.

This was not because they hoped that, in time, testimony would be forthcoming. On the contrary, when it did come, in the shape of a visit from an elderly neighbouring spinster asserting that she killed John Doe with her own hand because he had made a dastardly attempt upon her virtue, even the village constable (not an exceptionally bright lad, but kindly) advised her to go home and have some aspirin. Later in the day the village poacher came along and said that he had seen the squire's gamekeeper climbing in at John Doe's study window; testimony which was treated with even less deference. Finally the rector's daughter, in a state of great agitation, rushed in and said she had done it herself; the only effect of which was to make the village constable ring up the local Inspector and remind him that the girl's young man, Richard Roe, was a medical student, and presumably knew where to find a man's heart; and that he had spent Saturday night at the rectory, within a stone's throw of the dead man's house.

There had been a thunderstorm that night, with heavy rain, between twelve and one; and the Inspector, when he questioned the rectory parlour-maid (for the living was a good one), was told that Mr. Roe's shoes had been very wet in the morning. Questioned, Richard admitted having gone out in the middle of the night, but refused to say where or why.

John Doe was a blackmailer. For years he had been black-mailing the rector, threatening to publish the facts about a certain youthful escapade of his dead wife. Of this escapade the rector's supposed daughter, born six months after marriage, was the fruit; and John Doe had letters in his possession that proved it. By now he had absorbed the whole of the rector's private fortune, and on the morning of the fatal Saturday he demanded an instalment of his wife's, which she had left to him in trust for her child. The rector made up his mind to end it. He knew that John Doe sat at his desk late into the night; he knew that behind him, as he sat, there was a french window on the left and a trophy of Eastern weapons on the right; and that on hot nights the window was left open until he went to bed. At mid-night, wearing gloves, he slipped out; but Richard, who had noticed his state of mind and was troubled about it, happened to be leaning out of his window and saw the rector cross the garden. He hurried into his clothes and followed; but by the time he reached the garden the rector was gone. At this moment the thunderstorm broke. Meanwhile the rector's plan had succeeded perfectly. John Doe was asleep, his head fallen forward on a pile of old letters. Only after the dagger had reached his heart did the rector look at them, and see his wife's handwriting. The envelopes were addressed 'John Doe, Esq.' Until that moment, he had never known who his wife's seducer had been.

It was Detective-Inspector Jenkins of Scotland Yard, called in by the Chief Constable at the entreaty of his old friend's little girl, who found in the rectory dustbin a lot of ashes, mostly from writing paper, but including some from leather, probably a pair of gloves. The wet paint on John Doe's garden gate—he had painted it himself that day, after tea—explained why the gloves might have been destroyed; and among the ashes were metal buttons bearing the name of a famous glove-maker in Oxford Street whom the rector always patronized. More of John Doe's paint was found on the right cuff of a jacket, ruined as to shape by a recent wetting, which on Monday the rector bestowed on a deserving parishioner. The Detective-Inspector was severely blamed, later on, for allowing the rector to see in what direction his inquiries were tending, and thus giving him an opportunity to take cyanide and cheat the hangman.

The methods of criminal detection are not at every point identical with those of scientific history, because their ultimate purpose is not the same. A criminal court has in its hands the life and liberty of a citizen, and in a country where the citizen is regarded as having rights the court is therefore bound to do something and do it quickly. The time taken to arrive at a decision is a factor in the value (that is, the justice) of the decision itself. If any juror says: 'I feel certain that a year hence, when we have all reflected on the evidence at leisure, we shall be in a better position to see what it means,' the reply will be: 'There is something in what you say; but what you propose is impossible. Your business is not just to give a verdict; it is to give a verdict now; and here you stay until you do it.' This is why a jury has to content itself with something less than scientific (historical) proof, namely with that degree of assurance or belief which would satisfy it in any of the practical affairs of daily life.

The student of historical method will hardly find it worth his while, therefore, to go closely into the rules of evidence, as these are recognized in courts of law. For the historian is under no obligation to make up his mind within any stated time. Nothing matters to him except that his decision, when he reaches it, shall be right: which means, for him, that it shall follow inevitably from the evidence.

So long as this is borne in mind, however, the analogy between legal methods and historical methods is of some value for the understanding of history; of sufficient value, I think, to justify my having put before the reader in outline the above sample of a literary genre which in the absence of any such motive it would, of course, be beneath his dignity to notice.

(viii) *The question*

Francis Bacon, lawyer and philosopher, laid it down in one of his memorable phrases that the natural scientist must 'put Nature to the question'. What he was denying, when he wrote this, was that the scientist's attitude towards nature should be one of respectful attentiveness, waiting upon her utterances and building his theories on the basis of what she chose to vouchsafe him. What he was asserting was two things at once: first, that the scientist must take the initiative, deciding for himself what he wants to know and formulating this in his own mind in the shape of a question; and secondly, that he must find means of compelling nature to answer, devising tortures under which she can no longer hold her tongue. Here, in a single brief epigram, Bacon laid down once for all the true theory of experimental science.

It is also, though Bacon did not know this, the true theory of historical method. In scissors-and-paste history the historian takes up a pre-Baconian position. His attitude towards his authorities, as the very word shows, is one of respectful attentiveness. He waits to hear what they choose to tell him, and lets them tell it in their own way and at their own time. Even when he has invented historical criticism, and his authorities have become mere sources, this attitude is at bottom unchanged. There is a change, but it is only superficial. It consists merely in the adoption of a technique for dividing witnesses into sheep and goats. One class is disqualified from giving testimony; the other is treated exactly as authorities were treated under the old dispensation. But in scientific history, or history proper, the Baconian revolution has been accomplished. The scientific historian no doubt spends a great deal of time reading the same books that the scissors-and-paste historian used to read— Herodotus, Thucydides, Livy, Tacitus, and so forth—but he reads them in an entirely different spirit; in fact, a Baconian spirit. The scissors-and-paste historian reads them in a simply receptive spirit, to find out what they said. The scientific historian reads them with a question in his mind, having taken the initiative by deciding for himself what he wants to find out from them. Further, the scissors-and-paste historian reads them on the understanding that what they did not tell him in so many words he would never find out from them at all; the scientific historian puts them to the torture, twisting a passage ostensibly about something quite different into an answer to the question he has decided to ask. Where the scissors-and-paste historian said quite confidently 'There is nothing in such-and-such an author about such-and-such a subject', the scientific or Baconian historian will reply 'Oh, isn't there? Do you not see that in this passage about a totally different matter it is implied that the author took such-and-such a view of the subject about which you say his text contains nothing?'

To illustrate from my fable. The village constable does not arrest the rector's daughter and beat her periodically with a rubber truncheon until she tells him that she thinks Richard did the murder. What he tortures is not her body, but her statement that she killed John Doe. He begins by using the methods of critical history. He says to himself: 'The murder was done by somebody with a good deal of strength and some knowledge of anatomy. This girl certainly hasn't the first, and probably hasn't the second; at any rate, I know she has never attended ambulance classes. Further, if she had done it she wouldn't be in such a hurry to accuse herself. The story is a lie.'

At this point the critical historian would lose interest in the story and throw it in the waste-paper basket: the scientific historian begins to be interested in it, and tests it for chemical reactions. This he is able to do because, being a scientific thinker, he knows what questions to ask. 'Why is she telling a lie? Because she is shielding someone. Whom is she shielding? Either her father or her young man. Is it her father? No; fancy the rector! Therefore it is her young man. Are her suspicions of him well founded? They might be; he was here at the time; he is strong enough; and he knows enough anatomy.' The reader will recollect that in criminal detection probability is required, of a degree sufficient for the conduct of daily life, whereas in history we demand certainty. Apart from that, the parallel is complete. The village constable (not a clever lad, as I explained; but a scientific thinker does not have to be clever, he has to know his job, that is, know what questions to ask) has been trained in the elements of police work, and this training enables him to know what questions to ask and thus to interpret the untrue statement that she did it herself into evidence for the true conclusion that she suspects Richard Roe.

The constable's only mistake was that in the excitement of answering the question 'Whom does this girl suspect?' he lost sight of the question 'Who killed John Doe?' This is where Inspector Jenkins, not so much because he was a cleverer man as because he had learned the job more thoroughly, had the advantage of him. The way I see the Inspector going to work is like this.

'Why does the rector's daughter suspect Richard Roe? Probably because she knows that he was involved in something queer which happened at the rectory that night. We know that one queer thing happened at the rectory: Richard was out in the storm, and that was quite enough to make the girl suspicious. But what we want to know is, did he kill John Doe? If he did, when did he do it? After the thunderstorm broke, or before? Not before, because here are his tracks going both ways in the mud of the rectory garden path: you see them beginning a few yards from the garden door, going away from the house; so that is where he was, and that is the direction he was going in, when the downpour began. Well, did he carry mud into John Doe's study? No: none there. Did he take off his shoes before going in? Think a moment. What position was John Doe in when he was stabbed? Was he leaning back or sitting upright in his chair? No; because the chair would have protected his back. He must have been leaning right forward. Possibly, indeed probably, asleep in the position in which he still lies. How exactly did the murderer proceed? If Doe was asleep, nothing easier: step quietly inside, take the dagger and in it goes. If Doe was awake and merely leaning forward, the same might be done, but not so easily. Now, did the murderer pause outside to take off his shoes? Impossible. In either case, speed was the first thing necessary: the job had to be done before he leaned back, or woke up. So the absence of mud in the study lets Richard out.

'Then, once more, why did he go into the garden? For a walk? Not with that thunderstorm growling about. For a smoke? They smoke all over the house. To meet the girl? No signs that she was in the garden; and why should he? They had had the drawing-room to themselves ever since dinner, and the rector isn't one to shoo young people off to bed. Broad-minded sort of chap. Had trouble, I shouldn't wonder. Now, why did young Richard go into that garden? Something must have been going on there. Something queer. A second queer thing that night at the rectory, one we don't know about.

'What could it have been? If the murderer had come from the rectory, which that paint suggests he did, and if Richard saw him from his window, it might have been that; because the murderer got to Doe's house before the rain began, and Richard was caught in it ten yards from the garden door. Just time. Let's see what would follow, if the murderer did come from the rectory. Probably he went back there afterwards. No tracks in the mud; why? Because he knew the garden well enough to keep on the grass all the way, even in that pitch darkness. If so, he knew the rectory very well and also spent the night there. Was it the rector himself?

'Now why does Richard refuse to say what made him go into the garden? It must be to keep somebody out of trouble; almost certainly, trouble about the murder. Not himself, because I've told him we know he didn't do it. Somebody else. Who? Might be the rector. Can't think of anybody else it might be. Suppose it was the rector; how would he have worked it? Very easy. Go out about midnight, in tennis shoes and gloves. Quite silent on the rectory paths—no gravel on them. Reach that little iron gate into John Doe's garden. Does he know it's wet paint? Probably not; it was only painted after tea. So he grabs it. Paint on glove. Probably paint on jacket too. Walk on the grass to Doe's study window. Doe is leaning forward in his chair, or likelier asleep. Now for a bit of quick work, easy for a good tennis-player. Left foot inside, right foot to the right, grab that dagger thing, left foot forward, in it goes.

'But what had John Doe been doing at that desk? Nothing on it, you know. Queer. Does a man spend the evening sitting at an empty desk? There must have been something there. What do we know about the chap at the Yard? Blackmailer, that's it. Had he been blackmailing the rector? and gloating over the letters, or what not, all evening? And did the rector, if it was the rector, find him asleep on top of them? Well, that's not our business. We'll pass it on to the defence, for what it's worth. I'd rather not use a motive like that in prosecution.

'Now then, Jonathan, don't go ahead too fast. You've got him in there, you've got to get him out again. What exactly does he do? About now it begins to rain cats and dogs. Back he goes through it. More paint at the gate. Walk on grass, no mud brought in. Back in the house. All soaked: gloves covered with paint, too. Wipe paint off door-knob. Lock up. Put letters (if it was letters), and anyhow gloves, in the hot-water furnace— the ashes may be in the dustbin now. Put all clothes in the bath-room cupboard; they will be dry by morning. And so they are; but the jacket will be hopelessly out of shape. Now what did he do with that jacket? First, he'd look for paint on it. If he found paint, he'd have to destroy the thing; and I pity the man who tries to destroy a jacket in a house overrun with women. If he didn't find any, he would certainly give it away on the quiet to a poor man.

'Well, well: there's a pretty story for you; but how can we tell whether it's true or not? There are two questions we've got to ask. First: can we find the ashes of those gloves? And the metal buttons, if they are like most of his gloves? If we can, the story is true. And if we can find a lot of writing-paper ash as well, the blackmail bit is true, too. Second: where is that jacket? Be-cause if we can find the tiniest speck of John Doe's paint on it, there's our case.'

I have gone to some length in this analysis because I wish to bring home to the reader the following points about the question-ing activity which is the dominant factor in history, as it is in all scientific work.

(1) Every step in the argument depends on asking a question. The question is the charge of gas, exploded in the cylinder-head, which is the motive force of every piston-stroke. But the metaphor is not adequate, because each new piston-stroke is produced not by exploding another charge of the same old mixture but by exploding a charge of a new kind. No one with any grasp of method will go on asking the same question all the time, 'Who killed John Doe?' He asks a new question every time. And it is not enough to cover the ground by having a catalogue of all the questions that have to be asked, and asking every one of them sooner or later: they must be asked in the right order. Descartes, one of the three great masters of the Logic of Questioning (the other two being Socrates and Bacon), insisted upon this as a cardinal point in scientific method, but so far as modern works on logic are concerned, Descartes might never have lived. Modern logicians are in a conspiracy to

pretend that a scientist's business is to 'make judgements', or 'assert propositions', or 'apprehend facts', and also to 'assert' or 'apprehend' the relations between them; suggesting that they have no experience whatever of scientific thinking, and wish to palm off, as an account of science, an account of their own haphazard, unsystematic, unscientific consciousness.

(2) These questions are not put by one man to another man, in the hope that the second man will enlighten the first man's ignorance by answering them. They are put, like all scientific questions, to the scientist by himself. This is the Socratic idea which Plato was to express by defining thought as 'the dialogue of the soul with itself', where Plato's own literary practice makes it clear that by dialogue he meant a process of question and answer. When Socrates taught his young pupils by asking them questions, he was teaching them how to ask questions of themselves, and showing them by examples how amazingly the obscurest subjects can be illuminated by asking oneself intelligent questions about them instead of simply gaping at them, according to the prescription of our modern anti-scientific epistemologists, in the hope that when we have made our minds a perfect blank we shall 'apprehend the facts'.

(ix) *Statement and evidence*

It is characteristic of scissors-and-paste history, from its least critical to its most critical form, that it has to do with ready-made statements, and that the historian's problem about any one of these statements is whether he shall accept it or not: where accepting it means reasserting it as a part of his own historical knowledge. Essentially, history for the scissors-and-paste historian means repeating statements that other people have made before him. Hence he can get to work only when he is supplied with ready-made statements on the subjects about which he wants to think, write, and so forth. It is the fact that these statements have to be found by him ready-made in his sources that makes it impossible for the scissors-and-paste historian to claim the title of a scientific thinker, for this fact makes it impossible to attribute to him that autonomy which is everywhere essential to scientific thought; where by autonomy I mean the condition of being one's own authority, making statements or taking action on one's own initiative and not because those statements or actions are authorized or pre-scribed by anyone else.

It follows that scientific history contains no ready-made state-ments at all. The act of incorporating a ready-made statement into the body of his own historical knowledge is an act which, for a scientific historian, is impossible. Confronted with a ready-made statement about the subject he is studying, the scientific historian never asks himself: 'Is this statement true or false?', in other words 'Shall I incorporate it in my history of that subject or not?' The question he asks himself is: 'What does this statement mean?' And this is not equivalent to the question 'What did the person who made it mean by it?', although that is doubtless a question that the historian must ask, and must be able to answer. It is equivalent, rather, to the question 'What light is thrown on the subject in which I am interested by the fact that this person made this statement, meaning by it what he did mean?' This might be expressed by saying that the scientific historian does not treat statements as statements but as evi-dence: not as true or false accounts of the facts of which they profess to be accounts, but as other facts which, if he knows the right questions to ask about them, may throw light on those facts. Thus in my fable the rector's daughter tells the constable that she killed John Doe. As a scientific historian, he begins attending seriously to this statement at the point where he stops treating it as a statement, that is, as a true or false account of her having done the murder, and begins treating the fact that she makes it as a fact which may be of service to him. It is of service to him because he knows what questions to ask about it, beginning with the question: 'Now why does she tell this story?' The scissors-and-paste historian is interested in the 'content', as it is called, of statements: he is interested in what they state. The scientific historian is interested in the fact that they are made.

A statement to which an historian listens, or one which he reads, is to him a ready-made statement. But the statement that such a statement is being made is not a ready-made state-ment. If he says to himself 'I am now reading or hearing a statement to such and such effect', he is himself making a state-ment; but it is not a second-hand statement, it is autonomous. He makes it on his own authority. And it is this autonomous statement that is the scientific historian's starting-point. The evidence from which the constable infers that the rector's daughter suspects Richard Roe is not her statement 'I killed John Doe', but his own statement 'the rector's daughter tells me that she killed John Doe'.

If the scientific historian gets his conclusions not from the statement that he finds ready-made, but from his own autonomous statement of the fact that such statements are made, he can get conclusions even when no statements are made to him. The premises of his argument are his own autonomous statements: there is no need for these autonomous statements to be themselves statements about other statements. To illustrate once more from the story of John Doe. The premises from which the Detective-Inspector argued to the innocence of Richard Roe were all premises of the Detective-Inspector's own stating, autonomous statements resting on no authority but his own: and not one of them was a statement about statements made by anybody else. The essential points were that Richard Roe had got his shoes muddy while going away from the rectory, that no mud was to be seen in John Doe's study, and that the circumstances of the murder had been such that he would not have stopped to clean or remove his shoes. Each of these three points, in its turn, was the conclusion of an inference, and the statements upon which they severally rested were no more statements about other people's statements than were these three points themselves. Again: the ultimate case against the rector did not logically depend upon any statements made by the Detective-Inspector about statements made by other persons. It depended upon the presence of certain objects in a certain dustbin, and of certain paint-smears on the cuff of a jacket made in the conventional clerical style and shrunk by wetting; and these facts were vouched for by his own observation. I do not mean that the scientific historian can work better when no statements are made to him about the subjects on which he is working; it would be a pedantical way of avoiding scissors-and-paste history, to avoid occasions of this type which might be a trap for the weaker brethren; what I mean is that he is not dependent on such statements being made.

This is important because it settles by appeal to principle a controversy which, even if it is no longer so urgent as it was, has not yet ceased to echo in the minds of historians. This was the controversy between those who maintained that history was ultimately dependent on 'written sources', and those who maintained that it could also be constructed from 'unwritten sources'. The terms were unhappily chosen. 'Written sources' were not conceived as excluding oral sources, or as having any special connexion with handwriting as distinct from chiselling in stone or the like. 'Written sources', in fact, meant sources containing ready-made statements asserting or implying alleged facts belonging to the subject in which the historian was interested. 'Unwritten sources' meant archaeological material, potsherds, and so forth, connected with the same subject. Of course, the word 'source' was in no sense applicable to these, for a source means something from which water or the like is drawn ready made; in the case of history, something from which the historian's statements are drawn ready made, and the point of describing potsherds as 'unwritten sources' was to indicate that, not being texts, they contained no ready-made statements and were therefore not sources. (Inscribed potsherds or 'ostraka' were, of course, 'written sources'.)

In effect, this was a controversy between people who believed that scissors-and-paste history was the only possible kind and people who, without impugning the validity of scissors-and-paste methods, claimed that there could be history without them. According to my own recollection the controversy was alive, though giving one an impression of obsolescence, in academic circles in this country thirty years ago; all statements of the issue, so far as I can recall them, were extremely confused, and the philosophers of the time, though it gave them an excellent opportunity for doing a useful job of work on a subject of high philosophical interest, cared for none of these things. My impression is that the controversy fizzled out in the feeblest of compromises, the partisans of scissors-and-paste history accepting the principle that 'unwritten sources' could give valid results, but insisting that this could happen only on a very small scale and when they were used as an auxiliary arm to 'written sources'; and only about low matters like industry and commerce, into which an historian with the instincts of a gentleman would not inquire. This amounted to saying that historians brought up to regard history as an affair of scissors and paste were beginning, very timidly, to recognize the possibility of something quite different; but that when they tried to convert this possibility into an actuality they were still too incompletely fledged for any but the shortest flights.

(x) *Question and evidence*

If history means scissors-and-paste history, where the historian depends on ready-made statements for all his knowledge about his subject, and where the texts in which he finds these statements are called his sources, it is easy to define a source in a way which has some practical utility. A source is a text containing a statement or statements about the subject; and this definition has some practical utility because it helps the historian to divide the whole of extant literature, once he has determined his subject, into texts which might serve him as sources, and must therefore be looked at, and those which cannot, and may therefore be ignored. What he has to do is to run over his library shelves, or his bibliography of the period, asking himself at every title: 'Could this contain anything about my subject?' And, in case he cannot give the answer out of his head, aids of several kinds have been provided: notably indexes and specialized or classified bibliographies. Even with all these aids, he may still miss an important piece of testimony, and thus provide sport for his friends; but on any given question the amount of testimony that exists is a finite quantity, and it is theoretically possible to exhaust it.

Theoretically, but not always practically: for the amount may be so large, and some parts of it so difficult of access, that no historian can hope to see it all. And one sometimes hears people complaining that nowadays so much raw material for history is being preserved that the task of using it is becoming impossible; and sighing for the good old days when books were few and libraries small, and an historian could hope to master his subject. What these complaints mean is that the scissors-and-paste historian is on the horns of a dilemma. If he possesses only a small amount of testimony about his subject, he wants more; because any new piece of testimony about it would, if really new, throw new light on it, and might make the view he is actually putting forward untenable. So, however much testimony he has, his zeal as an historian makes him want more.

But if he has a large amount of testimony, it becomes so difficult to manipulate and work up into a convincing narrative that, speaking as a mere weak mortal, he wishes he had less.

Consciousness of this dilemma has often driven men into scepticism about the very possibility of historical knowledge. And quite rightly, if knowledge means scientific knowledge and history means scissors-and-paste history. Scissors-and-paste historians who brush the dilemma aside with the blessed word 'hypercriticism' are only confessing that in their own professional practice they do not find that it troubles them, because they work to such a low standard of scientific cogency that their consciences become anaesthetized. Such cases in contemporary life are highly interesting, because in the history of science one often meets with them and wonders how such extraordinary blindness was possible. The answer is that the people who exhibit it have committed themselves to an impossible task, in this case the task of scissors-and-paste history, and since for practical reasons they cannot back out of it they have to blind themselves to its impossibility. The scissors-and-paste historian protects himself from seeing the truth about his own methods by carefully choosing subjects which he is able to 'get away' with, exactly as the nineteenth-century landscape-painter protected himself from seeing that his theory of landscape was all wrong by choosing what he called paintable subjects. The subjects must be those about which a certain amount of testimony is accessible, not too little and not too much; not so uniform as to give the historian nothing to do, not so divergent as to baffle his endeavours to do it. Practised on these principles, history was at worst a parlour game, and at best an elegant accomplishment. I have used the past tense; I leave it to the conscience of historians who are capable of self-criticism to decide how far I might justly have used the present.

If history means scientific history, for 'source' we must read 'evidence'. And when we try to define 'evidence' in the same spirit in which we defined 'sources', we find it very difficult. There is no short and easy test by which we can decide whether a given book is or is not capable of providing evidence about a given subject, and indeed no reason why we should limit our search to books. Indexes and bibliographies of sources are of no use at all to a scientific historian. This is not to say that he cannot use indexes and bibliographies; he can and does; but they are indexes and bibliographies not of sources but of monographs or the like: not of evidence, but of previous discussions which he can take as a starting-point for his own. Consequently, whereas the books mentioned in a bibliography for the use of a scissors-and-paste historian will be, roughly speaking, valuable in direct proportion to their antiquity, those mentioned in a bibliography for the use of a scientific historian will be, roughly speaking, valuable in direct proportion to their newness.

In my fable there is only one obvious characteristic common to all the pieces of evidence used by the Detective-Inspector in his argument: they are all things observed by himself. If we ask what kind of things, it is not easy to give an answer. They include such things as the existence of certain footprints in certain mud, their number, position, and direction, their resemblance to prints produced by a certain pair of shoes, and the absence of any others; the absence of mud on the floor of a certain room; the position of a dead body, the position of a dagger in its back, and the shape of the chair in which it is sitting; and so on, a most variegated collection. This, I think, we can safely say about it: that no one could possibly know what could or could not find a place in it until he had got all his questions not only formulated but answered. In scientific history anything is evidence which is used as evidence, and no one can know what is going to be useful as evidence until he has had occasion to use it.

Let us put this by saying that in scissors-and-paste history, if we allow ourselves to describe testimony—loosely, I admit— by the name of evidence, there is potential evidence and there is actual evidence. The potential evidence about a subject is all the extant statements about it. The actual evidence is that part of these statements which we decide to accept. But in scientific history the idea of potential evidence disappears; or, if we like to put the same fact in these other words, everything in the world is potential evidence for any subject whatever. This will be a distressing idea to anyone whose notions of historical method are fixed in a scissors-and-paste mould; for how, he will ask, are we to discover what facts are actually of service to us, unless we can first of all round up the facts that might be of service to us? To a person who understands the nature of scientific thinking, whether historical or any other, it will present no difficulty. He will realize that, every time the historian asks a question, he asks it because he thinks he can answer it: that is to say, he has already in his mind a preliminary and tentative idea of the evidence he will be able to use. Not a definite idea about potential evidence, but an indefinite idea about actual evidence. To ask questions which you see no prospect of answering is the fundamental sin in science, like giving orders which you do not think will be obeyed in politics, or praying for what you do not think God will give you in religion. Question and evidence, in history, are correlative. Anything is evidence which enables you to answer your question—the question you are asking now. A sensible question (the only kind of question that a scientifically competent man will ask) is a question which you think you have or are going to have evidence for answering. If you think you have it here and now, the question is an actual question, like the question 'What position was John Doe in when he was stabbed?' If you think you are going to have it the question is a deferred question, like the question 'Who killed John Doe?'

It was a correct understanding of this truth that underlay Lord Acton's great precept, 'Study problems, not periods'. Scissors-and-paste historians study periods; they collect all the extant testimony about a certain limited group of events, and hope in vain that something will come of it. Scientific historians study problems: they ask questions, and if they are good historians they ask questions which they see their way to answering. It was a correct understanding of the same truth that led Monsieur Hercule Poirot to pour scorn on the 'human bloodhound' who crawls about the floor trying to collect everything, no matter what, which might conceivably turn out to be a clue; and to insist that the secret of detection was to use what, with possibly wearisome iteration, he called 'the little grey cells'. You can't collect your evidence before you begin thinking, he meant: because thinking means asking questions (logicians, please note), and nothing is evidence except in relation to some definite question. The difference between Poirot and Holmes in this respect is deeply significant of the change that has taken place in the understanding of historical method in the last forty years. Lord Acton was preaching his doctrine in the heyday of Sherlock Holmes, in his inaugural lecture at Cambridge in 1895;

but it was caviare to the general. In Monsieur Poirot's time, to judge by his sales, the general cannot have too much of it. The revolution which dethroned the principles of scissors-and-paste history, and replaced them by those of scientific history, had become common property.

§ 4. *History as Re-enactment of Past Experience*

How, or on what conditions, can the historian know the past? In considering this question, the first point to notice is that the past is never a given fact which he can apprehend empirically by perception. *Ex hypothesi*, the historian is not an eyewitness of the facts he desires to know. Nor does the historian fancy that he is; he knows quite well that his only possible knowledge of the past is mediate or inferential or indirect, never empirical. The second point is that this mediation cannot be effected by testimony. The historian does not know the past by simply believing a witness who saw the events in question and has left his evidence on record. That kind of mediation would give at most not knowledge but belief, and very ill-founded and improbable belief. And the historian, once more, knows very well that this is not the way in which he proceeds; he is aware that what he does to his so-called authorities is not to believe them but to criticize them. If then the historian has no direct or empirical knowledge of his facts, and no transmitted or testimoniary knowledge of them, what kind of knowledge has he: in other words, what must the historian do in order that he may know them?

My historical review of the idea of history has resulted in the emergence of an answer to this question: namely, that the historian must re-enact the past in his own mind. What we must now do is to look more closely at this idea, and see what it means in itself and what further consequences it implies.

NB

In a general way, the meaning of the conception is easily understood. When a man thinks historically, he has before him certain documents or relics of the past. His business is to discover what the past was which has left these relics behind it. For example, the relics are certain written words; and in that case he has to discover what the person who wrote those words meant by them. This means discovering the thought (in the widest sense of that word: we shall look into its preciser meaning in § 5) which he expressed by them. To discover what this thought was, the historian must think it again for himself.

Suppose, for example, he is reading the Theodosian Code, and has before him a certain edict of an emperor. Merely reading the words and being able to translate them does not amount to knowing their historical significance. In order to do that he must envisage the situation with which the emperor was trying to deal, and he must envisage it as that emperor envisaged it. Then he must see for himself, just as if the emperor's situation were his own, how such a situation might be dealt with; he must see the possible alternatives, and the reasons for choosing one rather than another; and thus he must go through the process which the emperor went through in deciding on this particular course. Thus he is re-enacting in his own mind the experience of the emperor; and only in so far as he does this has he any historical knowledge, as distinct from a merely philological knowledge, of the meaning of the edict.

Or again, suppose he is reading a passage of an ancient philosopher. Once more, he must know the language in a philological sense and be able to construe; but by doing that he has not yet understood the passage as an historian of philosophy must understand it. In order to do that, he must see what the philosophical problem was, of which his author is here stating his solution. He must think that problem out for himself, see what possible solutions of it might be offered, and see why this particular philosopher chose that solution instead of another. This means re-thinking for himself the thought of his author, and nothing short of that will make him the historian of that author's philosophy.

It cannot, I think, be denied by anybody that these descriptions, whatever their ambiguities and shortcomings, do actually call attention to the central feature of all historical thinking. As descriptions of that experience, their general accuracy is beyond question. But they still require a great deal of amplification and explanation; and perhaps the best way of beginning this is to expose them to the criticism of an imaginary objector.

Such an objector might begin by saying that the whole conception is ambiguous. It implies either too little or too much. To re-enact an experience or re-think a thought, he might argue, may mean either of two things. Either it means enacting an experience or performing an act of thought resembling the first, or it means enacting an experience or performing an act of thought literally identical with the first. But no one experience can be literally identical with another, therefore presumably the relation intended is one of resemblance only. But in that case the doctrine that we know the past by re-enacting it is only a version of the familiar and discredited copy-theory of knowledge, which vainly professes to explain how a thing (in this case an experience or act of thought) is known by saying that the knower has a copy of it in his mind. And in the second place, suppose it granted that an experience could be identically repeated, the result would only be an immediate identity between the historian and the person he was trying to understand, so far as that experience was concerned. The object (in this case the past) would be simply incorporated in the subject (in this case the present, the historian's own thought); and instead of answering the question how the past is known we should be maintaining that the past is not known, but only the present. And, it may be asked, has not Croce himself admitted this with his doctrine of the contemporaneity of history?

Here we have two objections, which we must consider in turn. I suppose the person who maintained the first would be implying some such view of experience as this. In every experience, at any rate so far as it is cognitive, there is an act and an object; and two different acts may have the same object. If I read Euclid and find there the statement that the angles at the base of an isosceles triangle are equal, and if I understand what is meant and recognize that it is true, the truth which I recognize, or the proposition which I assert, is the same truth which Euclid recognized, the same proposition which he asserted. But my act of asserting it is not the same act as his; that is sufficiently proved by either of the two facts that they are done by different persons and are done at different times. My act of apprehending the equality of the angles is therefore not a revival of his act, but the performance of another act of the same kind; and what I know by performing that act is not that Euclid knew the angles at the base of an isosceles triangle to be equal, but that they are equal. In order to know the historical fact that Euclid knew them to be equal I shall have not to copy his act (that is, to perform one like it) but to perform a quite different one, the act of thinking that Euclid knew them to be equal. And the question how I manage to achieve this act is not at all illuminated by saying that I repeat Euclid's act of knowing in my own mind; for if repeating his act means apprehending the same truth or asserting the same proposition which he apprehended or asserted, the statement is untrue, for Euclid's proposition 'the angles are equal' and mine 'Euclid knew the angles to be equal' are different; and if repeating his act means performing the same act over again, it is nonsense, for an act cannot be repeated.

On this view, the relation between my act of now thinking 'the angles are equal' and my act of thinking it five minutes ago is a relation of numerical difference and specific identity. The two acts are different acts but acts of the same kind. They thus resemble one another, and either of these acts resembles Euclid's act in the same way; hence the conclusion that the doctrine we are considering is a case of the copy-theory of knowledge.

But is this a true account of the relation between these two acts? Is it the case that when we speak of two persons performing the same act of thought or of one person as performing the same act at two different times, we mean that they are performing different acts of the same kind? It is, I think, clear that we mean nothing of the sort; and that the only reason why anyone should fancy that we do is because he has accepted a dogma that whenever we distinguish two things and yet say that they are the same (which, as everyone admits, we often do) we mean that they are different specimens of the same kind, different instances of the same universal, or different members of the same class. The dogma is not that there is no such thing as identity in difference (nobody believes that), but that there is only one kind of it, namely specific identity in numerical difference. Criticism of the dogma, therefore, turns not on proving that this kind of identity in difference does not exist, but on proving that other kinds exist, and that the case we are considering is one of them.

It is contended by our supposed objector that Euclid's act of thought and mine are not one but two: numerically two though specifically one. It is also contended that my act of now thinking 'the angles are equal' stands in the same relation to my act of thinking 'the angles are equal' five minutes ago. The reason why this seems quite certain to the objector is, I believe, that he conceives an act of thought as something that has its place in the flow of consciousness, whose being is simply its occurrence in that flow. Once it has happened, the flow carries it into the past, and nothing can recall it. Another of the same kind may happen, but not that again.

But what precisely do these phrases mean? Suppose that a person continues for an appreciable time, say five seconds together, to think 'the angles are equal'. Is he performing one act of thought sustained over those five seconds; or is he performing five, or ten, or twenty acts of thought numerically different but specifically identical? If the latter, how many go to five seconds? The objector is bound to answer this question, for the essence of his view is that acts of thought are numerically distinct and therefore numerable. Nor can he defer answering until he has appealed to further research, for example in the psychological laboratory: if he does not already know what constitutes the plurality of acts of thought, the psychological laboratory can never tell him. But any answer he gives must be both arbitrary and self-contradictory. There is no more reason to correlate the unity of a single act of thought with the time-lapse of one second, or a quarter of a second, than with any other. The only possible answer is that the act of thought is one act sustained through five seconds; and the objector, if he likes, may admit this by saying that such identity in a sustained act of thought is 'the identity of a continuant'.

But does a continuant, here, imply continuousness? Suppose that, after thinking 'the angles are equal' for five seconds, the thinker allows his attention to wander for three more; and then, returning to the same subject, again thinks 'the angles are equal'. Have we here two acts of thought and not one, because a time elapsed between them? Clearly not; there is one single act, this time not merely sustained, but revived after an interval. For there is no difference in this case that was not already present in the other. When an act is sustained over five seconds, the activity in the fifth second is just as much separated by a lapse of time from that in the first, as when the intervening seconds are occupied by an activity of a different kind or (if that be possible) by none.

The contention that an act cannot happen twice because the flow of consciousness carries it away is thus false. Its falsity arises from an *ignoratio elenchi*. So far as experience consists of mere consciousness, of sensations and feelings pure and simple, it is true. But an act of thought is not a mere sensation or feeling. It is knowledge, and knowledge is something more than immediate consciousness. The process of knowledge is therefore not a mere flow of consciousness. A person whose consciousness was a mere succession of states, by whatever name these states are called, could have no knowledge whatever. He could not remember his own past states, for (even granting that his states are connected together by certain psychological laws, *ex hypothesi* to him unknowable) he would not remember being burnt but would only fear the fire. Nor could he perceive the world around him; he would fear, but would not recognize that which he feared as the fire. Least of all would he, or anyone else, know that his consciousness was the mere succession of states that it is alleged to be.

If, then, mere consciousness is a succession of states, thought is an activity by which that succession is somehow arrested so as to be apprehended in its general structure: something for which the past is not dead and gone, but can be envisaged together with the present and compared with it. Thought itself is not involved in the flow of immediate consciousness; in some sense it stands outside that flow. Acts of thought certainly happen at definite times; Archimedes discovered the idea of specific gravity at a time when he was in the bath; but they are not related to time in the same way as mere feelings and sensations. It is not only the object of thought that somehow stands outside time; the act of thought does so too: in this sense at least, that one and the same act of thought may endure through a lapse of time and revive after a time when it has been in abeyance.

Take a third case, then, where the interval covers the whole lapse of time from Euclid to myself. If he thought 'the angles are equal' and I now think 'the angles are equal', granted that the time interval is no cause for denying that the two acts are one and the same, is the difference between Euclid and myself ground for denying it? There is no tenable theory of personal identity that would justify such a doctrine. Euclid and I are not (as it were) two different typewriters which, just because they are not the same typewriter, can never perform the same act but only acts of the same kind. A mind is not a machine with various functions, but a complex of activities; and to argue that an act of Euclid's cannot be the same as an act of my own because it forms part of a different complex of activities is merely to beg the question. Granted that the same act can happen twice in different contexts within the complex of my own activities, why should it not happen twice in two different complexes?

The objector, although explicitly denying that this can happen, is covertly assuming that it can and does. He maintains that although the object of two people's acts of thought may be the same, the acts themselves are different. But, in order that this should be said, it is necessary to know 'what someone else is thinking' not only in the sense of knowing the same object that he knows, but in the further sense of knowing the act by which he knows it: for the statement rests on a claim to know not only my own act of knowing but someone else's also, and compare them. But what makes such comparison possible? Anyone who can perform the comparison must be able to reflect 'my act of knowledge is *this*'—and then he repeats it: 'from the way he talks, I can see that his act is *this*'—and then he repeats it. Unless that can be done, the comparison can never be made. But to do this involves the repetition by one mind of another's act of thought: not one like it (that would be the copy-theory of knowledge with a vengeance) but the act itself.

Thought can never be mere object. To know someone else's activity of thinking is possible only on the assumption that this same activity can be re-enacted in one's own mind. In that sense, to know 'what someone is thinking' (or 'has thought') involves thinking it for oneself. To reject this conclusion means denying that we have any right to speak of acts of thought at all, except such as take place in our own minds, and embracing the doctrine that my mind is the only one that exists. Against anyone who accepts that form of solipsism I shall not stay to argue. I am considering how history, as the knowledge of past thoughts (acts of thought), is possible; and I am only concerned to show that it is impossible except on the view that to know another's act of thought involves repeating it for oneself. If a person who rejects that view is driven in consequence to this kind of solipsism, my point is proved.

We now pass to the second objection. It will be said: 'Has not this argument proved too much? It has shown that an act of thought can be not only performed at an instant but sustained over a lapse of time; not only sustained, but revived; not only revived in the experience of the same mind but (on pain of solipsism) re-enacted in another's. But this does not prove the possibility of history. For that, we must be able not only to re-enact another's thought but also to know that the thought we are re-enacting is his. But so far as we re-enact it, it becomes our own; it is merely as our own that we perform it and are aware of it in the performance; it has become subjective, but for that very reason it has ceased to be objective; become present, and therefore ceased to be past. This indeed is just what Oakeshott has explicitly maintained in his doctrine that the historian only arranges *sub specie praeteritorum* what is in reality his own present experience, and what Croce in effect admits when he says that all history is contemporary history.'

The objector is here saying two different things. First, he is saying that mere re-enactment of another's thought does not make historical knowledge; we must also know that we are re-enacting it. Secondly, he is arguing that this addition, the knowledge that we are re-enacting a past thought, is in the nature of the case impossible; since the thought as re-enacted is now our own, and our knowledge of it is limited to our own present awareness of it as an element in our own experience.

The first point is obviously right. The fact that someone performs an act of thought which another has performed before him does not make him an historian. It cannot, in such a case, be said that he is an historian without knowing it: unless he knows that he is thinking historically, he is not thinking historically. Historical thinking is an activity (and not the only one, unless the others are somehow parts of it) which is a function of self-consciousness, a form of thought possible only to a mind which knows itself to be thinking in that way.

The second point is that the *condicio sine qua non* demanded by the first can never be realized. The argument adduced to prove this point is important; but let us look first at the point proved. It is that although we can re-enact in our own minds another's act of thought, we can never know that we are re-enacting it. But this is an explicit self-contradiction. The objector confesses to a knowledge that something happens and at the same time denies that such knowledge is possible. He might try to remove the paradox by saying 'I did not mean that it does happen; I only meant that, for all I know, it may; what I maintain is that, if it did, we could not know that it was happening'. And he might cite, as a parallel case, the impossibility of knowing that any two persons experience indistinguishably similar colour-sensations on looking at the same blade of grass. But the parallel is not exact; what he was actually saying was something very different. He was saying not that, if it happened, some other circumstance would prevent us from knowing it: he was saying that if it did happen the very fact of its happening would make us unable to know that it was happening. And this makes it an event of a very peculiar kind.

There is only one kind of thing which may happen in a mind, of which it can be said that the very fact of its happening would render it impossible for us to know that it was happening: namely being under an illusion or error. What the objector is saying, therefore, is that the first of the two indispensable conditions of historical knowledge is an illusion or error on just that point of which knowledge is required. No doubt this in itself would not make historical knowledge impossible. For a condition of something's existing may be related to that thing in either of two ways: either as something that must exist first, but ceases to exist when that thing comes into existence, or as something that must exist so long as that thing exists. If the contention were that historical knowledge can only come into existence as replacing historical error, it would at any rate be worth considering. But the re-enactment of past thought is not a pre-condition of historical knowledge, but an integral element in it; the effect of the contention, therefore, is to make such knowledge impossible.

We must turn to the argument on which this contention rests. It was urged that an act of thought by becoming subjective ceases to be objective, and thus, by becoming present, ceases to be past; I can only be aware of it as the act I am here and now performing, not as the act which someone else has performed at another time.

Here again there are various points to be distinguished. Perhaps the first is the meaning of the phrase 'be aware of it.' The term 'awareness' is often used in an equivocal manner. To be aware of a pain is loosely used for simply feeling it, without knowing that it is a toothache or a headache or even a pain at all: the phrase refers simply to the immediate experience of having or undergoing the pain. Some philosophers would call this immediate experience by the name 'acquaintance': but that is a most misleading term for it, since acquaintance is a familiar English word denoting the kind of way in which we know individual persons or places or other things as permanent objects that recur, recognizably identical with themselves, in the course of our experience: something far removed from immediate feeling. But the term 'awareness' is also used in two other ways. It is used as a name for self-consciousness, as when a person is said to be aware of losing his temper; where what is meant is not only that he immediately experiences a feeling of anger which, as a matter of fact, is increasing, but that he knows this feeling to be his feeling, and an increasing one: as distinct from the case, for example, where he experiences the feeling but attributes it, as people often do, to his neighbours. And thirdly, it is used for perception, as when a person is said to be aware of a table, especially when the perception is somewhat dim and uncertain. It is well to clear up this ambiguity by settling how to use the word; and the best English usage would suggest its restriction to the second meaning, reserving feeling for the first and perception for the third.

This requires a reconsideration of the thesis. Does it mean that I merely feel the act going on, as an element in the flow of immediate experience; or that I recognize it as my act with a determinate place in my mental life? Clearly the second, though this does not exclude the first. I am aware of my act not only as an experience but as my experience, and an experience of a determinate kind: an act, and an act of thought which has arisen in a certain way, and has a certain cognitive character, and so forth.

If that is so, it can no longer be said that the act, because it is subjective, cannot be objective. Indeed, to say that would be to contradict oneself. To say that an act of thought cannot be objective is to say that it cannot be known; but anyone who said this would be claiming thereby to state his knowledge of such acts. He must therefore modify it, and will perhaps say that one act of thought may be an object to another act, but not to itself. But this again needs modification, for any object is properly the object not of an act but of an agent, the mind that performs that act. True, a mind is nothing except its own activities; but it is all these activities together, not any one separately. The question is, then, whether a person who performs an act of knowing can also know that he is performing or has performed that act. Admittedly he can, or no one would know that there were such acts, and so no one could have called them subjective; but to call them merely subjective, and not objective too, is to deny that admission while yet continuing to assume its truth.

The act of thinking, then, is not only subjective but objective as well. It is not only a thinking, it is something that can be thought about. But, because (as I have already tried to show) it is never merely objective, it requires to be thought about in a peculiar way, a way only appropriate to itself. It cannot be set before the thinking mind as a ready-made object, discovered as something independent of that mind and studied as it is in itself, in that independence. It can never be studied 'objectively', in the sense in which 'objectively' excludes 'subjectively'. It has to be studied as it actually exists, that is to say, as an act. And because this act is subjectivity (though not mere subjectivity) or experience, it can be studied only in its own subjective being, that is, by the thinker whose activity or experience it is. This study is not mere experience or consciousness, not even mere self-consciousness: it is self-knowledge. Thus the act of thought in becoming subjective does not cease to be objective; it is the object of a self-knowledge which differs from mere consciousness in being self-consciousness or awareness, and differs from being mere self-consciousness in being self-knowledge: the critical study of one's own thought, not the mere awareness of that thought as one's own.

Here it is possible to answer a tacit question which was left open when I said that a person who performs an act of knowing can also know that he 'is performing or has performed' that act. Which is it? Clearly, the first: for the act of thought has to be studied as it actually exists, that is, as an act. But this does not exclude the second. We have already seen that if mere experience is conceived as a flow of successive states, thought must be conceived as something that can apprehend the structure of this flow and the forms of succession which it exhibits: that is, thought is able to think the past as well as the present. Where thought studies the activity of thinking itself, therefore, it is equally able to study past acts of thinking and compare them with the present act. But there is a difference between the two cases. If I now think about a feeling which I had in the past, it may be true that thinking about it occasions, or else perhaps depends for its possibility on the independent occurrence of, an echo of that feeling in the present: that, for example, I could not think of the anger I once felt except so far as I now experience at least a faint vibration of anger in my mind. But whether this is true or not, the actual past anger of which I am thinking is past and gone; that does not reappear, the stream of immediate experience has carried it away for ever; at most there reappears something like it. The gap of time between my present thought and its past object is bridged not by the survival or revival of the object, but only by the power of thought to overleap such a gap; and the thought which does this is memory.

If, on the contrary, what I think about is a past activity of thought, for example a past philosophical inquiry of my own, the gap is bridged from both sides. To think at all about that past activity of thought, I must revive it in my own mind, for the act of thinking can be studied only as an act. But what is so revived is not a mere echo of the old activity, another of the same kind; it is that same activity taken up again and re-enacted, perhaps in order that, doing it over again under my own critical inspection, I may detect in it false steps of which critics have accused me. In thus re-thinking my past thought I am not merely remembering it. I am constructing the history of a certain phase of my life: and the difference between memory and history is that whereas in memory the past is a mere spectacle, in history it is re-enacted in present thought. So far as this thought is mere thought, the past is merely re-enacted; so far as it is thought about thought, the past is thought of as being re-enacted, and my knowledge of myself is historical knowledge.

The history of myself is thus not memory as such, but a peculiar case of memory. Certainly, a mind which could not remember could not have historical knowledge. But memory as such is only the present thought of past experience as such, be that experience what it may; historical knowledge is that special case of memory where the object of present thought is past thought, the gap between present and past being bridged not only by the power of present thought to think of the past, but also by the power of past thought to reawaken itself in the present.

To return to our supposed objector. Why did he think that the act of thought, by becoming subjective, ceased to be objective? The answer should by now be plain. It is because he understood by subjectivity not the act of thinking, but simply consciousness as a flow of immediate states. Subjectivity for him means not the subjectivity of thought but only the subjectivity of feeling or immediate experience. Even immediate experience has an object, for in every feeling there is something felt and in every sensation there is something sensed: but in seeing a colour what we see is the colour, not our act of seeing the colour, and in feeling cold we feel the cold (whatever exactly cold may be) but not the activity of feeling it. The subjectivity of immediate experience is thus a pure or mere subjectivity; it is never objective to itself: the experiencing never experiences itself as experiencing. If, then, there were an experience from which all thought were excluded (whether such an experience really exists or not, it is beside the point to inquire), the active or subjective element in that experience could never be an object to itself, and if all experience were of the same kind it could never be an object at all. What the objector was doing, therefore, was to assume that all experience is immediate, mere consciousness, devoid of thought. If he denies this, and says that he fully recognizes the presence of thought as an element in experience, we must reply that he may have recognized it in name but that he has not recognized it in fact. He has found a place for thought only by the expedient of selecting some items in the flow of consciousness and conferring upon them the title of thought, without asking what it implied; so that what he calls thought is in fact just one kind of immediate experience, whereas thought differs precisely from sensation or feeling in that it is never an immediate experience. In the immediate experience of sight, we see a colour; only by thinking can we know ourselves to be seeing it and also know that what we see is what we do not see it to be: an object at a distance from us, for example, which we have seen before. And even if he went so far as to recognize this, he failed to take the next step, and realize that by thinking we know ourselves to be thinking.

There is still one point in the objection that has not been cleared up. Granted that it is possible to reconstruct the history of one's own mind, by an extension of the general act of memory to the special case where what is remembered is an act of thinking, does it follow that the past which can be thus knowingly re-enacted is any past but my own? Does it not rather seem that, since history has been described as a special case of memory, each of us can be the historian only of his own thought?

In order to answer this question we must inquire further into the relation between memory and what, as distinct from memory, I will call autobiography, using that name for a strictly historical account of my own past. If anyone of us were setting out to compose such an account, he would be confronted with two kinds of task of which one must come before the other. I do not mean that one must be completed before the other begins, but only that in every part of the work one side of it must be taken in hand before the other can be carried out. The first task is that of recollecting: he must search his memory for a vision of past experiences, and use various means of stimulating it, for example by reading letters and books that he once wrote, revisiting places associated in his mind with certain events, and so forth. When this is done, he has before his mind a spectacle of the relevant parts of his own past life: he sees a young man undergoing such and such experiences, and knows that this young man was himself. But now begins the second task. He must not merely know that this young man was himself, he must try to rediscover that young man's thoughts. And here recollection is a treacherous guide. He remembers how he walked in the garden at night, wrestling with a thought; he remembers the scent of the flowers, and the breeze in his hair; but if he relies on these associations to tell him what the thought was, he is more than likely to be misled. He will probably fall into the mistake of substituting for it another which came to him later. Thus politicians, in writing their autobiographies, remember very well the impacts and emotions of a crisis, but are apt, in describing the policy they then advocated, to contaminate it with ideas that belonged in fact to a later stage in their career. And this is natural: because thought is not wholly entangled in the flow of experience, so that we constantly reinterpret our past thoughts and assimilate them to those we are thinking now.

There is only one way in which this tendency can be checked. If I want to be sure that twenty years ago a certain thought was really in my mind, I must have evidence of it. That evidence must be a book or letter or the like that I then wrote, or a picture I painted, or a recollection (my own or another's) of something I said, or of an action that I did, clearly revealing what was in my mind. Only by having some such evidence before me, and interpreting it fairly and squarely, can I prove to myself that I did think thus. Having done so, I rediscover my past self, and re-enact these thoughts as my thoughts; judging now better than I could then, it is to be hoped, their merits and defects.

Now it is certainly true that, unless a man could do this for himself, he could not do it for anybody else. But there is nothing which the autobiographer does, in this second part of his task, that the historian could not do for another. If the autobiographer, although from the point of view of simple recollection his past thoughts are inextricably confused with his present ones, can disentangle them with the help of evidence, and decide that he must have thought in certain ways although at first he did not remember doing so, the historian, by using evidence of the same general kind, can recover the thoughts of others; coming to think them now even if he never thought them before, and knowing this activity as the re-enactment of what those men once thought. We shall never know how the flowers smelt in the garden of Epicurus, or how Nietzsche felt the wind in his hair as he walked on the mountains; we cannot relive the triumph of Archimedes or the bitterness of Marius; but the evidence of what these men thought is in our hands; and in re-creating these thoughts in our own minds by interpretation of that evidence we can know, so far as there is any knowledge, that the thoughts we create were theirs.

We put into the objector's mouth the statement that if experience could be repeated, the result would be an immediate identity between the historian and his object. This deserves further discussion. For if a mind is nothing but its own activities, and if to know the mind of a person in the past—say Thomas Becket—is to re-enact his thought, surely in so far as I, the historian, do this, I simply become Becket, which seems absurd.

Why is it absurd? It might be said, because to be Becket is one thing, to know Becket is another: and the historian aims at the latter. This objection, however, has already been answered. It depends on a false interpretation of the distinction between subjectivity and objectivity. For Becket, in so far as he was a thinking mind, being Becket was also knowing that he was Becket; and for myself, on the same showing, to be Becket is to know that I am Becket, that is, to know that I am my own present self re-enacting Becket's thought, myself being in that sense Becket. I do not 'simply' become Becket, for a thinking mind is never 'simply' anything: it is its own activities of thought, and it is not these 'simply' (which, if it means any-thing, means 'immediately'), for thought is not mere immediate experience but always reflection or self-knowledge, the know-ledge of oneself as living in these activities.

It may be well to enlarge on this point. An act of thought is certainly a part of the thinker's experience. It occurs at a cer-tain time, and in a certain context of other acts of thought, emotions, sensations, and so forth. Its presence in this context I call its immediacy; for although thought is not mere imme-diacy it is not devoid of immediacy. The peculiarity of thought is that, in addition to occurring here and now in this context, it can sustain itself through a change of context and revive in a different one. This power to sustain and revive itself is what makes an act of thought more than a mere 'event' or 'situation', to quote words that have been applied to it, for example, by Whitehead. It is because, and so far as, the act of thought is misconceived as a mere event that the idea of re-enacting it seems paradoxical and a perverse way of describing the occur-rence of another, similar, event. The immediate, as such, can-not be re-enacted. Consequently, those elements in experience whose being is just their immediacy (sensations, feelings, &c. as such) cannot be re-enacted; not only that, but thought itself can never be re-enacted in its immediacy. The first discovery of a truth, for example, differs from any subsequent contempla-tion of it, not in that the truth contemplated is a different truth, nor in that the act of contemplating it is a different act; but in that the immediacy of the first occasion can never again be experienced: the shock of its novelty, the liberation from perplexing problems, the triumph of achieving a desired result, perhaps the sense of having vanquished opponents and achieved fame, and so forth.

But further: the immediacy of thought consists not only in its context of emotions (together, of course, with sensations, like the buoyancy of Archimedes' body in the bath) but in its context of other thoughts. The self-identity of the act of thinking that these two angles are equal is not only independent of such matters as that a person performing it is hungry and cold, and feels his chair hard beneath him, and is bored with his lesson: it is also independent of further thoughts, such as that the book says they are equal, or that the master believes them to be equal; or even thoughts more closely relevant to the subject in hand, as that their sum, plus the angle at the vertex, is 180 degrees.

This has sometimes been denied. It has been said that anything torn from its context is thereby mutilated and falsified; and that in consequence, to know any one thing, we must know its context, which implies knowing the whole universe. I do not propose to discuss this doctrine in its whole bearing, but only to remind the reader of its connexion with the view that reality is immediate experience, and its corollary that thought, which inevitably tears things out of their context, can never be true. On such a doctrine Euclid's act of thinking on a given occasion that these angles are equal would be what it was only in relation to the total context of his then experience, including such things as his being in a good temper and having a slave standing behind his right shoulder: without knowing all these we cannot know what he meant. If (which the doctrine in its strict form would not allow) we brush aside as irrelevant everything except the context of his geometrical thought, we do not even so escape absurdity; for in composing his proof of the theorem he may have thought 'this theorem enables me to prove that the angle in a semicircle is a right angle', and a hundred other things which it is just as impossible for us to know. Very likely he never thought of his fifth theorem without some such context; but to say that because the theorem, as an act of thought, exists only in its context we cannot know it except in the context in which he actually thought it, is to restrict the being of thought to its own immediacy, to reduce it to a case of merely immediate experience, and so to deny it as thought. Nor does anyone who attempts to maintain such a doctrine maintain it consistently. For example, he tries to show that a rival doctrine is untrue. But the doctrine he criticizes is a doctrine taught by somebody else (or even one accepted in unregenerate days by himself). On his own showing, this doctrine is what it is only in a total context that cannot be repeated and cannot be known. The context of thought in which his adversary's doctrine has its being cannot ever be the context which it has in the critic's experience; and if an act of thought is what it is only in relation to its context, the doctrine he criticizes can never be the doctrine taught by his opponent. And this not owing to any defects in exposition or comprehension, but owing to the self-frustrating character of the attempt to understand another's thought, or indeed to think at all.

Others, who have taken warning by these consequences, have embraced the opposite doctrine that all acts of thought are atomically distinct from one another. This makes it both easy and legitimate to detach them from their context; for there is no context; there is only a juxtaposition of things standing to one another in merely external relations. On this view, the unity of a body of knowledge is only that kind of unity which belongs to a collection: and this is true both of a science, or system of things known, and of a mind, or system of acts of knowing. Once more I am not concerned with the whole bearing of such a doctrine, but only to point out that by substituting logical analysis for attention to experience (the constant appeal to which was the strength of the rival doctrine) it overlooks the immediacy of thought, and converts the act of thinking, from a subjective experience, into an objective spectacle. The fact that Euclid performed a certain operation of thought becomes just a fact, like the fact that this paper rests on this table; mind is merely a collective name for such facts.

History is no more possible on this view than on the other. That Euclid performed a certain operation of thought may be called a fact, but it is an unknowable fact. We cannot know it, we can only at most believe it on testimony. And this appears a satisfactory account of historical thought only to persons who embrace the fundamental error of mistaking for history that form of pseudo-history which Croce has called 'philological history': persons who think that history is nothing more than scholarship or learning, and would assign to the historian the self-contradictory task of discovering (for example) 'what Plato thought' without inquiring 'whether it is true'.

To disentangle ourselves from these two complementary errors, we must attack the false dilemma from which they both spring. That dilemma rests on the disjunction that thought is either pure immediacy, in which case it is inextricably involved in the flow of consciousness, or pure mediation, in which case it is utterly detached from that flow. Actually it is both immediacy and mediation. Every act of thought, as it actually happens, happens in a context out of which it arises and in which it lives, like any other experience, as an organic part of the thinker's life. Its relations with its context are not those of an item in a collection, but those of a special function in the total activity of an organism. So far, not only is the doctrine of the so-called idealists correct, but even that of the pragmatists who have developed that side of it to an extreme. But an act of thought, in addition to actually happening, is capable of sustaining itself and being revived or repeated without loss of its identity. So far, those who have opposed the 'idealists' are in the right, when they maintain that what we think is not altered by alterations of the context in which we think it. But it cannot repeat itself *in vacuo*, as the disembodied ghost of a past experience. However often it happens, it must always happen in some context, and the new context must be just as appropriate to it as the old. Thus, the mere fact that someone has expressed his thoughts in writing, and that we possess his works, does not enable us to understand his thoughts. In order that we may be able to do so, we must come to the reading of them prepared with an experience sufficiently like his own to make those thoughts organic to it.

This double character of thought provides the solution of a logical puzzle that has a close connexion with the theory of history. If I now re-think a thought of Plato's, is my act of thought identical with Plato's or different from it? Unless it is identical, my alleged knowledge of Plato's philosophy is sheer

error. But unless it is different, my knowledge of Plato's philosophy implies oblivion of my own. What is required, if I am
to know Plato's philosophy, is both to re-think it in my own
mind and also to think other things in the light of which I can
judge it. Some philosophers have attempted to solve this puzzle
by a vague appeal to the 'principle of identity in difference',
arguing that there is a development of thought from Plato to
myself and that anything which develops remains identical with
itself although it becomes different. Others have replied with
justice that the question is how exactly the two things are the
same, and how exactly they differ. The answer is that, in their
immediacy, as actual experiences organically united with the
body of experience out of which they arise, Plato's thought and
mine are different. But in their mediation they are the same.
This perhaps calls for further explanation. When I read Plato's
argument in the *Theaetetus* against the view that knowledge is
merely sensation, I do not know what philosophical doctrines
he was attacking; I could not expound these doctrines and say
in detail who maintained them and by what arguments. In its
immediacy, as an actual experience of his own, Plato's argument must undoubtedly have grown up out of a discussion of
some sort, though I do not know what it was, and been closely
connected with such a discussion. Yet if I not only read his argument but understand it, follow it in my own mind by re-arguing
it with and for myself, the process of argument which I go
through is not a process resembling Plato's, it actually is Plato's,
so far as I understand him rightly. The argument simply as
itself, starting from these premises and leading through this
process to this conclusion; the argument as it can be developed
either in Plato's mind or mine or anyone else's, is what I call the
thought in its mediation. In Plato's mind, this existed in a
certain context of discussion and theory; in my mind, because
I do not know that context, it exists in a different one, namely
that of the discussions arising out of modern sensationalism.
Because it is a thought and not a mere feeling or sensation, it can
exist in both these contexts without losing its identity, although
without some appropriate context it could never exist. Part of
the context in which it exists in my mind might, if it was a fallacious argument, be other activities of thought consisting in
knowing how to refute it; but even if I refuted it, it would still

be the same argument and the act of following its logical structure would be the same act.

§ 5. *The Subject-matter of History*

If we raise the question, Of what can there be historical knowledge? the answer is, Of that which can be re-enacted in the historian's mind. In the first place, this must be experience. Of that which is not experience but the mere object of experience, there can be no history. Thus there is and can be no history of nature, whether as perceived or as thought by the scientist. No doubt nature contains, undergoes, or even consists of, processes; its changes in time are essential to it, they may even (as some think) be all that it has or is; and these changes may be genuinely creative, no mere repetitions of fixed cyclical phases but the development of new orders of natural being. But all this goes no way towards proving that the life of nature is an historical life or that our knowledge of it is historical knowledge. The only condition on which there could be a history of nature is that the events of nature are actions on the part of some thinking being or beings, and that by studying these actions we could discover what were the thoughts which they expressed and think these thoughts for ourselves. This is a condition which probably no one will claim is fulfilled. Consequently the processes of nature are not historical processes and our knowledge of nature, though it may resemble history in certain superficial ways, e.g. by being chronological, is not historical knowledge.

Secondly, even experience is not as such the object of historical knowledge. In so far as it is merely immediate experience, a mere flow of consciousness consisting of sensations, feelings, and the like, its process is not an historical process. That process can, no doubt, be not only directly experienced in its immediacy, but also known; its particular details and its general characteristics can be studied by thought; but the thought which studies it finds in it a mere object of study, which in order to be studied need not be, and indeed cannot be, re-enacted in the thinking about it. In so far as we think about its particular details, we are remembering experiences of our own or entering with sympathy and imagination into those of others; but in such cases we do not re-enact the experiences which we remember or with which we sympathize; we are merely contemplating them as objects external to our present selves, aided perhaps by the presence in ourselves of other experiences like them. In so far as we think about its general characteristics, we are engaging in the science of psychology. In neither case are we thinking historically.

Thirdly, even thought itself, in its immediacy as the unique act of thought with its unique context in the life of an individual thinker, is not the object of historical knowledge. It cannot be re-enacted; if it could, time itself would be cancelled and the historian would be the person about whom he thinks, living over again in all respects the same. The historian cannot apprehend the individual act of thought in its individuality, just as it actually happened. What he apprehends of that individual is only something that it might have shared with other acts of thought and actually has shared with his own. But this something is not an abstraction, in the sense of a common characteristic shared by different individuals and considered apart from the individuals that share it. It is the act of thought itself, in its survival and revival at different times and in different persons: once in the historian's own life, once in the life of the person whose history he is narrating.

Thus the vague phrase that history is knowledge of the individual claims for it a field at once too wide and too narrow: too wide, because the individuality of perceived objects and natural facts and immediate experiences falls outside its sphere, and most of all because even the individuality of historical events and personages, if that means their uniqueness, falls equally outside it; too narrow, because it would exclude universality, and it is just the universality of an event or character that makes it a proper and possible object of historical study, if by universality we mean something that oversteps the limits of merely local and temporal existence and possesses a significance valid for all men at all times. These too are no doubt vague phrases; but they are attempts to describe something real: namely the way in which thought, transcending its own immediacy, survives and revives in other contexts; and to express the truth that individual acts and persons appear in history not in virtue of their individuality as such, but because that individuality is the vehicle of a thought which, because it was actually theirs, is potentially everyone's.

Of everything other than thought, there can be no history. Thus a biography, for example, however much history it contains, is constructed on principles that are not only non-historical but anti-historical. Its limits are biological events, the birth and death of a human organism: its framework is thus a framework not of thought but of natural process. Through this framework—the bodily life of the man, with his childhood, maturity and senescence, his diseases and all the accidents of animal existence—the tides of thought, his own and others', flow crosswise, regardless of its structure, like sea-water through a stranded wreck. Many human emotions are bound up with the spectacle of such bodily life in its vicissitudes, and biography, as a form of literature, feeds these emotions and may give them wholesome food; but this is not history. Again, the record of immediate experience with its flow of sensations and feelings, faithfully preserved in a diary or recalled in a memoir, is not history. At its best, it is poetry; at its worst, an obtrusive egotism; but history it can never be.

But there is another condition without which a thing cannot become the object of historical knowledge. The gulf of time between the historian and his object must be bridged, as I have said, from both ends. The object must be of such a kind that it can revive itself in the historian's mind; the historian's mind must be such as to offer a home for that revival. This does not mean that his mind must be of a certain kind, possessed of an historical temperament; nor that he must be trained in special rules of historical technique. It means that he must be the right man to study that object. What he is studying is a certain thought: to study it involves re-enacting it in himself; and in order that it may take its place in the immediacy of his own thought, his thought must be, as it were, pre-adapted to become its host. This does not imply, in the technical sense of the phrase, a pre-established harmony between the historian's mind and its object; it is not, for example, an endorsement of Coleridge's saying that men are born Platonists or Aristotelians; for it has not prejudged the question whether a Platonist or an Aristotelian is born or made. A man who at one time of life finds certain historical studies unprofitable, because he cannot enter for himself into the thought of those about whom he is thinking, will find at another time that he has become able to do so, perhaps as a result of deliberate self-training. But at any given stage in his life the historian as he stands is certain to have, for whatever reason, a readier sympathy with some ways of thinking than with others. Partly this is because certain ways of thinking are altogether, or relatively, strange to him: partly it is because they are all too familiar, and he feels the need of getting away from them in the interests of his own mental and moral welfare.

If the historian, working against the grain of his own mind because it is demanded of him that he should study such uncongenial subjects, or because they are 'in the period' which his own misguided conscience fancies he ought to treat in all its aspects, tries to master the history of a thought into which he cannot personally enter, instead of writing its history he will merely repeat the statements that record the external facts of its development: names and dates, and ready-made descriptive phrases. Such repetitions may very well be useful, but not because they are history. They are dry bones, which may some day become history, when someone is able to clothe them with the flesh and blood of a thought which is both his own and theirs. This is only a way of saying that the historian's thought must spring from the organic unity of his total experience, and be a function of his entire personality with its practical as well as its theoretical interests. It need hardly be added that since the historian is a son of his time, there is a general likelihood that what interests him will interest his contemporaries. It is a familiar fact that every generation finds itself interested in, and therefore able to study historically, tracts and aspects of the past which to its fathers were dry bones, signifying nothing.

Historical knowledge, then, has for its proper object thought: not things thought about, but the act of thinking itself. This principle has served us to distinguish history from natural science on the one hand, as the study of a given or objective world distinct from the act of thinking it, and on the other from psychology as the study of immediate experience, sensation, and feeling, which, though the activity of a mind, is not the activity of thinking. But the positive meaning of the principle needs further determination. How much or how little is meant to be included under the term 'thought'?

The term 'thought', as hitherto used in this section and its predecessor, has stood for a certain form of experience or mental activity whose peculiarity may be negatively described by saying that it is not merely immediate, and therefore is not carried away by the flow of consciousness. The positive peculiarity which distinguishes thought from mere consciousness is its power of recognizing the activity of the self as a single activity persisting through the diversity of its own acts. If I feel cold, and later feel warm, there is for mere feeling no continuity between the two experiences. It is true, as Bergson points out, that the feeling cold 'interpenetrates' the subsequent feeling warm, and gives it a quality which it would not otherwise have had; but the feeling warm, though it owes that quality to the previous feeling cold, does not recognize the debt. The distinction between mere feeling and thought may thus be illustrated by the distinction between simply feeling cold and being able to say 'I feel cold'. To say that, I must be aware of myself as something more than the immediate experience of cold: aware of myself as an activity of feeling which has had other experiences previously, and remains the same throughout the difference of these experiences. I need not even remember what these experiences were; but I must know that they existed and were mine.

The peculiarity of thought, then, is that it is not mere consciousness but self-consciousness. The self, as merely conscious, is a flow of consciousness, a series of immediate sensations and feelings; but as merely conscious it is not aware of itself as such a flow; it is ignorant of its own continuity through the succession of experiences. The activity of becoming aware of this continuity is what is called thinking.

But this thought of myself as an activity of feeling, which remains the same activity through its various acts, is only the most rudimentary form of thought. It develops into other forms by working outwards from this starting-point in various directions. One thing which it may do is to become more clearly aware of the precise nature of the continuity: instead of only conceiving 'myself' as having previously had some experiences, indeterminate in their nature, considering what in particular these experiences were: remembering them and comparing them with the immediate present. Another is to analyse the present experience itself, to distinguish in it the act of feeling from what is felt, and to conceive what is felt as something whose reality (like the reality of myself as the feeler) is not exhausted by its immediate presence to my feeling. Working along these two lines, thought becomes memory, the thought of my own flow of experiences, and perception, the thought of what I experience as something real.

A third way in which it develops is by recognizing myself as not only a sentient being but as a thinking being. In remembering and perceiving, I am already doing more than enjoying a flow of immediate experience; I am also thinking; but I am not (simply in remembering or perceiving as such) aware of myself as thinking. I am only aware of myself as feeling. This awareness is already self-consciousness or thought, but it is an imperfect self-consciousness, because in possessing it I am performing a certain kind of mental activity, namely thinking, of which I am not conscious. Hence the thinking which we do in memory or perception as such may be called unconscious thinking, not because we can do it without being conscious, for in order to do it we must be not only conscious but self-conscious, but because we do it without being conscious that we are doing it. To be conscious that I am thinking is to think in a new way, which may be called reflecting.

Historical thinking is always reflection; for reflection is thinking about the act of thinking, and we have seen that all historical thinking is of that kind. But what kind of thinking can be its object? Is it possible to study the history of what was just now called unconscious thinking, or must the thinking which history studies be conscious or reflective thinking?

This amounts to asking whether there can be a history of memory or perception. And it is clear that there cannot. A person who should sit down to write the history of memory or the history of perception would find nothing to write about. It is conceivable that different races of mankind, and for that matter different human beings, have had different ways of remembering or perceiving; and it is possible that these differences were sometimes due, not to physiological differences (such as the undeveloped colour-sense which has been ascribed, on very dubious grounds, to the Greeks), but to different habits of thought. But if there are ways of perceiving which for such reasons have prevailed here and there in the past, and are not practised by ourselves, we cannot reconstruct the history of them because we cannot re-enact the appropriate experiences at will; and this is because the habits of thought to which they are due are 'unconscious', and therefore cannot be deliberately revived. For example, it may be true that civilizations other than our own have enjoyed as part of their normal equipment the faculty of second sight or the power of seeing ghosts. It may be that, among them, these things arose out of certain habitual ways of thinking, and were therefore a familiar and understood way of expressing genuine knowledge or well-founded belief. Certainly, when Burnt Njál in the saga used his second sight as a means of giving advice to his friends, they were profiting by the wisdom of a sound lawyer and a shrewd man of the world. But, supposing all this to be true, it is still impossible for us to write a history of second sight; all we can do is to collect instances in which it has been alleged, and to believe that the statements about it are statements of fact. But this would be, at most, belief in testimony; and we know that such belief stops where history begins.

In order, therefore, that any particular act of thought should become subject-matter for history, it must be an act not only of thought but of reflective thought, that is, one which is performed in the consciousness that it is being performed, and is constituted what it is by that consciousness. The effort to do it must be more than a merely conscious effort. It must not be the blind effort to do we know not what, like the effort to remember a forgotten name or to perceive a confused object; it must be a reflective effort, the effort to do something of which we have a conception before we do it. A reflective activity is one in which we know what it is that we are trying to do, so that when it is done we know that it is done by seeing that it has conformed to the standard or criterion which was our initial conception of it. It is therefore an act which we are enabled to perform by knowing in advance how to perform it.

Not all acts are of this kind. Samuel Butler was confusing the issue from one side when he said that an infant must know how to suck, or it could not do it; others have confused it from the opposite side by maintaining that we never know what we are going to do until we have done it. Butler was trying to make out that acts which are unreflective are really reflective, exaggerating the place of reason in life, in order to oppose a prevailing materialism; these others are contending that reflective acts are really unreflective, because they conceive all experience as immediate. In its immediacy, as a unique individual, complete with all details and in the full context in which alone it can immediately exist, our future act can certainly never be planned in advance; however carefully we have thought it out, it will always contain much that is unforeseen and surprising; but to infer that therefore it cannot be planned at all is to betray the assumption that its immediate being is the only being it has. An act is more than a mere unique individual; it is something having a universal character; and in the case of a reflective or deliberate act (an act which we not only do, but intend to do before doing it) this universal character is the plan or idea of the act which we conceive in our thought before doing the act itself, and the criterion by reference to which, when we have done it, we know that we have done what we meant to do.

There are certain kinds of act which cannot be done except on these terms: that is to say, cannot be done except reflectively, by a person who knows what he is trying to do and is therefore able, when he has done it, to judge his own action by reference to his intention. It is characteristic of these acts that they should be done, as we say, 'on purpose': that there should be a basis of purpose upon which the structure of the act should be erected, and to which it must conform. Reflective acts may be roughly described as the acts which we do on purpose, and these are the only acts which can become the subject-matter of history.

From this point of view, it can be seen why certain forms of activity are, and others are not, matter of historical knowledge. It would be generally admitted that politics is a thing that can be historically studied. The reason is that politics affords a plain instance of purposive action. The politician is a man with a policy; his policy is a plan of action conceived in advance of its performance; and his success as a politician is proportional to his success in carrying out his policy. No doubt, his policy is not prior to his action in the sense of being fixed once for all before his action begins; it develops as his action develops; but at every stage of his action policy precedes its own fulfilment. If it were possible to say of any man that he acted with no idea whatever what would come of it, but did the first thing that came into his head and merely waited to see the consequences, it would follow that such a man was no politician, and that his action was merely the intrusion into political life of a blind and irrational force. And if it has to be said of a certain man that he doubtless had a policy but that we cannot discover what it was (and one sometimes feels inclined to say this of, for example, certain early Roman emperors), this is as much as to say that one's attempts to reconstruct the political history of his action have failed.

For the same reason, there can be a history of warfare. In a general way, the intentions of a military commander are easy to understand. If he took an army into a certain country and engaged its forces, we can see that he meant to defeat it, and from the recorded account of his acts we can reconstruct in our own minds the plan of campaign which he tried to carry out. Once more, this depends on the assumption that his acts were done on purpose. If they were not, there can be no history of them; if they were done on a purpose that we cannot fathom, then we at least cannot reconstruct their history.

Economic activity, too, can have a history. A man who builds a factory or starts a bank is acting on a purpose which we can understand; so are the men who accept wages from him, buy his goods or his shares, or make deposits and withdrawals. If we are told that there was a strike at the factory or a run on the bank, we can reconstruct in our own minds the purposes of the people whose collective action took those forms.

Again, there can be a history of morals; for in moral action we are doing certain things on purpose, in order to bring our practical life into harmony with the ideal of what it ought to be. This ideal is at once our conception of our own life as it should be, or our intention of what we mean to make it, and our criterion of whether what we have done has been done well or ill. Here too, as in the other cases, our purposes change as our activity develops, but the purpose is always in advance of the act. And it is impossible to act morally except when, and in so far as, one acts on purpose; duty cannot be done by accident or inadvertence; no one can do his duty except a person who means to do his duty.

In these cases we have examples of practical activities which are not merely as a matter of fact pursued on purpose, but could not be what they are unless they were so pursued. Now, it might be thought that all purposive action must be practical action, because there are two stages in it: first conceiving the purpose, which is a theoretical activity or act of pure thought, and then executing it, which is a practical activity supervening on the theoretical. On this analysis it would follow that acting, in the narrow or practical sense of the word, is the only thing that can be done on purpose. For, it might be argued, you cannot think on purpose, since if you conceived your own act of thought before executing it, you would have executed it already. The theoretical activities, it would follow, cannot be purposive: they must be, as it were, done in the dark, with no conception of what is to come from engaging in them.

This is an error, but it is an error of some interest for the theory of history, because it has actually influenced the theory and practice of historiography to the extent of making people think that the only possible subject-matter of history is the practical life of men. The idea that history concerns itself, and can concern itself, only with such matters as politics, warfare, economic life, and, in general, the world of practice, is still widespread and was once almost universal. We have seen how even Hegel, who showed so brilliantly how the history of philosophy should be written, committed himself in his lectures on the philosophy of history to the view that history's proper subject-matter is society and the state, the practical life, or (in his own technical language) objective mind, mind as expressing itself outwardly in actions and institutions.

To-day it is no longer necessary to argue that art, science, religion, philosophy, and so forth are proper subjects of historical study; the fact of their being studied historically is too familiar. But it is necessary to ask why this is so, in view of the argument to the contrary that has been stated above.

In the first place, it is not true that a person engaged in purely theoretical thinking is acting without a purpose. A man doing a certain piece of scientific work, such as inquiring into the cause of malaria, has a quite definite purpose in mind: to discover the cause of malaria. True, he does not know what this cause is; but he knows that when he finds it he will know that he has found it by applying to his discovery certain tests or criteria which he has before him from the start. The plan of his discovery, then, is the plan of a theory which will satisfy these criteria. Similarly for the historian or philosopher. He is never sailing an uncharted sea; his chart, however little detail it contains, is marked with the parallels of latitude and longitude, and his purpose is to discover what there is to put down on and between those lines. In other words: every actual inquiry starts from a certain problem, and the purpose of the inquiry is to solve that problem; the plan of the discovery, therefore, is already known and formulated by saying that, whatever the discovery may be, it must be such as to satisfy the terms of the problem. As in the case of practical activity, this plan of course changes as the activity of thought proceeds; some plans are abandoned as impracticable and replaced by others, some are carried out successfully and found to lead to new problems.

In the second place, the difference between conceiving and executing a purpose was not correctly described as the difference between a theoretical act and a practical one. To conceive a purpose or form an intention is already a practical activity. It is not thought forming an anteroom to action; it is action itself in its initial stage. If this is not at once recognized, it may be recognized by considering its implications. Thought, as theoretical activity, cannot be moral or immoral; it can only be true or false. That which is moral or immoral must be action. Now, if a man forms the intention of committing murder or adultery, and then decides not to carry out his intention, the intention itself already exposes him to condemnation on moral grounds. It is not said of him 'he accurately conceived the nature of murder or adultery, so his thought was true and therefore admirable'; it is said of him 'he is doubtless not so wicked as if he had carried his intention out to the end; but to intend such action at all was wicked'.

The scientist, the historian, and the philosopher are thus, no less than the practical man, proceeding in their activities according to plans, thinking on purpose, and thus arriving at results that can be judged according to criteria derived from the plans themselves. Consequently there can be histories of these things. All that is necessary is that there should be evidence of how such thinking has been done and that the historian should be able to interpret it, that is, should be able to re-enact in his own mind the thought he is studying, envisaging the problem from which it started and reconstructing the steps by which its solution was attempted. In practice, the common difficulty for the historian is to identify the problem, for whereas the thinker is generally careful to expound the steps of his own thought, he is talking as a rule to contemporaries who already know what the problem is, and he may never state it at all. And unless the historian knows what the problem was at which he was working, he has no criterion by which to judge the success of his work. It is the historian's endeavour to discover this problem that gives importance to the study of 'influences', which is so futile when influences are conceived as the decanting of ready-made thoughts out of one mind into another. An intelligent inquiry into the influence of Socrates on Plato, or Descartes on Newton, seeks to discover not the points of agreement, but the way in which the conclusions reached by one thinker give rise to problems for the next.

There might seem to be a special difficulty about the case of art. The artist, even if his work can be called reflective at all, seems a great deal less reflective than the scientist or philosopher. He does not appear to set out on a particular piece of work with a clearly formulated problem, and judge his result by reference to the terms of the problem. He seems to be working in a world of pure imagination, where his thought is absolutely creative, never in any sense knowing what he is going to do until he has done it. If thinking means reflection and judgement, it would seem that the genuine artist does not think at all; his mental labour seems to be a labour of pure intuition, where no concept either precedes or sustains or judges the intuition itself.

But the artist does not create his works out of nothing. He begins in every case with a problem before him. This problem, in so far as he is an artist, is not the problem of decorating a given room or designing a house to comply with given utilitarian requirements; these are the special problems of applied art, and in art as such they do not arise. Nor is it the problem of making something out of paint, or sounds, or marble; he only begins to be an artist when those problems cease to be problems at all, and the materials of his craft have become obedient servants of his imagination. The point at which he begins creating a work of art is the point at which that work is grafted on the body of his unreflective experience: his immediate sensitive and emotional life with its development, rational but unconscious, through memory and perception. The problem with which he is confronted is the problem of feeding this experience into a work of art. He has encountered some experience that stands out from the rest as significant or moving; its unexpressed significance lies on his mind as a burden, challenging him to find some way of uttering it; and his labour in creating a work of art is his response to that challenge. In this sense the artist knows very well what he is doing and what he is trying to do. The criterion of his having done it rightly is that, when it is done, it should be seen as expressing what he wanted to express. All that is peculiar to him is the fact that he cannot formulate his problem; if he could formulate it, he would have expressed it; and the work of art would have been achieved. But although he cannot in advance of the work itself say what the problem is, he knows that there is a problem, and he is aware of its peculiar nature; only not reflectively aware until the work has been done.

This indeed seems to be the special character of art and its peculiar importance in the life of thought. It is the phase of that life in which the conversion from unreflective to reflective thought actually comes about. There is therefore a history of art, but no history of artistic problems, as there is a history of scientific or philosophical problems. There is only the history of artistic achievements.

There is also a history of religion; for religion, no less than art or philosophy or politics, is a function of reflective thought. In religion man has a conception of himself as a thinking and active being, which he sets over against a conception of God in which his notion of thought and action, knowledge and power, are raised to the level of infinity. The task of religious thought and religious practice (for in religion the theoretical and practical activities are fused into one) is to find the relation between these two opposed conceptions of myself as finite and God as infinite. The absence of any definite relation, the mere difference of the two, is the problem and torment of the religious mind. The discovery of a relation is at once the discovery of my thought as reaching God and of God's thought as reaching me: and, indistinguishable from this, the performance of an act of mine by which I establish a relation with God and an act of God's by which he establishes a relation with me. To fancy that religion lives either below or above the limits of reflective thought is fatally to misconceive either the nature of religion or the nature of reflective thought. It would be nearer the truth to say that in religion the life of reflection is concentrated in its intensest form, and that the special problems of theoretical and practical life all take their special forms by segregation out of the body of the religious consciousness, and retain their vitality only so far as they preserve their connexion with it and with each other in it.

§ 6. *History and Freedom*

We study history, I have maintained, in order to attain self-knowledge. By way of illustrating this thesis, I shall try to show how our knowledge that human activity is free has been attained only through our discovery of history.

In my historical sketch of the idea of history I have tried to show how history has at last escaped from a state of pupilage to natural science. The disappearance of historical naturalism, however, entails the further conclusion that the activity by which man builds his own constantly changing historical world is a free activity. There are no forces other than this activity which control it or modify it or compel it to behave in this way or in that, to build one kind of world rather than another.

This does not mean that a man is always free to do what he pleases. All men, at some moments in their lives, are free to do what they want: to eat, being hungry, for example, or to sleep, being tired. But this has nothing to do with the problem to which I have referred. Eating and sleeping are animal activities, pursued under the compulsion of animal appetite. With animal appetites and their gratification or frustration history is not concerned. It makes no difference to the historian, as an historian, that there should be no food in a poor man's house; though it may and must make a difference to him as a man with feelings for his fellow creatures; and though as an historian he may be intensely concerned with the shifts by which other men have contrived to bring about this state of things in order that they should be rich and the men who take wages from them poor; and equally concerned with the action to which the poor man may be led not by the fact of his children's unsatisfied hunger, the fact, the physiological fact, of empty bellies and wizened limbs, but by his thought of that fact.

Nor does it mean that a man is free to do what he chooses; that in the realm of history proper, as distinct from that of animal appetite, people are free to plan their own actions as they think fit and execute their plans, each doing what he set out to do and each assuming full responsibility for the consequences, captain of his soul and all that. Nothing could be more false. Henley's rhyme does no more than utter the fantasy of a sick child who has discovered that he can stop himself crying for the moon by making believe that he has got it. A healthy man knows that the empty space in front of him, which he proposes to fill up with activities for which he accordingly now begins making plans, will be very far from empty by the time he steps into it. It will be crowded with other people all pursuing activities of their own. Even now it is not as empty as it looks. It is filled with a saturate solution of activity, on the point of beginning to crystallize out. There will be no room left for his own activity, unless he can so design this that it will fit into the interstices of the rest.

The rational activity which historians have to study is never free from compulsion: the compulsion to face the facts of its own situation. The more rational it is, the more completely it undergoes this compulsion. To be rational is to think; and for a man who proposes to act, the thing that it is important to think about is the situation in which he stands. With regard to this situation, he is not free at all. It is what it is, and neither he nor anyone else can ever change that. For though the situation consists altogether of thoughts, his own and other people's, it cannot be changed by a change of mind on the part of himself or anyone else. If minds change, as they do, this merely means that with the lapse of time a new situation has arisen. For a man about to act, the situation is his master, his oracle, his god. Whether his action is to prove successful or not depends on whether he grasps the situation rightly or not. If he is a wise man, it is not until he has consulted his oracle, done everything in his power to find out what the situation is, that he will make even the most trivial plan. And if he neglects the situation, the situation will not neglect him. It is not one of those gods that leave an insult unpunished.

The freedom that there is in history consists in the fact that this compulsion is imposed upon the activity of human reason not by anything else, but by itself. The situation, its master, oracle, and god, is a situation it has itself created. And when I say this I do not mean that the situation in which one man finds himself exists only because other men have created it by a rational activity not different in kind from that by which their successor finds himself to be in it and acts in it according to his lights; and that, because human reason is always human reason, whatever may be the name of the human being in whom it works, the historian can ignore these personal distinctions and say that human reason has created the situation in which it finds itself. I mean something rather different from that. All history is the history of thought; and when an historian says that a man is in a certain situation this is the same as saying that he thinks he is in this situation. The hard facts of the situation, which it is so important for him to face, are the hard facts of the way in which he conceives the situation.

If the reason why it is hard for a man to cross the mountains is because he is frightened of the devils in them, it is folly for the historian, preaching at him across a gulf of centuries, to say 'This is sheer superstition. There are no devils at all. Face facts, and realize that there are no dangers in the mountains except rocks and water and snow, wolves perhaps, and bad men perhaps, but no devils.' The historian says that these are the facts because that is the way in which he has been taught to think. But the devil-fearer says that the presence of devils is a fact, because that is the way in which he has been taught to think. The historian thinks it a wrong way; but wrong ways of thinking are just as much historical facts as right ones, and, no less than they, determine the situation (always a thought-situation) in which the man who shares them is placed. The hardness of the fact consists in the man's inability to think of his situation otherwise. The compulsion which the devil-haunted mountains exercise on the man who would cross them consists in the fact that he cannot help believing in the devils. Sheer superstition, no doubt: but this superstition is a fact, and the crucial fact in the situation we are considering. The man who suffers from it when he tries to cross the mountains is not suffering merely for the sins of his fathers who taught him to believe in devils, if that is a sin; he is suffering because he has accepted the belief, because he has shared the sin. If the modern historian believes that there are no devils in the mountains, that too is only a belief he has accepted in precisely the same way.

The discovery that the men whose actions he studies are in this sense free is a discovery which every historian makes as soon as he arrives at a scientific mastery of his own subject. When that happens, the historian discovers his own freedom: that is, he discovers the autonomous character of historical thought, its power to solve its own problems for itself by its own methods. He discovers how unnecessary it is, and how impossible it is, for him, as historian, to hand these problems over for solution to natural science; he discovers that in his capacity as historian he both can and must solve them for himself. It is simultaneously with this discovery of his own freedom as historian that he discovers the freedom of man as an historical agent. Historical thought, thought about rational activity, is free from the domination of natural science, and rational activity is free from the domination of nature.

The intimacy of the connexion between these two discoveries might be expressed by saying that they are the same thing in different words. It might be said that to describe the rational activity of an historical agent as free is only a roundabout and disguised way of saying that history is an autonomous science. Or it might be said that to describe history as an autonomous science is only a disguised way of saying that it is the science which studies free activity. For myself, I should welcome either of these two statements, as providing evidence that the person who made it had seen far enough into the nature of history to have discovered (*a*) that historical thought is free from the domination of natural science, and is an autonomous science, (*b*) that rational action is free from the domination of nature and builds its own world of human affairs, *Res Gestae*, at its own bidding and in its own way, (*c*) that there is an intimate connexion between these two propositions.

But at the same time I should find in either statement evidence that the person who made it was unable (or for some ulterior purpose had decided to profess himself unable) to distinguish between what a person says and what is implied in what he says: unable, that is, to distinguish the theory of language, or aesthetics, from the theory of thought, or logic; and was therefore committed, for the time being at least, to a verbalistic logic, in which the logical connexion between two thoughts which imply each other is confused with the linguistic connexion between two sets of words which 'stand for the same thing'.

I should see, too, that his attempt to burke the problems of logic by substituting for them problems in linguistics was not based on any very just appreciation of the nature of language, because I should see that, of two synonymous verbal expressions, he was assuming that one really and properly means the thing 'for which it stands', while the other means this only for the insufficient reason that the person who uses it means that by it. All of which is very disputable. Rather than approve such errors, I should prefer to leave the matter where I have left it; to say that these two statements (the statement that history is an autonomous science and the statement that rational activity is free in the sense described) are not synonymous forms of words, but express discoveries neither of which can be made without making the other. And arising out of this, I will observe that the 'free-will controversy' which was so prominent in the seventeenth century had a close connexion with the fact that the seventeenth century was the time when scissors-and-paste history in its simpler forms was beginning to dissatisfy people, and when historians were beginning to see that their own house needed setting in order or that historical studies ought to take example from the study of nature, and raise themselves to the level of a science. The desire to envisage human action as free was bound up with a desire to achieve autonomy for history as the study of human action.

But I do not leave the matter there; because I wish to point out that of the two statements I am considering, one is necessarily prior to the other. It is only by using historical methods that we can find out anything about the objects of historical study. No one will assert that he knows more than historians do about certain actions done in the past concerning which historians claim to have knowledge, and that he knows this in such a way that he can satisfy both himself and other people that that claim is groundless. It follows that we must first achieve a genuinely scientific and therefore autonomous method in historical study before we can grasp the fact that human activity is free.

This may seem contrary to facts; for surely, it will be said, many people were already aware that human activity is free, long before that revolution took place by which history raised itself to the level of a science. To this objection I will offer two answers, not mutually exclusive, but the one relatively superficial, the other, I hope, a little more profound.

(i) They were aware, perhaps, of human freedom; but did they grasp it? Was their awareness a knowledge that deserved the name of scientific? Surely not; for in that case they would not only have been convinced of it, they would have known it in a systematic way, and there would have been no room for controversy about it, because those who were convinced of it would have understood the grounds of their conviction and been able to state them convincingly.

(ii) Even if the revolution by which history has become a science is only about a half-century old, we must not be deceived by the word 'revolution'. Long before Bacon and Descartes revolutionized natural science by expounding publicly the principles on which its method was based, people here and there had been using these same methods, some more often, some more rarely. As Bacon and Descartes so justly pointed out, the effect of their own work was to put these same methods within the grasp of quite ordinary intellects. When it is said that the methods of history have been revolutionized in the last half-century, this is what is meant. It is not meant that examples of scientific history will be sought in vain before that date. It is meant that whereas, earlier, scientific history was a thing of rare occurrence, hardly to be found except in the work of outstanding men, and even in them marking moments of inspiration rather than the even tenor of study, it is now a thing within the compass of everyone; a thing which we demand of everybody who writes history at all, and which is widely enough understood, even among the unlearned, to procure a livelihood for writers of detective stories whose plot is based upon its methods. The sporadic and intermittent way in which the truth of human freedom was grasped in the seventeenth century might, to say the least of it, have been a consequence of this sporadic and intermittent grasp on the method of scientific history.

§ 7. *Progress as created by Historical Thinking*

The term 'progress', as used in the nineteenth century when the word was much in people's mouths, covers two things which it is well to distinguish: progress in history, and progress in nature. For progress in nature the word 'evolution' has been so widely used that this may be accepted as its established sense; and in order not to confuse the two things I shall restrict my use of the word 'evolution' to that meaning, and distinguish the other by the name 'historical progress'.

'Evolution' is a term applied to natural processes in so far as these are conceived as bringing into existence new specific forms in nature. This conception of nature as evolution must not be confused with the conception of nature as process. Granted the latter conception, two views of natural process are still possible: that events in nature repeat one another specifically, the specific forms remaining constant through the diversity of their individual instances, so that 'the course of nature is uniform' and 'the future will resemble the past', or that the specific forms themselves undergo change, new forms coming into existence by modification of the old. The second conception is what is meant by evolution.

In one sense, to call a natural process evolutionary is the same thing as calling it progressive. For if any given specific form can come into existence only as a modification of one already established, the establishment of any given form presupposes that of which it is a modification, and so on. If a form b is a modification of a, and c of b, and d of c, the forms a, b, c, d, can only come to exist in that order. The order is progressive in the sense that it is a series of terms which can come into existence only in that order. To say this, of course, implies nothing as to why the modifications arise, or whether they are large or small. In this sense of the word 'progress', progressive only means orderly, that is, exhibiting order.

But progress in nature, or evolution, has often been taken to mean more than this: namely the doctrine that each new form is not only a modification of the last but an improvement on it. To speak of improvement is to imply a standard of valuation. This, in the case of breeding new forms of domestic animals or plants, is intelligible enough: the value implied is the new form's utility for human purposes. But no one supposes that natural evolution is designed to produce such utilities; the standard implied, therefore, cannot be that. What is it?

Kant held that there was one form of value, and only one, that was independent of human purposes, namely the moral value of the good will. All other kinds of goodness, he argued, are merely goodness for some postulated purpose, but the goodness of morality does not depend on any postulated purpose, and thus moral goodness, as he put it, is an end in itself. On this view the evolutionary process has been truly progressive, because it has led through a determinate series of forms to the existence of man, a creature capable of moral goodness.

If this view is rejected, it is very doubtful whether any other standard of valuation can be found which would entitle us to call evolution progressive except merely in the sense of being orderly. Not because the idea of value finds no place in our view of nature, for it is difficult to think of any organism except as striving to maintain its own existence, and such effort implies that, at least for itself, its existence is not a mere matter of fact but something of value; but because all values seem merely relative. The archaeopteryx may in fact have been an ancestor of the bird, but what entitles us to call the bird an improvement on the archaeopteryx? A bird is not a better archaeopteryx, but something different that has grown out of it. Each is trying to be itself.

But the view of human nature as the noblest outcome of the evolutionary process did undoubtedly underlie the nineteenth-century conception of historical progress as guaranteed by a law of nature. That conception, in fact, depended on two assumptions or groups of assumptions. First, that man is or contains in himself something of absolute value, so that the process of nature in its evolution has been a progress in so far as it has been an orderly process leading to the existence of man. From this it followed that, since man obviously did not control the process leading to his own existence, there was in nature as such an inherent tendency towards the realization of this absolute value: in other words, 'progress is a law of nature'. Secondly, the assumption that man, as a child of nature, is subject to natural law, and that the laws of historical process are identical with the laws of evolution: that historical process is of the same kind as natural process. It followed that human history was subject to a necessary law of progress, in other words that of the new specific forms of social organization, art and science, and so forth, which it brings into existence each is necessarily an improvement on the last.

The idea of a 'law of progress' may be attacked by denying either of these two assumptions. It may be denied that man has in him anything of absolute value. His rationality, it may be said, only serves to make him the most maleficent and destructive of the animals, and is rather a blunder or a cruel joke of nature than her noblest work; his morality is only (as the modern jargon goes) a rationalization or ideology which he has devised to conceal from himself the crude fact of his bestiality. From this point of view, the natural process that has led to his existence can no longer be regarded as a progress. But further: if the conception of historical process as a mere extension of natural process is denied, as it must be by any sound theory of history, it follows that there is no natural and in that sense necessary law of progress in history. The question whether any particular historical change has been an improvement must consequently be a question to be answered on its merits in each particular case.

The conception of a 'law of progress', by which the course of history is so governed that successive forms of human activity exhibit each an improvement on the last, is thus a mere confusion of thought, bred of an unnatural union between man's belief in his own superiority to nature and his belief that he is nothing more than a part of nature. If either belief is true, the other is false: they cannot be combined to produce logical offspring.

Nor can the question, whether in a given case an historical change has or has not been progressive, be answered until we are sure that such questions have a meaning. Before they are raised, we must ask what is meant by historical progress, now that it has been distinguished from natural progress; and, if anything is meant, whether the meaning is one applicable to the given case we are considering. For it would be hasty to assume that, because the conception of historical progress as dictated by a law of nature is nonsensical, the conception of historical progress itself is therefore nonsensical.

Assuming, then, that the phrase 'historical progress' may still

have a meaning, we must ask what it means. The fact that it
has suffered confusion through contamination with the idea of
evolution does not prove it meaningless; on the contrary, it
suggests that it has a certain basis in historical experience.

As a first attempt to define its meaning, we might suggest
that historical progress is only another name for human activity
itself, as a succession of acts each of which arises out of the
last. Every act whose history we may study, of whatever kind
it is, has its place in a series of acts where one has created a
situation with which the next has to deal. The accomplished act
gives rise to a new problem; it is always this new problem, not
the old problem over again, which the new act is obliged to solve.
If a man has discovered how to get a meal, next time he is
hungry he must find out how to get another, and the getting of
this other is a new act arising out of the old. His situation is
always changing, and the act of thought by which he solves the
problems it presents is always changing too.

This is no doubt true, but it is not to our purpose. It is just
as true of a dog as of a man, that every meal must be a different
meal: just as true, that every time a bee gathering honey visits
a flower, it must be a different flower; just as true, that every
time a body moving in a straight line or an open curve comes
to a part of space, it must be a different part. But these processes are not historical processes, and to quote them as throwing light on the historical process would betray the old fallacy
of naturalism. Moreover, the novelty of the new situation and
the new act is not a specific novelty, for the new act may be a
new act of exactly the same kind (for example, setting the same
snare again in the same place); so that we are not even discussing the evolutionary aspect of natural process, which is the
point at which that process seems most akin to the historical.
The search for a fresh meal takes place even in the most completely static or non-progressive society.

The idea of historical progress, then, if it refers to anything,
refers to the coming into existence not merely of new actions
or thoughts or situations belonging to the same specific type,
but of new specific types. It therefore presupposes such specific
novelties, and consists in the conception of these as improvements. Suppose, for example, a man or a community had lived
on fish, and, the fish-supply failing, had sought food in a new

way, by digging for roots: this would be a change in the specific type of situation and activity, but it would not be regarded as a progress, because the change does not imply that the new type is an improvement on the old. But if a community of fish-eaters had changed their method of catching fish from a less to a more efficient one, by which an average fisherman could catch ten fish on an average day instead of five, this would be called an example of progress.

But from whose point of view is it an improvement? The question must be asked, because what is an improvement from one point of view may be the reverse from another; and if there is a third from which an impartial judgement can be passed on this conflict, the qualifications of this impartial judge must be determined.

Let us first consider the change from the point of view of the persons concerned in it: the older generation still practising the old method while the younger has adopted the new. In such a case the older generation will see no need for the change, knowing as it does that life can be lived on the old method. And it will also think that the old method is better than the new; not out of irrational prejudice, but because the way of life which it knows and values is built round the old method, which is therefore certain to have social and religious associations that express the intimacy of its connexion with this way of life as a whole. A man of the older generation only wants his five fish a day, and he does not want half a day's leisure; what he wants is to live as he has lived. To him, therefore, the change is no progress, but a decadence.

It might seem obvious that by the opposite party, the younger generation, the change is conceived as a progress. It has given up the life of its fathers and chosen a new one for itself: it would not do this (one might suppose) without comparing the two and deciding that the new is better. But this is not necessarily the case. There is no choice except for a person who knows what both the things are between which he is choosing. To choose between two ways of life is impossible unless one knows what they are; and this means not merely looking on one as a spectacle, and practising the other, or practising one and conceiving the other as an unrealized possibility, but knowing both in the only way in which ways of life can be known: by actual experience, or by the sympathetic insight which may take its place for such a purpose. But experience shows that nothing is harder than for a given generation in a changing society, which is living in a new way of its own, to enter sympathetically into the life of the last. It sees that life as a mere incomprehensible spectacle, and seems driven to escape from sympathy with it by a kind of instinctive effort to free itself from parental influences and bring about the change on which it is blindly resolved. There is here no genuine comparison between the two ways of life, and therefore no judgement that one is better than the other, and therefore no conception of the change as a progress.

For this reason, the historical changes in a society's way of life are very rarely conceived as progressive even by the generation that makes them. It makes them in obedience to a blind impulse to destroy what it does not comprehend, as bad, and substitute something else as good. But progress is not the replacement of the bad by the good, but of the good by the better. In order to conceive a change as a progress, then, the person who has made it must think of what he has abolished as good, and good in certain definite ways. This he can only do on condition of his knowing what the old way of life was like, that is, having historical knowledge of his society's past while he is actually living in the present he is creating: for historical knowledge is simply the re-enactment of past experiences in the mind of the present thinker. Only thus can the two ways of life be held together in the same mind for a comparison of their merits, so that a person choosing one and rejecting the other can know what he has gained and what he has lost, and decide that he has chosen the better. In short: the revolutionary can only regard his revolution as a progress in so far as he is also an historian, genuinely re-enacting in his own historical thought the life he nevertheless rejects.

Let us now consider the change in question, no longer from the standpoint of those concerned in it, but from that of an historian placed outside it. We might hope that, from his detached and impartial point of view, he would be able to judge with some chance of fairness whether it was a progress or not. But this is a difficult matter. He is only deceived if he fastens on the fact that ten fish are caught where five were caught before, and uses this as a criterion of progress. He must take into account the conditions and consequences of that change. He must ask what was done with the additional fish or the additional leisure. He must ask what value attached to the social and religious institutions that were sacrificed for them. In short, he must judge the relative value of two different ways of life, taken as two wholes. Now, in order to do this, he must be able to enter with equal sympathy into the essential features and values of each way of life: he must re-experience them both in his own mind, as objects of historical knowledge. What makes him a qualified judge, therefore, is just the fact that he does not look at his object from a detached point of view, but re-lives it in himself.

We shall see, later, that the task of judging the value of a certain way of life taken in its entirety is an impossible task, because no such thing in its entirety is ever a possible object of historical knowledge. The attempt to know what we have no means of knowing is an infallible way to generate illusions; and this attempt to judge whether one period of history or phase of human life, taken as a whole, shows progress as compared with its predecessor, generates illusions of an easily recognizable type. Their characteristic feature is the labelling of certain historical periods as good periods, or ages of historical greatness, and of others as bad periods, ages of historical failure or poverty. The so-called good periods are the ones into whose spirit the historian has penetrated, owing either to the existence of abundant evidence or to his own capacity for re-living the experience they enjoyed; the so-called bad periods are either those for which evidence is relatively scanty, or those whose life he cannot, for reasons arising out of his own experience and that of his age, reconstruct within himself.

At the present day we are constantly presented with a view of history as consisting in this way of good and bad periods, the bad periods being divided into the primitive and the decadent, according as they come before or after the good ones. This distinction between periods of primitiveness, periods of greatness, and periods of decadence, is not and never can be historically true. It tells us much about the historians who study the facts, but nothing about the facts they study. It is characteristic of an age like our own, where history is studied widely and successfully, but eclectically. Every period of which we have competent knowledge (and by competent knowledge I mean insight into its thought, not mere acquaintance with its remains) appears in the perspective of time as an age of brilliance: the brilliance being the light of our own historical insight. The intervening periods are seen by contrast as, relatively speaking and in different degrees, 'dark ages': ages which we know to have existed, because there is a gap of time for them in our chronology, and we have possibly numerous relics of their work and thought, but in which we can find no real life because we cannot re-enact that thought in our own minds. That this pattern of light and darkness is an optical illusion proceeding from the distribution of the historian's knowledge and ignorance is obvious from the different ways in which it is drawn by different historians and by the historical thought of different generations.

The same optical illusion in a simpler form affected the historical thought of the eighteenth century, and laid the foundations for the dogma of progress, as that was accepted in the nineteenth. When Voltaire laid it down that 'all history is modern history',[1] and that nothing could be genuinely known before about the end of the fifteenth century, he was saying two things at once: that nothing earlier than the modern period could be known, and that nothing earlier deserved to be known. These two things came to the same thing. His inability to reconstruct genuine history from the documents of the ancient world and the Middle Ages was the source of his belief that those ages were dark and barbarous. The idea of history as a progress from primitive times to the present day was, to those who believed in it, a simple consequence of the fact that their historical outlook was limited to the recent past.

The old dogma of a single historical progress leading to the present, and the modern dogma of historical cycles, that is, of a multiple progress leading to 'great ages' and then to decadence, are thus mere projections of the historian's ignorance upon the screen of the past. But, setting dogmas aside, has the idea of progress no other basis than this? We have already seen that there is one condition on which that idea can represent a genuine thought, and not either a blind feeling or a mere state of ignorance. The condition is that the person who uses the word should

[1] *Dictionnaire philosophique*, art. 'Histoire'; *Œuvres* (1784), vol. xli, p. 45.

use it in comparing two historical periods or ways of life, both of which he can understand historically, that is, with enough sympathy and insight to reconstruct their experience for himself. He must satisfy himself and his readers that no blind spot in his own mind, and no defect in his equipment of learning, prevents him from entering into the experience of either less fully than into the other's. Then, having fulfilled that condition, he is entitled to ask whether the change from the first to the second was a progress.

But when he asks this, what exactly is he asking? Obviously, he is not asking whether the second comes nearer to the way of life which he accepts as his own. By re-enacting the experience of either in his own mind he has already accepted it as a thing to be judged by its own standards: a form of life having its own problems, to be judged by its success in solving those problems and no others. Nor is he assuming that the two different ways of life were attempts to do one and the same thing, and asking whether the second did it better than the first. Bach was not trying to write like Beethoven and failing; Athens was not a relatively unsuccessful attempt to produce Rome; Plato was himself, not a half-developed Aristotle.

There is only one genuine meaning for this question. If thought in its first phase, after solving the initial problems of that phase, is then, through solving these, brought up against others which defeat it; and if the second solves these further problems without losing its hold on the solution of the first, so that there is gain without any corresponding loss, then there is progress. And there can be progress on no other terms. If there is any loss, the problem of setting loss against gain is insoluble.

According to this definition, it would be idle to ask whether any one period of history taken as a whole showed a progress over its predecessor. For the historian can never take any period as a whole. There must be large tracts of its life for which he has either no data, or no data that he is in a position to interpret. We cannot, for example, know what the Greeks enjoyed in the way of musical experience, though we know that they greatly valued it; we have not enough material; and on the other hand, though we have no lack of data about Roman religion, our own religious experience is not of such a kind as to qualify us for reconstructing in our own minds what it meant to them. We must select certain aspects of experience and confine our search for progress to these.

Can we speak of progress in happiness or comfort or satisfaction? Obviously not. Different ways of life are differentiated by nothing more clearly than by differences between the things that people habitually enjoy, the conditions which they find comfortable, and the achievements they regard as satisfactory. The problem of being comfortable in a medieval cottage is so different from the problem of being comfortable in a modern slum that there is no comparing them; the happiness of a peasant is not contained in the happiness of a millionaire.

Nor does it mean anything to ask whether there is progress in art. The artist's problem, so far as he is an artist, is not the problem of doing what his predecessor has done and going on to do something further which his predecessor failed to do. There is development in art, but no progress: for though in the technical processes of art one man learns from another, Titian from Bellini, Beethoven from Mozart, and so on, the problem of art itself consists not in mastering these technical processes but in using them to express the artist's experience and give it reflective form, and consequently every fresh work of art is the solution of a fresh problem which arises not out of a previous work of art but out of the artist's unreflective experience. Artists do better or worse work in so far as they solve these problems well or ill; but the relation between good and bad art is not an historical relation, because the problems arise out of the flow of unreflective experience, and that flow is not an historical process.

In one sense, there is no progress in morality. The life of morality consists not in the development of moral codes, but in their application to individual problems of conduct, and to a great extent these problems, like those of art, arise out of unreflective experience. The course of our moral life is conditioned by the succession of our desires; and, though our desires change, they do not change historically. They arise out of our animal nature, and though this may change from youth to old age, or vary in different peoples and climates, its differences are part of the process of nature, not of history.

In another sense, however, there is or may be moral progress. Part of our moral life consists of coping with problems arising not out of our animal nature but out of our social institutions, and these are historical things, which create moral problems only in so far as they are already the expression of moral ideals. A man who asks himself whether he ought to take voluntary part in his country's war is not struggling with personal fear; he is involved in a conflict between the moral forces embodied in the institution of the State, and those embodied not merely in the ideal, but in the equally actual reality, of international peace and intercourse. Similarly the problem of divorce arises not out of the whims of sexual desire, but out of an unresolved conflict between the moral ideal of monogamy and the moral evils which that ideal, rigidly applied, brings in its train. To solve the problem of war or of divorce is only possible by devising new institutions which shall recognize in full the moral claims recognized by the State or by monogamy, and shall satisfy these claims without leaving unsatisfied the further claims to which, in historical fact, the old institutions have given rise.

The same double aspect appears in the economic life. So far as that consists in finding from moment to moment the means of satisfying demands which spring not from our historical environment but from our nature as animals with certain desires, there can be no progress in it; that would be a progress in happiness or comfort or satisfaction, which we have seen to be impossible. But not all our demands are for the satisfaction of animal desires. The demand for investments in which I can put my savings to support me in old age is not an animal desire; it arises out of an individualistic economic system in which the old are supported neither statutorily by the State nor customarily by their families, but by the fruits of their own labour, and in which capital commands a certain rate of interest. That system has solved a good many problems, and therein lies its economic value; but it gives rise to a good many others which as yet it has failed to solve. A better economic system, one whose substitution for this would be a progress, would continue to solve the same problems which are solved by individualist capitalism, and solve these others as well.

The same considerations apply to politics and law, and I need not work out the application in detail. In science, philosophy, and religion the conditions are rather different. Here, unless I am mistaken, the question of coping with our animal nature and satisfying its needs does not arise. The problem is a single one instead of a double.

Progress in science would consist in the supersession of one theory by another which served both to explain all that the first theory explained, and also to explain types or classes of events or 'phenomena' which the first ought to have explained but could not. I suppose that Darwin's theory of the origin of species was an example. The theory of fixed species explained the relative permanence of natural kinds within the recorded memory of man; but it ought to have held good for the longer stretch of geological time, and it broke down, too, for the case of selectively-bred animals and plants under domestication. Darwin propounded a theory whose claim to merit rested on its bringing these three classes under one conception. I need hardly quote the now more familiar relation between Newton's law of gravitation and that of Einstein, or that between the special and general theories of relativity. The interest of science, in relation to the conception of progress, seems to be that this is the simplest and most obvious case in which progress exists and is verifiable. For this reason, those who have believed most strongly in progress have been much in the habit of appealing to the progress of science as the plainest proof that there is such a thing, and often, too, have based their hope of progress in other fields on the hope of making science the absolute mistress of human life. But science is and can be mistress only in her own house, and forms of activity which cannot progress (such as art) cannot be made to do so by subjecting them, if that phrase meant anything, to the rule of science; whereas those which can must progress by finding out for themselves how to improve in doing their own work.

Philosophy progresses in so far as one stage of its development solves the problems which defeated it in the last, without losing its hold on the solutions already achieved. This, of course, is independent of whether the two stages are stages in the life of a single philosopher, or are represented by different men. Thus, suppose it true that Plato grasped the necessity for an eternal object, the world of Ideas or Idea of the Good, and also for an eternal subject, the soul in its double function of knower and mover, as solutions for the problems with which his predecessors' work had left him confronted: but was baffled to say how these two were related; and suppose Aristotle saw that the problem of the relation between them, as Plato had stated it, or rather as he himself saw it in his long apprenticeship to Plato's teaching, could be solved by thinking of them as one and the same, pure intellect being identical with its own object, and its knowledge of that object being its knowledge of itself; then, so far (though conceivably not in other respects) Aristotle's philosophy would mark a progress on Plato's, granted that by that new step Aristotle sacrificed nothing that Plato had achieved by his theory of Ideas and his theory of soul.

In religion, progress is possible on the same terms. If Christianity, bating no jot or tittle of what Judaism had won by its conception of God as one God, just and terrible, infinitely great over against man's infinite littleness and infinitely exacting in his demands on man, could bridge the gulf between God and man by the conception that God became man in order that we might become God, that was a progress, and a momentous one, in the history of the religious consciousness.

In such senses and in such cases as these, progress is possible. Whether it has actually occurred, and where and when and in what ways, are questions for historical thought to answer. But there is one other thing for historical thought to do: namely to create this progress itself. For progress is not a mere fact to be discovered by historical thinking: it is only through historical thinking that it comes about at all.

The reason for this is that progress, in those cases (common or rare) when it happens, happens only in one way: by the retention in the mind, at one phase, of what was achieved in the preceding phase. The two phases are related not merely by way of succession, but by way of continuity, and continuity of a peculiar kind. If Einstein makes an advance on Newton, he does it by knowing Newton's thought and retaining it within his own, in the sense that he knows what Newton's problems were, and how he solved them, and, disentangling the truth in those solutions from whatever errors prevented Newton from going further, embodying these solutions as thus disentangled in his own theory. He might have done this, no doubt, without having read Newton in the original for himself; but not without having received Newton's doctrine from someone. Thus Newton stands, in such a context, not for a man but for a theory, reigning during a certain period of scientific thought. It is only in so far as Einstein knows that theory, as a fact in the history of science, that he can make an advance upon it. Newton thus lives in Einstein in the way in which any past experience lives in the mind of the historian, as a past experience known as past— as the point from which the development with which he is concerned started—but re-enacted here and now together with a development of itself that is partly constructive or positive and partly critical or negative.

Similarly with any other progress. If we want to abolish capitalism or war, and in doing so not only to destroy them but to bring into existence something better, we must begin by understanding them: seeing what the problems are which our economic or international system succeeds in solving, and how the solution of these is related to the other problems which it fails to solve. This understanding of the system we set out to supersede is a thing which we must retain throughout the work of superseding it, as a knowledge of the past conditioning our creation of the future. It may be impossible to do this; our hatred of the thing we are destroying may prevent us from understanding it, and we may love it so much that we cannot destroy it unless we are blinded by such hatred. But if that is so, there will once more, as so often in the past, be change but no progress; we shall have lost our hold on one group of problems in our anxiety to solve the next. And we ought by now to realize that no kindly law of nature will save us from the fruits of our ignorance.

INDEX

Acton, Lord, 147, 281.
Alexander, S., 142, 210, 211.
— the Great, 31, 32, 37.
Alfred, King, 52, 69.
Ambrose, St., 51.
anthropology, 79, 91, 148, 155, 224.
apocalyptic history, 50, 52, 80.
archaeology, 58, 127, 199, 210, 212, 253, 260.
Archimedes, 287, 296, 298.
Aristotle, 29, 329.
— *Ethics* of, 229.
— metaphysics of, 333.
— on happiness, 212.
— — logic, 253–4, 255.
— — poetry, 27, 239.
— — substance, 42.
— — the State, 210.
— quoted, 44.
Arnold, T., 135.
art and history, 168, 191–4.
— freedom of, 108.
— history of, 88, 105, 121–2, 132, 213, 313–14.
— no progress in, 330, 332.
— theory of, 104, 191–4, 236, 279.
Augustine, St., 47, 51.
authorities, the historian's, 33, 37–8, 62, 69, 71, 135, 234–8, 242–5, 256–9, 260, 265, 269, 282.
— *see also* testimony.
autobiography, 27, 295–6.
autonomy of history, 125–6, 155, 159, 201–4, 236–8, 256, 274–6, 318–20.
awareness', meanings of, 291.

Babylonia, 15, 17.
Bacon, Francis, defines history as realm of memory, 58, 62, 69, 252.
— 'idols' in, 68.
— logic of questioning, 273.
— map of knowledge, 58, 59.
— methodology of science, 6, 63, 84, 237, 265, 269, 320.
— on truth, 72.
Barbarians and Greeks, 32.
Barth, P., 176.
Bauer, W., 175.
Baumgarten, A. G., 93.
Baur, F. C., 122, 135.
Baynes, N. H., 151.
Becket, Thomas, 297.
Bede, 51.
Beethoven, 329, 330.
Bergson, H., 185, 187–9, 198, 211, 306.
Berkeley, Bishop, 47, 71–3, 84.

Bernheim, E., 176.
bibliographies, 278–80.
biography, 94, 304.
Bodin, J., 57.
Bollandists, the, 61, 62, 77.
Bosanquet, B., 143, 155.
Boutroux, E., 186.
Bradley, F. H., 134–43, 151, 152, 238–40.
Bréhier, E., quoted, 209.
Breysig, K., 176, 178.
Buchanan, G., 61.
Buckle, H. T., 144.
Burnt Njál, 308.
Bury, J. B., 147–51, 155, 177, 249.
Butler, S., 308.

Cambridge histories, 147, 260.
Camden, W., 58.
Campanella, T., 68.
cats, 197–8, 227.
causation in science, 23, 230.
causes in history, 80–1, 125, 149, 176–7, 178, 179–80, 185, 214–15, 300.
China, 14, 22, 69, 90, 91.
chronicle, 202–3.
civilization, downfall of, 56.
Cleopatra's nose, 80, 149.
Cochrane, C. N., 29.
Coleridge, S. T., 304.
compilation, 33, 40, 51.
Comte, A., 128, 222, 264, 265.
Condorcet, Marquis de, 80, 86.
contingency in history, 149–51, 180.
Copernican revolution, 50, 60, 236, 240.
Cornford, F. M., 18.
Cournot, A. A., 149.
creation, doctrine of, 47, 49, 65, 255.
criterion of history, 60, 61, 137–8, 139–40, 238–40, 244–5.
critical history, 61, 62, 209, 259–61, 269, 270, 274.
Croce, B., 118–19, 140, 190–204, 284, 289, 300.
Croesus, 23, 24.
Croiset, A., quoted, 19.
cycles, historical, 67–8, 181, 264, 32⁸.

Daniel, Book of, 57.
Dante, 76.
Darwin, Charles, 115, 129, 332.
data, the historian's, 222–3, 243–4, 329.
decay never absolute in history, 164–5.